Fundamentals of
Income Taxation

Huebner School Series   *Gary K. Stone, Editor*

Huebner School Series

Fundamentals of Income Taxation
Second Edition

Edited by James F. Ivers III

The American College/*Bryn Mawr, Pennsylvania*

This publication is designed to provide accurate and authoritative information about the subject covered. While every precaution has been taken in the preparation of this material, the editor and The American College assume no liability for damages resulting from the use of the information contained in this publication. The American College is not engaged in rendering legal, accounting, or other professional advice. If legal or other expert advice is required, the services of an appropriate professional should be sought.

Library of Congress Catalog Card Number 00-135880
ISBN 1-57996-033-2

Printed in the United States of America

To my mother
Natalie Ann Gormley Ivers

Contents

Acknowledgments

I wish to express my appreciation and gratitude to all the individuals who were involved in the development and production of this book, including (but certainly not limited to) the following:

Patricia G. Berenson for her production skills and indispensable assistance.

Maria Marlowe for her fastidious and cooperative efforts in editing the manuscript, and Renee Heron, manuscript editor, for her assistance with the index.

Charlene McNulty for her assistance with the graphics.

Each of the authors and co-authors of chapters in this text: Burton T. Beam, Jr., associate professor of insurance at The American College; Thomas M. Brinker, Jr., professor of accounting at Beaver College (Arcadia University as of July 2001); Fred J. Dopheide, former vice president of Educational Resources at the Society of Financial Service Professionals; Edward E. Graves, associate professor of insurance and Charles J. Zimmerman Chair in Life Insurance Education at The American College; Michael R. Harris, attorney at law; Deborah A. Jenkins, assistant librarian at The American College; Stephen N. Kandell of Consolidated Brokerage Services, Inc.; Ted Kurlowicz, professor of taxation and Charles A. Drimal Professor of Estate Planning at The American College; Stephan R. Leimberg, former professor of taxation at The American College; John J. McFadden, professor of taxation at The American College; and Alban Salaman, attorney at law.

David A. Littell, associate professor of taxation at The American College, for his benevolent peer review.

Gary K. Stone, vice president of Academics and professor of insurance, and C. Bruce Worsham, associate vice president and director of the Solomon S. Huebner School and associate professor of taxation and insurance, for their management and support in the development of this project and for their faith in me to deliver it.

All the capable students, American College instructors, and other colleagues, friends, and family members whose constructive suggestions have been incorporated in this text.

It should also be noted that chapter 16 of this text, "Income Taxation of Life Insurance," is an updated revision of a reading copyrighted in 1973 by Richard D. Irwin, Inc., as a chapter in the third edition of *The Life and Health Insurance Handbook,* edited by Davis W. Gregg and Vane B. Lucas, portions of which are used herein by permission and with all rights reserved.

James F. Ivers III

About the Editor

James F. Ivers III, JD, LLM, ChFC, is professor of taxation at The American College. He has professional experience in the areas of estate, gift, and income taxation as well as business and personal financial planning. He received his JD and LLM in taxation from the Boston University School of Law and his ChFC from The American College. He is a member of the bar in Florida and Pennsylvania.

Fundamentals of
Income Taxation

1

Access to Sources of Tax Law and New Legislation

James F. Ivers III and Deborah A. Jenkins[*]

Our tax code is so long it makes *War and Peace* seem breezy.

Steven LaTourette

Chapter Outline

INTRODUCTION

A student or financial services professional will frequently need information regarding a particular issue or new piece of legislation in the area of federal income taxation. This chapter will ease the process of basic tax research as well as point out means of access to new law and related explanatory material.

Effective research of court decisions involves techniques whose explanations are beyond the scope of this chapter. However, the use of the basic tax services, encyclopedias, periodicals, and material published on new law is addressed.

For the tax practitioner, the basic services and encyclopedias are well worth their substantial cost. This cost includes annual charges for periodic revisions. However, unless the student is a specialist in taxation, he or she is likely to use these services at a library.

The remainder of this chapter explains how to acquire the most current tax information.

---

[*] Deborah A. Jenkins, MLS, is assistant librarian at The American College.

MAJOR TAX SERVICES AND RESEARCH TOOLS

Two of the major reporting services in the area of federal income tax are

- *Federal Tax Coordinator 2d,* published by The Research Institute of America (RIA)
- *Standard Federal Tax Reporter,* published by Commerce Clearing House (CCH)

Each of these services consists of multivolume sets with updates provided regularly in the form of replacement sheets or add-ons for the loose-leaf format each service uses.

Each includes the Internal Revenue Code sections and the current regulations promulgated thereunder. In addition, each includes explanatory material and case citations or annotations that summarize court decisions and provide references to the full text of opinions related to a particular subject or issue.

The RIA service is organized by topic, and volumes run alphabetically in sequence. To find the explanatory material for a particular topic, the researcher can consult either the *Topic Index* or *Finding Tables* volumes.

The CCH service is organized by sequential treatment of Internal Revenue Code sections. CCH also contains a thorough subject index volume.

It may be easier for the fledgling researcher to use the RIA service, since it is organized by subject and contains lengthy explanatory text. The RIA service offers a *Practice Aids* volume, which contains tax ideas along with reprints of IRS audit manuals. It also provides two volumes of proposed regulations as well as reprints of recent revenue rulings and revenue procedures.

The CCH service, on the other hand, offers more verbatim reprints of various elements of primary-source tax law. It also offers more extensive annotations of court decisions. CCH also offers a two-volume *Citator* that shows where each listed decision has been cited and discussed in later court decisions.

Each service has its own advantages and character. The researcher will likely become more familiar with one and will develop a preference based on that familiarity. Both services (and others) can be found in most law libraries as well as in other selected libraries.

The researcher should note that these services are referenced by paragraph number, not page number. The upper corner of each page contains the paragraph numbers, while the page number appears in the bottom corner of the page.

Both the CCH and RIA services are also available on CD-ROM.

A major encyclopedia-type multivolume tax treatise is Rabkin and Johnson, *Federal Income, Gift, and Estate Taxation.* Rabkin and Johnson is a multivolume treatise organized by subject and is characterized by its economy of language and its clear explanatory material. It is supplemented monthly. Rabkin and Johnson includes congressional committee reports to inform the researcher of legislative history with respect to various Code sections. It is also available in a single-volume desk edition, which is a condensed version of the full encyclopedia.

PERIODICALS

There are a host of periodicals that publish tax articles, and this chapter is not intended to recommend a selective list over any others.

Commerce Clearing House publishes *Federal Tax Articles,* a comprehensive list of tax-related articles published in all types of professional journals.

Among the periodicals devoted exclusively to taxation are the *Journal of Taxation, Taxes—The Tax Magazine, Tax Notes,* and the *Monthly Digest of Tax Articles.*

The *Journal of Financial Service Professionals* also publishes many tax-related articles in addition to other articles of interest. Numerous other periodicals include tax articles of interest to the financial services professional.

NEW LEGISLATION AND RELATED MATERIAL

Each of the major tax services publishes verbatim reprints of new tax legislation and accompanying legislative history, explanatory material, and analysis. These separate volumes can be obtained by contacting the publishers.

Within the basic tax services are sections covering current developments. A volume of CCH, entitled *New Matters,* contains new legislation, recent cases, and rulings that have not yet been incorporated into the main body of the Service. It also includes a cumulative index to new developments. Additional volumes of CCH provide advance sheets on court decisions in tax cases in the federal courts.

The RIA service contains a tab section at the end of each volume entitled "Developments." This section features decisions, rulings, and other developments occurring since the last periodic revision. The new developments are referenced by way of specific paragraph numbers to the main body of the service.

In addition to materials published by the major tax services, major accounting firms also publish summaries of each new piece of federal tax legislation both in printed form and on the Internet. These are generally easy to read, although depth of coverage is not comparable to the publications of the major services. However, these summaries can be quite satisfactory for an overview of the highlights of new tax legislation. They are generally available by contacting the local office or Web site of major accounting firms shortly after new tax legislation is signed by the president.

Various government Web sites on the Internet, such as the "Thomas" site, also provide text of new legislation, committee reports, and related material.

The leading printed report for the latest tax developments is the *Daily Tax Report* published by the Bureau of National Affairs (BNA). The *Daily* is thorough, well written, and appropriate not only for the tax specialist but also for the financial planner. It is also available as an online service.

CCH has an Internet service that provides quick access to the latest developments in all areas of tax law. This service is called "OMNITAX." For information regarding features, cost, and computer compatibility, contact the publisher. The LEXIS database service also offers a tax research library called FEDTAX. RIA also has an Internet product available by subscription called "Checkpoint" that provides information comparable to *Federal Tax Coordinator 2d.*

CONCLUSION

A few trips to the tax section of a law library will make the student familiar with the ways in which tax law is developed and reported. Researchers who prefer working by computer can also develop effective researching skills that way. In view of the importance of tax matters in virtually every aspect of the financial planning process, basic research techniques should be of interest to the student.

2

A History of the Income Tax Law and a Glance at the Sources of Current Law

James F. Ivers III and Stephan R. Leimberg[*]

What at first was plunder assumed the softer name of revenue.

Thomas Paine

That most delicious of all privileges—spending other people's money.

John Randolph

Chapter Outline

---

[*] Stephan R. Leimberg, JD, CLU, is a former professor of taxation and estate planning at The American College.

EARLY TAX LAW

The tax history of the United States mirrors the general history of this country. Under the Articles of Confederation, the first governing instrument adopted by the Continental Congress in 1777, the federal government had no taxing power or right to collect custom duties. Several attempts to amend the Articles and give Congress a power to tax failed.

Because the Articles of Confederation proved to be too weak, the Constitution, written in 1787 and ratified in 1789, enlarged the powers of the federal government. However, the framers of the Constitution feared that the accumulation of power by the federal government would result in tyranny similar to the absolute monarchy of King George III of England. Therefore the government was divided into three coequal branches of government (legislative, executive, and judicial) with a system of checks and balances. The original taxing power of the federal government under the Constitution was sharply limited by the uniformity and apportionment clauses—Article I, Sections 8 and 9, of the Constitution. A detailed explanation is beyond the scope of this chapter, but it is sufficient to say, in retrospect, that these clauses precluded the federal government from imposing an income tax.

INCREASED PRESSURE FOR REVENUES

The high cost of the Civil War brought about the first governmental attempt to collect a tax on income. The tax soon expired, but by 1894 governmental needs for revenue led to the adoption of another income tax. Within a year, the constitutional validity of this tax was tested. In the famous case of *Pollock v. Farmers' Loan and Trust Company,* the U.S. Supreme Court held that the tax was neither apportioned among the states nor uniform and was therefore unconstitutional, as Pollock had claimed.

Congressional reaction to the *Pollock* decision was shaped by the increasing pressures as well as the demands for a steady and sufficient source of revenue. The result was a political compromise in 1909 that levied a tax on corporations. However, even while the constitutionality of the Revenue Act of 1909 was being considered, Congress realized the need for a broader tax base.

THE 16TH AMENDMENT

In 1909, the 16th Amendment to the Constitution, which nullified the *Pollock* decision, was adopted by Congress. After appropriate action by the states, it was declared ratified on February 25, 1913. The 16th Amendment says the following:

> The Congress shall have the power to lay and collect taxes on income, from whatever source derived, without apportionment

among the several States, and without regard to any census or enumeration.

It is this amendment that dispensed with the apportionment requirement and therefore became the foundation for the basic framework of our modern tax law. The broad and sweeping language that permitted "income, from whatever source derived" to be taxed pervades the entire income tax law and has far-reaching implications.

Congress quickly utilized the newly sanctioned revenue source. The corporate income tax created by the Revenue Act of 1909 was discontinued. Individuals, as well as corporations, then became subject to the broad new income tax introduced by Congress in 1913.

THE CODE

The Revenue Act of 1913 was quickly followed by a series of additional revenue acts. In 1939 the entire federal tax law was codified and entitled the Internal Revenue Code of 1939. The crucial need to raise revenue to finance World War II turned the income tax from a tax on wealthy taxpayers to a tax on the majority of the population. This period also saw the introduction of the withholding provisions for employees. After the war the Code provisions were rearranged and revised. The result was the Internal Revenue Code of 1954. The Code is now called the Internal Revenue Code of 1986, however, as a result of the voluminous changes wrought by the Tax Reform Act of 1986. Numerous additional changes have been made since 1986.

FUNCTIONS OF THE INCOME TAX SYSTEM

Revenue-Producing Function

The income tax law originated as a revenue-producing mechanism to supply money for the administration and operation of the federal government. The bulk of the government's net receipts are still produced by the federal income tax. Congress, however, does not enact tax laws solely to raise revenue. The tax law also serves economic, social, and regulatory functions.

Economic Function

The Internal Revenue Code plays an important role in the management of the nation's economy. According to current economic thinking, greater taxes result in lower spending by consumers. The reasoning concludes that by reducing consumer spending (without increasing governmental expenditures) the income tax system can be used to reduce inflationary trends. Conversely, the use of tax incentives or lower tax rates leaves consumers with more cash that, in turn, translates into increased spending, saving, and investment. The hoped-for result is an increase in the national product that will increase the demand for new workers and thus reduce unemployment. Thus the tax system can prevent or reduce the impact of recessions.

Some economic experts feel that the very nature of a progressive income tax will automatically perform both antiinflationary and antirecessionary functions without Congress actually changing the rates. The theory is that when more dollars (through increased salaries) are available to consumers, their income taxes will increase more than proportionately, resulting in a dampening of their ability to make inflationary expenditures with their increased incomes. During a recession the amount of money collected through the federal income tax decreases more than proportionately as the amount of a taxpayer's income decreases. Thus the relative reduction in income available to taxpayers is less than the reduction in their wages and salaries. Consequently, recessionary forces should be smaller than they otherwise would be. However, at the present time, recessionary signs are not coupled with a reduction in salaries. The value of the dollar is continually being eroded. Salary increases push the taxpayer into increasingly higher tax brackets, leaving less spendable income than before. As a result, our progressive tax structure does not automatically provide an anti-inflationary function during the type of combined recession-inflation that the United States encountered in the 1980s.

Further, the Code used incentives to encourage economic activity at the taxpayer level. For example, liberal depreciation rules as well as an investment credit encouraged taxpayers to invest capital in their businesses that, in turn, created more jobs for the nation. These incentives are now being questioned.

Social Function

As the tax base grew wider and rates became higher, Congress found that in addition to producing revenue, the tax structure could be used as a method of effectuating governmental policy. For example, the income tax, as a progressive tax, could be used to redistribute the national wealth. A progressive tax is one in which the amount of tax increases more than proportionately as the amount of the taxpayer's taxable income increases. Therefore in theory, if not in practice, by taking a higher proportion of tax dollars from higher incomes rather than from lower incomes (and using those dollars for governmental expenditures that benefit lower income taxpayers), the distribution of national wealth could be changed significantly. The social function of the income tax has been increasing in importance.

Regulatory Function

The income tax system performs a regulatory function as well as the revenue and social functions mentioned above. Two extreme examples of this use of the tax system to discourage socially undesirable activities are the punitive tax on marijuana and the tax on automatic weapons.

Counterbalancing Factors

There are, of course, factors that shape the methods used to achieve these ends. Balancing the need of the federal government for revenues is the desire of Congress to be fair to the parties affected. Generally, *fairness* is recognized as being "equal treatment of equals" and reasonable differences in the treatment of unequals. The test of this fairness is how well the tax imposed matches a taxpayer's ability to pay. Counterbalancing a desire to be fair, Congress is keenly aware of the political consequences of its actions. For example, it is generally politically more expedient to tax a small and unorganized group of voters than to tax a large, organized group with an effective and well-financed lobby.

Thus a tax law is a compromise between purposes and people—with great pressures exerted by the economic, political, and social groups who are affected by particular laws, and who constantly lobby in Congress in an attempt to have tax laws changed to their advantage.

SOURCES OF TAX LAW TODAY

Each of the three coequal branches of the federal government has a major role in the federal income tax system. These roles can be shown graphically by the illustration on the following page.

Legislative

The 16th Amendment to the U.S. Constitution empowered Congress to enact an income tax law now compiled in the Internal Revenue Code. The importance of the Code is that federal taxation must proceed from a statutory origin. The present Code came into effect in 1986. It is revised and updated almost annually by Congress. Specific Code sections or parts of sections can be amended or repealed through the passage of revenue bills, which then supersede the older law as to those provisions. The House of Representatives has the constitutional responsibility for initiating revenue bills. A revenue bill becomes law, in most cases, through the following process:

- Revenue bills are written by the Ways and Means Committee of the House of Representatives, or bills are received by the Ways and Means Committee through referral by the House of Representatives (1) from a member of the House or (2) by suggestion of the Joint Committee on Internal Revenue and Taxation (this is a committee of 10 members— five from the House Ways and Means Committee and five from the Senate Finance Committee).

- The Ways and Means Committee conducts hearings on the revenue bill. Expert opinion will be heard that may influence the form and meaning of the statute.

SOURCES OF TAX LAW

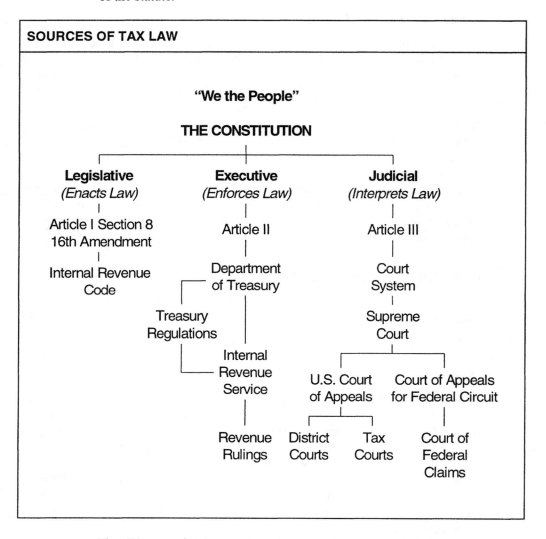

"We the People"

THE CONSTITUTION

Legislative	**Executive**	**Judicial**
(Enacts Law)	*(Enforces Law)*	*(Interprets Law)*
Article I Section 8 16th Amendment	Article II	Article III
Internal Revenue Code	Department of Treasury	Court System
	Treasury Regulations	Supreme Court
	Internal Revenue Service	
		U.S. Court of Appeals — Court of Appeals for Federal Circuit
	Revenue Rulings	District Courts — Tax Courts — Court of Federal Claims

---

- The Ways and Means Committee sends an amended bill with the committee's report to the House for adoption.
- The adopted bill is sent to the Senate.
- The Senate sends the bill to the Senate Finance Committee where it is studied, hearings on it are held, and amendments to the bill are made. The amended bill and the committee report are then forwarded to the Senate for passage.

- Sometimes—where there are material differences between the House's version of the bill and the Senate's—a joint conference committee consisting of members from both sides develops a compromise version.
- The compromise version must be passed by both houses of the Congress.
- The bill is sent to the president for his signature or veto.
- If the president vetoes the bill, a two-thirds majority of both houses can revise the bill and make it law over the president's veto.

Once a law becomes effective, all taxpayers must follow it unless the law is declared unconstitutional. For example, a law taxing the income of men and women at different rates would be unconstitutional.

Once effective, the law is subject to a great deal of interpretation. The House Ways and Means Committee and the Senate Finance Committee reports become extremely important. Both the courts and the Department of Treasury Regulations (discussed below) rely heavily on these reports to determine the intent of the creators before an interpretation is made.

The Code itself contains seven subtitles. Subtitle A is concerned with income taxes; Subtitle B is concerned with estate and gift taxes; and the rest are concerned with other areas of taxation. The Code is then further subdivided. Each subtitle consists of chapters, subchapters, parts, subparts, sections, subsections, paragraphs, subparagraphs, and subparagraph subdivisions known as clauses.

Executive

The president, as the chief enforcer of the law under Article II of the Constitution, has the duty to enforce the collection of tax. He has delegated his responsibility to the Department of the Treasury that, in turn, has delegated the responsibility to its subdivision, the Internal Revenue Service.

The Department of the Treasury has also been granted the power by Congress to enact regulations under the Code. Congress, recognizing that the Code must be written in legal language but that it would not be the proper place to explain how the law will be applied to specific taxpayers, empowered the secretary of the Treasury or his or her delegate to promulgate the rules and regulations that are necessary to enforce the law. Thus the Code itself provides for the Treasury Department to prescribe the rules and regulations needed for the enforcement of the Code. Actually, the Internal Revenue Service writes these regulations, and the secretary of the Treasury approves them. Regulations are issued first in proposed form so that interested taxpayers may file objections or participate in public hearings before the proposed regulations are finalized.

The regulations, or "regs" as they are often called, constitute the official Treasury interpretation of the Code. Regulations may particularize, define, clarify, illustrate, or even amplify the Code. To the extent that these regs are not inconsistent with the Code, they are said to have the force and effect of law. Generally they are presumed to be correct, are followed by Treasury personnel, and are seldom invalidated by the courts. Because they are carefully prepared and unlikely to be quickly changed, taxpayers can ordinarily rely on them in everyday transactions.

Regulations can be held invalid by the courts for a number of reasons. The two principal ones are (1) the regulation is ambiguous and without persuasive force in determining the true construction of a statute, and (2) the regulation goes beyond the statute (the Code) and thus has no effect. Even if a regulation is held invalid by a lower court, the Treasury can still continue to enforce it unless the Supreme Court itself holds the regulation invalid.

Thus the IRS does not consider itself bound (beyond that particular case) where a regulation is held invalid by any court lower than the Supreme Court, although it now conforms to circuit court decisions for the taxpayer's circuit. At times, therefore, the Service will continue to enforce a regulation (held invalid in a given case) against other taxpayers (even in almost identical circumstances) until the issue is decided by the Supreme Court itself.

The regulations can be accessed in a manner similar to the Code. For example, the regulations pertaining to Section 303 of the Code would use the number 303. Income tax regulations are preceded by the number 1 (one). Therefore the regulations pertaining to Code Section 303, "Distributions in Redemption of Stock to Pay Death Taxes," could be found under the number 1.303 of the regulations.

Revenue Rulings and Private Rulings

It would be impossible for the Code and regulations to cover the tax consequences of every possible factual situation that can arise. Frequently taxpayers request the Internal Revenue Service's view on the interpretation of a doubtful point of law. In response to these requests, the Service issues various types of administrative rulings.

Revenue rulings are based on a stated set of facts that usually involve a problem common to a number of taxpayers. These pronouncements are binding on officials of the IRS, and they follow them in their handling of issues arising in particular cases. For example, suppose the law is unclear as to whether a taxpayer can deduct the cost of moving a pet under the moving-expense deduction. If the Internal Revenue Service issues a revenue ruling to the effect that the cost of moving a pet is not deductible, all revenue agents will adhere to the ruling. The taxpayer has the choice of (1) relying upon rulings if the facts and circumstances are substantially the same or (2) challenging rulings in the courts. Unlike Treasury regulations, the courts need not give rulings any weight.

Revenue rulings are published in a weekly bulletin called the Internal Revenue Bulletin. They can be found in the following manner. The first number following the abbreviation "Rev. Rul." gives the year the ruling was issued. This is followed by a dash. The second number is in numerical sequence, denoting the order in which the ruling was issued. Rev. Rul. 64-19 would be a ruling issued in 1964 and the 19th such revenue ruling issued in that year. The citation in the Internal Revenue Bulletin would include (1) the year, (2) the number of the weekly bulletin of that year, and (3) the page under which the ruling could be found. For example, Rev. Rul. 69-173, IRB 1969-15, 12, means that the particular ruling in 1969 was the 173d of that year. It would be found in the 15th weekly bulletin issued in 1969 on page 12.

Private rulings arise when a taxpayer requests an administrative interpretation on a prospective transaction or on completed transactions that are not involved in returns already filed. Although private rulings are personal to the taxpayer, they have been made available to the public in recent years and are now published after the deletion of certain information. Deleted materials include names and addresses of taxpayers, trade secrets, classified matter, and so forth. Even though published, they still have the same effect—they may not be claimed by another taxpayer as a precedent.

Revenue Procedures

Revenue procedures describe internal practices and procedures within the IRS. Like revenue rulings, they are published in the Internal Revenue Bulletin. Generally revenue procedures state changes in techniques and administrative procedures used by the Internal Revenue Service. Revenue procedures are generally designated by the abbreviation "Rev. Proc."

Determination Letters

The National Office of the Internal Revenue Service issues revenue rulings. IRS officials within specific operating divisions have the power to write determination letters regarding various transactions to be reflected on returns that will be filed by various types of taxpayers and organizations. Determination letters are issued only if the answer to the question presented is covered specifically by statute, Treasury decision, or regulation, or specifically by a court decision or ruling opinion published in the Internal Revenue Bulletin. Determination letters contrast with revenue rulings in that such letters are never issued about unclear points of law.

Conflict between Taxpayers and the Internal Revenue Service

Individual taxpayers must generally file returns by April 15 for the previous calendar year or, if they are fiscal taxpayers, by the 15th day of the fourth month after their fiscal year ends. Corporations must file tax returns by March 15, or the 15th day of the third month after their fiscal year ends.

Once a return is filed, the Internal Revenue Service processes the form for mathematical accuracy and audit selection at its service center. The IRS has 3 years from the time the return is filed within which to assess additional taxes.

Early returns are deemed to be filed on their due date. An important exception to the 3-year statute of limitations exists when fraud is involved. In this situation, there is unlimited time to audit.

Taxpayers who file incorrect returns may be subject to an accuracy-related penalty that is equal to 20 percent of the amount of the underpayment of tax actually due. The penalty applies to situations involving negligence or disregard of tax laws, substantial understatement of income tax, and substantial valuation misstatements. If fraud is involved, additional civil and criminal penalties can be imposed.

Tax return preparers may also be subject to one or more of several different penalties. These include a penalty of $1,000 per return for a willful or reckless understatement of a taxpayer's tax liability.

An initial income tax audit by an IRS examiner may take place at an IRS office or at the taxpayer's home or business. A preliminary letter advising the taxpayer of the agent's recommendation and a 30-day right to appeal from that determination will then be sent. If the taxpayer disagrees with the conclusion, he or she may write to the IRS to request a hearing before its Appeals organization.

When a dispute with the IRS is being considered in Appeals, the appeals officers are not permitted to engage in substantive discussions regarding a specific case with other IRS officials in the absence of the taxpayer or his or her representative.

While a case is pending with the Appeals officers, the taxpayer also has the right to request that the issue be referred to the National Office staff for technical advice. Grounds for referral include a lack of uniformity in the disposition of the issue or significant complexity or uniqueness of the issue. Dispute resolution methods in Appeals now also include mediation and arbitration.

If no agreement is reached with Appeals, statutory notice of deficiency is issued by the commissioner of Internal Revenue. Following this notice, taxpayers have 90 days to file a petition with the U.S. Tax Court to have their cases heard. If taxpayers allow the 90 days to pass without either paying the tax and/or instituting suit, the IRS can assess a tax deficiency, enter judgment, and seize the taxpayers' property to collect the deficiency.

No tax need be paid in advance for cases to be litigated in the U.S. Tax Court. Once a case has been docketed there, an appeals officer is assigned to the case and given exclusive authority to settle within a 4-month period. If no settlement is reached in that time, the case is scheduled for trial.

Alternatively, the taxpayer may choose to pay the tax deficiency and then file a claim for a refund with the IRS. Unless a notice of claim disallowance is sent before 6 months expire, the taxpayer must wait that time period before he or she can file suit for a refund in either the U.S. District Court or the U.S. Court of Federal Claims. Various factors discussed below will affect the taxpayer's choice of the best tribunal before which to try the case. By statute, the taxpayer has 2 years from the date the notice of the claim disallowance was mailed in which to sue the government for a refund. This 2-year period may be extended only by a written agreement between the taxpayer and the secretary of the Treasury.

A privilege of confidentiality generally applies to communications between a taxpayer and a tax adviser authorized to practice before the IRS, including an attorney, CPA, or enrolled agent. The privilege may be asserted in noncriminal tax disputes. It does not apply to disputes involving tax shelter promotions.

Judicial

Article III of the U.S. Constitution states that judicial power shall be vested in one Supreme Court and in such lower courts as Congress shall establish. The jurisdiction of the federal courts includes all cases arising under the laws of the United States, including revenue laws.

The court system that Congress has established comprises trial courts that decide issues of fact and law, appellate courts for a review of issues of law, and the Supreme Court, which is the ultimate reviewer of questions of law.

U.S. Tax Court

The U.S. Tax Court was established for taxpayers who seek a redetermination of a deficiency asserted against them but do not wish first to pay the deficiency. A large majority of tax cases are heard by the Tax Court for this reason. Trial by jury is not available in the Tax Court. Questions of law and fact are decided by Tax Court judges.

The Tax Court has its main offices and trial rooms in Washington, D.C., but trials are conducted also in principal cities throughout the United States. The Tax Court is a special court designed principally for taxpayers who appeal tax deficiencies imposed by the Treasury Department.

To expedite hearings on deficiencies of $50,000 and under, the Tax Court has a small tax case division. These cases are handled much less formally and much more quickly than other Tax Court cases. Decisions of this division may not be appealed or treated as authority in other cases. The small case procedure is optional at the taxpayer's request.

The IRS does not consider itself bound by a Tax Court decision any more than it does by a Court of Federal Claims or district court decision (except for the particular case in which an adverse decision has been rendered). Thus the IRS often will continue to litigate the same issue in other cases before the same court or in other courts. However, rather than have the Tax Court rule against it in a number of cases (which establishes precedent), the IRS will often negotiate a settlement. When the Service loses a Tax Court case, it will indicate its willingness or unwillingness to follow the case in the future by reporting in the Internal Revenue Bulletin its acquiescence ("acq.") or nonacquiescence ("non-acq.") to the principle of tax law established in that case.

Appeals from the Tax Court by either an unsuccessful taxpayer or the IRS are heard by the U.S. Court of Appeals in the region of the country in which the taxpayer resides. If there is a difference of opinion in the various courts of appeal as to the interpretation of the tax law, the Tax Court follows the decisions of that court of appeals to which the taxpayer may appeal.

U.S. Court of Federal Claims

The U.S. Court of Federal Claims (called the U.S. Claims Court until its name was changed in December 1992) is a trial court that became operative on October 1, 1982, when the U.S. Court of Claims ceased to exist as such. It continues to hear cases that would have been heard by the old Court of Claims, whose jurisdiction was limited to refund cases (the tax must be paid before jurisdiction can be invoked). Appeals from the Court of Federal Claims are heard by another court simultaneously created under the Federal Courts Improvement Act of 1982. This appellate court is called the Court of Appeals for the Federal Circuit and is, in fact, a merger of the old U.S. Court of Claims and the Court of Customs and Patents Appeals. Both of these courts generally follow the tax precedents of the Court of Claims as opposed to following the tax precedents established by the taxpayer's home district court. Since the abolishment of the U.S. Court of Claims, there is no longer any tax forum where appeal is taken directly to the U.S. Supreme Court.

U.S. District Court

The U.S. District Court (of which there is at least one for each state) like the U.S. Court of Federal Claims can only hear tax cases in which the taxpayer has first paid the deficiency and has been denied a refund by the Internal Revenue Service.

The U.S. District Court is unique in that it is the only court in which a taxpayer may request a jury trial. In a case where there is a jury, the jury decides questions of fact; the judge decides questions of law. For example, sometimes the taxpayers will choose to institute suit in a district court because their battles with the IRS are essentially factual, and they believe they will obtain a sympathetic jury. As to questions of law, a district court in a certain location must follow decisions of that particular court's corresponding court of appeals as precedent. Appeals from a district court can be made to the U.S. Court of Appeals and then further to the Supreme Court.

U.S. Court of Appeals

The U.S. Court of Appeals comprises 12 circuit courts located throughout the country. These courts hear appeals that are taken by either taxpayers or the Treasury from decisions rendered by the Tax Court or a district court. The U.S. Court of Appeals is the second highest level in the court system. The importance of this court is underscored by the fact that the only appeal from a decision of such a court is to the Supreme Court itself. Both the district courts and the Tax Court must follow decisions of the Court of Appeals to which the taxpayer may appeal. The Court of Appeals of one region is not bound to follow decisions by the Court of Appeals in another region. Although a favorable decision in a sister court may be persuasive, it is not controlling. Taxpayers who must use the Court of Appeals in a region other than where the favorable decision was rendered cannot be sure of the outcome of their cases, even if the facts of their cases are almost identical to the facts of the case previously decided elsewhere. Of course, a favorable decision in one circuit may be relied upon by other taxpayers in that same circuit.

U.S. Supreme Court

The United States Supreme Court is the highest court in the land. Supreme Court decisions are required to be followed by taxpayers as well as by the Internal Revenue Service. However, there are few tax cases that the high court decides. This is because Supreme Court review of tax cases is generally available only if the Court itself grants petitions for appeal. Supreme Court review, therefore, is a matter of discretion with the Supreme Court and not a matter of right. The Supreme Court will most probably review a tax case if (1) there is a conflict between the courts of appeal for different circuits, or (2) an important and recurring problem in tax law administration is involved, or (3) many taxpayers are involved, or (4) the decision of a lower court conflicts with long-standing practice or existing legal authority.

A Supreme Court interpretation of tax law is the law of the land until (1) Congress enacts a new statute, tantamount to overturning a decision interpreting the Internal Revenue Code, or (2) the Court overrides its own prior decision in rare situations.

SUMMARY

The history of the income tax parallels the history of the financial needs of the United States. The strain of a modern government attempting to meet the costs of both wartime expenditures and peacetime services created a demand for additional revenues. Once established, the overriding importance of the individual and corporate income taxes in the federal revenue structure has never diminished.

Aside from revenue purposes, the income tax has been used with varying degrees of success to perform social, economic, and regulatory functions.

The source of the federal income tax law is ultimately the people. The intent of the people was expressed through the Constitution, which in turn gives legislative power to Congress. Congress exercises this power in the form of the Internal Revenue Code, which is further modified and expanded by the Internal Revenue Service's regulations and rulings. Court decisions on particular issues further interpret and expound on statutory law as well as IRS regulations and rulings. The importance and effect of these court cases is in turn determined by the status of the court. The hierarchy of the court system (and hence the weight given to a decision of that particular court) at the highest level starts with the Supreme Court and works its way down to courts of original jurisdiction known as the United States Court of Federal Claims, the United States District Court, and the United States Tax Court.

3

An Introduction to Four Basic Income Tax Concepts

James F. Ivers III, Stephen N. Kandell, and Stephan R. Leimberg[*]

The hardest thing in the world to understand is the Income Tax.

This [preparing my tax return] is too difficult for a mathematician. It takes a philosopher.

Albert Einstein

Chapter Outline

INTRODUCTION

In this chapter, we will examine four concepts that are essential in gaining a fundamental understanding of how the income tax laws work. The first is the concept of gross income. This concept is a guide to items and transactions that are subject to taxation. The second concept is the doctrine of constructive receipt, which applies in determining when an item of income will be taxed to a particular taxpayer. The third concept is the economic benefit theory. This theory helps to ascertain under what circumstances a taxpayer has realized income subject to taxation, even though no cash has been directly received by the taxpayer. The fourth concept is the principle of assignment of income. This principle deals with the question of to whom income is taxed in situations where

---

[*]Stephen N. Kandell is director of estate and business analysis at Consolidated Brokerage Services, Inc., Conshohocken, Pennsylvania.

the income is received by a taxpayer other than the taxpayer whose efforts generated the income.

In order to highlight some of the basic issues involved in these areas, a question and answer format will be used.

GROSS INCOME UNDER THE INTERNAL REVENUE CODE

Question: What is the meaning of the term "gross income"?

Answer: Gross income is income that must be included on a taxpayer's income tax return. The Internal Revenue Code defines gross income as "all income from whatever source derived," including (but not limited to) the following items:

- compensation for services, including fees, commissions, fringe benefits, and similar items
- gross income derived from business
- gains derived from dealings in property
- interest
- rents
- royalties
- dividends
- alimony and separate maintenance payments
- annuities
- income from life insurance and endowment contracts
- pensions
- income from discharge of indebtedness
- distributive share of partnership gross income
- income in respect of a decedent
- income from an interest in an estate or trust

Under this definition, the fifteen items listed are examples of items includible in a taxpayer's gross income. They are by no means an exclusive list. In fact, the general rule for inclusion is that any item of income received by a taxpayer is includible in gross income unless a specific provision in the Internal Revenue Code specifically states that the item may be excluded. The rule that all items of income are includible in gross income unless the Code explicitly provides otherwise is an important fundamental income tax concept.

Question: What is the difference between "income" and "capital" for income tax purposes?

Answer: To begin with, "income" is subject to income taxation, while "capital" (including transactions in which a taxpayer receives a return of capital) is not. The trick is how to differentiate the receipt of income from the receipt, return, or replacement of a capital item. An example of a return of capital is where a taxpayer purchases 100 shares of corporate stock for $50 a share and later sells the stock for the same amount per share. The sales proceeds of $50 per share do not constitute gross income to the taxpayer, because the taxpayer already had that much money invested in the property. To the extent the taxpayer is receiving back only what was paid for the property, he or she does not have "gains derived from dealings in property."

On the other hand, if the stock had been sold for $70 a share, the difference of $20 per share between the amount the taxpayer invested in the property and the amount he or she received for it would be includible in gross income.

Another example of an item that is not considered "income" is where a creditor receives repayment of the principal amount of a debt. The repayment of the principal by the debtor is not gross income to the creditor. The creditor is simply receiving back the amount of money that was, in a sense, "invested" in the debtor. However, any interest payments on the debt received by the creditor would generally be includible in gross income.

Question: What is the significance of the term "realization of income" for tax purposes?

Answer: In order for income to be taxable, the income must be "realized" or obtained by the taxpayer. For example, gain is generally not realized from dealings in property until there is a disposition of the property. The disposition is the event that causes the gain in the property to be realized by the taxpayer and therefore taxed. An increase in value without an event such as a disposition of the property does not result in taxation of gain. An individual taxpayer who uses the cash-basis method of tax accounting (discussed in more detail later in this chapter) is not taxed on income unless and until the income is actually or constructively received. As a general rule, there must be a "taxable event" (such as a sale of property, payment of a salary, or receipt of an economic benefit) that brings the income into the taxpayer's possession.

In certain situations, there can be a dispute as to whether a taxpayer has realized an item of income. The tax concept of realization has been fairly well developed both in court decisions and in the Internal Revenue Code, and it will be touched upon in certain other portions of this text. In general, income is taxable when it is realized by the taxpayer, although the Code does contain certain rules that defer or even eliminate the taxation of certain types of realized income.

Question: What are some examples of situations in which a taxpayer may unexpectedly be subject to income tax?

Answer: Certain items of gross income may result from situations in which the taxpayer does not expect to be taxed. A good example is the rule that imposes taxation on a debtor when that debtor is discharged or relieved of the obligation to pay a debt. As a general rule, the release of an obligation to pay a debt results in "income from discharge of indebtedness" to the debtor. The extent to which such income is taxed may be limited by specific rules regarding the financial position of the debtor. The underlying concept is that the debtor has received a monetary benefit from no longer having to repay money that was borrowed under a legal obligation to repay. Therefore the discharge of indebtedness is a taxable event that results in gross income, unless the discharge of the debt can be treated as a nontaxable gift.

As discussed in chapter 6, a gift is specifically excludible from the gross income of the donee under the Internal Revenue Code. However, there is frequently an issue of fact as to whether a given transaction is really a gift. The taxation of income from discharge of indebtedness is one area where the issue can arise. It may also arise in determining whether a given transaction is a taxable payment for the taxpayer's personal services or merely a gift. In order for a payment to be treated as a gift, the donor must intend for the payment to be a gift and not a payment for services. Donative intent is a must in order to properly characterize a transaction as a gift. In an employer-employee relationship, it will generally be presumed that payments are for services rendered and not a result of the employer's generosity or concern for the employee's personal welfare even if the employer was not legally obligated to make the payment. However, in certain cases, courts have decided that payments received by employees were nontaxable gifts from the employer. In any event, this is not a fertile ground for income tax planning because the IRS will generally treat such payments as taxable, unless the gift is a "de minimis" (minimal) payment such as a holiday turkey or a similar item. The Code also specifically excludes certain (but not all) employee fringe benefits from the gross income of employees. A detailed discussion of fringe benefits is beyond the scope of this text.

Income does not have to be received in cash in order to be taxable. If income is received in a form other than cash, the general rule is that the fair market value of the property received is the amount includible in gross income. An example of noncash income subject to taxation is a barter transaction. If two taxpayers agree to exchange the performance of valuable services for each other, the exchange is taxable to each. For example, if an attorney performs legal services for a dentist in exchange for receiving root canal work, both the attorney and the dentist have realized gross income equal to the value of the services received. Although many transactions in the so-called "barter" economy are not actually reported on tax returns, they are still taxable as a matter of law.

Other common examples of noncash income will be discussed below in the context of the economic benefit theory.

DOCTRINE OF CONSTRUCTIVE RECEIPT

Question: What is the doctrine of constructive receipt?

Answer: Before answering that question directly, it is necessary to review what is meant by the *cash receipts and disbursements* or *cash-basis* method of accounting. Most financial services professionals and their clients are cash-basis taxpayers, which means that they report income and pay taxes on that income only if it is received during the taxable year. Almost all individual taxpayers who do not own a trade or business (and many who do) use this method of accounting.

For example, suppose your client—a doctor using the cash-basis method of accounting—renders services but is not paid for them until January of next year. The income will not be includible in the doctor's income for this year (even though the services were performed this year) but it will be reportable next year.

In a nutshell, the cash-basis method of accounting means that an individual reports income in the year it is received. More formally stated, the amount of any item of gross income is included in the taxpayer's gross income for the taxable year in which it is received, unless an accounting method is used in which such income is to be properly accounted for in a different taxable year.

Question: Generally, then, a cash-basis taxpayer does not have to report income until and unless this person actually receives it. How does the doctrine of constructive receipt apply to this general rule?

Answer: There is an exception to the general rule that income is reported by a cash-basis taxpayer only when it is actually received. The exception is known as the theory or doctrine of constructive receipt. This doctrine might best be illustrated by restating two questions often asked of financial services professionals:

1. Is the interest earned on life insurance policy dividend accumulations currently taxable to the policyholder at the time it is credited to the policyholder's account, even though the interest is not actually received by the policyholder at that time?
2. If a policyholder takes the maturity proceeds or cash surrender value of the life, endowment, or annuity contract in the form of a life income or in installments (rather than as a lump sum), is the entire gain on the policy taxable to him or her in the year of maturity or surrender?

Question: What is the problem? It is evident that in either case the policyholder does not have actual receipt of income.

Answer: In both situations above, the policyholder might have received income *constructively,* even though he or she has not actually reduced income to his or her possession. The problem is caused by a section of the income tax regulations that provides that income must be included in the taxpayer's gross income for the taxable year in which it is "actually or constructively received." This means that a taxpayer does not have to reduce income to actual possession before it has to be reported. An individual must report it as soon as it is either actually received or constructively received.

Regulations elaborate by stating that even though income is not actually reduced to a taxpayer's possession, the taxpayer is deemed to have constructively received it in the taxable year during which (1) it is credited to the taxpayer's account, (2) set apart for the taxpayer, or (3) otherwise made available to be drawn from at any time.

Question: These rules seem very strict. Are there exceptions?

Answer: The regulations qualify the constructive-receipt rules by stating that income is *not* constructively received if the taxpayer's control of its receipt is subject to substantial limitations or restrictions. In essence, therefore, the implications of these regulations to cash-basis life underwriters and their cash-basis policyholders is that they must currently report any income that has become unconditionally subject to their demand, although in fact they have not chosen to actually receive or reduce that income to their possession.

The doctrine of constructive receipt might be considered the "Can I get it when I want it?" doctrine. When taxpayers decide to actually obtain items of income and only their volition stands between them and the income, they have constructively received the income at that time (and are therefore taxed on it).

Question: What is the reason for the doctrine?

Answer: The purpose of the constructive-receipt rules is to prevent taxpayers from unilaterally determining the tax year when an item of income is "received by" them for federal income tax purposes. Were it not for this doctrine, cash-basis taxpayers could shift, at will, the year in which they will report an item of income merely by not taking any steps to reduce that income to their possession. The rule prevents cash-basis taxpayers from avoiding taxes by putting off actual receipt of income until their tax circumstances are more favorable, tax rates are lower, or they have a lower amount of other includible income.

The thrust of the doctrine of constructive receipt may therefore be capsulized by the statement that a cash-basis taxpayer "may not deliberately turn his back upon income and thus select the year for which he will report it." If income is payable on the demand of a taxpayer in a given taxable year, he or she must include such amounts in his or her taxable income for that year. To hold otherwise would permit a taxpayer to defer taxable income by merely choosing not to exercise the right to receive it. Therefore the owner of a savings account cannot defer the year in which interest earnings must be reported by deciding in

December not to walk into a bank but instead to wait until the following January to have that interest credited on his or her passbook.

Question: What is the effect when there are substantial limitations or restrictions placed on a taxpayer's right to receive income?

Answer: The regulations qualify the rules on inclusion of constructively received income by stating that income will not be constructively received if the taxpayer's control of its receipt is subject to substantial limitations or substantial restrictions. For example, suppose Lee, a pension consultant, signs a contract to perform actuarial services during this year. Lee actually performs those services during this year. However, the contract specifies that payment will not be made until 5 years from now. Lee has no right to require earlier payment. Because payment to Lee (a cash-basis taxpayer) was subject to a substantial restriction (that is, it was not payable until 5 years later), it should not be considered constructively received this year. Thus where a taxpayer is not legally entitled to receive payment in a year prior to actual receipt, this individual will not be held to have constructively received that income in the prior year.

This raises the central question of whether the taxpayer merely refrained from exercising a legal right to receive current payment or whether there was actually never a legal right to receive payment in the prior year. The answer is a question of fact that will be determined by examining the agreement between the parties in each situation. Court cases indicate that if there is any substantial limitation or restriction on either the time or the manner of payment of income, there can be no constructive receipt until the limitation or restriction is removed. There would be no constructive receipt, for example, if the Tyler Corporation raises Robert's salary but does not pay that salary increase until a later year when wage freeze rules are changed to permit payment. Robert will not be deemed to be in constructive receipt in the earlier year.

Question: How does the effect of substantial limitations or restrictions apply to life insurance?

Answer: The cash value of a life insurance policy earns interest, which is reflected in the increase in the policy cash value from year to year. Although a policyholder could easily reduce any gain reflected by the excess of the cash value over the cost of the contract, the policyholder is not required to include such gain in his or her gross income each year. This is because the right to receive that income is subject to substantial limitations or restrictions. In other words, to receive the gain the policyholder must complete a transaction that will affect the nature and extent of his or her valuable insurance coverage and contractual rights.

Question: Suppose amounts are credited or set apart for a taxpayer, but there are no funds to pay the promised amounts. What is the effect on an inability to pay amounts credited?

Answer: If the financial condition of the debtor makes payment of the income in question impossible, there will be no constructive receipt by the creditor. For example, suppose Pam loaned the Esposito Corporation $10,000. In return Pam received an interest-bearing note. If the Esposito Corporation had insufficient funds to pay the interest, Pam would have no constructive receipt even if her account was credited with the interest on the corporation's books. Likewise, if the Martin Corporation issued a salary check to Oliver, an officer, but the corporation lacked the funds to pay the check, Oliver would not be taxed. This result would hold even if the Martin Corporation could have borrowed money or sold assets to pay the check.

Question: Specifically, how does the doctrine of constructive receipt affect life insurance?

Answer: At this point it is appropriate to answer the two questions asked earlier:

1. Is the interest earned on life insurance policy dividend accumulations currently taxable to the policyholder as soon as it is credited to the policyholder's account, even if the policyholder has not actually received the interest?
2. If a policyholder takes the maturity proceeds or cash surrender value of the life, endowment, or annuity contract in the form of a life income or in installments (rather than in a lump sum), is the gain on the policy taxable to him or her in the year of maturity or surrender?

The first question pertains to the time at which interest earned on policy dividends becomes taxable. The general rule is that the interest earned on policy dividends must be included in the policyholder's gross income for the first taxable year during which the policyholder has the right to withdraw the interest. This result applies even if the taxpayer, in fact, does not withdraw the interest. The key issue is the following: When can the policyholder withdraw the interest on the policy dividends? If the policy provides that interest can be withdrawn only on the policy's anniversary date, the interest income is not constructively received in the year prior to the anniversary date.

The second question pertains to the result that occurs when the maturity proceeds or cash surrender value of a policy are taken in the form of installments of lifetime payments rather than in the form of a lump sum. When an endowment contract matures (or an ordinary life contract is surrendered), gain on the lump sum available to the policyholder will be immediately taxable. However, if a policyholder decides to select an installment payment or annuity settlement option rather than taking the lump sum that could be chosen at will, is the policyholder in constructive receipt of the lump sum? If there is a gain on the contract and if proceeds are constructively received, the full gain would be taxable—just as if the policyholder had actually received a lump-sum payment.

A constructive-receipt problem can occur in three typical situations. The first situation is when the policyholder elects *before* the maturity or surrender date to postpone receipt of the proceeds and take income in the form of an annuity or installments. In this case, however, the policyholder avoids constructive receipt since there is no point in time when he or she had an unqualified right to take the lump sum. The policyholder will be taxed on the gain reflected in each installment when he or she actually receives it.

The second situation is when a policyholder does *not* make an election before the maturity or surrender date. Were it not for a special provision in the Internal Revenue Code, the policyholder would be considered to be in constructive receipt of the lump sum when it became available. However, because of this special provision, a policyholder will not be deemed to be in constructive receipt of the lump sum (1) within 60 days after the lump sum becomes payable and (2) if before receiving any payment in cash, the policyholder exercises an option or agrees with the insurer to take the proceeds in the form of a life income annuity or other installment-type settlement.

The third situation occurs when a policyholder decides to give up the right to withdraw principal, leaves proceeds on deposit, and receives only the interest that those proceeds generate. Constructive receipt in this case can be avoided only if an election to receive interest is made *before* the maturity or surrender date. Thus the 60-day extension is allowed only for the election of a life income or other installment-type settlement and not for an election to leave proceeds on deposit at interest.

Question: Does the doctrine of constructive receipt affect agreements to defer compensation?

Answer: It is in the area of deferred compensation that the doctrine of constructive receipt proves to be most complex and troublesome. The reason for deferring compensation is quite simple: If all or a part of an individual's current earnings are not payable by an employer until a specified date, or if those earnings are spread out over a number of years in the future when the individual is in a lower income tax bracket, the net after-tax compensation will be increased. Therefore it is possible to defer the tax of a cash-basis employee or independent contractor, but this deferral requires careful planning.

Basically there are two types of deferred-compensation methods: funded and unfunded. A funded deferred-compensation agreement entails the actual deposit of funds by the employer into a trust, escrow, or custodial account. Unfunded deferred compensation implies that no funds are irrevocably set aside (that is, outside the corporation's control and beyond the reach of its creditors) by an employer. In this case, the employee must rely solely on the employer's unsecured promise and ability to pay the deferred amount (plus any interest that is applicable) in the future. Taxation generally depends not only on whether the agreement is funded or unfunded but also on whether the rights of the employee whose income is deferred are forfeitable or nonforfeitable.

Where the agreement can be classified as funded (according to the definition above), the deferred compensation will be taxable to the employee in (1) the first year the employee's rights are not subject to a substantial risk of forfeiture, or (2) the first year the employee's rights can be transferred to another party (that is, assigned free of the substantial risk of forfeiture).

If the agreement can be classified as unfunded (according to the definition above), such compensation will not be taxable until it is actually paid to the employee provided (1) the agreement to defer the compensation is made *prior* to the time the compensation is earned, and (2) the employer's promise is not secured by specific assets. In other words, the obligation may not be evidenced by specified financial instruments, such as a negotiable note. If these two requirements are met, constructive receipt will be avoided until the deferred compensation is actually received. This is because receipt of the compensation is not within the employee's control. This result will apply regardless of whether such compensation was or was not forfeitable by the employee. Therefore even if the employee had a nonforfeitable right to such compensation, no tax would be imposed until actual receipt since the agreement was unfunded.

For example, suppose the Rawlins Corporation offered Elaine a 5-year employment contract to entice her to join. The agreement provides that Elaine will be paid $50,000 a year currently, plus an additional $10,000 of nonforfeitable deferred compensation credited to a reserve account each year. However, Elaine will receive the money only upon her retirement, death, or disability. Elaine receives neither notes from the corporation nor evidence of its debt other than the agreement signed by the corporation and Elaine. She is to receive the deferred salary in 10 equal annual installments.

Even though the compensation that has been deferred is nonforfeitable, Elaine does not have constructive receipt. The agreement to defer the compensation was made before Elaine earned it. The Rawlins Corporation did not put aside funds in an escrow account for her benefit. In no way did the Rawlins Corporation secure its promise to Elaine other than through an employment agreement, and thus she has no right to the funds. They have not been credited or set apart so that she may draw from them at will. All Elaine has is a promise by the Rawlins Corporation to be paid income upon her retirement, death, or disability. Nothing has been placed beyond the access of the corporation's creditors, and no control over the funds has been given to Elaine. Likewise, upon retirement, death, or disability, when the Rawlins Corporation's promise matures and Elaine becomes entitled to receive installment payments, there is still no constructive receipt. The only income subject to her unqualified control is the installment payment she actually receives each year. These payments, of course, will be taxable income when actually paid to Elaine.

The Internal Revenue Service has allowed the use of so-called *rabbi trusts* in connection with deferred-compensation agreements without imposing current taxation on the funds placed in the trust to be paid later to the employee. The employee will escape current taxation only if the funds in the trust can be reached by the creditors of the employer and if the deferred-compensation agreement does not require that a *specific* asset (such as a particular life insurance policy) be maintained in the trust to fund the agreement. The rabbi trust has been a significant development in terms of how the IRS regards the doctrine of constructive receipt, since it involves setting aside funds for the payment of deferred compensation without the arrangement being treated as a "funded" agreement.

Question: How is the use of life insurance in deferred-compensation agreements affected by the doctrine of constructive receipt?

Answer: Life insurance or annuity policies are often used by an employer to finance its obligation under the deferred-compensation agreement. For example, suppose the Mitchell Corporation executed a deferred-compensation contract with Sam, a key employee. The agreement stated that Mitchell would credit a specific sum on behalf of Sam to a bookkeeping account each month for the entire term of the contract. (This agreement is unfunded, since no amounts are set aside in trust or in an escrow account beyond the reach of the corporation's creditors.)

The Mitchell Corporation could invest all or any portion of the amount credited to Sam. Payout would not commence until the earlier of (1) Sam's 65th birthday, (2) his death prior to retirement, or (3) his disability. At that time the value of the account would be paid out in equal installments over a period of 10 years to Sam or to his named beneficiary. To finance this liability under the agreement, Mitchell purchased a life insurance contract. Mitchell applied for, owned, and was beneficiary of the contract. The policy was carried as a corporate asset on the Mitchell Corporation's books and was subject at all times to the claims of its general creditors.

The employee under this type of deferred-compensation contract will be successful in avoiding constructive receipt of the money set aside. The employee will recognize no income until the taxable year in which the income is actually received (or it is made available to the employee in some other way). The rationale is that the employee has no present interest in either the account or the policy, both of which are general assets of the employer. Note that the agreement gave the employee or his or her beneficiary no direct interest in any specific account, insurance or annuity policy, or in any other employer assets. The account merely served as a measure of the employer's liability for bookkeeping purposes.

ECONOMIC-BENEFIT THEORY

Question: What is the economic-benefit theory?

Answer: Sec. 61 of the Internal Revenue Code defines gross income as including "income from whatever source derived. . . ." In cases dealing with this section of the Code, courts have held that the language of the section is "broad enough to include as taxable income any economic or financial benefit conferred on the employee as compensation, whatever the form or mode by which it is effected." This concept has appropriately been entitled the *economic-benefit theory* or *doctrine.* Its purpose is to force an employee to include in income any compensation regardless of its form. It has been applied to situations involving a *payment in kind* or where an employer has made available to an employee the *equivalent of cash.*

Question: How does this principle differ from the doctrine of constructive receipt?

Answer: The constructive-receipt doctrine forces the inclusion of income when the employee has an unqualified choice—to take or not to take income set apart or credited to his or her account. The economic-benefit theory or doctrine, on the other hand, forces the inclusion of income, even if the employee *cannot* take the income. All that is necessary under the economic-benefit theory is that the employee receive from an employer the equivalent of cash, something with a (1) current, (2) real, and (3) measurable value.

For example, if Pete is given the right to receive his bonus in cash or in the form of a nontransferable annuity with no currently accessible cash values, he has constructive receipt of the bonus regardless of the choice he makes. The reason is that he has the unrestricted right to take the cash. Alternatively, if Pete was given no choice as to the form of his bonus—if it was only available to him in the form of a nontransferable, single-premium deferred annuity with no accessible cash value—he would not have constructively received his bonus. This is because he can neither take cash nor draw down cash values from the annuity. Still, he would realize current income. He has received a promise from an insurance company, a financial institution in the business of making such promises, that he will receive benefits (his bonus) in the future.

The second situation illustrates the economic-benefit theory. The secured promise of an insurance company or banking company to pay income in the future can be currently and adequately valued and is therefore immediately taxable. This is unlike the naked promise of an employer that is, in effect, a non-negotiable, nonassignable agreement generally incapable of valuation. This is so because the employer's promise is subject, according to the courts, to the hazards of economic and business conditions regardless of the size or financial state of the employer.

Perhaps the following case will further illustrate the distinction between the doctrine of constructive receipt and the economic-benefit theory. An employer established a trust in 1945 for the benefit of one of its key employees. The employer placed $10,500 in the trust that year. The trustee was directed to pay that employee $5,000 in 1946 and the balance in 1947. In other words, the deferred compensation was irrevocably set aside in a trust and payable over a 2-year period. The court held that in 1945 the amount of $10,500 was fixed and irrevocably paid out by the employer for the sole benefit of the taxpayer. The court recognized that the employee technically had neither actual nor constructive receipt of the trust money. During 1945 he had no right whatsoever to draw from those funds. Therefore the court reasoned that there was a substantial limitation on the employee's control that prevented constructive receipt. However, the court concluded that the employee did have an *actual receipt of the economic or financial benefit* conferred on him in 1945. This was the year in which the employer established the irrevocable trust for the employee's benefit in which the employee's rights were nonforfeitable. In such a case, the employee would pay tax on the present value (1945 value) of the right to receive $5,000 one year later (1946) and an additional $5,500 2 years later (1947).

Even though the funds were not immediately subject to his actual expenditure, they were there solely for his benefit. Therefore the amount of income he is to realize in the year in which the funds were set apart for his benefit must be measured by the amount of money paid, appropriately discounted to reflect the postponement of possession or enjoyment. Even this discount would not be allowed if the funds were placed in an interest-bearing account on which the employee would ultimately receive the interest.

Question: How might the economic-benefit theory be applied in a life insurance situation?

Answer: There are several life insurance related situations in which the economic-benefit theory is applied. One such situation is the taxation of employees covered under a qualified pension or profit-sharing plan that contains life insurance on their lives. Another situation is where an employee receives group insurance in excess of the excludible limit. Perhaps the clearest example can be found in the taxation of split-dollar life insurance. Split-dollar insurance is an arrangement, typically between an employer and an employee, whereby policy premiums, cash values, dividends, and death benefits may be split. The classic example is where the employer pays that part of the annual premium that equals the current year's increase in the cash value. The employee pays the balance of the premium, if any. Death benefits will be apportioned so that the employer recovers the total outlay, while the employee's family receives any balance. There are several variations on this traditional arrangement that are currently being used.

The employee is taxed currently on the value of the economic benefit received from the employer's participation in the split-dollar agreement. The benefit in question is the current insurance protection available to the employee under the basic policy. The value of this benefit is measured by government tables that contain one-year term insurance rates, so-called P.S. 58 premium rates.

The employee is deemed to have received a currently taxable economic benefit measured by the premium cost that would have been incurred for the net protection at this individual's attained age. Government tables (P.S. 58 rates) are used to determine this term cost. Policy dividends used to purchase one-year term insurance under a dividend option or applied to purchase insurance in which the employee has a nonforfeitable interest likewise constitute an economic benefit to the employee (just as if those dividends had been received in cash). The value of this benefit is the actual dollar amount of dividends so used or received.

If the policy realizes cash value buildup in excess of the amount ultimately payable to the employer, the IRS maintains that such amounts are also taxable to the employee. The total value of all such economic benefits is added. The employee may then subtract from the total value of the economic benefit received any premium contribution that the employee makes. Any remaining balance is taxable to the employee as ordinary income during the current year. This amount represents the entire economic benefit the employee has received.

THE PRINCIPLE OF ASSIGNMENT OF INCOME

Question: What is the principle of assignment of income?

Answer: The principle of assignment of income requires the taxpayer whose personal efforts generate income or who is the owner of property that generates income to report or declare the income on his or her own tax return. It provides that the taxation of income cannot be shifted from one taxpayer to another merely by transferring or assigning to another taxpayer the right to receive the income. This principle was developed in the tax law mostly through judicial decisions. Litigation with the IRS arose as a result of the efforts of crafty taxpayers to shift the taxation of income to other taxpayers (such as family members) whose marginal rate of taxation was lower than their own. Such techniques would result in lower overall taxes for the parties concerned. The issue here is not what income is taxable or when it is taxable, but rather *to whom* it is taxable.

Question: How does the principle of assignment of income operate?

Answer: The principle operates in two basic ways: first, by requiring that income that is generated by the performance of personal services be taxed to the person who performed the services; and second, by requiring that income generated by property be taxed to the taxpayer who owns the property. For example, suppose an executive of a large corporation enters into a written contract with her son providing that his salary from the corporation be paid directly to her son. Even though the son actually receives the income under this arrangement, it will still be taxable to the executive because it was her personal services rendered for the company that produced the income. The income would also be treated as a gift to the son. Another example would be where a father arranges for the income from his portfolio of corporate securities to be paid directly to his daughter. Again, even though the daughter receives the income, the father is still taxed on the income because he is the owner of the underlying property.

Question: How can a taxpayer successfully shift the burden of taxation of income to another taxpayer who is in a lower tax bracket?

Answer: In the case of income generated by most types of personal services, there is no reliable planning technique that can legally shift taxation to another taxpayer. In addition to the general assignment of income principle, there are various statutory roadblocks set up in the tax law to defeat or discourage such efforts. The best example of a legitimate shift in the taxation of personal service income is not useful for planning purposes: where a taxpayer dies before receiving income for services rendered and the income becomes "income in respect of a decedent" that is taxable to the beneficiary who receives it.

In the case of income generated by the ownership of property, a bona fide transfer of the ownership of the property will result in the income from the property being shifted for tax purposes to the transferee. Suppose that in the example discussed above, the father transferred outright ownership of his portfolio of securities to his daughter rather than merely assigning the income to her. The income earned on the securities after the transfer would then be taxable to the daughter because she would be the owner of the property.

This requirement of transfer of property ownership is often referred to as the doctrine of "the fruit and the tree." This metaphor indicates that in order to shift the burden of taxation, the entire "tree" or underlying asset—and not merely the "fruit" or income generated by it—must be transferred to another taxpayer. The economic reality of such situations is that the property owner must relinquish control of property in order to avoid taxation on its income. This is a more difficult decision than simply assigning the income from the property to another person or entity.

Question: Must there be an outright transfer of property to another person to shift the burden of taxation of income from the property?

Answer: There need not always be an outright transfer. For example, minor children are limited by law in how they are able to control and manage property. In situations where parents wish to shift the taxation of income to children, certain types of trusts can be used to hold ownership of property while effectively shifting taxation. However, the principle that the donor must relinquish ownership and control over the property still holds. The trust must be drafted in a way that complies with applicable federal, state, and local tax and property laws. Trusts used for income-shifting purposes include so-called "Sec. 2503(b) income trusts" and "Sec. 2503(c) accumulation trusts," which are named for the Internal Revenue Code provisions that govern them. The specific provisions and techniques used in such trusts are not covered in detail in this text.

CONCLUSION

The four concepts discussed in this chapter are fundamental to an understanding of the income tax law. Each of them is represented in various ways by portions of the Internal Revenue Code, by judicial decisions, by IRS practices, and by other elements of tax law authority. These concepts help students of the tax law to know the specific tax result of a given transaction or situation and also to understand why the result occurs.

4

Determination of Income
Tax Liability

James F. Ivers III

The Higher the Tax Bracket, the Better the View.
Advertisement for luxury Florida real estate development

Chapter Outline

INTRODUCTION

This chapter will examine the basic steps in determining an individual's income tax liability. It begins with a discussion of how an individual's adjusted gross income is determined using gross income as a starting point. Then the determination of taxable income is examined, followed by the calculation of actual tax payable.

In the course of following this process, several fundamental tax rules applicable to individuals will be covered including the general concepts of exclusions and deductions, the standard deduction, personal and dependency exemptions, filing status, tax rates, and the "kiddie tax."

THE DETERMINATION OF ADJUSTED GROSS INCOME

The Nature of Exclusions

The concept of gross income was discussed in chapter 3. Gross income is essentially all income that a taxpayer realizes during the tax year minus any available exclusions from gross income.

In chapters 5 and 6, various items that are includible or partially includible in gross income will be examined. Items of income that are excludible from a taxpayer's gross income will also be discussed. An exclusion may be defined as an item of income that is not required to be included in gross income pursuant to a specific provision of the income tax law. It is something quite different from a deduction. A deduction is an expense paid or incurred by a taxpayer that the tax law specifically allows to be subtracted from the amount of income that is otherwise subject to tax. It is an item of expense. An exclusion, on the other hand, is an item of income that may be received by a taxpayer without being included in gross income. As previously stated, a taxpayer's gross income equals all items of income received by the taxpayer during the year minus all available exclusions from gross income.

Once gross income has been determined, the next step is to reduce gross income by all deductions that are allowable in determining adjusted gross income.

What Is Adjusted Gross Income?

The calculation of an individual taxpayer's adjusted gross income (AGI) is an intermediate step in the process of calculating taxable income. To calculate adjusted gross income, certain deductions are subtracted from the individual's gross income.

There are two fundamental categories of deductions for individual taxpayers: deductions allowable in determining adjusted gross income and deductions allowable in determining taxable income. Deductions subtracted from gross income in determining adjusted gross income are referred to as "above-the-line" deductions. Deductions subtracted from adjusted gross income in determining taxable income are referred to as "below-the-line" deductions.

Although the calculation of AGI is an intermediate step, it is an important one. Two of the most significant reasons why are as follows:

- Above-the-line deductions allowable in determining adjusted gross income are available regardless of whether the taxpayer claims "itemized" deductions. As explained below, the taxpayer claims itemized or below-the-line deductions only if the total of such deductions exceeds the available standard deduction. For this reason, above-the-line deductions are often more valuable to the taxpayer.

- Many tax benefits, including the availability of several deductions and the amount of the taxpayer's personal and dependency exemptions, are reduced or "phased out" if the taxpayer's AGI exceeds certain specified amounts. Several of these "phaseouts" are discussed in this text. Certain other deductions are available only to the extent the amount of such deductions exceeds a specified percentage of AGI (a deduction "floor"). Also the deduction for charitable contributions is allowed only to the extent that contributions do not exceed specified percentage of AGI (a deduction "ceiling").

The reduction of an individual's AGI results in the increased availability of other tax benefits. In fact, the maximum allowable reduction of an individual's AGI is one of the most important individual tax planning objectives. Above-the-line deductions reduce AGI, while below-the-line deductions do not.

With a few exceptions, above-the-line deductions generally relate to business or income-producing activities of the taxpayer. On the other hand, the majority of the taxpayer's itemized or below-the-line deductions are expenses or losses of a personal nature for which Congress has provided income tax deductions for social and economic policy reasons.

Deductions Allowable in Determining Adjusted Gross Income

The following expenses are some of the more important deductions that are claimed above-the-line by individual taxpayers. This list is not all-inclusive.

- all deductions attributable to a trade or business carried on by the taxpayer, if such trade or business does not consist of the performance of services by the taxpayer as an employee
- certain business expenses of employees including expenses reimbursed by the taxpayer's employer, business expenses of performing artists, and business expenses of certain public officials
- losses from the sale or exchange of property (Property sales will be discussed in later chapters of this text.)
- deductions attributable to rents and royalties
- deductible contributions to pension and profit-sharing plans of self-employed individuals
- deductible contributions to IRAs
- penalties or other forfeitures resulting from premature withdrawals from time savings accounts or deposits (including certificates of deposit)
- deductible alimony payments
- the portion of jury duty pay remitted to the taxpayer's employer

- deductions for clean-fuel vehicles and certain refueling property
- deductible moving expenses
- contributions to medical savings accounts
- deductible interest payments made on qualified education loans

THE DETERMINATION OF TAXABLE INCOME

Introduction

An individual's taxable income is determined by subtracting the following items from adjusted gross income:

- either the total of the taxpayer's allowable itemized deductions or the taxpayer's applicable standard deduction amount, whichever is greater, and
- the total allowable amount of the taxpayer's personal and dependency exemptions

The amount of the taxpayer's standard deduction is based on filing status. Increased amounts are available for blind taxpayers and taxpayers aged 65 and over. Personal and dependency exemptions are "phased out" for upper income taxpayers as explained below.

The Standard Deduction

The standard deduction is a specified amount, indexed annually for inflation, that may be claimed in calculating taxable income by taxpayers who do not itemize their deductions. As stated above, taxpayers claim itemized deductions if the total amount of such deductions exceeds the available standard deduction. For tax years beginning in 2001,[*] the standard deduction amounts are

Filing Status	Amount
Married filing jointly	$7,600
Unmarried head of household	6,650
Single	4,550
Married filing separately	3,800

---

[*] The numbers in this text applicable to the year 2001 that are adjusted annually for inflation are based on published estimates available at the time of printing and, though usually accurate, are not the official numbers.

Standard Deduction for Dependents

A special rule applies to taxpayers who are dependents. A dependent is an individual for whom another taxpayer claims a dependency exemption. Dependents are not eligible to claim the regular standard deduction amounts on their own returns. As indexed for inflation for the 2001 tax year, the special standard deduction amount allowable on a dependent's tax return is the greater of:

- a sum equal to the amount of the dependent's earned income for the year plus $250 (but not more than the regular standard deduction amount), or
- $750 (for 2001)

For example, a dependent with earned income of $1,000 would be entitled to a standard deduction of $1,250 ($1,000 plus $250). A dependent with earned income of $400 would be entitled to a standard deduction of $750 because that amount is greater than his or her earned income plus $250 ($650).

Aged or Blind Taxpayers

Another special rule applies to taxpayers who are 65 years of age or older and/or are legally blind. Such taxpayers (including dependents) are entitled to increase their standard deduction by specified amounts. For married taxpayers filing jointly, each spouse who qualifies may add the additional amount or amounts to the standard deduction claimed on the joint return. As indexed for inflation for the 2001 tax year, these "additional amounts" are as follows:

- $1,100 for taxpayers who are unmarried and are not filing as surviving spouses using tax rates applicable to joint returns
- $900 for other taxpayers

> *Example:* Mr. and Mrs. Volare file a joint return for 2001. Mr. Volare is 64 years old, and Mrs. Volare is 67. Their standard deduction amount is $8,500, the sum of the regular amount of $7,600 plus the applicable additional amount of $900. Mr. and Mrs. Volare will claim the standard deduction in calculating their taxable income unless the total of their itemized deductions exceeds $8,500. If so, they will itemize their deductions and not claim the standard deduction.

The Overall Limitation on Itemized Deductions

The rules applicable to specific itemized deductions will be discussed in chapter 9. However, in discussing the process of calculating individual income tax liability, it is important to consider the "overall limitation" on itemized deductions. This rule is one of the many "phaseout" provisions in the Internal Revenue Code that reduce or eliminate tax benefits for taxpayers with income above certain levels in a given year.

If an individual taxpayer's adjusted gross income exceeds a specified threshold amount that is indexed annually for inflation, the taxpayer's itemized deductions are reduced by 3 percent of the amount by which AGI exceeds the threshold amount. For 2001, that specified amount is $132,950 ($66,475 or half of the regular amount for married taxpayers filing separately). If itemized deductions are reduced by the overall limitation, the reduction cannot exceed 80 percent of the total itemized deductions that are subject to the reduction. A significant modification to this rule is that the overall limitation does not apply to deductions for medical expenses, investment interest expenses, or casualty and theft losses.

> *Example:* Mark and Terry Sellers are married taxpayers filing jointly. For 2001, their adjusted gross income is $265,000. Mark and Terry have the following itemized deductions: $25,000 of charitable contributions, $18,000 of deductible interest on a home mortgage, and a deductible casualty loss from uninsured flood damage of $40,000 (after all the specific restrictions on the deduction for personal casualty losses have been applied). Their AGI exceeds the threshold amount of $132,950 by $132,050 ($265,000 − $132,950). Three percent of that amount is $3,962 ($132,050 x .03). The couple's charitable contributions and their home mortgage interest are subject to the overall limitation, but their deductible casualty loss is not. Therefore the total amount subject to the limit is $43,000 ($25,000 + $18,000). Mark and Terry will lose $3,962 of this $43,000 amount, reducing that deductible amount to $39,038. If their AGI increases for the year, they could lose up to $34,400 of the $43,000 of deductions, which would be the maximum 80 percent reduction ($43,000 x .8).

The overall limitation on itemized deductions is applied after the rules and limits for each specific itemized deduction have been applied. These specific rules include the 50 percent of AGI "ceiling" on charitable contributions, the dollar amount loan limits for qualified residence interest, and the 2 percent of AGI "floor" on most miscellaneous itemized deductions. All of these topics are covered in detail in later chapters of this text.

Personal and Dependency Exemptions

Introduction

In the computation of taxable income, taxpayers are permitted to subtract from AGI the total amount of their allowable personal and dependency exemptions. Each exemption is the equivalent of a deduction for a specified amount that is indexed annually for inflation. This amount is referred to as an "exemption" rather than as a "deduction" because it is not attributable to any actual or determinable expense made by the taxpayer. Rather, it is an arbitrary amount that is granted to taxpayers under the tax law to help reduce the net cost of their personal expenses. Personal and dependency exemptions are allowable regardless of whether the taxpayer claims the standard deduction or itemizes deductions.

These exemptions are available in two forms: personal exemptions and dependency exemptions. The amount is the same for each type of exemption. For the year 2001, the exemption amount is $2,900. For each individual with respect to whom either a personal or dependency exemption is claimed on a tax return, a taxpayer identification number must be included on the return.

Personal Exemptions

Each taxpayer is generally permitted to claim one personal exemption for himself or herself on the individual tax return. Married taxpayers filing jointly are allowed one personal exemption for each spouse. If married taxpayers file a separate return, generally only one exemption is allowed. However, if the spouse of the taxpayer filing the separate return has no gross income and is not the dependent of another taxpayer, an exemption for that spouse is allowed.

A special rule applies to individuals with respect to whom a dependency exemption is claimed by another taxpayer. Taxpayers who are "dependents" in this sense are not permitted to claim their own personal exemption on their individual returns. In this way, a total of only one exemption is claimed for each person. The rules for dependency exemptions are discussed below.

Dependency Exemptions

Taxpayers are entitled to claim one additional exemption for each individual who is a dependent of the taxpayer. In order to claim an individual as a dependent, the taxpayer must meet the following requirements:

- The dependent person must have one of the relationships with the taxpayer prescribed by the Internal Revenue Code. These relationships include parent-child and other family relations, and also cover other individuals who are members of the taxpayer's household for the entire tax year. For purposes of this test, a "child" of the taxpayer includes a legally adopted child, a child placed in the taxpayer's home by an authorized placement agency for the purpose of legal adoption, or a foster child who was a member of the taxpayer's household for the year.
- The taxpayer must have provided more than half of the dependent's support for the tax year. The term "support" generally means expenses for the necessities of life and other important expenses such as those for education. Recreational expenses are generally not included in the

calculation of support for purposes of the "more than one half" rule. Also scholarships granted to full-time students are not included in the calculation of support.

- The dependent person must have gross income of less than the exemption amount for the tax year, unless the person is a child of the taxpayer who is either under age 19 or a full-time student under age 24.
- The dependent person must not file a joint return with his or her spouse.

These rules or tests for claiming an individual as a dependent are shown in more detail in table 4-1.

TABLE 4-1 Tests for Claiming Dependency Exemption*				
Relationship of Dependent Person	Support Test	Gross Income Test	Joint Return Test	Social Security Numbers
• son, daughter, stepson, step-daughter, brother, sister, stepbrother, stepsister, father, mother or other lineal ancestor, stepfather, stepmother, niece, nephew, aunt, uncle, son-in-law, daughter-in-law, father-in-law, mother-in-law, brother-in-law, or sister-in-law of the taxpayer • an individual other than the taxpayer's spouse who was a member of the tax-payer's house-hold for the year	Taxpayer claiming exemption must have provided more than half of the qualifying person's support for the year. Scholar-ships received by full-time students do not count as support under this "support" test. This rule makes it easier for students to qualify as dependents.	Dependent person must *either:* • have gross income for the year less than the exemption amount or • be a child of the taxpayer who is either under age 19 or a full-time student under age 24	No person who files a joint return with his or her spouse may be claimed as a dependent.	Social Security number of dependent *must* be furnished on return of taxpayer claiming the exemption

*These are the basic rules. There are some other wrinkles that apply in certain situations.

"Phaseout" Rule for Personal and Dependency Exemptions

Another "phaseout" provision applies to the personal and dependency exemptions of upper-income taxpayers. The dollar amount of each available exemption is phased out in increments of 2 percent of the exemption amount for taxpayers with income above specified threshold levels. All the taxpayer's personal and dependency exemptions are phased out simultaneously rather than sequentially, "one by one." The threshold income levels for the phaseout are based on adjusted gross income, are indexed annually for inflation, and vary according to the filing status of the taxpayer.

The AGI amounts at which the phaseout begins and at which the exemption amounts are completely phased out are as follows for 2001:

Filing Status	AGI Threshold Phaseout Amount	AGI Amount at which Phaseout Is Completed
Married filing jointly	$199,450	$321,951
Head of household	166, 200	288,701
Single	132,950	255,451
Married filing separately	99,725	160,976

Each personal and dependency exemption otherwise allowable to a taxpayer is phased out by 2 percent of each $2,500 or any fraction of $2,500 by which AGI is in excess of the threshold phaseout amount. The term "any fraction of $2,500" essentially means that the first dollar of each $2,500 increment of AGI above the threshold phaseout amount results in the loss of 2 percent of the exemption amount. For example, a taxpayer with AGI of $2,501 above the threshold amount would lose 4 percent of the exemption amount for all personal and dependency exemptions. If the taxpayer's income reaches the applicable "completion of phaseout" amount, the amount of the taxpayer's personal and dependency exemptions is zero.

Example: Louise and Don McGill are married and file a joint return. In 2001, their adjusted gross income is $350,000. Except for their income level, they would be entitled to two personal exemptions on their return. Because of their income level, their exemption amount is phased out by 2 percent for each $2,500 or fraction thereof by which their AGI exceeds $199,450. The range of income over which their exemption amount is reduced is $122,501 ($321,951 – $199,450). This amount is equal to $2,500 x 49, plus one dollar under the fractional rule. The first 49 increments of $2,500 of AGI over the threshold amount reduce their exemption by 98 percent. The next dollar of income eliminates the last 2 percent of the exemption amount. Since their AGI is equal to or greater than $199,450 plus $122,501 (the "completion" amount of $321,951), their exemption amount is reduced to zero.

This and other phaseout rules essentially increase the effective rate of income tax on upper-income taxpayers.

Other Phaseout Rules

Many taxpayers are subject to more than one phaseout. For example, the same taxpayer could often be subject to both the phaseout of the exemption amount and the overall limitation on itemized deductions. Such combinations of the loss of tax benefits results in additional increments of the taxpayer's income being taxed at effective rates higher than the marginal rate of tax imposed by the Internal Revenue Code, so long as the taxpayer's income is still within the ranges of income at which tax benefits are being phased out.

In addition to the marginal rate of tax imposed by the rate system as discussed below, taxpayers are also losing deductions (and/or credits) with each additional increment of income that results in phaseouts. Therefore the actual effective tax rate on the increments of income that result in the phaseout of tax benefits may be significantly higher than the statutory marginal rate.

Phaseouts have become widespread in the tax law. Many of them will be covered in later chapters of this text. Some of the other tax benefits that are subject to variations of the phaseout concept include the following:

- tax credit for children
- tax credits for higher education
- contributions to traditional IRAs, Roth IRAs, and education IRAs
- tax credit for adoption expenses
- "active participation" exception to the passive loss rules
- exclusion for certain income from U.S. savings bonds used for higher education
- deduction for interest on qualified higher education loans
- tax credit for child-care expenses
- earned income credit

The above list, although not all inclusive, is indicative of how Congress has become enamored of the phaseout concept in the income tax law.

Divorced or Separated Parents

The general rule for claiming a dependency exemption for a child of divorced or separated parents is that the custodial parent is entitled to the dependency exemption. However, if the custodial parent signs a written declaration that he or she will not claim the child as a dependent for tax purposes, the noncustodial parent may claim the exemption if the written declaration is attached to his or her tax return. A "custodial parent" for this purpose is the parent who has custody of the child for the greater portion of the calendar year.

Multiple Support Agreements

There is a special rule for certain situations in which no one individual provides over half of a dependent's support. The most common example of such a situation is probably where siblings provide combined support to an elderly parent. Normally, each individual providing support would be entitled to claim the dependent for tax purposes, except that the "more than half" support test is not met by any one individual providing support. The rule for such cases is that an individual who contributed more than 10 percent of the dependent's support for the year and who is entitled to claim the exemption except for the support test may claim the dependency exemption. However, every other individual who provided more than 10 percent of the dependent's support (and is also eligible to claim the exemption except for the support test) files a written declaration with the IRS stating that he or she will not claim the dependency exemption.

TAX RATES AND FILING STATUS

Tax Rates and Brackets

Once taxable income has been determined, tax rates are applied to determine the individual's tentative income tax liability. That liability may then be reduced by any tax credits for which the taxpayer is eligible. For taxpayers other than corporations, there are five sets of tax rates that differ according to the taxpayer's filing status. Each filing status or set of rates includes different amounts of taxable income that are subject to each of the five basic federal income tax rates under current law. The five rates are 15 percent, 28 percent, 31 percent, 36 percent, and 39.6 percent. The filing status for taxpayers other than corporations includes the following five groups:

- married taxpayers filing jointly
- unmarried heads of households
- unmarried or "single" taxpayers
- married taxpayers filing separately
- estates and trusts

The amount of taxable income subject to each tax rate for each filing status can be referred to as a tax "bracket." These brackets are indexed annually for inflation. For 2001, the tax brackets (also referred to as "tax rate schedules") for each filing status are shown in table 4-2.

TABLE 4-2
Individual Tax Rate Schedules for 2001

	If taxable income is	The tax is
Married individuals filing joint returns and surviving spouses	Not over $45,200 Over $45,200 but not over $109,250 Over $109,250 but not over $166,500 Over $166,500 but not over $297,350 Over $297,350	15% of the taxable income $6,780 plus 28% of the excess over $45,200 $24,714 plus 31% of the excess over $109,250 $42,461.50 plus 36% of the excess over $166,500 $89,567.50 plus 39.6% of the excess over $297,350
Heads of households	Not over $36,250 Over $36,250 but not over $93,650 Over $93,650 but not over $151,650 Over $151,650 but not over $297,350 Over $297,350	15% of the taxable income $5,437.50 plus 28% of the excess over $36,250 $21,509.50 plus 31% of the excess over $93,650 $39,489.50 plus 36% of the excess over $151,650 $91,941.50 plus 39.6% of the excess over $297,350
Unmarried individuals (other than surviving spouses and heads of households)	Not over $27,050 Over $27,050 but not over $65,550 Over $65,550 but not over $136,750 Over $136,750 but not over $297,350 Over $297,350	15% of the taxable income $4,057.50 plus 28% of the excess over $27,050 $14,837.50 plus 31% of the excess over $65,550 $36,909.50 plus 36% of the excess over $136,750 $94,725.50 plus 39.6% of the excess over $297,350
Married individuals filing separate returns	Not over $22,600 Over $22,600 but not over $54,625 Over $54,625 but not over $83,250 Over $83,250 but not over $148,675 Over $148,675	15% of the taxable income $3,390 plus 28% of the excess over $22,600 $12,357 plus 31% of the excess over $54,625 $21,230.75 plus 36% of the excess over $83,250 $44,783.75 plus 39.6% of the excess over $148,675
Estates and trusts	Not over $1,800 Over $1,800 but not over $4,250 Over $4,250 but not over $6,500 Over $6,500 but not over $8,900 Over $8,900	15% of the taxable income $270 plus 28% of the excess over $1,800 $956 plus 31% of the excess over $4,250 $1,653.50 plus 36% of the excess over $6,500 $2,517.50 plus 39.6% of the excess over $8,900

Note that these tax rate schedules are those which apply to ordinary income and not to capital gains of individual taxpayers. For a detailed discussion of the taxation of capital gains as distinguished from ordinary income, refer to chapter 14.

Example: Garry and Karen are married taxpayers filing jointly. Their taxable income in 2001 is $189,000. Their tax due is $50,568, computed as follows:

- Their taxable income up to $45,200 is taxed at a rate of 15 percent, which equals a tax of $6,780.
- Their taxable income over $45,200 but not over $109,250 (or $64,050) is taxed at a rate of 28 percent, which equals a tax of $17,934.
- Their taxable income over $109,250 but not over $166,500 (or $57,250) is taxed at a rate of 31 percent, which equals a tax of $17,747.50.
- Their taxable income over $166,500 but not over $297,350 (or $22,500, the remainder of their taxable income) is taxed at a rate of 36 percent, which equals a tax of $8,100.
- The tax computed under each of the four brackets shown above is added together for a total of $50,561.50 ($6,780 + $17,934 + $17,747.50 + $8,100).

Filing Status for Individual Taxpayers

Married Taxpayers Filing Jointly

Taxpayers who are married at the end of the tax year are generally permitted to file a joint return. A joint return may also be filed if one of the spouses dies during the tax year. A taxpayer who qualifies as a "surviving spouse" as discussed below is also eligible to file as a married taxpayer filing jointly. If a couple have obtained a decree of divorce or of separate maintenance, they are not eligible to file jointly.

Married couples who file jointly are, as a general rule, jointly and severally liable for the tax due. However, if one of the spouses qualifies as an "innocent spouse" under a special set of rules, that spouse may be relieved of all or a portion of the liability to pay tax arising from the joint return.

Surviving Spouses

A "surviving spouse" is permitted to file and use the tax brackets applicable to joint returns for a period of 2 years beginning with the year following the year of the spouse's death. In order to qualify, the surviving spouse must maintain as his or her home a household that includes as a member of the household a son, stepson, daughter, or stepdaughter of the surviving spouse who is eligible to be claimed as the surviving spouse's dependent under the dependency exemption rules. The surviving spouse must furnish over half the cost of maintaining such a household.

Why would a surviving spouse wish to file as a married taxpayer filing jointly? The answer lies in the structure of the tax rate schedules. The tax rate schedules for joint returns produce the lowest tax payable for any one amount of income as compared with any other filing status. This is so because the brackets to which the lower income tax rates apply are larger for joint filers.

The "Marriage Penalty"

What is the meaning of the often quoted term "marriage penalty" in the context of joint return filing status? The term "marriage penalty" refers to the fact that in many situations, married couples who both earn income would pay less total income taxes if they were single rather than married. Even though their total income added together will produce the least amount of tax by using the joint return tax rate schedules or "brackets," it would be possible for the couple to pay less if they were permitted to each file their own return, report their respective incomes separately, and use the single taxpayer's rate schedules. By combining income on a joint return, the highest tax rate brackets are reached by joint filers at lower total income levels than such brackets would be reached if the income could be split into two returns filed by single taxpayers. This "penalty" occurs because the higher tax rate brackets, particularly the 36 percent and 39.6 percent brackets, begin for single taxpayers and married taxpayers at income levels that are relatively close. For example, the 39.6 percent bracket begins at the same level of income for both single taxpayers and joint filers.

Of course, married taxpayers are not permitted to file as single taxpayers. They are, however, permitted to file as married taxpayers filing separately. In certain situations, this may produce a better overall result than the joint tax rates schedules, but usually it does not. In addition, there are restrictions and limitations on the use of many tax benefits by married taxpayers filing separately.

Head of Household Filing Status

The rate schedules applicable to an unmarried head of household are more beneficial than those for single taxpayers but not as beneficial as joint return rate schedules. The rules for qualifying as an unmarried head of household are somewhat complicated. These rules can be summarized using four basic components:

- The marital status requirement. The taxpayer must be unmarried at the close of the taxable year, unless the taxpayer's spouse was not a member of the household for the last six months of the tax year and the household includes a child for whom the taxpayer is eligible to claim a dependency exemption (a so-called "abandoned spouse"). Taxpayers who are legally separated under a decree of divorce or separate maintenance (other than an interlocutory decree) are not considered to be married. Taxpayers who qualify as surviving spouses under the rules discussed above will use joint return rate schedules and are not treated as heads of households.

- The household requirement. The taxpayer must maintain as his or her home and furnish over half the cost of maintaining a household during the taxable year. At least one "qualifying person" must be a member of this household.

- The "qualifying person" requirement. The qualifying person must be a member of the household for more than one-half of the taxable year. Temporary absences due to special circumstances are not taken into account for this purpose. Qualifying persons include unmarried children, stepchildren, and grandchildren of the taxpayer, or any person for whom the taxpayer may claim a dependency exemption (including a married child). Adopted children are, of course, treated the same way as biological children.

- The rule for parents. A parent may be a "qualifying person," even if the parent does not live in the taxpayer's household, if the taxpayer is eligible to claim a dependency exemption for the parent, and the taxpayer furnishes over half the cost of maintaining the parent's household. This makes it possible for unmarried taxpayers who pay for a parent's residence in a long-term care facility to be treated as heads of households.

Other Filers

The remaining types of filing status include single taxpayers, married taxpayers filing separately, and estates and trusts. The tax rate schedules applicable to estates and trusts are the most "compressed"; that is, the highest tax rates take effect at the lowest levels of taxable income for these taxpayers. Single taxpayers use rate schedules that are less compressed than those applicable to both marrieds filing separately and estates and trusts. Corporations are subject to a different tax rate structure as discussed in chapter 18.

TAX CREDITS

After the tax has been computed on taxable income using the applicable filing status, the actual tax liability shown on the return may be reduced if the taxpayer qualifies for credits. Tax credits are dollar-for-dollar reductions in the actual tax owed; deductions, on the other hand, only reduce the amount of income subject to tax. Therefore credits are quite beneficial to taxpayers. Several significant tax credits that may be available to individual taxpayers are discussed in chapter 10.

THE "KIDDIE TAX"

One popular tax planning strategy is the shifting of income to a taxpayer who is subject to a lower marginal rate. Since parents generally have more income than young children, investment assets are often transferred to children by parents in order to gain the benefit of lower marginal tax rates. Custodial accounts or certain trusts can be used for this purpose.

Under current tax law, however, this planning strategy is significantly curtailed. Families are prevented from shifting large amounts of unearned income to children and making the shift effective for income tax purposes. The provision that limits such income shifting is referred to as the "kiddie tax."

The mechanics of the kiddie tax are essentially as follows:

- If a child under the age of 14 has unearned income above a specified amount, the excess is taxed at the highest marginal rate applicable to the child's parents for the year rather than at the child's marginal rate. The child's excess unearned income above the specified amount is called "net unearned income." The specified amount is the amount of a dependent child's regular standard deduction ($750 as adjusted for inflation in 2001) plus another $750, or $1,500 for 2001. Therefore unearned income in excess of $1,500 is "net unearned income" and is taxed at the parents' rates in 2001. Children 14 years of age or older at the end of the tax year are not subject to this rule.

- This prevention of the income-shifting technique applies to income generated by any asset the child under 14 owns, regardless of whether the asset was received from the child's parents or from another source. It also applies regardless of when any income-producing assets were transferred to the child. If the income is unearned and is included in the child's taxable income, it is subject to these rules.

- The additional tax paid with the child's return is equal to the difference between the tax payable at the child's rates and the amount of tax the parents would have paid on the net unearned income if it had been included on the parents' return. If more than one child in the same family has net unearned income, the total net unearned income is added together to determine the total tax on the income. Then the additional tax payable is allocated to the children's returns on a pro-rata basis. Instead of paying the kiddie tax on the child's return, the parents may elect to include the income of the child on their own return. This election can be made if the child has no income other than dividends and interest, and if such income is more than $750 and less than $7,500 (as adjusted for inflation for 2001).

- The kiddie tax applies only if the child has at least one parent living at the end of the taxable year.
- The rules become a bit more complicated if a child has both earned and unearned income. Dependent children are entitled to a standard deduction equal to the greater of $750 in 2001 or the amount of the child's earned income plus $250, up to the regular standard deduction amount. If a child has both earned and unearned income, up to $750 of the child's standard deduction is allocated to unearned income first. The next $750 of unearned income is taxed at the child's marginal rate. Any remaining standard deduction allowable to the child is allocated to the child's earned income.

Example: Kyle Bradford is 10 years old. He lives with his mother, Melody, who is unmarried. In 2001, he has $1,000 in earned income from doing work for neighbors, and $2,000 in interest income from a custodial bank account. Kyle's standard deduction is $1,250 ($1,000 of earned income plus $250). The first $750 of his standard deduction is allocated to his $2,000 of unearned income. The remaining $1,250 of Kyle's unearned income is subject to taxation. Of this amount, $750 will be taxed at Kyle's marginal rate. The remaining $500 of his unearned income is "net unearned income" and will be taxed at Melody's highest marginal rate. The remaining $500 of Kyle's standard deduction ($1,250 − $750) is allocated to his $1,000 of earned income. The remaining $500 of his earned income ($1,000 − $500) is subject to taxation and will be taxed at Kyle's marginal rate.

DUE DATES FOR FILING INCOME TAX RETURNS

Tax returns other than returns of a corporation are generally due on or before the fifteenth day of the fourth month following the close of the taxable year. Taxpayers whose tax year is the calendar year (including almost all individual taxpayers) are therefore required to file tax returns by April 15. Individuals can receive an automatic 4-month extension by filing Form 4868 on or before the due date. However, this is an extension of the due date for filing a return and not an extension of the time for payment of tax. Therefore any tax due with the return should be paid with Form 4868 to avoid interest and penalty charges.

Corporations are generally required to file returns on or before the fifteenth day of the third month following the close of the taxable year. Corporations file Form 1120 (1120-S for S corporations). Therefore a corporation using the calendar year as its tax year would be required to file its return by March 15. However, some corporations may have a tax year that operates on a 12-month period other than the calendar year. For example, the tax year might begin on

April 1 and end on March 31. If so, the corporation's return would be due on June 15.

Items of Gross Income

Burton T. Beam, Jr., James F. Ivers III, and John J. McFadden[*]

[A] tax lawyer is a person who is good with numbers but does not have
enough personality to be an accountant.

James D. Gordon III

Chapter Outline

[*] Burton T. Beam, Jr., MBA, CLU, ChFC, CPCU, is associate professor of insurance, and John
J. McFadden, JD, is professor of taxation and pensions, both of The American College.

INTRODUCTION

In chapter 3, the concept of gross income as it is defined under the tax law was explored. This chapter will examine some specific items of income and the rules under which they are taxed.

The Internal Revenue Code contains many provisions that exclude specific items from the calculation of a taxpayer's gross income. These provisions are called exclusions. Exclusions will be examined more closely in chapter 6, "Exclusions from Gross Income." Many items of income may be partially includible in gross income and partially excludible from gross income. Alternatively, some items are either includible in or excludible from the taxpayer's gross income, depending on whether the circumstances under which the item received meets the requirements of a specific exclusion rule. In this regard, there are similarities between the topics covered in this chapter and those covered in chapter 6. Many of the items covered in each chapter are either partially includible in gross income or excludible only if they meet certain rules and definitions. For example, annuity payments are generally partially includible in gross income. Also, the value of employer-provided group life insurance coverage may be includible if certain requirements are not met or if the amount of the coverage exceeds a specified limit. As a result, this and the next chapter should be viewed together in developing a familiarity with the ways in which the Internal Revenue Code provides definitions and limitations for the taxation of certain items of income that are treated in special ways.

PAYMENTS IN CONNECTION WITH SEPARATION OR DIVORCE

Alimony or Separate Maintenance Payments

The basic rule for alimony or separate maintenance payments is that they are includible in the gross income of the payee. Correspondingly, alimony payments includible in the gross income of the payee are deductible for income tax purposes from the gross income of the payer. The term "alimony or separate maintenance payments" means payments that are

- received by or on behalf of a spouse under a divorce or separation agreement
- not designated under the divorce or separation agreement as payments for the support of minor children, which are not includible in the gross income of the payee spouse and not deductible by the payer spouse
- not required under the divorce or separation agreement to be made for any period or in any other form after the death of the payee spouse and are not in fact so paid, and
- are made in cash or cash equivalent

In the case of spouses who are legally separated under a legal decree of divorce or of separate maintenance, in order for payments to qualify as alimony the payee spouse and the payer spouse must not be members of the same household at the time the payment is made.

Because of the requirement that alimony payments be made in cash, such benefits as rent-free occupancy of a home by one spouse and the couple's children will not be treated as alimony payments for tax purposes.

Excess "Front-Loading" of Alimony Payments

If a payer makes "excess" alimony payments, a special rule applies to include the excess payment in the gross income of the payer in the third postseparation year. At first glance, it seems illogical to include a payment in the income of the taxpayer who made the payment. However, the inclusion of an excess payment in the payer's income eliminates the prior tax benefit of the deduction that was claimed for the payment before it was characterized as an excess payment. Correspondingly, if there is an "excess" alimony payment includible in the payer's income, the payee spouse receives a deduction for such amount that was previously included in his or her gross income to balance the tax treatment of the excess payment.

The calculation of an "excess" alimony payment is based on the relative amounts of the payments made during the first three postseparation years. In the payer's first postseparation tax year, the "excess" payment is computed by taking the average of the alimony payments in the second and third postseparation years and adding $15,000 to that figure. Any alimony payment for the first postseparation year that is in excess of that amount is the "excess alimony payment."

Example: Roberta has paid her former husband, Bobby, alimony in each of the 3 years since their divorce settlement. In the first year Roberta paid Bobby $100,000 and deducted that amount on her tax return. Bobby included the $100,000 in his gross income for that year. In the second postseparation year, the payment was $60,000. In the third year, it was $50,000. The average of the payments for the second and third postseparation years is $55,000 [($60,000 + $50,000) ÷ 2]. To this amount is added $15,000 for a total of $70,000. Any alimony payment in excess of $70,000 for the first year is an excess payment. Therefore Roberta's excess alimony payment for the first postseparation year is $30,000 ($100,000 − $70,000). Roberta will have to include $30,000 in her income in the third postseparation year. Bobby will receive a corresponding deduction in that year to equalize the tax treatment of the excess alimony payment.

For the second postseparation year, the "excess" payment is the amount in excess of the payment in the third postseparation year plus $15,000.

If either spouse dies before the end of the third postseparation year, or if either spouse remarries before the end of that year and payments cease as a result of such event, then the front-loading rules for excess alimony payments do not apply.

Treatment of Child Support Payments

As stated above, payments for support of minor children are not treated as alimony for tax purposes. Such payments are not deductible by the payer spouse and not includible in the gross income of the payee spouse. Payments are treated as child support to the extent that the terms of the applicable divorce or separation agreement fix or designate them as such. For purposes of this rule, a provision in the agreement calling for a reduction in payments based on certain specified contingencies relating to a child is considered to be designating such payments as child support. These contingencies include a reduction in payments happening at the time or associated with the time when a child attains a specified age, marries, leaves school, or dies. The amount of the reduction in the payment that would result from the occurrence of one of these contingencies under the agreement is the amount treated as child support for tax purposes.

The application of the terms of the divorce agreement to fix certain payments as child support provides certainty for planning for the tax consequences of periodic payments. Under these rules, both parties can be confident of the applicable tax treatment. In fact, the divorce or separation agreement may also provide that payments that are not child support under the contingency rules will not be treated as alimony for tax purposes. The tax law respects such a characterization according to the intent of the parties. Therefore spouses can basically choose whether or not they wish to have payments deductible by the payer and taxable to the payee.

Use of Life Insurance Arrangements in Property Settlements

Life insurance contracts will often be involved in property settlement agreements incident to a divorce. The protection afforded by life insurance coverage may be an important component of the settlement. Perhaps the most common arrangement is to transfer the ownership of an existing life policy that insures the life of one spouse to the other spouse. The transfer of the policy itself does not have income tax consequences for either spouse regardless of the policy's cash value. Such a transfer is neither alimony nor child support, but a nontaxable transfer of property incident to a divorce. However, if the spouse who transferred the policy is obligated to continue to pay premiums on the transferred policy, the payment of such premiums is generally treated as an alimony payment. The same is true for premiums paid on other insurance coverages that benefit the other spouse.

The transfer of a life insurance policy will not cause the subsequent payment of death benefits to be subject to income tax under the "transfer-for-value" rule discussed in chapter 16. Transfers incident to divorce are not subject to the transfer for value rule. Therefore such death benefits retain their income-tax-free character.

Alternatively, the ownership of an existing policy might be retained by the insured spouse, while premium payments continue to be made by the policyowner spouse with the other spouse named as policy beneficiary. In such a case, the payments of the premiums by the policyowner spouse are not alimony payments and are not deductible. Clearly, the ownership rights of the insured spouse may be compromised by a provision in the divorce agreement requiring him or her to pay premiums and/or to maintain the other spouse as the death beneficiary under the policy. Even so, the payment of premiums in such a situation does not constitute alimony payments. As in the case of a transferred policy, a subsequent payment of death benefits from a policy under such an arrangement will not be subject to income tax under the transfer-for-value rule.

A third possible arrangement is to set up a new life insurance policy that insures the life of one spouse and is owned by the other spouse. The policyowner spouse can pay premiums on the new policy and have death benefit protection in the event of the former spouse's death. A portion of alimony payments received from the former spouse could be used to fund the premium obligation.

INCOME TAXATION OF ANNUITIES

Introduction

Annuities may be a significant part of an individual's comprehensive financial plan. There are special income tax rules that apply to annuity contracts. These rules are derived from the unique nature of these contracts and the ways that they are used to enhance wealth accumulation. In this text, the discussion will focus on nonqualified commercial annuities, that is, annuity contracts issued by commercial insurers that are not used in connection with a qualified plan of deferred compensation.

An "annuity" may be defined as a systematic liquidation of a sum of money, including a principal amount and an interest element, over either a period of time determined by reference to the life expectancy of one or more individuals or a fixed period of time. A commercial annuity involves the payment of one or more premiums by the contract owner to an insurance company in return for the company's obligation to make annuity payments to one or more contract beneficiaries or "annuitants" at either a specified or an unspecified time in the future.

The taxation of the actual annuity payments under the contract is subject to specific tax rules. In addition, such payments are typically deferred for some period of time after the inception of the contract, either until the annuitant reaches a specified age or for some period thereafter at the discretion of the contract owner. During this period of "deferral," the funds in the contract are generally permitted to accumulate on a tax-deferred basis. However, if a withdrawal, loan, or other financial transaction involving the contract is done before the commencement of the stream of annuitized payments, additional tax rules apply to the transaction.

The general theory of annuity taxation involves the concept that the contract owner's capital investment in the contract may be recovered tax free when distributions are made. But the interest or other earnings on the contract funds must be subject to taxation at some point in time. When and how the earnings on the contract are taxed will be explained below.

The "Exclusion Ratio" for Annuitized Payments

The income taxation of a payment in the form of an annuity is determined by using a fraction called the "exclusion ratio." The numerator of the fraction is the amount of the "investment in the contract." The denominator of the fraction is the total "expected return" under the contract. The periodic annuity payment is multiplied by this fraction to calculate the portion of the payment that is received tax free by the annuitant as a return of the investment in the contract. The balance of the payment is taxable to the annuitant.

The "investment in the contract" may be defined as the aggregate amount of premiums or other consideration paid for the contract minus any distributions already made from the contract that were excludible from the recipient's gross income as a return of capital.

The "expected return" under the contract may be defined as the total of the amounts that are expected to be received in the form of an annuity under the contract. If the annuity payment is calculated using the life expectancy of one or more annuitants, the expected return is calculated by reference to actuarial tables found in the Treasury regulations promulgated pursuant to IRC Sec. 72.

Under the regulations, there are tables used to determine life expectancy for annuity taxation purposes. One set of tables applies to annuity contracts that were fully funded before July 1986, and a second set of tables applies to contracts that are fully or partially paid for after June 1986. The tables provide "expected return multiples" expressed as the number of years that the annuitant is expected to live beginning as of the annuity starting date. The older tables differ depending on the gender of the annuitant, while the newer tables are unisex. Taxpayers who funded contracts before July 1986 may generally elect to compute their exclusion ratio under the newer unisex tables.

Example: Jay is 60 years old and is the owner and annuitant under a contract that begins annuitized payments this year. Jay will receive annuity payments for as long as he lives. His investment in the contract is $100,000. His life expectancy under the regulations is 24.2 years. His annuity payment will be $10,000 per year for life. The expected return under the contract is $242,000 ($10,000 x 24.2). Jay's exclusion ratio for the annuity payments is 41.32 percent ($100,000/$242,000). Therefore Jay may exclude from his gross income $4,132 of his $10,000 annuity payment each year. The $5,868 balance of the payment ($10,000 − $4,132) will be taxable to Jay.

Sometimes an annuity payment is made over a fixed period of time rather than for the annuitant's lifetime. If the payment of the annuity is to be made over a fixed period (such as a number of years), and assuming the number of years is less than the annuitant's life expectancy, the expected return under the contract is calculated by multiplying the amount of the annuity payment by the number of payments that are to be made.

Example: Suppose that in the example above Jay will receive the same annuity payments except that he will be paid over a fixed 20-year period rather than over his lifetime. Jay's expected return will be $200,000 ($10,000 annual payment x 20 years). Therefore his exclusion ratio will be 50 percent: $100,000 investment in the contract/ $200,000 expected return.

Deduction for Unrecovered Investment in the Contract

If the annuitant lives beyond his or her period of life expectancy as determined under the regulations, no exclusion ratio is applied to payments received after the end of the life expectancy period. Therefore the full amount of payments received after the life expectancy period will be taxable. Correspondingly, if the annuitant dies after the stream of annuity payments begins but before the end of the life expectancy period, an income tax deduction may be claimed for the unrecovered amount of the investment in the contract. This deduction may be claimed on the annuitant's final income tax return. The "unrecovered investment" would be the total investment in the contract reduced by the total of all payments previously received under the contract that were excluded from gross income.

However, different rules apply to contracts with respect to which annuity payments commenced before January 1, 1987. For such contracts, there is no deduction available for unrecovered investment at the annuitant's death. Therefore, the tax benefit of the unrecovered investment is lost. However, a corresponding rule is more favorable: if the annuitant under such contracts lives beyond his or her life expectancy, the exclusion ratio is applied to payments for as long as the annuitant lives, making it possible for the annuitant to recover a total amount tax free that is more than the actual investment in the contract.

Refund or "Period Certain" Features

Some annuity contracts contain a feature providing that, in the event the annuitant dies after the stream of annuity payments has begun but before a specified number of annuity payments have been received, the annuitant's estate or designated beneficiary will receive the remainder of the specified number of payments. An example of this feature would be a so-called "10-year certain" annuity under which the annuitized payments, once begun, are guaranteed to be paid for at least 10 years.

Contracts that contain such refund features are subject to a special tax rule regarding the calculation of the investment in the contract for exclusion ratio purposes. In calculating the exclusion ratio, the actuarial value of the guarantee or "refund" feature must be subtracted from the amount paid for the contract to determine the "investment in the contract." This actuarial value is also calculated using the tables in the regulations. The investment in the contract, as adjusted, is then used to calculate the excludible portion of the annuity payment.

> *Example:* Suppose that in the previous example, Jay's annuity is to be paid over his lifetime but also has a feature that guarantees that Jay or his designated beneficiary will receive a total of at least 10 annual annuity payments even if Jay dies during that time. Assume that the actuarial value of that guarantee, based on Jay's life expectancy, is $4,000. In calculating Jay's exclusion ratio for his annuity payments, his $100,000 investment in the contract must be reduced to $96,000 ($100,000 − $4,000). Therefore his exclusion ratio for a contract with this guarantee will be 39.67 percent ($96,000/$242,000).

The taxpayer who receives payments under a refund feature after the death of the primary annuitant is subject to tax rules that are somewhat different from those that applied to the primary annuitant. These rules are contained in Treas. Reg. Sec. 1.72-11.

Certain guarantees provided by modern annuity contracts should be distinguished from the traditional refund feature or period-certain guarantee. For example, many annuity contracts provide for a repayment of premium paid (or premium plus interest) in the event the contract owner dies before annuity payments begin under the contract. Such a guarantee does not appear to be a "refund" feature for income tax purposes because it applies to the contract owner's death before annuitization of the contract rather than to the annuitant's death after the stream of annuity payments has begun. As a result, a guarantee that applies only in the event of the owner's death while the annuity is still in the deferral or accumulation stage would not reduce the investment in the contract for exclusion ratio purposes.

Joint and Survivor Annuities

Annuity payment arrangements may involve more than one annuitant. An annuity may be payable in a fixed amount over the life of an annuitant, then payable in the same amount after the first annuitant's death over the life of a second annuitant. For example, a married couple might receive a fixed payment for as long as either one of the spouses is still alive. A variation of this arrangement would be where the annuity payments cease after the death of one of the spouses. Another annuity arrangement could be the payment of a fixed amount to one annuitant followed by the payment of a lesser amount to a second annuitant for life after the first annuitant's death. In each of these variations, the expected return under the contract can be calculated by using various tables contained in Treasury regulations.

In the case of an annuity under which an annuity payment is made to a primary annuitant, then to a secondary annuitant in the same amount after the death of the primary annuitant, the multiple for calculating expected return under the contract under such a "last survivor" annuity arrangement is found in table VI in the regulations pursuant to IRC Sec. 72.

> *Example:* Howard and Janet, a married couple, will receive annual payments under an annuity contract beginning this year. They paid $40,000 for the contract and have taken no prior distributions from it. The annuity payment will be $2,200 per year for as long as either Howard or Janet is alive. Howard is 48 years old, and Janet is 50. Under table VI, their joint life expectancy is 40.2 years. Therefore their expected return under the contract is $88,440 ($2,200 x 40.2). Their applicable exclusion ratio is 45.23 percent ($40,000/$88,440). The excludible amount of their annual annuity payment will be $995 ($2,200 x .4523).

Special Rules for Variable Annuity Contracts

Variable annuities have become more popular in recent years. In a variable annuity, all or a substantial portion of the funds in the contract are placed in equity-based investments, such as publicly traded stocks and stock mutual funds. If the contract is annuitized and payments begin, the amount of the payments may vary under a calculation based on the investment performance of the contract funds. As a result, the "expected return" under the contract cannot be accurately calculated for purposes of determining an exclusion ratio for the annuity payments. Therefore the exclusion ratio calculation is not used to determine the taxation of the annuity payments under a variable contract. Rather, the investment in the contract is divided by the number of years of the annuitant's life expectancy to determine the dollar amount of each payment that is excludible from the annuitant's gross income.

Example: Tyler is the owner and annuitant under a variable annuity contract. Tyler's investment in the contract is $250,000. At the time that annual annuity payments commence, Tyler's life expectancy is 30 years. Therefore Tyler may exclude $8,333 of each annual payment from his gross income ($250,000/30).

Because the payments are subject to fluctuations, it is possible that the amount of an annuity payment under a variable contract will be less than the amount of each payment that was determined to be excludible. In such cases, the entire payment will be excludible from gross income, and the "unused" portion of the excludible amount can be recovered later for income tax purposes by recomputing the annual dollar amount of the annuity payment that is excludible from gross income. The recomputation of the excludible amount can be made at the election of the annuitant and is accomplished by the following steps:

- The dollar amount of the exclusion that was not utilized is determined.
- The annuitant's life expectancy at the time of the recomputation is found by consulting the appropriate table in the regulations.
- An additional excludible amount is determined by dividing the amount of the unused exclusion by the life expectancy of the annuitant at the time of the election to recompute.
- The additional amount is then added to the original excludible amount to determine the adjusted excludible amount.

Example: Assume that in the previous example Tyler receives an annual annuity payment of $5,000. His excludible amount is $8,333, so the amount of his unused exclusion is $3,333 ($8,333 – $5,000). Tyler elects to recompute his excludible amount. At that time, he is 70 years old, and his life expectancy is 16 years. The additional excludible amount is $208 ($3,333/16). This additional amount is added to Tyler's original excludible amount ($8,333) to arrive at the adjusted excludible amount of $8,541.

Remember that unless the annuity starting date was on or before December 31, 1986, the annuitant cannot exclude a cumulative total of more than his or her total investment in the contract. Therefore, if the annuitant lives beyond his or her life expectancy, payments will be fully taxable once the annuitant has excluded a cumulative amount equal to the investment in the contract.

Withdrawals and Other Transactions during the "Accumulation" Period

Introduction

Some annuity contracts are so-called "immediate" annuities, that is, contracts in which annuity payments begin no later than one year from the date the annuity is purchased. However, the majority of contracts sold in the nonqualified market are "deferred" annuities, that is, contracts in which the annuity payments do not commence within one year. In many contracts, it is possible that actual annuitized payments will never be made. The contract owner may be purchasing the annuity primarily for the purpose of obtaining tax deferral of the funds accumulating within the contract. Of course, at some point in time the income earned on the contract funds will be taxed. If the owner never annuitizes the contract, rules apply upon the death of the contract owner that provide for the taxation of interest or other investment gains that have been realized within the annuity contract. In the meantime, it is possible for the contract owner to make partial withdrawals from the contract, borrow funds from the contract, or even surrender the contract and obtain its cash surrender value.

Amounts "Not Received As an Annuity"

The funds in a deferred annuity contract accumulate free of income taxation until one of the following occurs: a loan, collateralization, or withdrawal from the contract; an annuitization of the contract; or the death of the contract owner. Partial withdrawals or loans from an annuity contract during the deferral or accumulation period are subject to different income tax rules than actual annuitized payments. Withdrawals and loans are treated as taxable events for income tax purposes. No exclusion ratio applies. The general rule is that the loan or withdrawal will be taxed to the extent of "income on the contract." "Income on the contract" is the amount by which the cash value of the contract (without regard to surrender charges) exceeds the owner's investment in the contract. This is, in effect, a form of "LIFO" (last-in, first-out) taxation in which the earnings on the contract are taxed before the investment in the contract can be recovered tax free as a return of capital.

> *Example:* Anna owns a deferred annuity under which annuity payments have not commenced. Her investment in the contract is $125,000. The cash value of the contract is currently $160,000. Anna withdraws $25,000 from the contract. The income on the contract is $35,000 ($160,000 − $125,000). Therefore all of Anna's $25,000

withdrawal will be taxed because her withdrawal is less than the existing income on the contract.

This "income first" or "LIFO" rule of income taxation applies to annuity contracts that were funded after August 13, 1982. If a taxpayer owns a contract that was funded on or before August 13, 1982, "FIFO" ("first-in, first-out") rather than LIFO taxation will apply to a withdrawal from the contract that is not in the form of an annuity payment. This means that the taxpayer will be able to treat the distribution as a nontaxable return of capital until the taxpayer's investment in the contract has been fully recovered.

> *Example:* Assume the same facts as in the example above, except that Anna's annuity was fully funded before August 14, 1982. Her $25,000 withdrawal will be nontaxable as a partial return of her investment in the contract. However, her investment in the contract for purposes of determining an exclusion ratio when the contract is annuitized or for purposes of determining the tax treatment of future withdrawals will be reduced from $125,000 to $100,000 by the $25,000 nontaxable withdrawal.

Complete surrenders of annuity contracts are taxable to the extent that the cash value of the annuity exceeds the investment in the contract. However, in the case of a complete surrender of the contract, the taxpayer is permitted to reduce the cash value by any surrender charges in order to determine the taxable amount.

The 10 Percent Penalty for Premature Distributions

There is a 10 percent penalty tax that generally applies to amounts received from annuity contracts that

- are not received in the form of annuity payments and
- are received by a taxpayer who has not attained the age of 59 1/2

This 10 percent penalty tax applies only to the portion of any withdrawal, loan, or collateralization of the contract that is taxable under the rules described above. It applies in addition to the regular income tax. It does not apply to any portion of the transaction that is treated as a nontaxable return of capital. In addition, the penalty tax does not apply to distributions that are part of a series of substantially equal periodic payments based on the taxpayer's life expectancy (that is, payments in the form of a life or joint life annuity). In addition to the life expectancy exception, the following types of distributions are also not subject to the 10 percent penalty tax:

- distributions allocable to an investment in the contract made before August 14, 1982
- distributions attributable to the disability of the recipient
- distributions under an immediate annuity contract
- distributions made on or after the death of the contract owner

These rules are similar but not identical to the 10 percent penalty rules applicable to certain distributions from qualified plans of deferred compensation and IRAs. Those rules are beyond the scope of this text.

Gifts of Annuity Contracts

Generally, a gift of an asset from one taxpayer to another involves transfer tax, but not income tax, consequences. The general rule for gifts is that the gift is not includible in the donee's gross income. However, when an annuity contract is transferred by gift, the donor of the annuity (not the donee) is subject to special income tax rules.

The first rule applies to contracts that were issued after April 22, 1987. If such contracts are gifted, the owner has a taxable event at the time of the gift. The amount taxable to the donor is the cash surrender value of the contract minus the investment in the contract.

> *Example:* Maxie owns an annuity contract with a cash surrender value of $100,000. His investment in the contract is $70,000. The contract was issued 5 years ago. Maxie gives the annuity to his brother, Jake. As a result of the gift, Maxie must include $30,000 ($100,000 – $70,000) in his gross income for the year in which the gift is made.

A second rule applies to gifts of annuity contracts that were issued on or before April 22, 1987. For such contracts, the donor does not have a taxable event at the time of the gift. However, if the donee later surrenders the contract, the donor will be taxed on an amount equal to the difference between the cash surrender value and the investment in the contract as of the time of the prior gift (not as of the time of surrender). The balance of the gain upon surrender of the contract will be taxable to the donee.

These rules make it important to remember that transfers of annuity contracts for less than adequate consideration can result in income tax problems as well as gift tax problems.

The "Non-natural Person" Rule

There is another special income tax rule that prospective purchasers of annuity contracts should be aware of. It is referred to as the "non-natural person" rule. This rule provides that a deferred annuity contract held by an owner other than a human being (such as a trust or business entity) will generally not be treated as an annuity for income tax purposes. If the rule applies, the tax deferral feature of the annuity will be lost, and the income earned on the contract will be taxed each year to the contract owner, regardless of whether any distributions from the contract are made. This is clearly an undesirable result. In almost all cases a deferred annuity contract should not be placed with an owner that would violate the non-natural person rule.

Fortunately, the rule does have some exceptions. It does not apply in the following situations:

- where the contract is owned by the estate of a deceased annuity owner
- where the annuity contract is an immediate annuity
- where the annuity contract is owned by an IRA or a qualified plan of deferred compensation
- where the entity owns the annuity as an "agent for a natural person." The "agent for a natural person" exception has been approved by the IRS in the case of annuity ownership by various types of trusts, including, but not limited to, single beneficiary trusts and certain trusts that are "grantor" trusts for income tax purposes. Any situation in which trust ownership is proposed for an annuity should be reviewed by a competent tax professional to evaluate the application of the non-natural person rule.

GROUP TERM LIFE INSURANCE

Introduction

The growth of group life insurance has been greatly influenced by the favorable income tax treatment afforded it under federal tax laws. This chapter discusses the effects of these tax laws on basic group term insurance, coverages that may be added to a basic group term insurance contract, and group life insurance with permanent benefits. A complete explanation of the federal income tax laws pertaining to group life insurance, as well as their interpretation by the Internal Revenue Service, would be lengthy and is beyond the scope of this chapter. Consequently, this discussion will only highlight these laws.

Deductibility of Premiums

In general, employer contributions for an employee's group term insurance coverage are fully deductible to the employer under Sec. 162 of the Internal Revenue Code as an ordinary and necessary business expense as long as the overall compensation of the employee is reasonable. The reasonableness of compensation (which includes wages, salary, and other fringe benefits) is usually only a potential issue for the owners of small businesses or the stockholder-employees of closely held corporations. Any compensation that is determined by the Internal Revenue Service to be unreasonable may not be deducted by a firm for income tax purposes. In addition, the Internal Revenue Code does not allow a firm to take an income tax deduction for contributions (1) that are made on behalf of sole proprietors or partners under any circumstances or (2) that are made on behalf of stockholders, unless they are providing substantial services to the corporation. Finally, no deduction is allowed under Sec. 264 of the Internal Revenue Code if the employer is named as beneficiary.

Contributions by any individual employee are considered payments for personal life insurance and are not deductible for income tax purposes by that employee. Thus the amount of any payroll deductions authorized by an employee for group term insurance purposes will be included in the employee's taxable income.

Income Tax Liability of Employees

In the absence of tax laws to the contrary, the amount of any compensation for which an employer receives an income tax deduction (including the payment of group insurance premiums) represents taxable income to the employee. However, Sec. 79 of the Internal Revenue Code provides favorable tax treatment to employer contributions for life insurance that qualifies as group term insurance.

Sec. 79 Requirements

In order to qualify as group term insurance under Sec. 79, life insurance must meet the following conditions:

- It must provide a death benefit excludible from federal income tax.
- It must be provided to a group of employees. A group of employees is defined to include all employees of an employer. If all employees are not covered, membership must be determined on the basis of age, marital status, or factors relating to employment.
- It must be provided under a policy carried directly or indirectly by the employer. This includes (1) any policy for which the employer pays any part of the cost or (2) if the employer pays no part of the cost, any policy arranged by the employer if at least one employee is charged less than his or her cost (under Table I, discussed below) and at least one other employee is charged more than his or her cost. If no employee is charged more than the Table I cost, a policy is not group term insurance for purposes of Sec. 79. A policy is defined to include a master contract of a group of individual policies. The term *carried indirectly* refers to those situations where the employer is not the policyowner, but rather provides coverage to employees through master contracts issued to

organizations such as negotiated trusteeships or multiple-employer trusts.

- The plan must be arranged in such a manner as to preclude individual selection of coverage amounts. However, it is acceptable to have alternative benefit schedules based on the amount an employee elects to contribute. Supplemental plans where an employee is given a choice, such as either 1, 1 1/2, or 2 times salary, are considered to fall within this category.

All life insurance that qualifies under Sec. 79 as group term insurance is considered to be a single plan of insurance, regardless of the number of insurance contracts used. For example, an employer might provide coverage for union employees under a negotiated trusteeship, for other employees under an individual employer group insurance contract, and additional coverage for top executives under a group of individual life insurance policies. Under Sec. 79 these would all constitute a single plan. This plan must be provided for at least 10 full-time employees at some time during the calendar year. For purposes of meeting the 10-life requirement, employees who have not satisfied any required waiting periods may be counted as participants. In addition, employees who have elected not to participate are also counted as participants—but only if they would not have been required to contribute to the cost of other benefits besides group term insurance if they had participated. As will be described later, a plan with fewer than 10 full-time employees may still qualify for favorable tax treatment under Sec. 79 if more restrictive requirements are met.

Exceptions to Sec. 79

Even when all the previous requirements are met, there are some situations in which Sec. 79 does not apply. In some cases different sections of the Internal Revenue Code provide alternative tax treatment. For example, when group term insurance is issued to the trustees of a qualified pension plan and is used to provide a death benefit under the plan, the full amount of any life insurance paid for by employer contributions will result in taxable income to the employee.

There are three situations in which employer contributions for group term insurance will not result in taxable income to an employee, regardless of the amount of insurance: (1) if an employee has terminated employment because of disability; (2) if a qualified charity (as determined by the Internal Revenue Code) has been named as beneficiary for the entire period during the tax year for which the employee receives insurance; or (3) if the employer has been named as beneficiary for the entire year.

Coverage on retired employees is subject to Sec. 79, and these persons are treated in the same manner as active employees. Thus they will have taxable income in any year in which the amount of coverage received exceeds $50,000. However, a grandfather clause to this new rule stipulates that it does not apply to group term life insurance plans (or to comparable successor plans or to plans of successor employers) in existence on January 1, 1984, for covered employees who (1) retired before 1984 or (2) were at least 55 years of age before 1984 and were employed by the employer any time during 1983. There is one exception to this grandfather clause: it does not apply to persons retiring after 1986 if a plan is discriminatory.

General Tax Rules

Under Sec. 79 the cost of the first $50,000 of coverage is not taxed to the employee. Since all group term insurance that qualifies under Sec. 79 is considered to be one plan, this exclusion applies only once to each employee. For example, an employee who has $10,000 of coverage under a policy for all employees and $75,000 of coverage under a separate insurance policy for executives would have a single $50,000 exclusion. The cost of coverage in excess of $50,000, less any employee contributions for the entire amount of coverage, represents taxable income to the employee. For purposes of Sec. 79, the cost of this excess coverage is determined by a government table called the Uniform Premium Table I. This table will often result in a lower cost than would be calculated by using the actual premium paid by the employer for the coverage.

UNIFORM PREMIUM TABLE I	
Age	Cost per Month per $1,000 of Coverage
Under 25	$ .05
25–29	.06
30–34	.08
35–39	.09
40–44	.10
45–49	.15
50–54	.23
55–59	.43
60–64	.66
65–69	1.27
70 and over	2.06

To calculate the cost of an employee's coverage for one month of protection under a group term insurance plan, the Uniform Premium Table I cost shown for the employee's age bracket (based on the employee's attained age at the end of the tax year) is multiplied by the number of thousands in excess of 50 of group term insurance on the employee. For example, if an employee, aged 57, was provided with $150,000 of group term insurance, the employee's monthly cost (assuming no employee contributions) would be calculated as follows:

Coverage provided	$150,000
Less Sec. 79 exclusion	50,000
Amount subject to taxation	$100,000
Uniform Premium Table I monthly cost	
per $1,000 of coverage at age 57	$ 0.43
Monthly cost ($0.43 x 100)	$43.00

The monthly costs are then totaled to obtain an annual cost. Assuming no change in the amount of coverage during the year, the annual cost would be $516. Any employee contributions for the entire amount of coverage are subtracted from the annual cost to determine the taxable income that must be reported by an employee. If the employee contributed $.15 per month ($1.80 per year) per $1,000 of coverage, the employee's total annual contribution for $150,000 of coverage would be $270. This reduces the amount reportable as taxable income from $516 to $246.

It is important to note that group term insurance coverage can often be purchased at a lower cost than Table I rates. There are some who argue that, in these instances, the actual cost of coverage can be used in place of the Table I cost for determining an employee's taxable income. From the standpoint of logic and consistency with the tax laws, this view makes sense. However, the law clearly provides that Table I costs must be used.

Nondiscrimination Rules

Any plan that qualifies as group term insurance under Sec. 79 is subject to nondiscrimination rules, and the $50,000 exclusion will not be available to key employees if a plan is discriminatory. Such a plan might favor key employees in either eligibility or benefits. If the plan is discriminatory, the value of the full amount of coverage for key employees, less their own contributions, will be considered taxable income, based on the greater of actual or Table I costs. A key employee of a firm is defined as any person who at any time during the current plan year or the preceding 4 plan years is any of the following:

- an officer of the firm who earns from the firm more than 50 percent of the Internal Revenue Code limit on the amount of benefits payable by a defined-benefit plan. This amount (50 percent of $140,000, or $70,000 for 2001) is indexed annually. For purposes of this rule the number of employees treated as officers is the greater of 3 or 10 percent of the firm's employees, subject to a maximum of 50. In applying the rule certain employees can be excluded. These include persons who are part-time, under 21, or have less than 6 months of service with the firm.
- one of the 10 employees owning the largest interests in the firm and having an annual compensation from the firm of more than $35,000

- a more-than-5-percent owner of the firm
- a more-than-one-percent owner of the firm who earns over $150,000 per year
- a retired employee who was a key employee when he or she retired or terminated service

Note that the definition of key employee includes not only active employees but also retired employees who were key employees at the time of retirement or separation from service.

Eligibility requirements are not discriminatory if (1) at least 70 percent of all employees are eligible, (2) at least 85 percent of all employees who are participants are not key employees, or (3) participants comprise a classification that the IRS determines is nondiscriminatory. For purposes of the 70 percent test employees with less than 3 years' service, part-time employees, and seasonal employees may be excluded. Employees covered by collective-bargaining agreements may also be excluded if plan benefits were the subject of good-faith bargaining.

Benefits are not discriminatory if neither the type nor amount of benefits discriminates in favor of key employees. The act specifies that it is permissible to base benefits on a uniform percentage of salary.

One issue that arose after the passage of the nondiscrimination rules in 1984 was whether they applied separately to active and to retired employees. A technical correction in the Tax Reform Act of 1986 clarified the issue stating that the rules do apply separately to the extent provided in IRS regulations. However, such regulations have yet to be issued.

Groups with Fewer than 10 Full-Time Employees

A group insurance plan that covers fewer than 10 employees must also satisfy another set of nondiscrimination requirements before it is eligible for favorable tax treatment under Sec. 79. These requirements, which are set forth in Treasury regulations, make smaller groups subject to two separate and somewhat overlapping sets of rules.

It should again be noted that Sec. 79 applies to an employer's overall plan of group insurance, not to separate group insurance contracts. For example, an employer providing group insurance coverage for its 50 hourly employees under one group insurance contract and for its 6 executives under a separate contract is considered to have a single plan covering 56 employees, and thus is exempt from the under-10 requirements. While the stated purpose of the under-10 requirements is to preclude individual selection, their effect is to prevent the group insurance plan from discriminating in favor of the owners or stockholder-employees of small businesses.

With some exceptions, plans covering fewer than 10 employees must provide coverage for all full-time employees. For purposes of this requirement, employees who are not customarily employed for more than 20 hours in any one week or 5 months in any calendar year are considered part-time employees. It is permissible to exclude full-time employees from coverage under the following circumstances:

- The employee has reached age 65.
- The employee has not satisfied the waiting period under the plan. However, the waiting period may not exceed 6 months.
- The employee has elected not to participate in the plan but only if the employee would not have been required to contribute to the cost of other benefits besides group term life insurance if he or she had participated.
- The employee has not satisfied the evidence of insurability required under the plan. However, this evidence of insurability must be determined solely on the basis of a medical questionnaire completed by the employee and not by a medical examination.

The amount of coverage must be either a flat amount, a uniform percentage of salary, or an amount based on different employee classifications. These employee classifications, which are referred to as coverage brackets in Sec. 79, may be determined in the manner described earlier. The amount of coverage provided each employee in any classification may be no greater than 2 1/2 times the amount of coverage provided each employee in the next lower classification. In addition, each employee in the lowest classification must be provided with an amount of coverage that is equal to at least 10 percent of the amount provided each employee in the highest classification. There must also be a reasonable expectation that there will be at least one employee in each classification. The following benefit schedule would be unacceptable for two reasons. First, the amount of coverage provided for the hourly employees is only 5 percent of the amount of coverage provided for the president. Second, the amount of coverage on the supervisor is more than 2 1/2 times the amount of coverage provided for the hourly employees.

Classification	Amount of Coverage
President	$100,000
Supervisor	40,000
Hourly employees	5,000

The following benefit schedule, however, would be acceptable:

Classification	Amount of Coverage
President	$100,000
Supervisor	40,000
Hourly employees	20,000

If a group insurance plan that covers fewer than 10 employees does not qualify for favorable tax treatment under Sec. 79, any premiums paid by the employer for such coverage will represent taxable income to the employees. The employer, however, will still receive an income tax deduction for any premiums paid on behalf of the employees, as long as overall compensation is reasonable.

Income Taxation of Proceeds

In most instances the death proceeds under a group term insurance contract do not result in any taxable income to the beneficiary if they are paid in a lump sum. If the proceeds are payable in installments over more than one taxable year of the beneficiary, only the interest earnings attributable to the proceeds will be included in the beneficiary's income for tax purposes. The tax treatment of so-called "accelerated death benefits" paid to or on behalf of insureds who are terminally or chronically ill is discussed in chapter 16. Such benefits can be excluded from gross income if certain requirements are met. The law provides specific definitions of what constitutes a terminally ill or chronically ill individual for purposes of the exclusion for such benefits.

Prior to the Tax Reform Act of 1986, a spouse could exclude the first $1,000 of interest from gross income if it was paid under any settlement option other than an interest-only option. This exclusion is no longer available with respect to proceeds payable as the result of a death occurring after October 22, 1986. Under certain circumstances the exemption of the proceeds from income taxation does not apply if the coverage was transferred (either in whole or in part) for a valuable consideration. Such a situation will arise when the stockholder-employees of a corporation name each other as beneficiaries under their group term insurance coverage as a method of funding a buy-sell agreement. The mutual agreement to name each other as beneficiaries is the valuable consideration. Under these circumstances any proceeds paid to a beneficiary constitute ordinary income to the extent that the proceeds exceed the beneficiary's tax basis, as determined by the Internal Revenue Code.

In many cases benefits paid by an employer to employees or their beneficiaries from the firm's assets receive the same tax treatment as benefits provided under an insurance contract. This is not true for death benefits. If they are provided other than through an insurance contract, the amount of the proceeds will represent taxable income to the beneficiary. For this reason employers are less likely to use alternative funding arrangements for death benefits than for disability and medical expense benefits.

Treatment of Added Coverages

Supplemental life insurance can be written as either a separate contract or as part of the contract providing basic group term life insurance coverage. If it is a separate contract and if the supplemental group life insurance meets the conditions of qualifying as group term insurance under Sec. 79, the amount of coverage provided is added to all other group term insurance for purposes of calculating the Uniform Premium Table I cost. Any premiums paid by the employee for the supplemental coverage reduce the taxable income resulting from the coverage. In all other ways, supplemental life insurance is treated the same as group term insurance.

When supplemental life insurance coverage is written in conjunction with a basic group life insurance plan, employers have the option of treating the supplemental coverage as a separate policy of insurance as long as the premiums are properly allocated between the two portions of the coverage. There is no advantage in treating the supplemental coverage as a separate policy if it, by itself, would still qualify as group term insurance under Sec. 79. However, this election will minimize taxable income to employees if the cost of the supplemental coverage is paid entirely by the employees and all employees are charged rates that are at or below Table I rates. There is no taxable income if the employee pays the entire cost of the coverage.

Premiums paid for accidental death and dismemberment insurance are considered to be health insurance premiums rather than group term insurance premiums. However, these are also deductible to the employer as an ordinary and necessary business expense the same as they are for group term insurance. Benefits paid to an employee under the dismemberment portion of the coverage are treated like benefits received under a health insurance contract and are received income tax free. Death benefits received under the coverage are treated like death benefits received under group term life insurance.

For federal tax purposes, survivor income benefit insurance is considered to be a group term insurance coverage. Under Sec. 79, the amount of benefit is equal to the commuted value of benefit payments that would have been received by eligible survivors if the employee had died during the year. This amount normally is provided annually by the insurance company. A commuted value is also used for estate tax purposes. In all other respects survivor income benefit insurance is treated the same as group term insurance.

Employer contributions for dependent life insurance coverage are fully deductible by the employer as an ordinary and necessary business expense if overall compensation of the employee is reasonable. Employer contributions do not result in taxable income to an employee as long as the value of the benefit is *de minimis*. This means that the value is so small that it is administratively impractical for the employer to account for the cost on a per-person basis. Dependent coverage of $2,000 or less on any person falls into this category. The Internal Revenue Service considers amounts of coverage in excess of $2,000 on any dependent to be more than *de minimis*. If more than $2,000 of coverage is provided for any dependent from employer contributions, the cost of the entire amount of coverage for that dependent (as determined by Uniform Premium Table I rates) will be considered taxable income to the employee.

Death benefits will be free of income taxation and will not be included in the taxable estate of the dependent for estate tax purposes.

State Taxation

In most instances state tax laws affecting group term insurance are similar to the federal laws. However, two major differences do exist. In most states the payment of group term insurance premiums by the employer will not result in any taxable income to the employee, even if the amount of insurance exceeds $50,000. In addition, death proceeds receive favorable tax treatment under the estate and inheritance tax laws of most states. Generally the death proceeds are partially, if not totally, exempt from such taxation.

Group Life Insurance with Permanent Benefits

With the exception of the income tax liability of employees, group paid-up insurance and group ordinary insurance are treated in essentially the same manner as group term insurance. Favorable tax treatment for the term portion of group insurance contracts that have permanent benefits (that is, cash value life insurance) has been available for many years to employees under Sec. 79, if certain requirements are satisfied. However, no favorable tax treatment is given to the premium for the permanent portion of the coverage. If paid by an employer, the premiums for permanent coverage will be fully taxable to the employee as additional compensation.

The Sec. 79 regulation pertaining to group insurance with permanent benefits can be divided into three segments:

- the general requirements that a policy having permanent benefits must satisfy in order to have a portion of the policy considered as group term life insurance for purposes of Sec. 79
- a mandatory actuarial procedure for determining the cost of the permanent benefits
- the provisions for the tax treatment of dividends

General Requirements

The regulations define a *policy* as including two or more obligations of an insurer (for its affiliates) that are offered to a group of employees as a result of their employment relationship. The definition is broad enough to include a group of individual policies provided to a group of employees. In addition, term insurance benefits and permanent benefits provided under separate contracts can be considered a policy, even if one of the benefits is provided to employees who decline the other. The regulations also specify that a *permanent benefit* is an economic value extending beyond one policy year. This includes, for example, paid-up insurance or cash surrender values.

Before any part of a policy may be treated as group term life insurance, two requirements must be met:[1]

- The policy or the employer must designate in writing the portion of each employee's death benefit that is considered group term insurance.
- The portion of each employee's death benefit that is designated as group term insurance for any policy year must not be less than the difference between the total death benefit provided under the policy and the employee's *deemed death benefit*[2] at the end of the policy year.

If these requirements are met, the portion of the policy representing group term insurance will receive favorable income tax treatment under Sec. 79. When added to any other coverage that qualifies for Sec. 79 treatment, only the cost of the total term protection that exceeds $50,000 will represent taxable income to an employee. The cost is calculated by using Uniform Premium Table I rates and is reduced by the aggregate of any employee contributions for the entire term coverage but not for the permanent coverage.

The Cost of Permanent Benefits

The regulations also establish a mandatory allocation procedure of determining the cost of permanent benefits for an employee in a given policy year.[3] This cost represents taxable income to the employee to the extent that it is paid by the employer. It should be noted that the cost as determined by this formula is independent of the annual premium for permanent benefits actually specified in the policy. For example, if an employee is required to pay the cost of permanent benefits and this cost is specified in the policy as $300, the employee will have taxable income to the extent the mandatory allocation procedure yields a cost in excess of $300.

Treatment of Dividends

If the employer pays the entire cost of the permanent benefits, any dividends that are actually or constructively received by the employee must be included in the employee's income for federal income tax purposes. In all other cases, the amount of dividends included in an employee's taxable income is determined by a formula specified in the regulations.[4] The effect of this formula is that any dividend will result in currently taxable income unless an employee has paid more than the aggregate costs (from the inception of coverage) for the permanent protection, as determined by the mandatory allocation formula.

PROPERTY TRANSFERRED IN CONNECTION WITH THE PERFORMANCE OF SERVICES

Introduction

In the early days of the tax law employers frequently tried to reduce their employees' tax liability by paying them with noncash items—cars, houses, clothing, and so forth—on the theory that such items were not taxable income. The courts quickly held otherwise; taxable income includes noncash as well as cash receipts. Moreover, if the property transferred to the employee has restrictions that temporarily eliminate or reduce its value to the employee, taxable income must ultimately be reported. The courts have held that the recipient of the property must include its value in income in the year in which the recipient becomes vested in the value of the property.[5] The court-made rules in this area are sometimes summarized as the "economic benefit doctrine." The doctrine focuses on the vested benefits provided to the employee rather than on the type of property or its form of ownership.

Currently this issue affects "restricted stock" plans, under which an employer compensates an employee for services with stock of the employer corporation, subject to provisions under which the stock must be paid back to the employer if the employee fails to complete specified services. The issue also arises in plans providing life insurance for employees, affecting both the pure death benefit (term insurance) amount and also the year of inclusion of any policy cash values owned by or benefiting the employee.

The economic benefit doctrine as it applies to property transferred for services is codified in IRC Sec. 83, which provides specific rules for (1) the year in which the value of the property is included, and (2) the amount to be included in that year.

Year of Inclusion

Sec. 83 provides that the value of property (the excess over the amount paid by the recipient for the property) that is transferred for services is included in income "at the first time the rights of the person having the beneficial interest in such property are transferable or are not subject to a substantial risk of forfeiture. . . ." Sec. 83(c)(1) provides that "the rights of a person in property are subject to a substantial risk of forfeiture if such person's rights to full enjoyment of such property are conditioned upon the future performance of substantial services by any individual."

Example: Fothrex Corporation transfers 1,000 shares of Fothrex stock to employee Hanson under the condition that Hanson may not sell the stock during a 5-year period. If Hanson leaves employment with Fothrex during the 5-year period, he must return the stock to the company. Hanson pays nothing for the stock. He must include the value of the stock in his income in the year in which the 5-year period expires.

Employers may wish to adopt restricted property plans that are more complex and custom-designed than the simple illustration above. Understanding the term "substantial risk of forfeiture" is the key to designing appropriate forfeiture provisions in restricted property plans. As discussed below, the regulations under Sec. 83 provide some specific rules and illustrations that are helpful.

Discharges for Cause

The regulations state that requirements that the property be returned to the employer if the employee is discharged for cause or for committing a crime will not be considered to result in a substantial risk of forfeiture.[6]

Noncompetition and Consulting Provisions

The Sec. 83 regulations in effect create a presumption against the existence of a substantial risk of forfeiture where the forfeiture will occur only if the employee accepts a job with a competing firm. In that case, a "facts and circumstances" test will apply. Factors taken into account in determining whether the noncompetition provision constitutes a substantial risk of forfeiture include

- the age of the employee
- the availability of alternative employment opportunities
- the likelihood of the employee's obtaining such other employment and the employee's degree of skill
- the employee's health
- the practice (if any) of the employer to enforce such covenants

For example, a consulting provision applicable to a majority shareholder of the employer would not generally be given much weight because there would be little likelihood of his competing with his own business. The enforcement of such a provision would be entirely at his discretion as majority owner of the company.

The regulations also state that property transferred to a retiring employee subject to the sole requirement that the property will be returned unless he renders consulting services upon the request of his former employer will not be considered subject to a substantial risk of forfeiture unless he is in fact expected to perform substantial services.[7]

Organizational Performance and Other Forfeiture Provisions

The regulations state that where an employee receives property from an employer subject to a requirement that it be returned if the total earnings of the employer do not increase, such property is subject to a substantial risk of forfeiture.[8] Note that this "performance" standard does not actually involve a requirement that services be performed; it appears from this provision in the regulations that the IRS finds this acceptable although it does not strictly fit the language of Sec. 83.

The regulations state that a forfeiture provision can be valid if it is "related to the purpose of the transfer." The performance standard discussed in the preceding paragraph may be an example of this type of provision. One case dealt with a provision under which stock was transferred to an employee under a condition that if he wished to dispose of it within one year he had to sell it back to the employer at the original cost. The court viewed this as a substantial risk of forfeiture and noted that this provision served a substantial corporate purpose of avoiding insider trading.[9] This is arguably also a purpose related to the transfer, though it is not specifically related.

The Committee Reports for Sec. 83 state that "In other cases [besides those involving service conditions] the question of whether there is a substantial risk of forfeiture depends upon the facts and circumstances."[10]

Employee Election to Include in Current Income

If an employee receives restricted property and wants to include it in income currently (perhaps because he expects it to increase considerably in value) he can elect under Sec. 83(b) to include the current value (the fair market value at the time of transfer) in income currently. The fair market value of the property is determined without regard to restrictions (except a restriction that by its terms will not lapse).

> *Example:* Hott Software transfers stock this year to employee Geeke, with the provision that if Geeke leaves employment during the next 10 years, her stock is forfeited. The fair market value of the stock at the time of transfer is $20,000. Geeke expects it to more than quadruple in value in 10 years, so she elects to pay taxes at that time on the $20,000 current value.

An employee making a Sec. 83(b) election like that in the example is betting on the company to succeed, since if the value of the stock drops below its value at the time of transfer. no loss deduction is allowed.

Amount to Be Included under Sec. 83

The general rule under Sec. 83 is that property is included in income at its fair market value (determined without regard to any restriction other than a restriction that by its terms will never lapse) at the first time when the rights to the property are transferable or no longer subject to a substantial risk of forfeiture, as discussed above. If the employee paid any consideration for the property, the taxable amount is reduced by the amount paid.

The amount included is the value at the time of vesting, not at the time of transfer.

> *Example:* This year, Fothrex corporation transfers 1,000 shares of Fothrex stock to employee Hanson, subject to a provision that Hanson must continue in employment for 5 years. The stock is worth $30,000 at the time of transfer. Hanson sticks it out and is still working for Fothrex on the fifth anniversary of the transfer, at which time the stock is worth $50,000. Hanson must report the $50,000 as compensation income at that time. There is no discount to reflect the fact that the stock was restricted during the preceding 5 years.

As the example notes, the existence of a restriction that eventually lapses does not affect the valuation of the stock. However, if the stock was subject to a nonlapsing restriction it would affect valuation. Suppose that in the example the Fothrex stock that Hanson received continued after 5 years to be subject to a provision that any shares that Hanson wanted to dispose of would have to be first offered to the company for $40 per share. (This is *not* considered to be a forfeiture provision.) This provision would affect the value of the stock at that time and would reduce the amount that Hanson would have to report in that year. The actual reduction in value is an issue of facts and circumstances, and some kind of independent valuation would probably have to be made for tax purposes.

Employer's Deduction

Under Sec. 83(h), the employer's deduction is equal to the amount included in income by the employee and is included in the year in which the employee includes the amount. (The exact Code provision is that the deduction is allowed in the employer's taxable year in which or with which ends the taxable year in which the amount is included in the gross income of the person who performed the services.) Restricted property is a form of compensation that does not provide the employer with an "upfront" deduction—a deduction in the year the services are performed—as is the case with a qualified pension or profit-sharing plan. For compensation governed by Sec. 83, the year of deduction is tied to the year of the employee's inclusion of income.

NOTES

1. In addition, plans covering fewer than 10 lives and providing permanent protection must also satisfy the same requirements as those for group term life insurance plans covering fewer than 10 lives.

2. The deemed death benefit for a given policy year is defined as R/Y where

    R = the net level premium reserve at the end of that policy year for all benefits provided to the employee by the policy or, if greater, the cash value of the policy at the end of that policy year

    Y = the net single premium for insurance (the premium for one dollar of paid-up whole life insurance) at the employee's age at the end of that policy year

3. The cost of permanent benefits for any employee is X ($DDB^2 - DDB^1$) where

    DDB^2 = the employee's deemed death benefit at the end of the policy year

    DDB^1 = the employee's deemed death benefit at the end of the preceding policy year

    X = the net single premium for insurance (the premium for one dollar of paid-up whole life insurance) at the employee's attained age at the beginning of the policy year

4. The amount included in an employee's income is (D + C) – (PI + DI + AP) where

    D = the total amount of dividends actually or constructively received under the policy by the employee in the current and all preceding tax years of the employee

    C = the total cost of the permanent benefits for the current and all preceding tax years of the employee (determined under the formulas above)

    PI = the total amount of premium included in the employee's income under the formulas for the current and all preceding tax years of the employee

    DI = the total amount of dividends included in the employee's income under this dividend formula in all preceding tax years of the employee

    AP = the total amount paid for permanent benefits by the employee in the current and all preceding taxable years of the employee

5. *Sproull v. Commissioner,* 16 TC 244 (1951), aff'd per curiam, 194 F.2d 541 (6th Cir. 1952).

6. Treas. Reg. Sec. 1.83-3(c)(2).

7. Treas. Reg. Sec. 1.83-3(c)(2).

8. Treas. Reg. Sec. 1.83-3(c)(2).

9. *Robinson v. Comm'r,* 805 F.2d 38 (1st Cir. 1986), rev'g 82 TC 444.

10. H.R. Rep. No. 413 (Part 1), 91st Cong., 1st Sess 88 (1969) and S. Rep. No. 552, 91st Cong., 1st Sess. 121 (1969).

6

Exclusions from Gross Income

Thomas M. Brinker[*]

The income tax has made more liars out of the American people than golf has. Even when you make a tax form out on the level, you don't know when it's through if you are a crook or a martyr.

Will Rogers

Chapter Outline

INTRODUCTION

Although the majority of items a taxpayer receives are includible in gross income, there are exceptions. This chapter will focus on that which is excludible

---

[*] Thomas Brinker, Jr., CPA, is an accounting professor at Beaver College (Arcadia University as of July 2001) in Glenside, Pa. He also maintains a private tax practice in Springfield, Pa.

from gross income. These items are commonly referred to as *exclusions*. Obviously, an item of income that can be excluded from tax is worth more than an item of income that is subject to taxation. The Internal Revenue Code identifies which items—in the form of money, property, or benefits—are includible or excludible from gross income.

As discussed in chapter 3, items specifically included in gross income are fairly comprehensive. However, income may be defined in a much broader sense. Income, in the broadest of terms, represents all wealth that flows to the taxpayer other than as a mere return of capital. Income includes gains and profits from any source. For example, it includes any gain realized from the sale, exchange, or other disposition of a capital asset. However, income does not include a mere increase in capital, but a gain or a profit derived from the capital. It is normally evidenced by a closed and completed transaction fixed by identifiable events. Income is not a "return of capital," nor is it a "growth" or "increase" in the investment's value.

> *Example:* John owns AG&Z stock that he acquired 15 years ago for $20,000. This year the stock's value is $45,000. This growth in value is not taxable to John until the stock is sold or exchanged. When the stock is sold or exchanged, John will have a gain representing the difference between the selling price and his basis in the stock. If the stock's fair market value is $45,000 when John sells the stock, he will have a taxable gain of $25,000. His $20,000 investment represents a return of capital and therefore is not taxable.

As previously discussed, *"gross income"* represents *all income less exclusions*. Gross income is the starting point in preparing an individual income tax return. Items included in gross income are often termed *inclusions*. An *exclusion* is an item that is exempt from taxation. Exclusions should not be confused with *deductions*. Deductions are expense items that reduce gross income in arriving at adjusted gross income or taxable income.

What Are Exclusions?

An exclusion represents an item that is not included in gross income, which is the starting point in calculating the income tax. Items may be excluded for any one of the following reasons:

1. An item is not defined as "income."
2. An item is not taxable under the U.S. Constitution.
3. An item is expressly excluded under a provision in the Internal Revenue Code.

Items falling under (1) or (2) are entirely exempt from federal taxation. However, items falling under (3) may be either partially or wholly exempt, depending on the Internal Revenue Code statute.

In addition to the specific areas of exclusions covered in this chapter, other types of exclusions are addressed in later chapters of this text.

GIFTS AND INHERITANCES

General Rule

The value of money or property received as a gift, bequest, devise, or inheritance is generally excluded from gross income under IRC Sec. 102. However, the income from the property received is taxable. If income from property is assigned, the donor of the income is taxable, because income is taxed to the property owner. However, if the donor permanently disposes of the income-producing property, the income generated from the property is taxed to the recipient.

A gift can be defined as any voluntary transfer of property by one person to another that is not made as compensation and in return for which no consideration is given. If there is valuable consideration in money or money's worth for the transfer of the property, the transaction is not treated as a gift—it is a sale. A gift is defined as a gratuitous transfer of property. To be considered a gift, the following elements are essential:

- a donor competent to make the gift
- a clear and unmistakable intention on the donor's behalf to make the gift
- a donee capable of receiving the gift
- an irrevocable conveyance, assignment, or transfer sufficient to vest legal title to the property in the donee
- a donor's relinquishment of dominion and control of the property by delivery to the donee

In order to have a valid gift for federal income tax purposes, the donor must have acted out of a "detached and disinterested" generosity in transferring the property. Gifts are normally made out of "affection, respect, admiration, charity, or like impulses."[1] Valid gifts have *no strings attached.*

Questions regarding gift or compensation normally arise as to payments where there is a past or present employment relationship. For federal income tax law purposes, a voluntary transfer without compensation is not necessarily a gift. It is not a gift if there is a legal or moral obligation for the transfer or if the donor expects to receive a benefit from the "gift." However, the mere absence of a legal or moral obligation for the transfer does not necessarily qualify the transfer as a gift. As previously stated, a transfer is a gift if it is made from detached or disinterested generosity. Ultimately, the question of gift or compensation is resolved by reviewing the donor's dominant reason for making the transfer.

> *Example 1:* Mrs. Adams hires Julie to baby-sit her two young children while she goes shopping. Upon returning, Mrs. Adams gives Julie $20 for minding the children. Julie has $20 of taxable income. She

has given consideration (rendered services) in return for the amount received.

Example 2: On another occasion, Mrs. Adams contacts Julie for additional baby-sitting. Moments before Julie is scheduled to arrive, Mrs. Adams's event is canceled. She contacts Julie to cancel her "employment." In addition, she mails Julie $20 out of kindness. Since Julie provided no consideration to Mrs. Adams, her payment of $20 to her is considered a gift.

Example 3: Michael is a tax accountant for a CPA firm. During tax season, he works 300 hours of overtime. The firm's policy is to compensate all employees at time and one-half for all overtime hours up to a maximum of 250 hours of overtime. During his post-tax season review, the firm announces to Michael that in recognition of his outstanding work ethic and overtime contributions, the firm will make a gift to him of $2,500.

Because of the employer-employee relationship, Michael has taxable income. The "gift" has been made to Michael in recognition of his work ethic and overtime hours. The IRS will treat the $2,500 payment as compensation for past services rendered and not as a gift.

As illustrated, amounts transferred from an employer to an employee will not generally be treated as gifts.

Income from Gifts

Sec. 102 of the Code does not apply to the income generated from excludible property or to a gift of income. For example, if a father gifts a mutual fund investment to his daughter, the value of the mutual fund is not taxable to her. However, any dividends or capital gains earned on that fund subsequent to the gift would be taxable to her.

Gifts of Income

Similar to the concept of income from gifts is that of gifts of income. Neither income from gifts nor gifts of income is excludible from gross income. *If* payments under the terms of a gift are to be made at intervals, the payments are taxable to the donee to the extent they are made out of income.

Example: A father establishes a trust for his daughter. The daughter is given a life interest in the trust. She is not permitted to invade the principal of the trust. On an annual basis, she receives the income from the trust. The annual income from the trust is not a gift and is taxable to the daughter upon receipt.

However, a bequest of a specific sum of money or property is excluded, even if it is paid out of income. This exemption is met only if the "gift" is paid or credited all at once or in not more than three installments. If the gift or bequest is paid in more than three installments, it is taxable to the recipient to the extent it is actually paid from the income generated.

> *Example:* A decedent's will directs that a trustee will pay her husband $40,000 a year for 5 years. The husband is scheduled to receive the $40,000 regardless of how much income is earned on the trust's assets. Since payments extend for more than 3 years, the husband will be taxed annually on the amount he receives to the extent of income earned on the trust's assets. If trust earnings are $50,000 and $45,000 during the first 2 years, the husband will be taxed on the full $40,000 he receives each year. However, if in years 3 through 5, the trust's earnings dip to $35,000, $31,000, and $28,500, respectively, the outcome is different. Since the trustee is required to distribute $40,000 annually to the husband, he or she will be forced to invade principal to make the payments. As a result, the husband will only be taxed to the extent of the trust's income—$35,000, $31,000, and $28,500 in years 3, 4, and 5, respectively.

Inheritances

The rules pertaining to gifts also extend to inheritances. The value of property acquired by inheritance is tax-free to the recipient. However, income earned on that property subsequent to the transfer is taxable to the recipient.

Although the exclusion rules are similar for gifts and inheritances, the basis rules are significantly different. The recipient's basis in inherited property is generally the fair market value of the property at the decedent's death. As a result, appreciation of the property prior to the decedent's death escapes federal income taxation. In contrast, a donee's basis in property acquired by gift is generally the donor's basis in the property at the time of the gift. A more complete discussion of these rules appears in chapter 13.

INTEREST ON CERTAIN GOVERNMENTAL OBLIGATIONS

State and Municipal Bonds

Sec. 103 of the Internal Revenue Code provides that interest paid on certain obligations of a state, a U.S. territory, or a U.S. possession is tax exempt and therefore excluded from gross income. This exemption applies specifically to the interest earned on these obligations. In addition, interest earned on any political subdivision (that is, county, city, town, and/or the District of Columbia) is also exempt from federal income taxation. Such "tax-exempt" state and municipal bonds are generally "public purpose" bonds; that is, bonds used to finance essential governmental activities.

The exclusion exists to encourage taxpayers to invest in state and municipal bonds. Because of their tax-exempt status, the states and municipalities are able to borrow at relatively low interest rates when compared with taxable investments. To an investor, 100 percent of the interest income received is generally free from federal taxation. Prior to acquiring a tax-exempt obligation, investors need to compare the after-tax return of both tax-exempt and taxable obligations. A taxable obligation yields a before-tax interest rate. This interest rate can also be expressed as an after-tax rate of return. An overall comparison requires knowledge of the investor's federal, state, and local marginal tax brackets. The following examples illustrate comparisons using federal income tax brackets only.

Example 1: Mr. and Mrs. Joe Investor are married and file a joint tax return. Their projected current taxable income is $175,000 (a 36 percent marginal federal income tax bracket). The Investors have the option of acquiring a tax-free bond fund yielding 4 percent or a corporate bond earning a 6 percent interest rate. The key for the Investors is to determine the after-tax return. The after-tax return on the tax-free bond fund is 4 percent. This represents a 6.25 percent equivalent to a taxable alternative [4% ÷ (1 − .36 tax rate)]. The after-tax return on the corporate bond is only 3.84 percent [6% x (1 − .36 tax rate)].

Example 2: If Mr. and Mrs. Joe Investor are in the 15 percent federal tax bracket, the investment choice is not as clear. Similar to the above example, the Investors have the option of acquiring a 4 percent tax-free bond fund or a corporate bond earning a 6 percent interest rate. The after-tax return on the tax-free bond fund is 4 percent (or a 4.71 percent equivalent to a taxable alternative). The after-tax return on the corporate bond is 5.1 percent.

As illustrated, the exclusion is beneficial to both governments and investors. State and local governments benefit by paying a "below-market" interest rate to investors. Wealthier investors also benefit because of their higher marginal federal and state income tax brackets. Also, the majority of states exempt the interest income earned on their own state's obligations. As income tax rates increase, a tax-free investment's taxable equivalent also increases.

However, the exclusion for municipal bond interest does not extend to:

- private activity bonds that are not "qualified bonds"
- arbitrage bonds
- certain bonds not in registered form

The interest income of arbitrage bonds, industrial development bonds, and most other private activity bonds is subject to the regular federal income tax. Obligations issued under this category may include sports facilities, convention or trade show facilities, parking facilities, and air and water pollution control facilities. These bonds are considered taxable municipal bonds.

The interest income from "nongovernmental purpose" bonds, including bonds used to finance subsidized housing and student loans and redevelopment bonds, is not subject to the regular federal income tax. However, the income from these bonds is subject to the alternative minimum tax. The activities financed by such bonds are of a quasi-governmental nature.

Generally, the more essential the bond is to the issuing authority, the better the tax treatment. Tax-free public purpose municipal bonds typically include obligations issued to finance highway construction or school financing, airports, docks, wharves, mass commuting facilities, sewage, and solid waste disposal facilities.

In addition, municipal bonds issued before August 7, 1986, generate tax-exempt interest to the extent they were exempt under prior law.

U.S. Treasury Obligations

As a general rule, interest on U.S. obligations and obligations issued by U.S. agencies or instrumentalities are included in gross income. For example, interest income earned on U.S. Treasury Bills and Notes is included in gross income. In addition, interest income earned on U.S. savings bonds is also taxable. Although taxpayers have a choice of including the incremental interest income annually, most taxpayers report the entire amount of interest income over the life of the bond upon redemption. Note that interest on U.S. obligations may be exempt from state and local taxation.

Educational Savings Bonds

Despite the general rule stated above, an exception exists for U.S. savings bonds redeemed to finance certain educational expenses. Accrued interest income on certain Series EE savings bonds may be excluded from gross income if the bonds are redeemed to pay for qualified higher educational expenses of the taxpayer, the taxpayer's spouse, or the taxpayer's dependents. IRC Sec. 135 defines "qualified higher education expenses" as tuition and required fees (net of scholarships, fellowships, employer-provided educational assistance, and other tuition-reduction amounts) for enrolling in or attending a college or eligible vocational school. The qualified expenses must also be exclusive of expenses used in computing the Lifetime or Hope credits. The Code also stipulates that the taxpayer must be at least 24 years of age when the bonds are purchased. The exclusion is available only to the original purchaser of the bond or his or her spouse. The exclusion therefore precludes a gift of qualified Series EE savings bonds.

To qualify for the interest exclusion, the total of the interest and principal on the U.S. savings bonds redeemed must be less than the qualified higher education expenses for the year. If the interest and principal exceed the educational expenses, the amount of the interest exclusion must be reduced.

Example: This year, Kathy Jones, aged 58, redeems Series EE savings bonds for $10,000, $2,500 of which is accrued interest. Kathy's son Joe attends a local university and has qualified educational expenses of $12,000. Kathy may exclude the entire $2,500 from her gross income. However, if Joe's qualified expenses were only $8,500, Kathy could exclude from her gross income only $2,125 determined as follows:

$$\frac{\text{qualified expenses}}{\text{Series EE proceeds}} \ \times \ \text{interest} \ = \ \frac{\$ \ 8,500}{\$10,000} \ \times \ \$2,500 \ = \ \$2,125$$

This special exclusion is designed to benefit only those taxpayers with moderate incomes. The exclusion for 2001 is phased out between the following modified adjusted gross income levels: $55,750 to $70,750 for taxpayers filing as single or head of household and $83,650 to $113,650 for married taxpayers filing jointly. This phaseout range is adjusted annually for inflation. Married taxpayers who file separate tax returns are not eligible for the exclusion.

Sales of Nontaxable Municipal Bonds

Although the interest earned on certain bonds and other obligations of state and local municipalities is excluded from gross income, Sec. 103 does not extend the exemption to any gain or loss upon their sale. If a tax-exempt security is sold at a gain, the gain is taxable in computing gross income. However, if a sale results in a loss, the loss may prove deductible in computing taxable income. These rules are covered in chapters 13 and 14.

Example: On July 1 of last year, Mary purchased a $25,000, 10-year tax-exempt municipal bond at par value. The bond's yield was 5 percent. On May 30 of this year, Mary sells the municipal bond for $25,875. During the period Mary owned the bond, she also received $625 of interest. Although the tax-exempt interest of $625 is excludible, the capital gain of $875 ($25,875 − $25,000) is taxable (short-term capital gain) in this year.

SOCIAL SECURITY BENEFITS AND SIMILAR BENEFITS

Prior to 1984, Social Security and railroad retirement benefits were excluded from gross income. During the period from 1984 through 1993, a maximum of 50 percent of these benefits was exposed to federal taxation. Starting in 1994, an additional amount of these benefits became exposed to federal taxation.

Currently, recipients of Social Security and railroad retirement benefits may have up to 85 percent of their benefits subjected to tax. Sec. 86 of the Internal Revenue Code outlines the procedures for determining if a benefit is taxable.

Social Security and railroad retirement benefits are included in gross income when the individual's "provisional income" exceeds certain threshold amounts. Provisional income is defined as "modified adjusted gross income" plus one-half of the Social Security or tier 1 railroad retirement benefits. Modified adjusted gross income is generally adjusted gross income plus any tax-exempt income (interest or interest/dividends) received. Social Security recipients should be aware that tax-exempt interest from municipal bonds and bond funds could indirectly increase the amount of Social Security benefits subject to tax. (Note: If Social Security benefits are subject to taxation, recipients should consider shifting money from their tax-free municipal bond portfolio to tax-deferred investments—growth stocks, Series EE savings bonds, annuities, and so forth.)

The calculation used to determine the taxable portion of the benefits involves two tiers. Figure 6-1 illustrates the taxation of Social Security benefits at various income levels. If the taxpayer's provisional income is less than the first-tier base amount, there is no taxable benefit to report. However, if the provisional income exceeds the first-tier base amount but does not exceed the second-tier base amount, the taxable portion of the Social Security or railroad retirement benefit is limited to the *lesser* of

- one-half (50 percent) of the benefits received or
- one-half (50 percent) of the excess of the provisional income over the first-tier base amount

The base amounts (thresholds) are

	First-Tier	*Second-Tier*
Married filing jointly	$32,000	$44,000
Single	25,000	34,000
Married filing separately	0	0

If the taxpayer's provisional income exceeds the applicable second-tier base amount, the amount of Social Security or railroad retirement benefits exposed to taxation increases to 85 percent. In this case, the taxpayer must then include in gross income the *lesser* of

- 85 percent of the Social Security or railroad retirement benefits received or the total of
- 85 percent of the amount of provisional income in excess of the second-tier base amount plus the lesser of the amount of the first-tier income or the statutory amount ($6,000 if married filing jointly; $4,500 if filing as a single person; or zero if married filing separately)

Example 1: Bob, a single taxpayer, has an adjusted gross income for the year of $26,000. He has no tax-exempt interest and has received

FIGURE 6-1

Calculation of Taxable Portion of Social Security Benefits

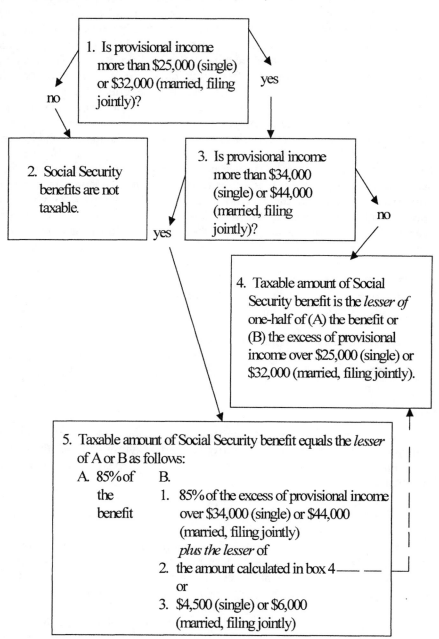

$6,000 of Social Security benefits this year. Therefore his provisional income is $29,000 ($26,000 plus $3,000). According to figure 6-1, the taxable portion of his benefits is calculated as follows:

A. one-half of the benefits received = $6,000/2 or $3,000, or
B. one-half of the excess of the provisional income over the first-tier base amount ($25,000)

   $4,000 / 2 or $2,000

The lesser of A or B is B, or $2,000. Therefore $2,000 of Bob's benefits are taxable.

Example 2: Jack and Ruby are married taxpayers filing a joint tax return. Their adjusted gross income is $60,000 this year. They also received $10,000 in tax-exempt interest and $15,000 in Social Security benefits. Consequently, their provisional income is $77,500 [$60,000 + $10,000 + ($15,000/2)]. Using figure 6-1, the taxable portion of their benefits is calculated as follows:

A. 85 percent of the benefits received = $12,750 ($15,000 x .85) or
B. 85 percent of the amount of provisional income in excess of the second-tier base amount ($44,000) equals $28,475 ($77,500 – $44,000 = $33,500 x .85 or $28,475) plus the lesser of
   (a) the amount of the first-tier income of $7,500 (one-half of the Social Security benefits received: $15,000 / 2) or
   (b) the statutory amount of $6,000 (married filing jointly)

   Since the $6,000 amount in (b) is less than the $7,500 amount in (a), $6,000 is added to $28,475 for a total potential taxable benefit of $34,475.

According to figure 6-1, Jack and Ruby are required to include $12,750 of their Social Security benefits in gross income (the lesser of A or B).

These complex formulas for the taxation of Social Security benefits are an example of the convoluted calculations that can result in the tax law from what once was a simple concept in a human mind that a portion of the benefits should be taxable.

ACCIDENT AND HEALTH BENEFITS

Medical and Disability Benefits

Internal Revenue Secs. 104 through 106 deal with a variety of benefits that may be received tax free by individuals on account of injuries or sickness. Such benefits include

- medical expense reimbursement plans
- disability policies
- workers' compensation acts
- certain damages
- government disability programs

Medical expense reimbursements from accident and health insurance plans are excluded from gross income to the extent the taxpayer has not claimed a medical expense deduction for the underlying medical costs as an itemized deduction (Schedule A of Form 1040).

Example: Mr. Apple had $10,000 of deductible medical expenses last year. In itemizing his deductions, he deducted a net medical expense of $2,000 (after subtracting 7.5 percent of adjusted gross income). This year, he received a medical reimbursement check for $7,500 covering some of the costs incurred last year. Mr. Apple must include $2,000 of the reimbursement as income this year (representing the tax benefit he derived on last year's return). The balance of the reimbursement, $5,500, is excluded from gross income.

A disability policy or income replacement policy protects the insured against a financial loss that may occur if the individual is incapacitated and unable to work. If the taxpayer purchases the policy with after-tax dollars, the entire proceeds from the policy are excluded from gross income.

Example: Tom Hanes missed 12 weeks of work after falling two stories from a building in June. Because of the multiple fractures he suffered, he was unable to work in any capacity until September. As a result, Tom received $8,000 from a disability policy he had purchased several years ago. The entire amount of the proceeds are tax free because Tom had personally purchased the policy.

Amounts received by an employee under Social Security or workers' compensation as compensation for physical injury or sickness are excluded from gross income. In addition, workers' compensation acts extend to the survivors of a deceased employee and allow the recipients to exclude any benefits received on behalf of the deceased employee.

Government disability payments are also excluded from gross income if the payments (pension, annuity, or similar allowance) are received for the personal physical injuries or sickness of the taxpayer. These awards are tax exempt if attributable to active service in the armed forces of any country, or in the Coast Guard and Geodetic Survey or Public Health Service, or as a disability annuity payable under the Foreign Service Act of 1980.

In addition, the law provides an exclusion for amounts received by an individual as disability income attributable to injuries incurred as a direct result of a terrorist attack. The attack must have occurred while the individual was an employee of the United States and engaged in performing official duties outside of the United States.

Damages

Certain damages may also be excluded from gross income. The exclusion applies to financial awards for damages received because of personal physical injury or sickness. The exclusion is limited to non-punitive damages. Sec. 104 prohibits the exclusion of punitive damages. However, an exception to this rule exists for wrongful death cases. If under a state law in effect on September 13, 1995, the only damages awarded in a wrongful death action are punitive damages, then the wrongful death award is excluded from gross income.

Nonpunitive damages for personal injury are currently excludible from gross income only if they are paid on account of a physical injury or sickness. Financial awards related to emotional distress are generally not excludible under current law. The exclusion would apply only if the emotional distress award is attributed to a physical injury or sickness or represents reimbursement for medical expenses arising from the emotional distress. This same logic now applies to the taxation of financial awards for loss of employment, age and gender discrimination, and civil rights violations. The key test for excludibility is physical injury or sickness. Without this requirement, these awards are included in gross income. The exclusion extends to both court awards and settlement agreements received outside of litigation.

Employer-Provided Accident and Health Plans

Employers often contribute to the cost of an employee's accident and health care insurance. The plan will often make payments directly to the employee or health care provider. Under certain conditions, benefits received from the employer-sponsored plan may be excluded from the employee's gross income. IRC Sec. 105 addresses amounts received under accident and health plans. Employer contributions to accident and health plans are covered under Sec. 106.

In general, the tax treatment of amounts received under accident and health plans depends on why benefits are paid, who pays the premiums, and how the benefits are computed.

Although Sec. 104 permits the tax-free receipt of a disability or income replacement policy's proceeds, there is one catch. The exclusion from gross income results from the taxpayer's purchasing of the policy with after-tax dollars. Sec. 104 is therefore addressing self-purchased disability and income replacement policies. However, if the taxpayer's employer pays the premiums on a disability or income replacement policy as a tax-free fringe benefit to the employee, the tax issue regarding policy proceeds is somewhat different. Sec. 105 requires the employee to include in gross income the proceeds received from employer-purchased disability and income replacement policies.

If the employer and employee share the premium costs of a disability or income replacement policy, only part of the policy's proceeds are excluded from gross income.

The exclusion from gross income is proportional to the employee's after-tax contribution of the policy's premium.

> *Example:* The ABC Corporation maintains a disability plan. The plan provides for regular wages to employees missing work because of personal injury or sickness. The corporation requires that all employees participate in the premium cost of the policy. Employees are required to contribute 35 percent of the policy's premium cost through after-tax payroll deductions.
>
> Johnson, an employee, suffered a personal injury during the year. As a result, Johnson missed 6 weeks of work. During his absence, Johnson received $3,000 in disability proceeds under the corporation's plan. Johnson must include $1,950 of the proceeds in gross income. The balance, $1,050, is excluded from gross income. The exclusion (35 percent of $3,000) is proportional to Johnson's premium payments.

As illustrated, the general rule is to tax amounts received for personal injuries or sickness under accident and health plans to employees where the employer pays for the cost of the plan. However, there are two significant exceptions to this general rule:

- amounts expended for medical care
- payments unrelated to absence from work

The first exception excludes from gross income amounts received as reimbursements from an accident or health plan for the medical care of the taxpayer, his or her spouse, or dependents. These benefits are excludible if an insurance company provides the accident and health insurance benefits. However, as discussed below, comprehensive nondiscrimination tests are applied to self-funded (uninsured) medical reimbursement plans.

> *Example:* Sicck Corporation provides all employees with health care insurance. Amy, a Sicck Corporation employee, receives a $500 reimbursement for medical bills incurred during the year. The reimbursement is excluded from gross income even though Sicck Corporation paid the health care insurance premiums.

The second exception excludes payments unrelated to absence from work. If a taxpayer, a spouse, or a dependent incurs an injury that results in permanent disfigurement, loss or loss of using a body part, or loss of a bodily function, then the amounts received under the employer's accident or health care plan are excluded from gross income. For example, benefits paid for the loss of an arm, leg, or other bodily function are tax exempt. In addition, amounts received under an accident policy based on the nature of the injury are tax free. However, as previously stated, no exclusion is permitted if the length of time an employee is absent is a factor in determining the amount of the payment (that is, disability income proceeds).

> *Example:* The Reading Railroad Corporation maintains an accident plan that provides payments for certain injuries. The plan provides for a $15,000 payment in the event an employee loses a limb. John, an employee who lost a leg, receives $15,000 from the corporation's plan. The $15,000 payment is excludible from John's gross income.
>
> The Reading Railroad Corporation's plan also provides for payments of $400 weekly to each employee missing work on account of an injury. The corporation's plan covers employees for a maximum period of 26 weeks, regardless of the employee's injury. John received the maximum benefit ($10,400) under the plan. The entire amount received by John is included in gross income (disability income).

Qualified long-term care insurance is treated as accident or health insurance under Secs. 104 through 106 (the related deduction rules appear under Sec. 213). As a medical expense reimbursement, long-term care reimbursements are excluded from gross income, subject to certain restrictions. For 2001, the exclusion for benefits paid from qualified long-term care insurance contracts is $200 a day per covered individual, as adjusted for inflation. Amounts in excess of the daily exclusion are also excluded from gross income to the extent that actual long-term care expenses exceed the daily benefit and are not otherwise reimbursed. In an employer-provided long-term care insurance plan, amounts received are treated in generally the same way as amounts received for medical care.

An employee's gross income does not include premiums paid by an employer for accident or health care insurance coverage for the employee, the employee's spouse, and the employee's dependents. Sec. 106 addresses contributions by employers to accident and health plans. This section specifically excludes contributions made by an employer to an accident or health plan to provide compensation, through insurance or otherwise, directly to an employee for personal injuries or sickness. This exclusion applies to both insured and self-funded (uninsured) plans regardless of the number of employees. However, if an employee is indemnified beyond the medical costs incurred under the accident and health insurance plan, the excess reimbursement represents taxable income to the employee.

Contributions continuing after an employee's death or retirement are also excluded under the statute.

In general, the employer may claim a tax deduction for premiums paid for accident and health care coverage for employees.

Self-Funded Medical Reimbursement Plans

The tax situation may be different than the above if an employer provides medical expense benefits through a self-funded plan (referred to in Sec. 105 of the Internal Revenue Code as a self-insured medical reimbursement plan) under which employers either (1) pay the providers of medical care directly or (2) reimburse employees for their medical expenses. If a self-funded plan meets certain nondiscrimination requirements for highly compensated employees, the employer can deduct benefit payments as they are made, and the employee will have no taxable income. If a plan is discriminatory, the employer will still receive an income tax deduction. However, all or a portion of the benefits received by "highly compensated individuals," but not by other employees, will be treated as taxable income. A highly compensated individual is (1) one of the five highest-paid officers of the firm, (2) a shareholder who owns more than 10 percent of the firm's stock, or (3) one of the highest-paid 25 percent of all the firm's employees. There are no nondiscrimination rules if a plan is not self-funded and provides benefits through an insurance contract, a Blue Cross–Blue Shield plan, an HMO, or a PPO.

Nondiscriminatory Plans

To be considered nondiscriminatory, a self-funded plan must meet certain requirements regarding eligibility and benefits. The plan must provide benefits for 70 percent or more of "all employees" or for 80 percent or more of all eligible employees if 70 percent or more of all employees are eligible. Certain employees can be excluded from the all-employees category without affecting the plan's nondiscriminatory status. These include

- employees who have not completed 3 years of service
- employees who have not attained age 25
- part-time employees. Anyone who works less than 25 hours per week is automatically considered a part-time employee. Persons who work 25 or more hours but less than 35 hours per week may also be counted as part-time as long as other employees in similar work for the employer have substantially more hours.
- seasonal employees. Anyone who works less than 7 months of the year is automatically considered a seasonal employee. Persons who work between 7 and 9 months of the year may also be considered seasonal as long as other employees have substantially more months of employment.

- employees who are covered by a collective-bargaining agreement if accident and health benefits were a subject of collective bargaining

Even if the plan fails to meet the percentage requirements regarding eligibility, it can still qualify as nondiscriminatory as long as the IRS is satisfied that the plan benefits a classification of employees in a manner that does not discriminate in favor of highly compensated individuals. This determination is made on a case-by-case basis.

To satisfy the nondiscrimination requirements for benefits, the same type and amount of benefits must be provided for all employees covered under the plan regardless of their compensation. In addition, the dependents of other employees cannot be treated less favorably than the dependents of highly compensated individuals. However, because diagnostic procedures are not considered part of a self-funded plan for purposes of the nondiscrimination rule, a higher level of this type of benefit is permissible for highly compensated employees.

Discriminatory Plans

If a plan is discriminatory in either benefits or eligibility, highly compensated individuals must include the amount of any "excess reimbursement" in their gross income for income tax purposes. If highly compensated individuals receive any benefits that are not available to all employees covered under the plan, then these benefits are considered an excess reimbursement. For example, if a plan pays 80 percent of covered expenses for employees in general, but 100 percent for highly compensated individuals, the extra 20 percent of benefits constitutes taxable income for the highly compensated.

If a self-funded plan discriminates in the way it determines eligibility, then highly compensated individuals will have excess reimbursements for any amounts they receive. The amount of this excess reimbursement is determined by a percentage that is calculated by dividing the total amount of benefits received by highly compensated individuals (exclusive of any other excess reimbursements) by the total amount of benefits paid to all employees (exclusive of any other excess reimbursements).

A plan might discriminate with respect to both eligibility and benefits. Using the example above, assume a highly compensated individual receives $2,000 in benefits during a certain year. If other employees received only 80 percent of this amount (or $1,600), then the highly compensated individual would have received an excess reimbursement of $400. If the plan also discriminates in the area of eligibility, the highly compensated individual will incur additional excess reimbursement. For example, if 60 percent of the benefits (ignoring any benefits already considered excess reimbursement) were given to highly compensated individuals, then 60 percent of the remaining $1,600 ($2,000 − $400), or $960, would be added to the $400, for a total excess reimbursement of $1,360.

If a plan provides benefits only for highly compensated individuals, then all benefits received will be considered an excess reimbursement, as the percentage of total benefits received by the highly compensated group would be 100 percent. [2]

DEPENDENT-CARE ASSISTANCE PROGRAMS

Under IRC Sec. 129, an employee may exclude from gross income the value of child- and dependent-care costs provided by an employer under a written nondiscriminatory plan. The dollar amount of the exclusion cannot exceed $5,000 for single parents and married couples filing jointly. The exclusion is reduced to $2,500 if the filing status is married filing separately. However, the amount excludible from income cannot exceed the employee's earned income for the year. In the event the employee is married, the earned income limitation applies to the lower earner's wages.

In addition to dependent-care assistance programs, the tax law allows a child-care credit under Sec. 21. This section allows employed individuals a limited credit for their child-care expenses (a 20 to 30 percent credit based on qualifying expenses of $2,400 to $4,800 depending on the employee's income and number of children). A more detailed discussion of the child-care credit appears in chapter 10. Although the law allows these two tax benefits related to child care, they are mutually exclusive. Sec. 129 prohibits utilizing both provisions by reducing any benefits qualifying for the credit by the amount of any excluded benefits under this section. Therefore reimbursements under dependent-care assistance programs reduce the dollar limit on expenses qualifying for the child-care credit.

> *Example:* Mrs. Thomson works for R&H Corporation. The corporation provides a day-care facility for the children of its employees. Every working morning, Mrs. Thomson leaves her two young children at her employer's day-care center prior to commencing work. The employer estimates the value of the day-care center to Mrs. Thomson at $5,000. Mrs. Thomson may exclude the $5,000 from her income to the extent that both she and her husband have earned income up to $5,000. Alternatively, if Mrs. Thomson personally pays for the day-care center and is reimbursed for $5,000, the reimbursement is excluded from gross income. The amount of her qualifying child-care expenses for purposes of the tax credit would be zero. However, if Mrs. Thomson paid for all or part of the cost of the day-care center and was not reimbursed by her employer, up to $4,800 of her payments would qualify for the child-care credit.

In order to claim the dependent-care assistance exclusion or child-care credit, a series of special rules must be followed. For example, an employer's payments for dependent-care services to an employee's child under the age of 19 (or to anyone for whom the employee can claim a dependency exemption) do not qualify for the exclusion. These rules are also outlined in chapter 10.

NOTES

1. *Placko v. Comm'r.,* 74 T.C. 452 (1980).
2. This portion of the text (Self-Funded Medical Reimbursement Plans) was excerpted from *Group Benefits: Basic Concepts and Alternatives,* 7th ed., by Burton T. Beam, Jr. (Bryn Mawr, Pa.: The American College, 1997).

Business Expenses and Expenses for the Production of Income

James F. Ivers III and Alban Salaman[*]

The income tax created more criminals than any other single act of government.

Barry M. Goldwater

Chapter Outline

---

[*] Alban Salaman, JD, LLM, CLU, is a partner at Holland and Knight, Washington, D.C.

INTRODUCTION

This chapter will focus on the specific rules for deductibility of certain expenses paid or incurred for business or for the production of income. The broad subject of income tax deductions has previously been touched on in this text. A more specific look at various deduction rules is taken here. There are many different types of deductible expenses, many of which are covered in this text. In this chapter, the following areas will be examined:

- specific types of business expenses
- business entertainment and related expenses
- expenses that are not business expenses but that are made in connection with the production of income
- home office expenses
- vacation home expenses
- the "2 percent floor" on individual miscellaneous itemized deductions

Deductible business expenses may generally be claimed by both individual taxpayers and business entities. However, the manner in which expenses are deductible can vary depending on both the type of taxpayer involved and the nature of the taxpayer's relationship to the business. For example, the business expenses of a regular or "C" corporation are deducted on the corporation's tax return to provide a benefit for the corporation as a tax-paying entity. In the case of so-called "pass-through" tax entities including partnerships and "S" corporations, the deductions are reported on the entity's tax return, but the individual business owners are the taxpayers who actually receive the benefit of the deductions because they are the actual taxpayers for the business. For individual owners of partnerships and "S" corporations, business deductions are, in effect, claimed on Schedule E of Form 1040. The tax treatment of business entities is discussed in more detail in later chapters of this text.

For individual taxpayers who are sole proprietors for income tax purposes, business expenses are claimed on Schedule C of Form 1040. Like partners and shareholders in "S" corporations, sole proprietors claim their business expenses "above the line," that is, such expenses are subtracted from gross income in determining adjusted gross income.

Individual taxpayers who are employees must generally claim their allowable business expenses as miscellaneous itemized deductions on Schedule A of Form 1040. A few employee business expenses (including deductions for reimbursed business expenses, moving expenses, and certain expenses of performing artists) are deductible "above the line" in calculating adjusted gross income. The rest are treated as miscellaneous itemized deductions that are "below-the-line" deductions and are also generally subject to the limitations of the "2 percent floor" that will be covered in this chapter.

Expenses of individual taxpayers that are not business expenses but that are paid in connection with an activity engaged in for the production of income are also generally deductible. These deductions are often loosely referred to as "investor's expenses," although that terminology is not always appropriate. Expenses for the production of income are deductible in various ways depending on the nature of the income-producing activity. For example, expenses associated with a nonbusiness rental activity would be shown on Schedule E of Form 1040 and deducted above the line. On the other hand, expenses for financial planning or investment advisory fees would be miscellaneous itemized deductions subject to the 2 percent floor.

This chapter also covers the specific limitations applicable to the deductibility of expenses attributable to the business use of a home. In addition, the special restrictions on deducting expenses for the rental of a vacation home will be discussed. Although these are two different topics, they are covered in the same section of the Internal Revenue Code.

Later chapters will focus on additional deductible expenses with particular reference to items deductible by individual taxpayers.

BUSINESS EXPENSES

Fundamental Rules

Internal Revenue Code Sec. 162 states that "there shall be allowed as a deduction all the ordinary and necessary expenses paid or incurred during the taxable year in carrying on any trade or business. . . ." The Code then goes on to list special rules and requirements applicable to specific types of business expenses. However, the fundamental rules for deductibility are contained in the sentence quoted. The expense must be attributable to a business, be paid or incurred during the taxable year, and be both "ordinary" and "necessary" in the conduct of the business.

The terms "ordinary" and "necessary" have been the subject of considerable interpretation by both the IRS and the courts. Essentially, an expense is "ordinary" if it is a customary or usual expense made by many taxpayers involved in the same business activity. The expense does not necessarily have to be made at regular intervals in order to be considered ordinary. However, not all business expenses are considered to be ordinary. An example of an expense that is not ordinary is where a corporation pays the cost of a wedding reception for a majority stockholder's daughter. Even if most of the guests are customers of the corporation, such an expense is not customary and therefore not ordinary.

The term "necessary" has been accepted as including expenses that are appropriate and helpful to the taxpayer's business, even if the expense is not necessary in the strictest sense. In most situations, an expense that is ordinary will also be considered necessary.

The phrase "paid or incurred during the taxable year" means that the taxpayer cannot arbitrarily select the tax year in which to claim a deduction but must claim it in the year the deductible expense is paid or accrued. The term "accrued" refers to taxpayers on the accrual method of tax accounting. Such taxpayers deduct expenses in the tax year in which the liability to pay the expense becomes fixed, ascertainable, and certain. Taxpayers who use the cash methods of tax accounting must deduct expenses in the year they are paid.

The phrase "in carrying on any trade or business" means that the expense must be business related. An activity must be engaged in with the intent and expectation of making money in order to be a business activity for tax purposes. There must also be an element of regularity and continuousness in the taxpayer's participation in the activity. Certain activities are engaged in with the primary intention of making money, but they are treated for tax purposes as nonbusiness activities engaged in for the production of income. This type of activity has its own income tax rules that will be discussed later in this chapter. If an activity is engaged in primarily for personal satisfaction or pleasure, expenses associated with the activity will generally be nondeductible unless the activity actually becomes a profitable business.

Another fundamental rule for deductibility of expenses is that the expense must not be a capital expenditure. Expenses of a capital nature generally cannot be fully deducted in the year they are made but must either be deducted over a period of years or not be deducted at all. Capital expenditures include the cost of acquiring or improving property with a useful life of more than one year. The distinction between currently deductible expenses and capital expenditures is discussed in more detail in chapter 9.

Specifically Nondeductible Expenses

Although business expenses are generally deductible, the Code describes certain payments that are specifically nondeductible. Among these are payments that are illegal under federal or state law. Examples of illegal payments are bribes to government officials and kickbacks in consideration of the referral of a client, patient, or customer. Expenses paid in the conduct of an illegal business such as drug trafficking are nondeductible. Illegal payments include payments in violation of any federal law or of any state law that is generally enforced and subjects the payer to either a criminal penalty or the loss of a license or privilege to engage in a business. There is also a specific Code provision that disallows deductions for bribes and kickbacks made by any provider of services furnished under Medicare or Medicaid coverage.

A fine or penalty paid to a government for the violation of any law is also nondeductible. Such payments include penalties assessed with respect to a federal tax liability and fines for traffic violations or other criminal offenses. For example, payments for speeding or parking tickets received while traveling on business are nondeductible. Similarly, if a taxpayer makes treble damage payments in judgment or settlement of a lawsuit brought in connection with the taxpayer's criminal conviction or plea of nolo contendere under the antitrust laws, two-thirds of the damage payments (essentially the punitive portion) is nondeductible.

Certain expenses of a political nature are also nondeductible. These include the following:

- expenses in connection with influencing legislation
- expenses for participation in a political campaign on behalf of or in opposition to a candidate for public office
- expenses for influencing public opinion on a political issue
- expenses for communication with certain executive branch officials to influence their official positions

Note that expenses for influencing legislation at the local level are not subject to this rule and are therefore deductible. Also, if the taxpayer is a professional lobbyist who is paid to influence legislation, he or she may deduct expenses related to that activity as business expenses.

Payments in Compensation for Services

Reasonable Compensation

When a taxpayer engaged in a trade or business makes payment to an individual for services rendered, the general rule is that the payment is a deductible business expense. However, the amount of the payment must be reasonable to be deductible. In other words, the payment of any compensation in excess of a reasonable amount is nondeductible.

The tax issue of reasonable compensation has historically arisen mostly in cases involving compensation paid to employees of a corporation who are also its shareholders. The IRS typically seeks to recharacterize the excess portion of the compensation as a nondeductible dividend payment to the shareholder-employee. In such cases, the corporation has an incentive to characterize payments to the shareholder-employee as compensation rather than as dividends, because compensation payments are deductible by the corporation while dividend payments are not. As a result, the factual issue of reasonableness arises and is often decided by a court.

"Reasonable" compensation may be loosely defined as that amount that would ordinarily be paid to an employee for similar services by similar companies operating in similar circumstances. Under the judicial decisions on this issue (of which there are many), several factors are taken into account in making the factual determination of reasonableness. These factors include (but are not limited to)

- the degree and nature of the employee's responsibility in his or her position (including responsibility for the production of profits)
- the amount the employee could have earned in similar employment for another company
- the salary paid in prior years for the same services
- the time the employee devotes to the performance of the services
- the nature of the services and any unique or peculiar abilities of the employee in rendering those services
- the amount of salaries paid to other employees providing similar services who are not shareholders
- general economic conditions in the region

The employee's total compensation is considered in determining reasonableness including commissions, overrides, bonuses, and payments to pension, profit-sharing, or 401(k) plans.

One factor that may work in favor of taxpayers in a dispute over this issue is that a court will allow a larger payment in a later year for the same services rendered in prior years if it can be shown that the total amount paid over the years is reasonable for the total services rendered. This means that a company can "make up" compensation in later years that an employee earned or deserved but the company was not previously able to pay.

In anticipation of possible dispute with the IRS over this issue, a privately owned corporation might enter into an agreement with an officer-stockholder of the corporation that provides for a repayment of a portion of his or her compensation to the corporation in the event that it is determined by the IRS to be unreasonable and therefore partially nondeductible. The officer-stockholder may deduct such a repayment on his or her tax return if the agreement was made before the time of the payment and is otherwise enforceable. The problem with such agreements is that they may become a self-fulfilling prophecy: The IRS may use them as evidence that the parties themselves had an inkling that the compensation was unreasonable.

The Rule of "Excessive Employee Remuneration"

One special rule limiting deductions for compensation applies only to payments by publicly held corporations. The general definition of "excessive employee remuneration" is remuneration paid to a "covered employee" that is in excess of $1 million for the taxable year. A "covered employee" is either one of the following:

- the chief executive officer of the corporation or an individual acting in such capacity at the close of the taxable year
- one of the four most highly paid officers of the corporation for the taxable year (other than the chief executive officer)

Under this definition, the rule applies to no more than five employees of a company for any taxable year.

There are also qualifying provisions that apply to the $1 million maximum amount. The following types of compensation or "remuneration" do not count toward the $1 million deductible limit:

- commissions generated by the taxpayer to whom the compensation is paid
- contributions to a qualified plan of deferred compensation
- the value of employee benefits that are excludible from the gross income of the employee (such as employer contributions to health plans)
- so-called "performance-based" compensation. In order to be treated as "performance-based," the compensation must be payable solely on account of the attainment of one or more performance goals, must be disclosed to and approved by a majority vote of the corporation's shareholders, and must be determined by a compensation committee of the corporation's board of directors comprised solely of two or more outside directors.

This provision has been criticized by commentators as not being strong enough to truly discourage the excessive compensation being paid to executives of public companies. However, it is at least a step in that direction by the income tax law.

In certain situations, the IRS may assert that compensation paid to an employee is unreasonably low rather than unreasonably high. This problem arises in partnershps and "S" corporations where low salaries are paid to owner-employees in order to allow more of the company's income to be allocated to lower-bracket owners (typically family members) of the so-called "pass-through" business entity, resulting in lower overall taxes. In such cases, the IRS may reallocate income to high-bracket owner-employees whose efforts actually generated the income.

Expenses for Business-Related Education

Treasury Regulations deal with the question of whether expenses for education that is related to a business activity are deductible. Such expenses are deductible if they meet either of the two following criteria:

- The expenses are deductible if incurred primarily for the purpose of meeting the requirements of the taxpayer's employer or of local law as a condition for the taxpayer's retention of employment.
- The expenses are deductible if incurred primarily for the purpose of maintaining or improving skills needed by the taxpayer in his or her current employment or business activity.

On the other hand, expenses for education that qualifies a taxpayer for a new business or line of work are not deductible. Also, expenses for education leading to the minimum requirements necessary for obtaining employment (as distinguished from retaining employment) as determined by an employer or the standards of a profession or business are not deductible. For example, expenses for medical school would generally fall within this rule of disallowance.

Travel itself as a form of education is not a deductible expense. However, travel expenses incurred to and from an educational event are deductible if the education itself is deductible. Any meal expenses incurred in connection with deductible education may be deductible subject to the 50 percent limitation explained later in this chapter.

The availability of the deduction may be affected by interaction with other education tax incentives. For example, the same education expenses cannot be used to claim both the business expense deduction and the "Lifetime" learning credit described in chapter 10. The taxpayer may have to choose between the two tax benefits. The choice will generally depend on the taxpayer's marginal tax bracket and perhaps also on whether the business deduction would be claimed above the line or below the line.

If the taxpayer is a sole proprietor, the deduction would be claimed above the line on Schedule C of Form 1040. If the taxpayer is an employee, the deduction is a miscellaneous itemized deduction claimed on Schedule A and subject to the "2 percent floor" discussed later in this chapter.

Health Insurance Premiums Paid on Behalf of Self-Employed Individuals

If a sole proprietorship, partnership, or "S" corporation pays the health insurance premiums for a proprietor, partner, or more than 2 percent shareholder in the S corporation, this payment cannot be excluded from the gross income of such "self-employed" persons as it would be in the case of an employee. However, the covered person is entitled to an above-the-line deduction for a specified percentage of the amount paid. The deductible percentage is currently on an increasing schedule and is as follows:

Year	Deductible Percentage
1999 through 2001	60
2002	70
2003 and thereafter	100

Medical expense deductions of individuals are generally claimed below the line as itemized deductions. However, this particular deduction is taken above the line in determining adjusted gross income. The deduction cannot exceed the individual's earned income from the business that provides the health plan. It is available only if the self-employed person is not eligible to participate in any subsidized health plan maintained by any employer of the self-employed person or the person's spouse. Premiums for qualified long-term care insurance as well as for health insurance coverage are eligible for this deduction. The requirements and limits for the deduction are applied separately with respect to long-term care coverage.

Transportation and Travel Expenses

Business Transportation Costs

Expenses incurred for local transportation in the course of a business activity are generally deductible. Such expenses include taxi, railway, or bus fares, and expenses for the business use of a car.

Car expenses may be deducted in one of two different ways. The taxpayer may claim a standard mileage allowance for business transportation. This allowance is deemed to include depreciation, fuel, insurance, repairs, and other normal operating expenses. The only actual expenses that are deductible in addition to the mileage allowance are those for highway tolls, parking charges, and interest payments with respect to the car that are otherwise deductible under the tax law. Taxpayers who lease their cars may generally use the mileage allowance but it must be used for the entire lease period. The mileage allowance can be claimed only with respect to those miles actually driven for business purposes. For the year 2001, the standard allowance is 34.5 cents per mile. The basis of the car must be reduced by 15 cents for each mile claimed during 2001 under the standard allowance. These figures are subject to annual indexing for inflation. The standard mileage allowance cannot be used by taxpayers who

- use the car for livery or hire
- use two or more cars simultaneously for business purposes, or
- have previously claimed accelerated depreciation for the same car

In lieu of claiming the standard mileage allowance, taxpayers may claim their actual expenses (including depreciation) in using a car for business. Any depreciation deductions will be limited by that percentage of the overall use of the car that represents business use. Cars used for business are also subject to special "luxury auto" limits on depreciation that are discussed in chapter 11. Repairs made to the car will also be deductible only to the extent of the percentage of business use. The "actual expense" method requires significant recordkeeping to substantiate deductions. Many taxpayers find it easier to simply keep a log of business miles, and claim deductions under the standard mileage allowance.

Taxpayers who lease a car used for business are not permitted to claim depreciation for the car, since the required ownership does not exist. However, such taxpayers are permitted to deduct their lease payments to the extent the car is used for business if the standard mileage allowance is not used. This deduction is, however, subject to an "add-back" rule. Depending on the car's fair market value, a specified amount of the lease payment must be included in the taxpayer's gross income to offset part of the lease payment deduction. This rule corresponds to the "luxury auto" limitations that apply to taxpayers who claim depreciation for the business use of a car. These add-back amounts are relatively low and are published annually by the IRS to reflect adjustments for inflation.

Commuting Expenses

Expenses for commuting do not qualify as business transportation expenses and are not deductible. Therefore the trip between a taxpayer's home and his or her place of business is generally nondeductible. However, if the taxpayer engages in business activities at more than one location during the day, the cost of transportation between one business location and another such location are deductible.

If a taxpayer has an office at home that qualifies as a home office because it is the taxpayer's principal place of business, transportation expenses between the home office and other business locations are treated as deductible transportation expenses rather than nondeductible commuting expenses. The income tax rules for home offices are discussed in more detail later in this chapter.

"Temporary" Work Locations

Another situation in which transportation expenses from a taxpayer's home may be deductible involves so-called "temporary" business locations. Essentially, a temporary work location is one that is expected to last for no longer than one year, and actually lasts for no longer than one year.

For example, a work location will not be treated as temporary if it was expected to last more than one year, even if it actually does not last more than one year. In addition, the location is not temporary if it does in fact last longer than one year, even if it was not expected to.

If a taxpayer has a temporary work location that is outside the taxpayer's metropolitan area, a trip from the taxpayer's home to the temporary work location and back is deductible business transportation, rather than nondeductible commuting. However, if the temporary work location is within the taxpayer's metropolitan area, additional rules apply. In such cases, in order to deduct the trip from the residence to the temporary location, the taxpayer must either

- have a place of business in addition to the temporary work location or
- have a home office that is the taxpayer's principal place of business for the business conducted at the temporary location

Business Travel Away from Home

Ordinary and necessary expenses incurred in the course of traveling away from home on business are deductible. A taxpayer is generally considered to be "away from home" on a trip in which the taxpayer stays overnight or longer at a temporary business location.

Expenses that would be deductible for such trips include travel to the business location, lodging costs, meals (to the extent of 50 percent of the cost of the meal), local business transportation expenses, and other business expenses incurred while at the destination. Expenses for meals and lodging are deductible only to the extent they are not lavish or extravagant. Expenses incurred for personal activities at the business location are not deductible.

If the taxpayer's trip away from home is partially for business and partially for pleasure, the availability of travel expense and related deductions is subject to additional rules that are based on

- the taxpayer's principal purpose for making the trip
- the number of days spent on business during the trip
- whether the trip is to a destination within or outside of the United States

DEDUCTIONS FOR ENTERTAINMENT EXPENSES

Entertainment of clients, customers, employees, and associates is an expense that practically every business person incurs. However, such expenses may be disallowed as deductible business expenses unless the strict requirements in the Internal Revenue Code are followed. This chapter is intended to highlight the requirements that must be met to obtain the proper deduction for entertainment expenses.

Entertainment Defined

Entertainment is defined in the Treasury regulations as any activity that is considered "entertainment, amusement, or recreation." This includes entertaining at nightclubs, cocktail lounges, theaters, country clubs, or sporting events. It also includes activities satisfying the personal, living, or family needs of a business customer, such as providing food and beverages, a hotel room, or an automobile.[1] No deduction will be allowed for any entertainment or recreation that is lavish or extravagant.[2]

Special Requirements for Deduction

There are special requirements that apply specifically to entertainment expenses, in addition to the general requirement that the expense be "ordinary and necessary." Unless an entertainment activity is "directly related to" or "associated with" the active conduct of the trade or business,[3] a deduction will be disallowed. Furthermore, the taxpayer must be able to substantiate the entertainment expenditures with adequate records of the business-related event or with other sufficient corroborating evidence.

Directly Related Requirement

The *directly related* requirement generally refers to entertainment provided during a period in which the taxpayer is actively engaged in a business negotiation or discussion.[4] Thus food and beverages served to sales prospects during a business discussion are deductible subject to limitations. Under this requirement the taxpayer must have more than a general expectation of deriving some business benefit at some future, indefinite time. The expenditure must relate to the person with whom the taxpayer engaged in the active conduct of business. Thus the entertainment expenses paid for nonbusiness persons, such as spouses, are excluded here but may qualify under the *associated with* test discussed below.

The primary purpose of any combined business and entertainment activity must not be a social one, but one to further the taxpayer's business. For example, if incidental business discussions take place on hunting or fishing trips, it cannot be said that the principal aspect of the combined business and entertainment was the transaction of business.

The directly related test is also met when the expenditures are made in a clear business setting, such that the recipient knows that the taxpayer has no significant motive other than to further business (for example, the sponsorship of a *hospitality room* at a convention, or the entertainment of business representatives at the opening of a new hotel or theatrical production).[5] Large parties thrown by the taxpayer, such as a wedding where other than business associates are present, are not deductible under the directly related test as there is no clear business setting nor is the event related.

The expenses of entertainment are not directly related where there is little or no possibility of engaging in the active conduct of business, such as where the taxpayer is not present or when the distractions are substantial.[6] Discussions at nightclubs, cocktail parties, theaters, or sporting events are generally not considered directly related because of the substantial distractions.

Entertainment for goodwill purposes without business discussions is not deductible under the directly related requirement but may qualify under the *associated with* test discussed below.

Associated-with Requirement

As previously stated, entertainment expenses to promote goodwill (for example, expenses incurred in an effort to obtain new business or to encourage the continuation of existing business relationships) are not deductible under the *directly related* requirements. However, such goodwill entertainment expenses are considered *associated with* the conduct of business and may be deductible if the expenses "directly precede or follow" a bona fide business discussion.[7]

For example, Alan, a manufacturing representative, has complex business discussions during the day with Barbara. At night Barbara is Alan's guest at the theater. His entertainment expenses are deductible, because they are associated with the business as goodwill expenses and directly followed bona fide business discussions. However, if Alan merely invited Barbara, a long-time business associate, to the theater, Alan could not deduct expenses if there was no business discussion before or after the show. Similarly, cocktail parties for business associates and their spouses are not deductible under this test if there were no substantial business discussions preceding or following the party.

"Directly preceding or following" has been interpreted in the regulations to mean that the entertainment occurs on the same day as the business discussions. However, entertainment expenses incurred on a day other than the day of business discussion may still qualify depending on the facts and circumstances. To continue the previous example, assume Barbara lives in Los Angeles and travels to New York for the negotiations. If Barbara takes Alan to the theater the night before the negotiations, such entertainment expenses are still deductible.[8]

Unlike the directly related test, expenses allocable to the entertainment of spouses who are not business associates may be deductible under the associated-with test. Thus if Alan invites Barbara and her spouse to the theater after business negotiations, the entire cost of the spouse's ticket is deductible. If Alan's spouse comes also, the cost of this ticket is likewise deductible.[9] Stricter rules apply to travel expenses paid for spouses.

Exceptions to the General Requirements

Exceptions to the directly related and associated-with requirements in the Code basically relate to employers' entertainment expenses for their employees. Food and beverages furnished on the business premises to employees, whether for recreational or social purposes (such as Christmas parties or summer picnics), and expenses incurred for business meetings of employees (and stockholders, agents, or directors) are deductible without regard to the directly related or associated-with tests. An employer may also deduct entertainment expenses regarded as compensation to the employee, such as a paid vacation trip.[10]

Although the exceptions to the general rules need not meet directly related or associated-with tests, they still must meet the substantiation requirement discussed below in order to be deductible.

The 50 Percent Limitation

Deductions for all business meal and business entertainment expenses are limited to 50 percent of the amount that is deductible after taking into account all other limitations and restrictions. This rule applies to both business entertainment meals and meals taken while the taxpayer is traveling on business. It does not, however, apply to business travel expenses other than meal expenses.

There are some minor exceptions to the 50 percent rule, including meals provided at meetings of business leagues and meals provided to employees on the employer's business premises. Items that are treated as de minimis fringe benefits are excluded from the limitation. Also if a meal is treated as compensation to the recipient for tax purposes, rather than as entertainment, the limitation does not apply. Certain individuals in the transportation industry are also subject to different limitations on business meals.

The 50 percent limitation increases the after-tax cost of business meals and entertainment. For example, suppose Jane entertains a business client just after a meeting in New York. The total cost of the entertainment is $500. Her deduction is limited to 50 percent. Therefore the deductible amount is $250. If Jane is in a 36 percent bracket, her after-tax cost of the entertainment has been increased by $90 because of the 50 percent limitation ($250 nondeductible portion x .36).

Entertainment Facilities and Tickets

Deductions for expenses paid or incurred in connection with the operation and maintenance of an entertainment facility are generally disallowed. No depreciation deductions may be taken even when a facility is primarily used for business entertainment. By eliminating the deductibility of these expenses, Congress has sought to curtail excessive and abusive use of these facilities under the guise of business entertainment.

Facility refers to any real or personal property (such as a yacht, hunting lodge, swimming pool, apartment, or hotel suite in a resort area) that is owned, rented, or used by taxpayers for recreational, entertainment, or amusement activities. However, certain facilities, such as automobiles or airplanes, that are not necessarily recreational may not fall within the above limitation. Deductions for these items continue to be allowed for business trips. Generally deductions for depreciation and operating costs of facilities, such as yachts, lodges, and so forth, are a thing of the past. Those deductions otherwise allowable to individuals that are not predicated on a business connection (such as interest expense on mortgage debt, real estate taxes, and casualty losses) are still available to the taxpayer who owns a facility used for business entertaining.

Out-of-pocket expenses for entertaining at a facility, such as the cost of food and beverages, fall within the general entertainment rules. However, membership dues and fees for business, social, athletic, sporting, luncheon, and country clubs are no longer deductible, regardless of whether the taxpayer uses the club for business purposes. Professional and civic organizations are not considered clubs for this purpose, so membership fees paid to such organizations are not subject to the entertainment rules. They are deductible if they qualify as ordinary and necessary business expenses.[11]

Although fees and membership dues are nondeductible, out-of-pocket expenses incurred while entertaining at a club may be deductible as business expenses if the general requirements described in this chapter are met. Such expenses would, of course, be subject to the 50 percent limitation.

Deductions for tickets to entertainment events that qualify as business expenses are limited to the face value of the tickets. The face value limitation will make the premium paid to a scalper, as well as the premium paid to a legitimate ticket agency, nondeductible. The deduction, of course, is then further reduced by the 50 percent limitation.

Business Gifts

The deduction for business gifts that are ordinary and necessary business expenses will be disallowed to the extent they exceed $25 per donee.[12] A husband and wife are considered one donor, and they are limited to $25 per donee.[13] Gifts to spouses of business associates are deemed to be gifts to the business associate, unless the spouse is also a bona fide business associate of the taxpayer.[14]

Gifts of admission tickets to business associates for such entertainment as the theater or sporting events are considered *entertainment expenses* if the taxpayer accompanies the associates to the event. Thus the taxpayer would have to meet the associated-with test to obtain a deduction. The directly related test could not be met because of the distractions of such places.

On the other hand, if the taxpayer does not accompany the associates to the place of entertainment, the taxpayer has the choice of treating the expense as either a gift ($25 deduction limit) or *entertainment* (meeting the associated-with test) in order for it to be deductible. The taxpayer will probably elect to treat the expense as associated-with business only when the cost of the admission ticket is in excess of $25 and the event either precedes or follows a business discussion.

Substantiation Requirement for Travel and Entertainment Expenses

Even if the taxpayer meets the previously discussed requirements and limitations, travel and entertainment expense deductions will be disallowed unless the taxpayer can adequately substantiate the deductible expenses.[15] This requires the taxpayer either to maintain an account book or diary in which the expenditures are recorded at or near the time of expenditure or to substantiate the deductions with other sufficient evidence. The use of an account book is the better way to meet the substantiation requirements, and it must include the following:

- the amount of each expenditure
- the date of the entertainment and its duration
- the place of the travel or entertainment, including name and address
- the business purpose
- for entertainment expenses, the business relationship, meaning the name, title, or other description of the person entertained, sufficient to establish a business relationship to the taxpayer[16]

If entertainment is merely associated with the taxpayer's business, then the taxpayer must record the place and duration of the business discussion and must identify the persons entertained who participated in the discussion.[17]

Lodging expenses and other expenses of $75 or more require documentary evidence, such as a receipt, to support the deduction.[18] Incidental items, such as taxi fares or telephone calls, may be aggregated on a daily basis.[19]

The statutory substantiation requirements superseded the well-known *Cohan* case,[20] which held that if evidence indicated the taxpayer had incurred deductible travel or entertainment expenses, but these amounts could not be determined, then a court must make "as close an approximation as it can, rather than disallow the deduction entirely."

The substantiation requirements have been construed to require a detailed accounting.[21] For example, in one case the taxpayer offered a virtual blizzard of more than 1,700 chits, bills, and statements to support his deductions. The court denied the deduction, holding that his bills contained only monthly aggregates of time, place, or individual amount, and that almost all the exhibits failed to contain a record of the business purpose or business relationship of the persons entertained.[22]

Reporting of Deductible Business Travel and Entertainment Expenses

Depending on the business situation of the taxpayer, travel and entertainment expenses may or may not be one of the items deducted from gross income in determining adjusted gross income.

If the taxpayer is a sole proprietor or partner, travel and entertainment expenses are considered deductible from gross income to determine adjusted gross income.[23] These taxpayers may deduct such expenses from gross income.[24]

If a partnership pays for or reimburses the travel and entertainment expenses of its partners, the expenses are part of the partnership's deductions from gross income.[25] The partner's share of the taxable income of the partnership after all deductions is added to the partner's individual gross income.[26] If a partner is not reimbursed for these expenses, the partner is allowed to deduct them from gross income to determine adjusted gross income on an individual return, provided that the partnership agreement specifically requires that the partner pay expenses of the partnership without reimbursement.[27]

On the other hand, all employees who have unreimbursed business expenses must itemize their deductions on Schedule A of Form 1040 to take advantage of these deductions.[28] For employees, these deductions are taken from adjusted gross income to determine taxable income and are generally subject to the 2 percent floor on miscellaneous itemized deductions.

Employees who adequately account to their employer for reimbursed expenses are entitled to net the reimbursements and deductions in lieu of the more cumbersome method of including the reimbursements as income and then taking the deductions.[29] If reimbursements exceed the deductible expenses, the employee must include this excess income.

If taxpayers are fully reimbursed for their expenses for which they adequately account to their employers, they will not be required to substantiate the expenses again to the Internal Revenue Service.[30] However, the employer and employee must be unrelated for this rule to apply. Employees will have to substantiate expenses if they deduct amounts in excess of their reimbursements.

EXPENSES FOR THE PRODUCTION OF INCOME

Basic Rules

"Production of income" expenses are deductible by individual taxpayers. These are expenses that are paid in the course of an activity that is engaged in for profit but does not rise to the level of a business activity. The Code states that such deductible expenses must be "ordinary and necessary expenses paid or incurred during the taxable year." They must fall within one of the three following definitions:

- expenses made for the production or collection of income. An example of such an expense would be the costs of managing stock and bond investment and trading activities (but not the actual cost of an investment or an expense taken directly from the proceeds of a sale).
- expenses for the management, conservation, or maintenance of property held for the production of income. An example of this type of expense would be expenses for repair and maintenance of a rental property owned by the taxpayer.
- expenses made in connection with the determination, refund, or collection of any tax. An example of this type of expense would be the fee paid by an individual for the preparation of his or her income tax return or for representation at a tax return audit.

Such expenses are sometimes referred to as "nonbusiness" expenses or "investment" expenses.

Determining Whether a Particular Expense Is Deductible

There are certain guidelines that can be applied in determining whether a given expense is deductible as a nonbusiness expense. First, the expense must not be purely personal in nature. It must be clearly related to an activity engaged in for profit. For example, consider the cost of renting a safe deposit box. If the box contains only documents relating to the ownership of stocks, bonds, and other securities held for investment, the cost of the box would be deductible as a nonbusiness expense. However, if the safe deposit box contained personal effects or even valuable property that is owned by the taxpayer primarily for personal reasons, the cost would be nondeductible. As another example, fees paid to an investment adviser are deductible nonbusiness expenses. However, fees for music lessons paid by an amateur musician would be nondeductible personal expenses. The cost of a taxpayer's hobby is neither a business expense nor a deductible nonbusiness expense.

Amounts paid for sophisticated estate planning documents are deductible only to the extent that the documents or other work produced relate to the collection (or legitimate avoidance) of taxes including income, estate, and gift taxes. If the estate planning involves both tax planning and the implementation of personal dispositive intent, an allocation can be made between the deductible and nondeductible portions of the fees. Fees for the drafting of a simple will are nondeductible because the expense is essentially personal.

As in the case of a business expense, a nonbusiness expense must be a current expense and not a capital expenditure in order to be deductible. For example, it is settled that the costs of acquiring, perfecting, or defending a taxpayer's legal title to property are not deductible as nonbusiness expenses because such costs are included in the taxpayer's capital investment in the property and therefore do not qualify as current expenses. Such costs, however, may be recovered for tax purposes when the property is sold or depreciated for income tax purposes.

Another area where deductibility must be carefully considered is the cost of obtaining a divorce. Although a divorce proceeding will usually involve a property settlement that will have important financial consequences for both spouses, the legal fees and other costs associated with a divorce are generally nondeductible. This is so because of the origin of the nature of the claim and rights involved in a divorce. The marital relationship is not fundamentally an income-producing activity in the eyes of the law. Therefore the dissolution of that relationship is not considered to be an activity engaged in for the production of income. The same principle holds in the case of a taxpayer who is defending a tort action for a personal injury resulting from a personal auto accident. Although the taxpayer may lose a significant amount of money because of the action, the incident that gave rise to the claim is personal in nature, and therefore the cost of defending the claim is nondeductible. In determining the deductibility of costs incurred in legal actions, consider the fundamental nature of the right or claim that is being pursued or defended, not simply the monetary consequences of the action. However, it should be remembered that to the extent that legal fees or other costs are directly attributable to tax planning or tax advice, a deduction will be allowed because the Code specifically provides for that.

Expenses paid or incurred in connection with the production of tax-exempt income are specifically nondeductible, as discussed in chapter 9.

Claiming Deductible Nonbusiness Expenses

Most nonbusiness expenses are deductible as below-the-line miscellaneous itemized deductions on Schedule A of Form 1040. They are generally subject to the "2 percent floor" as discussed later in this chapter. However, deductible expenses with respect to rental property owned by the taxpayer are claimed on Schedule E of Form 1040 as an above-the-line deduction taken in determining the taxpayer's adjusted gross income.

DEDUCTIBILITY OF HOME-OFFICE EXPENSES

Basic Rules

Many businesses are operated partially or entirely out of the home. The Internal Revenue Code provides as a general rule that a taxpayer is not entitled to deductions for the business use of a home. Exceptions are made if the taxpayer qualifies under any one of certain tests.

Home-office deductions will be allowed if the residence or portion of the residence falls within any of the following categories of use:

- It is used exclusively and regularly as the principal business place of the taxpayer for the business under consideration.
- It is used exclusively and regularly by patients, clients, or customers in meeting or dealing with the taxpayer in the normal course of the taxpayer's trade or business.
- It is separate from the main home (an office, studio, garage, greenhouse, darkroom, or therapy room) and used exclusively and regularly in connection with the taxpayer's trade or business.
- (In the case of an employee) it is used for the convenience of the taxpayer's employer *and* if one of the above three requirements is met.

There are certain other home-office deduction rules that apply to taxpayers who store inventory or product samples in their homes or who provide day-care services.

"Principal Place of Business" Test

Congress has recently provided a special avenue for taxpayers to qualify under the "principal place of business" test listed above for home-office deductions. Since 1999, the principal place of business test is passed if the taxpayer uses the home office for "administrative or management activities," *and* there is no other fixed location where the taxpayer performs a substantial portion of such activities for the business conducted in the home office.

In the *Soliman* case, the U.S. Supreme Court had previously given its own interpretation of the principal place of business test. In short, *Soliman* held that there are two primary considerations in determining whether a home office is a principal place of business: the relative importance of the activities performed at each location of the business conducted in the home office, and the relative amount of time spent at each location. Some taxpayers could be considered to fail this test even if they have no fixed office outside the home office, especially taxpayers who spend most of their time at the business locations of their clients or customers. *Soliman* must still be considered under the principal place of business test. However, if the newer "administrative or management activities" rule is met, the taxpayer will qualify for home-office deductions under the principal place of business requirement even if the criteria of *Soliman* are not otherwise satisfied.

Limitation on Amount Deductible

Even if a taxpayer qualifies under one of these tests, the deduction permitted for business use is limited. Allowable home-office deductions cannot exceed the gross income derived from the business conducted in the home office less (1) the expense deductions that are allowable regardless of business use (such as mortgage interest and real estate taxes) and (2) deductions attributable to the business other than home-office deductions. Any amounts disallowed are deductible in succeeding years against income from the business conducted in the home office, subject to the same limits. In effect, a taxpayer cannot use home-office expenses to create a net loss from a business activity.

Example: Patrick Riley uses a room in his house exclusively and regularly as an office. The gross income from the business this year is $50,000. The mortgage interest and real estate taxes allocable to that space are $20,000. Patrick also has $30,000 of home-office expenses and $5,000 of business deductions that are not home-office expenses. The amount of home-office expenses that may be deducted is $25,000 ($50,000 income – $20,000 personal deductible home expenses – $5,000 other business expenses = $25,000).

Types of Expenses That May Be Deductible

Deductible home-office expenses for a qualifying home office include the following:

- depreciation on business furniture (studio furniture or equipment, office furniture, and so on)
- depreciation on the business premises. The portion of the acquisition costs and improvements allocable to the portion of the home used exclusively and on a regular basis for the conduct of a trade or business may be depreciated.
- rent. If the home is rented, rent for the portion of the home allocated to business use may be deducted.
- utilities. The cost of electricity, heating, and air conditioning for the portion of the home used for business is deductible.

DEDUCTIBILITY OF VACATION HOME EXPENSES

Introduction

For taxpayers who own a second or "vacation" home and rent that home to others for a portion of the year, the income tax treatment of deductions related to the home is hair-pullingly complex. Several different restrictions and limitations contained in the Internal Revenue Code converge on such taxpayers. Also, the mathematical calculation of how certain deductions are limited is a matter of judicial controversy with the IRS, which has not yet been settled by the Supreme Court. Taxpayers who own vacation homes that are used for both personal and rental purposes are in serious need of an unusually capable tax adviser. The following is a basic view of the three fundamental tax categories into which a vacation home may fall and how such property may be treated for income tax purposes. The reader is not expected to become an expert in this area. A detailed discussion of all the issues involved is beyond the scope of this text.

Treatment of the Property as Having Minimal Rental Use

The simplest tax treatment of a vacation home results where the taxpayer actually rents the home for less than 15 days during the taxable year. In such cases, the rental income is excludible from the taxpayer's gross income, and no deductions attributable to rental use are allowed. Therefore a home can be rented for up to 2 weeks during the year with no tax consequences. So long as the taxpayer owns no more than two homes, the mortgage interest will be treated as qualified residence interest as discussed in chapter 9. The property taxes on the home will be deductible on Schedule A of Form 1040.

Treatment of the Property as Rental Property

The vacation home will be treated for tax purposes as a rental property if the number of days that the home is used as a residence during the year does not exceed the greater of:

- 14 days or
- 10 percent of the number of days during the year that the property is rented at fair market value

For example, suppose a home is used as a residence for 21 days during the year and is rented for 240 days. The period of use as a residence (21 days) does not exceed 10 percent of the period of rental use (10 percent of 240 days, or 24 days). Therefore the home will be treated as a rental property for tax purposes, and deductions attributable to rental use may be allowed. There are, however, complications associated with rental property treatment. The two most significant complications are as follows:

- The rental property will be subject to the "passive loss" provisions discussed in chapter 12. These provisions may significantly restrict deductible expenses for the property. If the taxpayer has less than $150,000 of adjusted gross income for the year, he or she may be able to utilize the "active participation" exception to the passive loss rules.
- The portion of mortgage interest paid on the property that is allocable to days of personal use will be nondeductible personal interest and not deductible qualified residence interest because the property is not treated as a residence. This may be a significant tax trap for many property owners. Property taxes will be deductible, however, to the extent allowed by the passive loss limitations.

Treatment of the Property as a Residence

If the property is used for personal purposes for more than the greater of 14 days or 10 percent of the days it is rented during the year (in other words, if the taxpayer does not meet the requirement discussed above to have the home treated as a rental property), the tax treatment of the property becomes even more complicated. Suppose the taxpayer uses the property for personal purposes for 21 days during the year and rents it for 150 days. The 21 days are more than 10 percent of 150 days. Therefore the property is treated as a residence, not as a rental property, and the so-called "vacation home" rules apply.

How do the vacation home rules work? The basic intent of these rules is that the taxpayer should not be permitted to claim a tax loss with respect to a property that is essentially a residence. In other words, deductions in excess of the income generated by the property are not permitted. To enforce this limitation, the gross income from the rental use is computed first. Next, that portion of mortgage interest and property taxes that is allocable to the days of rental use is subtracted from the rental income. Next, any expenses such as advertising and broker's fees that are attributable solely to rental use are subtracted from the remaining income. The resulting figure is the maximum amount of expenses paid for depreciation, repairs, maintenance, and utilities for the property that is deductible. At any point in the calculation at which the rental income is reduced to zero, no further deductions are permitted. Any amounts disallowed by this calculation can be carried forward to future tax years subject to the same limitations.

The "judicial controversy" mentioned previously in this discussion of vacation homes relates to the percentage of the taxpayer's mortgage interest and property taxes that is "allocable" to rental use for purposes of the vacation home deduction limitation. Is the allocable percentage calculated by dividing the rental days by the total number of days the property is actually used? Or is it calculated by dividing the rental days by 365 days? The second method will allocate less interest and taxes to rental use, leaving more rental income to be "sheltered" by other rental expenses. Mortgage interest and taxes not allocable to rental use are deductible anyway on Schedule A of Form 1040 because the property is treated as a residence. Therefore the "365 days" allocation percentage is better for most taxpayers. This approach has been approved by courts but not accepted by the IRS.

Conclusion

The vacation home area is one in which several provisions of the Code interact and overlap, and this can paralyze taxpayers with mind-numbing complexity. In fact, one observer's opinion is that the tax treatment of second homes is enough to drive a person to own just one home and stay in a hotel for vacation.

THE "TWO PERCENT FLOOR" ON MISCELLANEOUS ITEMIZED DEDUCTIONS

Most miscellaneous itemized deductions can be made only to the extent that they exceed 2 percent of AGI for the taxable year. For example, if a taxpayer's adjusted gross income is $100,000, miscellaneous itemized deductions are allowable only to the extent the total of such deductions exceeds $2,000. Miscellaneous itemized deductions may be defined as itemized deductions other than medical expenses, interest, taxes, charitable contributions, and casualty and theft losses. The topic of itemized deductions will be covered in detail in chapter 9. Miscellaneous itemized deductions are covered here because the majority of these are either employee business expenses or expenses for the production of income that are discussed in this chapter. Miscellaneous itemized deductions are generally subject to the 2 percent floor, *except* for the following deductions:

- impairment-related work expenses of a handicapped taxpayer
- the deduction for estate tax related to income in respect of a decedent
- deductions related to personal property used in a short sale
- deduction for the restoration of the amount held under claim of right
- deduction for annuity payments ceasing before the taxpayer's recovery of investment in the contract
- amortizable bond premiums
- cooperative housing costs
- gambling losses to the extent of gambling winnings

Examples of the types of deductions that *are* subject to the 2 percent floor include the following:

- unreimbursed employee transportation travel and entertainment expenses
- union dues and dues to professional organizations
- cost of subscriptions to business and professional journals
- most investment expenses such as fees for investment advice, deductible safety deposit box fees, payments for clerical help, and other expenses incurred in caring for investments
- tax advice, including tax-return preparation fees and attorney's fees paid in connection with a dispute with the IRS
- depreciation on business property purchased by an employee
- employment-agency fees
- deductible employment-related education expenses of employees
- malpractice insurance premiums of employees
- expenses for a qualified home office used regularly and exclusively for the convenience of the taxpayer's employer
- work clothes and uniforms required for employment

NOTES

1. Treas. Reg. Sec. 1.274-2(b)(1)(i).
2. Treas. Reg. Sec. 1.274-1.
3. IRC Sec. 274(a).
4. Treas. Reg. Sec. 1.274-2(c)(2).
5. Treas. Reg. Sec. 1.274-2(c)(4).
6. Treas. Reg. Sec. 1.274-2(c)(7).
7. S. Rep. no. 1881, 87th Cong. 2d Sess. 26 (1962).
8. Treas. Reg. Sec. 1.274-2(d)(3)(ii).
9. Treas. Reg. Sec. 1.274-2(d)(4).
10. IRC Sec. 274(e).
11. Treas. Reg. Sec. 1.274-2(e)(3)(ii).
12. IRC Sec. 274(b). The $25 limitation relates to the donor's cost rather than to the value of the property at the time of the gift.
13. Treas. Reg. Sec. 1.274-3(e)(2).
14. Treas. Reg. Sec. 1.274-3(d). Under IRC Sec. 274(b)(1)(A) and (B) the following items are not regarded as constituting business gifts but would, of course, be otherwise deductible if incurred in connection with a taxpayer's trade or business: an item costing $4 or less on which the taxpayer's name is clearly and permanently imprinted, and which is one of a number of identical items generally distributed, such as pens, desk sets, plastic bags, calendars, and cases; signs, display racks, or other promotional material to be used on the business premises of the donee.
15. IRC Sec. 274(d).
16. IRC Sec. 274(d); Treas. Reg. Sec. 1.274-5(b).
17. Treas. Reg. Sec. 1.274-5(b)(4).
18. Treas. Reg. Sec. 1.274-5(c)(2)(iii); IRS Notice 95-50.
19. Treas. Reg. Sec. 1.274-5(c)(6)(i)(b).
20. *Cohan v. Comm'r*, 39 F.2d 540 (2d Cir. 1930).
21. *Phillip Handelman v. Comm'r*, 509 F.2d 1067 (2d Cir. 1975).
22. *Dowell v. U.S.*, 36 AFTR 75 6314 (5th Cir. 1975). Also see *Earle v. Comm'r*, 28 T.C.M. 138 (1969).
23. IRC Sec. 62(a)(2).
24. Sole proprietors report these deductions on Schedule C of the Form 1040.
25. These expenses are reported by the partnership on IRS Form 1065.
26. The partner must file Form 1065 K-1 with his or her individual return.
27. *Wallendal v. Comm'r*, 31 T.C. 1249 (1962).
28. Employees must report such expenses under miscellaneous deductions on Schedule A of the 1040 Form.
29. Treas. Reg. Sec. 1.274-5(e)(2).
30. Treas. Reg. Sec. 1.274-5(e)(2)(ii).

Losses and Bad Debts

James F. Ivers III

When everybody has got money they cut taxes, and when they're broke them [politicians] raise 'em. That's statesmanship of the highest order.

Will Rogers

Chapter Outline

INTRODUCTION

This chapter will examine the deductibility of losses sustained by individuals and business entities as well as the law applicable to the deductibility of bad debts. These are two different topics, but they are related in that they both deal with deductions attributable to events or transactions that have caused economic damage to a taxpayer. For both types of deductions there are restrictions on deductibility where the damage to the taxpayer does not arise in the course of a business activity. The rules applicable to both of these categories of deductions will be explained, and the manner in which the deductions are claimed on the tax return will also be mentioned.

DEDUCTIONS FOR LOSSES

Introduction

Sec. 165 of the Internal Revenue Code states as a general rule that "there shall be allowed as a deduction any loss sustained during the taxable year and not compensated for by insurance or otherwise." However simplistic this general rule may seem to be, there are many different categories of losses. Certain losses are exceptions to the general rule and are nondeductible. Certain deductible losses may not be deductible in full by most taxpayers. There are several different categories of deductible losses subject to their own rules and limitations.

The rules applicable to a loss depend on the nature of the activity the taxpayer engaged in that generated the loss, and also on the specific type of transaction that resulted in the loss.

An economic loss may result from the sale or exchange of property. A loss may also result from a fire, storm, accident, or other event that physically damages property. Other losses may be caused by theft, gambling, an event that results in property becoming worthless, or abandonment of property that has ceased to be useful. The loss may arise in the course of either the taxpayer's trade or business, or an income-producing (but nonbusiness) activity, or the taxpayer's personal affairs. There are, however, some general rules that apply to the deductibility of any of these categories of losses.

General Rules for Deductibility

Regardless of the activity or the specific transaction that gives rise to an economic loss, the following rules must be satisfied in order to claim a loss deduction:

- The loss must be suffered by the taxpayer who is claiming the deduction. One taxpayer cannot claim a deduction for a loss suffered by another taxpayer.
- The loss must result from an identifiable event. This means that the loss must be "realized" or "sustained" by the taxpayer from an economic standpoint. The identifiable event must be examined to reveal the nature and the extent of the loss. For example, a theft of property would be an

identifiable event that results in an ascertainable and measurable loss. The same would be true of a fire, shipwreck, or a sale of a publicly traded security for an amount less than what the taxpayer paid for the security. However, a reduction in the value of such a security owned by a taxpayer, without a sale, exchange, or other disposition of the asset, is not an identifiable event for purposes of a loss deduction.

- The property that is the subject of the loss must have had a determinable monetary value. Mere personal or emotional value is not sufficient for damage or loss with respect to the property to produce a deductible loss.
- There must be economic substance to the loss, and not just the form of a transaction that appears to result in a loss. This rule involves the general principle of "substance over form" that can look through the facade or formal structure of a transaction to its actual economic effect to determine the income tax result. For example, a sale of property between closely related parties at a loss would generally not result in a deductible loss because there is no actual realization of economic detriment suffered by the selling taxpayer.
- A loss of an expected economic benefit or item of income is not a deductible loss. To be deductible, the loss must be attributable to an asset or property that was already in the taxpayer's hands. In other words, the loss must occur with respect to the taxpayer's existing capital. For example, if an individual taxpayer was promised a large salary increase from her employer, and as a result of market changes the increase never materialized, the failure to receive the increase would not be a deductible loss.

Worthlessness or Abandonment of Property

Introduction

A loss deduction is allowable for property that has become worthless. Remember, however, that the taxpayer must be able to show that there was an identifiable event that resulted in the worthlessness of the property. The deduction cannot be taken for property that merely decreases in value, as mentioned above. The property must become completely worthless in order for a change in value to result in a deductible loss without a sale or exchange.

Corporate Securities

Stocks, bonds, or other corporate securities are examples of assets that may become worthless and produce a loss deduction. If a corporation is dissolved pursuant to a bankruptcy proceeding and the shareholders receive nothing for their stock, the dissolution in bankruptcy would be an identifiable event that could fix the time at which the loss occurs.

However, a problem can arise regarding the time the corporate security becomes worthless. The law specifies that the deduction is allowable for an asset that "becomes worthless during the taxable year. . . ." Even if there is an identifiable event that proves the worthlessness of the asset, there may be a timing problem in claiming the deduction. The deduction must be claimed in the year that worthlessness occurs, which may have been prior to the actual bankruptcy in the example just discussed. For this reason, the law allows a 7-year period for the amendment of a return or the filing of a claim with respect to a deduction for worthlessness of a corporate security. This 7-year period also applies to bad debt deductions, which are discussed later in this chapter. The 7-year period generally runs from the due date for filing of the tax return for the year in which the worthlessness or bad debt actually occurred. The normal time limit for filing a claim for a refund or an amended return is 3 years from the date the return was filed.

For purposes of calculating a deduction, losses from worthless securities are treated as a loss from the sale or exchange of a capital asset that takes place on the last day of the taxable year.

Demolition

A demolition of tangible property is one type of identifiable event that will generally show that the property has become worthless, unless the demolition actually increases the value of the property, or the taxpayer purchased the property with the intention of demolishing it.

Abandonment

A loss deduction may also arise from the abandonment of property. If the owner of the asset acts affirmatively and with manifest intent to abandon the property, the amount of the taxpayer's adjusted basis in the property is generally deductible as a loss.

Losses Covered by Insurance

The Code specifies that a deduction is allowed for losses "not compensated for by insurance or otherwise." This means that deductions are allowed only to the extent that the loss is not otherwise compensated for. If there is no insurance, the loss is deductible if it otherwise meets the loss deduction requirements. If the loss is partially compensated for by insurance or through some other arrangement, the portion of the loss not compensated for is deductible.

What if the company that insures the loss contests the taxpayer's claim for reimbursement? In such cases, the loss is deductible if the insurance company firmly disputes the payment of the claim. However, if the taxpayer prevails in the dispute with the insurance company and later receives compensation, the compensation must be included in the taxpayer's income to the extent that a loss deduction generated a tax benefit for the taxpayer.

A special rule applies to individual taxpayers claiming casualty or theft losses. In addition to the requirement that any insurance recovery must offset the amount of the deductible loss, a loss will be deductible for property that is insured only if a timely insurance claim is filed with respect to the loss. This means that individuals who suffer casualty or theft losses and have insurance coverage must file an insurance claim in order for any part of the loss to be deductible. Casualty and theft losses of individuals will be discussed in detail below.

The Identity of the Taxpayer

Business Entities

For business entities such as corporations and partnerships, losses are generally deductible in the year when they occur if the loss meets the overall requirements for deductibility. No special restrictions on losses generally apply to these entities. However, there are specific limitations on the types of losses that are deductible by individual taxpayers and on the extent to which they are deductible.

Individuals

Individual taxpayers may claim loss deductions if the loss is incurred in the course of a trade or business or in the course of any transaction entered into for profit. If a loss does not fall into either of these categories, it is a personal loss for income tax purposes. Personal losses are deductible only if they are theft losses or casualty losses (losses arising from fire, storm, shipwreck, or another type of casualty).

In other words, an individual's losses that result from a business or profit-seeking activity are deductible subject to the same rules that apply to a business entity. Other losses are nondeductible except for theft and casualty losses. Note, for example, that a loss on the sale of a personal residence is not deductible by an individual unless and only to the extent the residence had been rented or otherwise actually used in a business or income-producing activity.

Theft and casualty losses are subject to special limitations on deductibility as discussed later in this chapter.

Wagering Losses

The Code specifically provides that losses from wagering are deductible only to the extent that wagering gains are reportable as income. Unless the taxpayer can show that he or she is a professional gambler, such losses must be deducted as a miscellaneous itemized deduction on Schedule A of Form 1040. Such losses are not subject to the 2 percent floor that applies to most miscellaneous itemized deductions as discussed in chapter 7.

Personal Theft and Casualty Losses of Individuals

Introduction

An individual's losses that arise from theft or casualty and that are not incurred in the course of a business or profit-seeking activity are itemized deductions claimed on Schedule A of Form 1040. Theft and casualty losses are discussed in this chapter together with deductions for bad debts because these two subjects are related and have tax aspects that go beyond the deductibility of personal casualty losses on Schedule A. Other itemized deductions are the subject of chapter 9 of this text.

The term "casualty" may be generally defined as damage, destruction, or loss occurring to a taxpayer's property as a result of a sudden, unusual, or unexpected cause. Common examples include damage from storms, fire, flood, vandalism, or traffic accidents. However, a "loss" of property that has been mislaid or misplaced is not a casualty loss.

Rules for the Deductibility of Casualty Losses

The following basic rules apply to the deductibility of an individual's theft and casualty losses:

- Casualty losses must be deducted in the year the loss is incurred or sustained. For theft losses, the loss must be deducted in the year the theft is discovered.
- There must be a sudden event or sudden impact that results in the loss for a deduction to be allowed. This requirement of "suddenness" is discussed in more detail below.
- The amount of a casualty loss eligible for a deduction is reduced by $100 for each loss suffered by the taxpayer. In other words, the first $100 of a personal casualty or theft loss is nondeductible.
- Personal theft and casualty losses of individuals are also subject to a "floor" of 10 percent of the taxpayer's adjusted gross income. This means that the total amount of the taxpayer's personal casualty and theft losses for the year (after the subtraction of $100 per loss) can only be deducted to the extent the total of such losses exceeds 10 percent of adjusted gross income.
- The amount of a casualty loss is the difference in the fair market value of the property before and after the event that resulted in the casualty. However, if this amount is more than the taxpayer's adjusted basis in the

property, the deductible amount is limited to the taxpayer's adjusted basis. This computation will be discussed in more detail below.

The Requirement of a Sudden Event

Fires, storms, shipwrecks, accidents, floods, freezes, and earthquakes are examples of sudden and unexpected events that result in casualty losses. Normal wear and tear of property, and even gradual damage to property resulting from undiscovered causes, are not events that result in deductible personal casualty losses.

Termite damage has frequently been an issue in litigation over the claiming of a casualty loss deduction. The Internal Revenue Service has adhered to the position that this type of damage is not a sudden event or impact because of the gradual nature of the damage. Other more sudden damage resulting from infestation has sometimes been allowed as a casualty loss. The issue of suddenness is a question of fact over which taxpayers and the IRS have frequently disagreed.

Another issue is whether damage to property is a deductible loss resulting from a casualty or simply damage or breakage resulting from routine household activity. The dropping of a valuable plate during dishwashing would not be an event resulting in a deductible loss. However, the falling of the same plate from a breakfront during an earthquake would be.

The willfulness of the act that results in the damage to the property may also be an issue. For example, auto accidents are presumed to be events that result in casualty losses. However, if it can be shown that the taxpayer intentionally caused an accident rather than causing it from mere negligence, the deduction can be disallowed. Using the previous example, if, in a fit of anger, the taxpayer hurled the valuable plate against a wall, the loss would not be a deductible casualty loss.

Calculating the Deductible Loss

The mechanics of the casualty loss rules as discussed above may be best illustrated through a specific example of a deductible casualty.

Example: Nancy Fleet's home is damaged by flood. Her home is not insured for this loss because flood is specifically excluded under her homeowner's policy. Therefore she has no insurance reimbursement for her losses. The fair market value of her home and its contents before the flood was $135,000. After the flood, the value is $90,000. Her basis in her home and its contents is $100,000. The amount of her loss is $45,000 ($135,000 − $90,000). This loss amount is not in excess of her basis in the property. Nancy's adjusted gross income for the year is $95,000. She has suffered no other casualty losses during the year.

One hundred dollars must be subtracted from the amount of Nancy's loss. Thus her loss is now $44,900 for deduction purposes. She is permitted to deduct this loss only to the extent it exceeds 10 percent of her adjusted gross income of $95,000. Her deductible loss is therefore $35,400 [$44,900 − ($95,000 x .10)]. In this example, there is no insurance recovery. Of course, if Nancy's loss was covered by insurance, she would not be able to deduct any of it unless she filed a timely claim for reimbursement. Then her loss would be deductible only to the extent the amount of the loss exceeded the reimbursement.

Casualty Losses of Business and Income-Producing Property

Sometimes a sudden impact or event causes the complete destruction of a particular property. In the case of a personal loss, the deductible amount is computed the same way regardless of whether the loss is a complete or a partial one. The amount is the difference between the fair market value of the property before and after the casualty but not more than the taxpayer's adjusted basis in the property.

A somewhat different rule applies if the loss occurs with respect to business property or property held for the production of income. For such property that is completely lost or destroyed as a result of a casualty, the deductible amount is the greater of the property's fair market value immediately before the casualty or the taxpayer's adjusted basis in the property. In other words, the amount of the taxpayer's adjusted basis may be claimed as a casualty loss in such cases if that amount is greater than the property's fair market value before the loss.

If business or income-producing property is partially damaged by a casualty, but not completely lost or destroyed, then the deduction is the lesser of the property's adjusted basis or the difference in fair market value before and after the casualty.

With regard to casualty losses of business or income-producing property, three other points should be mentioned. First, losses to such property are not subject to the $100 per loss reduction that applies to personal casualty losses. Second, losses to business or income-producing property are not subject to the 10 percent "floor" of adjusted gross income that applies to personal casualty losses. Third, if a deductible loss occurs to property eligible for depreciation or other cost recovery deductions, the amount of the loss is measured or limited by the property's "adjusted basis." Such adjusted basis reflects depreciation deductions previously claimed. Therefore, such depreciation deductions, depending on the particular case, may reduce the allowable amount of the casualty loss. Depreciation and other cost recovery deductions are discussed in detail in chapter 11.

Tax Reporting and Treatment of Loss Deductions

Losses that may be deductible by individual taxpayers include casualty and theft losses, losses from the sale or exchange of property, losses from abandonment or worthlessness of property, wagering losses, and certain other losses. The type of event or transaction that gives rise to the loss and the character of the property involved will generally determine the specific tax treatment applicable to the loss.

Personal casualty and theft losses are claimed as itemized deductions on Schedule A of form 1040. These losses, to the extent allowable under the rules described in this chapter, are deductible against the taxpayer's ordinary income.

Wagering losses are deductible only to the extent of wagering gains. They must be deducted as a miscellaneous itemized deduction on Schedule A unless the taxpayer is a professional gambler.

Losses from the sale or exchange of property are treated differently. If the property is a capital asset of the taxpayer, then the loss is deductible as a capital loss on Schedule D of Form 1040. Losses from the sale of assets described in Sec. 1231 of the Internal Revenue Code may be deductible as ordinary losses arising from the sale of business property. The tax treatment of capital gains and losses and so-called "Sec. 1231" gains and losses is discussed in detail in chapter 14.

For individuals, the tax reporting of a deductible loss depends on the type of loss that occurs. The basic rule to remember is that if the taxpayer has a loss other than a casualty or theft loss, the loss must be sustained in the course of a business or an activity engaged in for profit in order for a deduction to be allowed. The loss will then be reported on the tax return in connection with the particular activity that produced it.

DEDUCTIONS FOR BAD DEBTS

Introduction

A bad debt deduction may arise when a debt becomes worthless, that is, when there is no longer a reasonable expectation that the debt will be repaid. The deduction is generally claimed by the primary creditor of the debt. However, under certain circumstances as discussed below, a guarantor of a debt may be eligible for the deduction. The deduction for bad debts is based on the unpaid principal amount of the debt.

Clearly, there must be a bona fide legal obligation of debt between the debtor and the creditor in order for a deduction to be available. For example, a gift of property that has merely been characterized as a debt obligation by the parties involved would not give rise to a bad debt deduction. The initial question is whether the taxpayer seeking the deduction (that is, the creditor) had obtained the unconditional obligation of the debtor to make repayment at the time the loan was made. Also, there must have been a reasonable expectation of repayment at that time. In common terms, a debt that was never "good" cannot become "bad" for purposes of an income tax deduction.

If the debt involves an item of income to the creditor, such as unpaid salary, unpaid rent, or an unpaid account receivable, the item cannot produce a bad debt deduction unless it was previously included in the gross income of the creditor. This requirement does not apply to a debtor's failure to repay the principal amount of a loan, because the loan principal itself is not an item of income to the creditor.

Once the existence of a bona fide debt is established, then the taxpayer must show that the debt became worthless during the taxable year. The debt must then be characterized as either business or nonbusiness bad debt for tax purposes. These two categories of bad debts are treated differently.

The Nature and Timing of Worthlessness of a Debt

The Code specifies that a bad debt deduction is allowed for a "debt which becomes worthless within the taxable year." The debt must become worthless for a deduction to be allowable, and it must be claimed for the tax year in which worthlessness occurs.

The occurrence and the timing of the worthlessness of a debt is a question of fact. Generally, the taxpayer (creditor) claiming the deduction makes a reasonable determination of the time when worthlessness occurs. Examples of situations that result in the worthlessness of a debt might include the bankruptcy of the debtor, the obtaining of a claim reduced to judgment against the debtor that cannot be collected because the debtor has no funds, the debtor's going out of business, or the disappearance, imprisonment, or other significant event in the life or business existence of the debtor that results in the creditor no longer having a reasonable expectation of repayment. The rules in this area are not hard and fast. The governing principle is the somewhat abstract concept that the debt has become worthless. Generally, the IRS has been reasonable in evaluating factual situations involving this issue.

Business Bad Debts

A more generous tax deduction is allowed for business bad debts as compared with nonbusiness bad debts. Business bad debts are deductible in full from the taxpayer's ordinary income, while nonbusiness bad debts are specifically characterized by the Internal Revenue Code as short-term capital losses. Therefore nonbusiness bad debts are subject to the limitations on deductions for capital losses as discussed in chapter 14. In most cases, worthless debts owed to business entities will be characterized as business bad debts. Corporations do not have nonbusiness bad debts.

Generally, the amount of the deduction is the actual amount of the debt that became worthless during the year. Certain financial institutions are permitted to use a reserve method for calculating bad debt deductions.

How is a business bad debt defined and distinguished from a nonbusiness bad debt? The law defines a business bad debt as either one of the following:

- a debt that is created or acquired (as the case may be) in connection with the taxpayer's trade or business, or
- a debt in which the worthlessness of the debt is incurred in the taxpayer's trade or business

This definition is intended to include situations in which the loan was made by the creditor in the course of conducting his or her business, but becomes worthless at a time during which the creditor is no longer in the business for which the debt was created or acquired. In such cases the debt is still treated as a business bad debt. Likewise, in any situation in which the worthlessness of the debt (as distinguished from its origination) occurs at a time when the debt is part of the creditor's business activity, the debt will be a business bad debt.

The most common example of a business bad debt is where the creditor is engaged in the specific business of lending money and the debt becomes worthless. However, the creditor does not always have to be in the business of lending money in order to have a business bad debt. For example, if a taxpayer lends money to a client or customer for the express purpose of improving the business relationship with that customer, the debt could be a business bad debt if it becomes worthless. The characterization of a bad debt as a business or nonbusiness bad debt is determined by reference to the nature of the creditor's activity in lending the money and not by reference to the purpose for which the borrower used the funds. One good reason for this approach is that it is the creditor, not the debtor, who seeks a bad debt deduction for a worthless obligation.

> *Example:* The Rentabuck Corporation is a private company in the business of lending money. Mr. Gamble has a loan of $50,000 outstanding from the company. He becomes insolvent during the year, files for bankruptcy, and then is arrested and imprisoned for writing false checks. Rentabuck no longer has a reasonable expectation of repayment of Gamble's debt and may claim a business bad debt deduction for the principal balance of the loan ($50,000) this year.

In some situations, taxpayers may seek to claim business bad debt deductions for worthless debts that the IRS views as nonbusiness bad debts. A common example is where a stockholder of a corporation loans money to the corporation and the debt becomes worthless. The IRS will generally take the position that this is a nonbusiness bad debt because the stockholder is seeking to protect his or her interest as an investor seeking to make a profit from ownership of the company rather than as a taxpayer engaged in a business activity. To claim a business bad debt deduction, it is not sufficient for the taxpayer to merely have a profit motive in making the debt. The debt must be created in the actual course of the taxpayer's business activities.

Partial Worthlessness of a Business Bad Debt

In the case of a business bad debt (but not a nonbusiness bad debt) a deduction may be claimed for partial worthlessness of the debt. The Code specifies that when a business debt is "recoverable only in part," a deduction may be allowed for the part of the debt that becomes worthless during the tax year.

Recovery of a Bad Debt Previously Deducted

As stated previously, the creditor must have no reasonable expectation of repayment in order to claim a bad debt deduction. However, in some cases the debt is later repaid unexpectedly, even though a bad debt deduction was legitimately claimed. When this occurs, the taxpayer who claimed the deduction must include the amount of the repaid debt in gross income to the extent that the previous deduction of the debt produced a tax benefit.

Investment Vehicles and the Bad Debt Deduction

Bank Accounts

If a taxpayer has a bank account in a financial institution that becomes insolvent or bankrupt and the funds are actually lost, two options are available. The taxpayer may elect to treat the loss as a casualty loss in the year it occurs with reasonable certainty. The loss is then subject to the rules and limitations applicable to personal casualty losses. This election cannot be made by a taxpayer who is an officer or one percent or greater stockholder of the financial institution. Alternatively, the taxpayer may treat the loss as a nonbusiness bad debt that is deductible as a short-term capital loss.

Corporate Debt Obligations

If an investment in a corporate debt security (such as a bond or debenture) becomes worthless, the loss is treated as a loss from a worthless security, as previously discussed in this chapter, and not as a bad debt. The security owner's deduction is calculated as if the owner had disposed of the worthless security on the last day of the taxable year. That is, it will be treated as a short-term or long-term capital loss depending upon the taxpayer's holding period for the security.

Tax Treatment of Nonbusiness Bad Debts

Any legitimate bad debt that does not meet the definition of a business bad debt is treated for tax purposes as a nonbusiness bad debt. The amount of the uncollectible debt is deductible as a short-term capital loss. An individual's net capital losses are deductible against ordinary income only to the extent of $3,000 per year, as discussed in chapter 14. Business bad debts, on the other hand, are deductible in full against ordinary income. This is significantly more favorable tax treatment than that which applies to nonbusiness bad debts. Consequently, the issue of whether the creditor entered into the debt in the actual course of a business activity, or merely to make a profit or investment, can be very significant for the taxpayer seeking to claim a deduction.

Loan Guarantees and the Bad Debt Deduction

A bad debt deduction may be available to a guarantor of a loan who is required to make payment when the loan becomes uncollectible from the debtor. Essentially, the same principles that apply to the lender also apply to the guarantor when evaluating the availability of the deduction. The payment of the guarantee will result in a business bad debt deduction only if the guarantor entered into the loan arrangement in the course of a business activity. If there was a profit motive in making the guarantee, but the guarantee was not actually part of the guarantor's business, then the payment on the guarantee will result in a nonbusiness bad debt deduction and short-term capital loss treatment. Guarantors should be mindful of these rules before entering into such arrangements.

If a loan is made purely for personal reasons (such as a loan between family members), there may be no "debt" at all, and therefore no bad debt deduction for either the creditor or the guarantor. There must be a legally enforceable debt and a legitimate profit motive on the part of the guarantor in order for payment on a loan guarantee to result in any bad debt deduction.

CONCLUSION

Loss deductions and bad debt deductions are different yet related topics. Each has its own rules and limitations depending on the type of loss or bad debt and the nature of the taxpayer's relationship to the loss or bad debt. An understanding of the fundamentals of these income tax rules can help the taxpayer and the adviser minimize the financial damage resulting from events or transactions that result in a loss of money or other property.

9

Itemized Deductions for Individuals

James F. Ivers III and Stephan R. Leimberg

[A tax loophole is] something that benefits the other guy. If it benefits you, it is tax reform.

Russell B. Long

Chapter Outline

INTRODUCTION

Individual taxpayers may "itemize," or claim, various deductions on Schedule A of Form 1040. The categories of deductions claimed on Schedule A include medical and dental expenses, certain taxes, certain interest payments, charitable contributions, casualty and theft losses, and miscellaneous itemized deductions.

Casualty and theft losses, and also "miscellaneous" itemized deductions, were covered in chapters 8 and 7, respectively. This chapter will focus mainly on the first four categories listed on Schedule A: medical expenses, taxes, interest, and contributions. The rules discussed in this chapter are those that apply to individual taxpayers. Business entities are entitled to claim many of the same types of items as deductions; however, for a business taxpayer most of these (except for charitable contributions) are treated as business expenses under the general principles of IRC Sec. 162. For individual taxpayers, these items are mostly expenses of a personal nature that Congress has decided should generate income tax benefits even though they are typically not associated with the production of income.

UNDERLYING PRINCIPLES GOVERNING DEDUCTIONS

Capital Expenditures versus Current Expenses

As a general principle of tax law, only items that are considered to be current expenses, as distinguished from capital expenditures, are deductible on a taxpayer's current income tax return. A capital expenditure is considered to be a new investment in property, while a current expense is more akin to a repair or a maintenance item that is necessary for the operation or well-being of a property or asset that the taxpayer already has. If a capital expenditure is made for an asset that is eligible for cost recovery deductions as discussed in chapter 11, the cost of the asset may be deducted over a number of tax years, but not, as a general rule, fully deducted in the year the expense is made. One important exception to this rule applies if the taxpayer acquires property that is eligible for the first-year expensing election under IRC Sec. 179, as also discussed in chapter 11.

What, then, is the specific test that distinguishes a capital expenditure from a deductible current expense? One principle is that if the expense is for the acquisition of property that has a useful life of more than one year, the expense is a capital expenditure. Another principle is that if the expense is for an enhancement or improvement to an asset the taxpayer already owns, it will be treated as a capital expenditure if the expense either enhances the value of the taxpayer's property or results in an improvement to the property that has a useful life of more than one year.

Examples of expenses that will generally be treated as capital expenditures rather than currently deductible expenses include the following:

- an individual's fees for obtaining a professional license such as a license to practice law or medicine
- expenses (such as attorney's fees) for perfecting or defending a taxpayer's legal title to property or for acquiring an ownership interest in property
- business investigation or start-up costs
- the cost of purchasing a building or of replacing substantial parts of a building, or the cost of machinery, equipment, furniture, and fixtures

Examples of expenses that are treated as current expenses and not capital expenditures include the following:

- routine repairs to property, such as painting, lawn maintenance, and repairs to equipment
- frequently recurring ordinary and necessary business expenses, such as expenses for advertising, marketing, and employee compensation
- rent paid on a taxpayer's business property (unless the rental payments are to be credited toward the purchase price of the property)

Tax Treatment of Personal Expenses

In discussing the concept of gross income in chapter 3, it was noted that all items of income received by a taxpayer during the year are includible in gross income unless the Internal Revenue Code expressly states otherwise. A similar principle applies to deductions. No expense is deductible unless the Code expressly provides a deduction for that specific expense or type of expense. Essentially, the Code allows deductions for current expenses paid or incurred in the course of conducting a business or an income-producing activity. Deductions for personal expenses, on the other hand, are generally disallowed. However, certain personal expenses are expressly deductible under the income tax law in spite of the general rule of disallowance. The most significant of these are the deductible personal expenses that are claimed on Schedule A of Form 1040; they are discussed in this chapter.

Among the personal expenses that are nondeductible under the general rule of disallowance are the following:

- payments for basic local telephone service for the first telephone line provided to any residence of a taxpayer
- homeowners insurance premiums including payments for fire and casualty insurance as well as additional premiums for specific personal property
- life insurance premiums paid for personally owned insurance contracts
- expenses for commuting to and from the taxpayer's place of employment
- attorney's fees for the drafting of a will or administration of an estate (except to the extent the legal services pertain to tax advice)
- expenses for groceries, utilities, and other normal expenses of maintaining a personal household
- expenses paid to obtain a divorce (except to the extent the expenses pertain to tax advice)

The following sections of this chapter will focus on those expenses that are deductible as itemized deductions on Schedule A. Most, but not all, of these expenses are personal expenses for which the Code allows deductions, subject to definitions, limitations, and restrictions.

MEDICAL AND DENTAL EXPENSES

Introduction

A deduction is allowed for expenses paid for the medical care of the taxpayer, the taxpayer's spouse, or the taxpayer's dependents (unless compensated for by insurance or otherwise) to the extent that the total of such expenses for the year exceeds 7.5 percent of the taxpayer's adjusted gross income. Medical expenses include amounts paid for the diagnosis, cure, treatment, or prevention of disease or for the purpose of affecting any structure or function of the body. Deductible expenses include expenses for dental care. Cosmetic surgery expenses, however, are deductible only under a narrow definition as set forth below. The deduction also encompasses premiums for medical expense insurance and expenses for qualified long-term care services and premiums for qualified long-term care insurance contracts. Certain expenses incidental to medical care may also be deductible subject to limitations, including transportation and lodging expenses incurred in the course of receiving medical treatment.

The 7.5 Percent "Floor" Applicable to Medical Expense Deductions

For a great many taxpayers, no medical expenses are actually deductible in most tax years because of the 7.5 percent "floor" that limits such deductions. As stated above, medical expenses can be deducted only to the extent that they exceed 7.5 percent of adjusted gross income for the year.

Example 1: Mr. Delaney's adjusted gross income for this year is $60,000. His total medical expenses for the year that were not compensated for by insurance equal $3,500. The floor applicable to his medical expense deduction is $4,500 ($60,000 x .075). Since the floor amount of $4,500 is greater than his otherwise deductible expenses of $3,500, no medical expense deduction is actually allowable on Mr. Delaney's return.

Example 2: Assume the same facts as in the previous example, except that Mr. Delaney's adjusted gross income is $40,000 rather than $60,000. His 7.5 percent floor amount is now $3,000 ($40,000 x .075). As a result, Mr. Delaney may deduct the excess of his expenses over the floor amount, or $500 ($3,500 − $3,000).

It is significant to note that for purposes of the alternative minimum tax, the floor on medical expenses is 10 percent of adjusted gross income rather than 7.5 percent. The alternative minimum tax is discussed in detail in chapter 15.

Eligible Medical Expenses under the Deduction Rules

Deductible medical expenses include such obvious expenses as doctor and hospital charges, expenses for nursing services, laboratory tests, and surgical procedures. Expenses for artificial limbs also qualify, as does the cost of prescription drugs and insulin. The cost of nonprescription drugs other than insulin is not a deductible medical expense.

Special restrictions apply to expenses for cosmetic surgery. Such expenses are deductible only if the surgery is done to correct a condition resulting from an accident, a congenital abnormality, or a disfiguring disease. Expenses for surgery performed to improve the appearance of an individual, such as a facelift procedure or similar surgery, do not qualify for the deduction. The question in evaluating the deductibility of cosmetic surgery is whether the procedure either meaningfully promotes the proper function of the body or prevents or treats illness or disease.

If a taxpayer travels away from home primarily to receive essential medical care, a deduction for the taxpayer's lodging while away from home is allowable up to a limit of $50 per night. Transportation expenses incurred in the course of receiving medical care are also deductible. For automobile travel, a standard mileage rate of 12 cents per mile may currently be claimed for travel necessary for medical care. However, parking fees and highway tolls may be deducted in addition to the mileage rate.

The following expenses have been accepted by the Internal Revenue Service as qualifying for the medical expense deduction:

- the cost of dentures and orthodontic treatment
- premiums for part B of Medicare (and also part A for taxpayers not covered by Social Security)
- the cost of guide animals, including hearing aid and seeing eye animals
- the cost of treatment for alcohol or drug addiction
- fees for psychiatric care
- the cost of legal abortions
- fees of chiropractors
- fees of osteopaths
- fees for psychological counseling
- the cost of eyeglasses, contact lenses, and hearing aids

One principle that the IRS will generally follow in determining whether a given expense qualifies as a deductible medical expense is the question of whether the service, product, or activity paid for is simply for the general preservation of the individual's health or well-being or rather is for the alleviation or treatment of a specific disease or defect. If the expense is for something that only promotes the individual's overall general health, it will generally not be deductible. On the other hand, if a physician prescribes an activity or program of treatment to improve or correct a specific medical condition, the expense is more likely to be deductible. In this regard, expenses for weight loss programs are generally not deductible unless prescribed by a physician as treatment for a specific disease. Likewise, fees paid to health clubs are generally not deductible. The same principle applies to trips to a therapeutic climate.

In a departure from its previous position, the IRS has decided that the cost of smoking cessation programs and prescription drugs to assist in nicotine withdrawal are deductible as medical expenses. In the past, the IRS had disallowed deductions for expenses for quitting tobacco use unless the taxpayer had a specific smoking-related disease.

Premiums paid for health insurance are deductible as medical expenses. Deductible premiums include those for both individually owned and group contracts. Premiums for supplemental policies are also generally deductible. However, premiums for a policy that provides a type of benefit that is associated with a disability policy, such as a benefit for the loss of a limb or a replacement of lost income while the covered individual is ill, are not deductible as medical expenses.

Medical Expenses That Are Capital Expenditures

As explained earlier in this chapter, capital expenditures are generally not deductible in the year in which they are made. A special rule applies to medical expenses that can also be categorized as capital expenditures. If an improvement is made to a taxpayer's property for medical reasons, and the improvement increases the value of the property, a medical expense deduction will be allowed only for the excess of the cost of the improvement over the increase in value to the property. Elevators, escalators, and swimming pools are examples of this type of expense.

> *Example:* Jordan's physician recommends that he install a swimming pool in his home as a therapeutic device for his problems with the connective tissue in his joints. The cost of the pool is $15,000. The value of Jordan's home increases by $10,000 as a result of the pool installation. Jordan can claim $5,000 ($15,000 cost – $10,000 value increase) as a medical expense deduction.

Note that capital expenditures that qualify as medical expenses and do not increase the value of property are deductible in full. The specific rule that applies to expenses that are both medical expenses and capital expenditures is more liberal than the general rule previously described that applies to most capital expenditures.

LONG-TERM CARE AND LONG-TERM CARE INSURANCE

Introduction

Expenses for qualified long-term care services are now generally deductible as medical expenses. Premiums for qualified long-term care insurance policies are also deductible as medical expenses, subject to dollar amount limitations based on the covered individual's age. Individual taxpayers and their financial advisers should be aware of the basic rules that apply to the deductibility of long-term care expenses. Although these expenses are generally subject to the 7.5 percent floor that applies to all medical expense deductions, the fact that long-term care expenses are often high enough to exceed the floor makes an understanding of the basic rules more important. With regard to qualified long-term care insurance policies, there are limitations on deductibility of premiums (in addition to the 7.5 percent floor) and also limits on the income tax exclusion that applies to benefits paid from such policies. The design of a long-term care policy that will qualify for these tax benefits is the responsibility of the issuing insurance company. However, the basic attributes of qualified long-term care services and insurance contracts should be understood so that individuals know what tax benefits to expect.

Qualified Long-Term Care Services

Qualified long-term care services for purposes of tax deductibility is defined as the diagnostic, preventive, therapeutic, rehabilitative, and other services required by a chronically ill person under a plan prescribed by a licensed health care professional. The income tax definition of a "chronically ill person" is the following: a person who is unable to perform at least two activities of daily living ("ADLs") for at least 90 days. "Activities of daily living" for purposes of that definition include the following activities: eating, toileting, transferring, bathing, dressing, and continence.

There is a restriction on the deductibility of services provided by a spouse or relative of the individual for whom the services are performed. Expenses paid for care rendered by a relative will not be deductible as medical expenses unless the spouse or relative is a licensed health care professional. A "relative" for this purpose includes a parent, child, grandparent, grandchild, sibling, niece, nephew, or in-law of the individual receiving care.

Individuals who are suffering from Alzheimer's disease or a related disorder involving cognitive impairment are considered to be "chronically ill" without regard to the requirement regarding ADLs.

Deductibility of Long-Term Care Insurance Premiums

Premiums paid for qualified long-term care insurance contracts are deductible as medical expenses. However, the deduction is limited to a maximum dollar amount per year that varies according to the age of the person covered under the policy. The dollar limits are indexed annually for inflation. For tax years beginning in the year 2001, the limits are as follows:

Age of Covered Person	Premium Deduction Limit
40 or under	$ 230
Above 40 but not above 50	$ 430
Above 50 but not above 60	$ 860
Above 60 but not above 70	$2,290
Above 70	$2,860

Example: Esther owns a qualified long-term care policy covering herself. At the end of 2001, she is 73 years old. She pays a premium of $3,500 for the policy in 2001. She may deduct $2,860 of the premium subject to the 7.5 percent medical expense deduction floor. The remaining $640 of the premium is nondeductible.

Note that the limits apply per covered individual and not with respect to each tax return. This means, for example, that a married couple filing jointly who each own a long-term care policy covering themselves could deduct the premiums paid for each policy subject to the applicable limitation. Remember too that the

7.5 percent floor is applied to all of the taxpayer's medical expenses taken together and not to each separate expense.

Qualified Long-Term Care Insurance Contracts

The medical expense deduction covers premiums paid for qualified long-term care contracts issued after 1996. However, under a grandfathering rule, most contracts in existence before 1997 are eligible for tax benefits as long as the applicable state legal requirements were met with respect to the contract when it was issued. Not all insurance contracts providing long-term care benefits are "qualified" for tax purposes, however. Individuals considering purchase of a long-term care policy should be fully informed regarding the income tax status of all contracts being considered.

The tax law requirements for a qualified long-term care insurance contract issued after 1996 include the following:

- It must not have a cash value.
- It must be guaranteed renewable.
- It must not have a forfeiture provision.

Tax qualification of a long-term care contract is the responsibility of the insurance company that issues the contract. Not all contracts are designed to be qualified.

Exclusion for Benefits Paid from Long-Term Care Contracts

Benefits received from qualified long-term care contracts are generally excludible from gross income. This exclusion was discussed in chapter 6. It is not a part of the medical expense deduction as discussed in this chapter, which covers only deductions for medical expenses and not exclusions for benefits paid from insurance contracts. However, the exclusion is mentioned in this context again for the sake of clarity. The benefits are fully excludible to the extent they are actually used for long-term care expenses. If benefits paid exceed actual long-term care expenses, they are excludible up to a fixed daily dollar amount that is indexed annually for inflation.

Long-Term Care Insurance in Business Situations

Premiums for qualified contracts are eligible for the "above-the-line" deduction for health insurance premiums paid by self-employed taxpayers as discussed in chapter 7. For other taxpayers, however, the deduction must be claimed as an itemized deduction subject to the 7.5 percent floor as discussed in this chapter.

Long-term care coverage cannot be provided to employees on a tax-favored basis as part of a cafeteria plan. In addition, if an employer offers a flexible spending account as part of its employee benefits package, employees may not use the tax-favored flexible spending account to pay for long-term care insurance premiums. A detailed discussion of cafeteria plans and flexible spending accounts is beyond the scope of this text.

TAXES

Introduction

Individuals may deduct payments for certain taxes on Schedule A of Form 1040. These are taxes that constitute personal expenses of the taxpayer for which the Internal Revenue Code allows a deduction. Because these deductions are claimed on Schedule A, they are "below-the-line" deductions (deductions taken from adjusted gross income in determining taxable income) rather than "above-the-line" deductions (deductions taken from gross income in determining adjusted gross income). This chapter will cover this category of deductible taxes.

Most taxes that are paid in connection with a business or an activity entered into for profit are also deductible but not on Schedule A. Those taxes are deductible on the portion of the tax return that includes items related to the business or profit-making activity. For individuals filing Form 1040, most of these taxes would be "above-the-line" deductions. For example, taxes paid on rental property owned by a taxpayer would be deducted on Schedule E of Form 1040 against the income generated by the rental property. The deductibility of such taxes would follow the general principles governing deductions for business expenses and profit-making activities discussed in chapter 7.

Federal income taxes (other than one-half of the self-employment tax) and certain other taxes are nondeductible regardless of the activity with which they are connected.

Taxes That Are Deductible on Schedule A

The following types of taxes not incurred in the course of a business or income-producing activity are deductible on Schedule A by individual taxpayers:

- state, local, and foreign real property taxes
- state and local personal property taxes
- state and local income taxes
- the generation-skipping transfer tax imposed on income distributions
- the environmental tax imposed by IRC Sec. 59A

Certain other taxes are deductible including foreign income, war profits, and excess profit taxes for taxpayers who do not claim a foreign tax credit for these taxes.

Categories of taxes that are not deductible include federal income, estate, and gift taxes, certain penalty taxes imposed by the Internal Revenue Code, and state and local sales taxes. Taxes paid on the purchase of alcohol, tobacco, or gasoline are not deductible. Transfer taxes on the conveyance of personally owned real estate are not deductible on Schedule A, although such taxes may reduce the gain realized by the taxpayer on the sale of such property.

Taxes on real property are deductible including property taxes paid on the taxpayer's principal residence. State and local income taxes are deductible, whether paid through withholding by the taxpayer's employer or paid with the filing of a return. These two types of taxes are generally the most important deductible taxes for individuals.

Nondeductible Assessments

Amounts that are assessed to pay for improvements or "betterments" to a taxpayer's property are not deductible as taxes because such amounts are really charges for capital improvements rather than actual taxes assessed with respect to property. For example, an assessment by a local municipality for improvements to the taxpayer's sidewalk or municipal waste disposal systems would not constitute a deductible tax.

Another type of expense that is not deductible as a tax is a charge for the use of a product or service provided by a municipality. For example, an annual sewer fee is not a deductible tax. Likewise, a taxpayer's bill for use of a municipal water supply is not deductible as a tax. Such nondeductible charges would also include highway tolls and municipal parking fees. Remember, however, that if a taxpayer incurs such charges with respect to a business or income-producing property, a deduction may be available on the portion of the taxpayer's return that reflects such activity.

Other Pertinent Rules

Generally, a deduction for taxes is allowed only to the taxpayer who is actually liable or responsible for the payment of the taxes. For example, if a mother paid her adult son's state income taxes, she would not be permitted to deduct that payment. Taxpayers who own property jointly (or as tenants by the entirety) are typically each liable for the full amount of any tax assessed on that property. Therefore any joint owner or owners who actually pay the taxes may deduct the amount paid on their returns.

One exception to this principle applies in the case of real property taxes assessed to a property owner (such as a homeowner) who sells the property during the period covered by an existing assessment. In such cases the property taxes are subject to a rule of apportionment. For deduction purposes, the taxes are treated as assessed to the seller of the property for the time period up to but not including the date of sale. As of the sale date, the taxes are treated as having been assessed to the buyer for deduction purposes. The apportionment is calculated based on the number of days of the assessment period that each party owns the property. This treatment is consistent with the usual apportionment of tax payments that appears on a closing statement or settlement sheet upon the sale of a home.

Homeowners frequently have escrow accounts with a mortgage lender from which real property taxes are paid. The homeowner makes a monthly or bimonthly payment into the escrow account, and the lending institution pays or arranges to pay the property tax before the due date. A deduction is available to the homeowner only for tax payments actually made to the taxing authority, not for the periodic payments made to the escrow account.

Finally, under IRC Sec. 266, taxpayers may elect to charge certain taxes and other expenses to a property's capital account rather than currently deduct those taxes. Such charges would then be added to the taxpayer's basis in the property for purposes of determining the gain or loss realized on a later sale. This election would typically be made in cases where the property does not produce income and the taxpayer will not obtain a tax benefit from claiming a current deduction.

DEDUCTIONS FOR INTEREST

Introduction

The term "interest" may be generally defined as payment by a borrower (or "debtor") for the use of money provided by a lender (or "creditor"). From an economic standpoint, there must be a bona fide debtor/creditor relationship between two or more parties in order to generate interest payments. Such a relationship is also required under the income tax law. For example, certain transactions between family members may not actually be bona fide loans for tax purposes, even though the parties characterize them as such.

Some interest payments are deductible for income tax purposes, and others are not. The distinctions between deductible and nondeductible interest will be explained below. The deductibility of interest is, for the most part, determined by how the interest payment is categorized for income tax purposes. However, no interest payment is deductible unless there is an enforceable obligation on the part of the debtor to pay a determinable sum to the creditor in exchange for the use of a determinable sum.

The amount of money provided by the lender for the borrower's use may be called the "principal" amount. The amount the borrower is obligated to pay the lender will consist of both a repayment of the principal amount at or over some period of time, plus an additional amount (interest) as payment for the use of the funds. There are many different ways in which the interest portion of a loan repayment can be calculated. The most common form is as a percentage of the principal amount. There are also many different economic methods by which a loan can be repaid, such as a direct reduction loan, a balloon loan, or a revolving credit arrangement.

Questions may arise as to whether a certain payment to a lender constitutes interest and therefore whether it may qualify under one of the categories of deductible interest. For example, "points" paid as a premium to a lender at the inception of a mortgage loan might be considered to be either a payment for the use of money (a prepaid interest payment) or a payment for services rendered by the lending institution. Generally, a prepayment of interest by a taxpayer not using the accrual method of tax accounting is not currently deductible. However, as discussed below, the tax law provides specific rules for the deductibility of points paid in connection with the acquisition or improvement of a taxpayer's personal residence.

A prepayment penalty on a loan is another type of payment that may be difficult to characterize. If the lender charges the borrower an extra amount in the event the borrower pays off the loan before full repayment is actually due, is such a payment an interest payment? Generally, for income tax purposes, if such a prepayment penalty is calculated as a percentage of the principal amount, the penalty will be treated as an interest payment.

In order for a payment of interest to qualify for a tax deduction, the taxpayer making the interest payment must have a legal obligation to repay the loan. For example, if a parent pays the interest on a loan incurred by the parent's adult child, the parent cannot claim a tax deduction for the payment. If there is a joint obligation on the part of two or more parties to repay a loan, the payment of part or all of the interest by any obligated party can be deducted if the payment otherwise qualifies for a deduction. The most significant exception to this principle is the fact that the IRS permits a purchaser of a home to deduct mortgage "points" that were actually paid by the seller of the home if the points would otherwise qualify for an interest deduction. This rule allows sellers to offer the incentive of paying points for the buyer without jeopardizing the buyer's income tax deduction. However, note that in this situation the points are not deductible by the party who pays them (the seller). Such points are, in turn, treated as a reduction of the property's purchase price. The deductibility of points is covered in more detail later in this chapter.

Categorization of Interest Payments

To determine whether the interest paid on indebtedness is a deductible expense, the interest payment must be properly categorized. This is so because the Internal Revenue Code expressly defines, limits, and allows or disallows deductions for interest payments based essentially on what type of interest payment the taxpayer has made. There are many types of debt arrangements that a taxpayer might enter into; consequently, there are numerous types of interest payments on indebtedness. The Internal Revenue Code provides several categories of interest payments and imposes rules for the deductibility or nondeductibility of each category. The most significant basic categories of interest payments for purposes of this text are as follows:

- interest on indebtedness incurred in the course of a trade or business ("business interest")
- interest on indebtedness incurred in the course of an activity entered into for profit that is not a business activity ("investment interest")
- interest on indebtedness incurred in connection with a passive activity as described in chapter 12 ("passive activity interest")

- certain interest on indebtedness secured by the taxpayer's residence ("qualified residence interest")
- personal interest

An interest payment is categorized by looking to the purposes for which the underlying loan was borrowed, that is, the specific activity for which the borrowed money was used. The Treasury regulations contain so-called "tracing" rules that generally help to determine which category a payment of interest should fall into. Each of these categories will be examined below.

Business Interest

The general rule for interest payments on indebtedness incurred in the course of a business activity is that the payments are deductible. If the payments are made by a regular or "C" corporation, they are deductible on the corporation's tax return. If the payments are made by an individual taxpayer or by a "pass-through" business entity such as a partnership or S corporation, they are ultimately deducted on the appropriate schedule of the business owner's individual tax return as an above-the-line deduction.

Even though business interest is generally deductible, there may be another set of rules that applies to the interest payment to limit or prevent its deductibility. For example, the interest payment, although incurred in the course of a business activity, may also be paid or incurred in connection with a passive activity. If so, it is subject to the limitations on passive activity losses as summarized in chapter 12. Or the interest may be paid with respect to a loan that is borrowed from or allocable to the values in a life insurance or annuity contract. If so, the interest is subject to the additional limitations described in chapter 16. Interest payments may be subject to multiple layers of complex rules. The first step is to determine the classification of the interest payment under one of the basic categories. Then, if the interest is deductible under that category, it must be determined whether there are other additional rules that may limit or prohibit a deduction.

Business interest, investment interest, qualified residence interest, and nondeductible personal interest are mutually exclusive categories. One interest payment cannot fall into more than one of these categories. However, the passive loss limitations might apply to interest that would otherwise be either business or investment interest. The limitations on interest deductions that are related to a life insurance or annuity contract can apply to any category of interest payment except qualified residence interest.

Investment Interest

Interest payments on a nonbusiness loan incurred in the course of an investment activity are referred to as investment interest. Deductions for investment interest expenses are allowed but are limited to the taxpayer's "net investment income" for the year.

To determine the applicable limitation on investment interest, the taxpayer's net investment income must be determined. The term "net investment income" means the excess of the taxpayer's investment income over the taxpayer's investment expenses. Investment income is the sum of gross income from property held for investment plus gain other than capital gain attributable to the disposition of property held for investment purposes. Investment expenses are generally all deductible expenses (other than interest expenses) that are connected with the production of the taxpayer's investment income.

Capital gain may, at the election of the taxpayer, be included in the calculation of investment income. Such inclusion will increase the taxpayer's investment income, thereby increasing the deductible amount of investment interest. The trade-off for such an election is that any capital gain so included in the calculation is not eligible for the lower maximum income tax rates on long-term capital gain of individual taxpayers, as discussed in chapter 14.

> *Example:* Muriel wishes to purchase shares of the Laramie Corporation, a publicly traded company that sells western-style fashions. She borrowed $250,000 from her bank last year and used all of the loan proceeds to fund the purchase. This year, Muriel paid $22,500 in interest on the loan. She also received $10,000 from Laramie in the form of dividends. In addition, Muriel received $3,000 of interest income this year from a money market account. Muriel has no other investment income or investment expenses this year. Muriel's deduction for investment interest on this year's tax return would be limited to $13,000, the total of her net investment income ($10,000 + $3,000).

Any investment interest that is nondeductible because of the net investment income limitation may be carried forward to future tax years and deducted (subject to the same limitation in that year) until the carryover of excess investment interest is fully used up. Therefore in the example above, Muriel could carry over her remaining $9,500 ($22,500 − $13,000) of investment interest to her future tax years. In no tax year, however, can either current or "carried over" investment interest be deducted in excess of the taxpayer's current net investment income.

Note that if an interest payment is made in connection with an activity that would be treated as an investment activity except that it meets the definition of a passive activity under the passive activity loss limitations, the interest is not treated as investment interest, but is instead included in the computation of passive activity income or loss under those rules.

An individual's investment interest deductions are generally claimed on Schedule A of Form 1040 as an itemized deduction.

Qualified Residence Interest

The term "qualified residence interest" means interest paid on a loan secured by the taxpayer's personal residence that is deductible for federal income tax purposes. For interest payments to be qualified residence interest, the loan must be secured by a "qualified residence." A qualified residence includes the taxpayer's principal residence plus one other residence (such as a vacation home) that the taxpayer selects to be treated as a qualified residence. Such other residence need not be a house but could include vehicles and water vessels that have sleeping and eating accommodations. If such other residence is rented by the taxpayer for part of the year, it must not qualify under the "rental use" test of the vacation home deduction limitations discussed in chapter 7. If it does qualify under that test, it cannot also be a "qualified residence" for purposes of deducting qualified residence interest.

For qualified residences, there are two types of qualified residence interest: interest paid on "acquisition indebtedness" and interest paid on "home equity indebtedness."

Acquisition Indebtedness

The term "acquisition indebtedness" means any indebtedness that is incurred in acquiring, constructing, or substantially improving a qualified residence, and that is secured by such residence. The term also includes the refinancing of such indebtedness, but only to the extent the principal amount of the refinancing does not exceed the amount of the refinanced indebtedness. Amounts refinanced in excess of the existing principal balance may qualify as home equity indebtedness as discussed below.

The maximum amount of acquisition indebtedness for any one taxpayer (including a married couple filing jointly) is $1 million. For married taxpayers filing separately, the limit is $500,000. Indebtedness in excess of these amounts will not be treated as acquisition indebtedness and will not give rise to deductible interest unless the debt qualifies as home equity indebtedness.

> *Example:* Ryan Lyon wins the lottery this year and purchases a home in the city and a vacation home at the beach. His mortgage on the city home is $500,000, and his mortgage on the beach home is $300,000. Both homes will be qualified residences. Since his total acquisition indebtedness is less than $1 million, the interest on both his mortgages will be deductible as qualified residence interest.

The $1 million limit applies to mortgages and refinancings beginning on or after October 14, 1987. If a mortgage loan was originally taken before that date, however, it may be refinanced in an amount not greater than the existing principal balance at the time of refinancing, and the $1 million limit will not apply to limit deductibility of the refinanced indebtedness.

Home Equity Indebtedness

The term "home equity indebtedness" means indebtedness other than acquisition indebtedness secured by a qualified residence to the extent that

- The total amount of acquisition and home equity indebtedness does not exceed the fair market value of the residence.
- The aggregate amount of the taxpayer's home equity indebtedness does not exceed $100,000 ($50,000 for married taxpayers filing separately).

Note that the $100,000 limit (as well as the $1 million limit on acquisition indebtedness) is a per-taxpayer, and not a per-residence, limitation. Also, the total of acquisition indebtedness and home equity indebtedness may exceed the taxpayer's cost for the home but may not exceed the fair market value of the home. Finally, home equity indebtedness does not have to be used for any specific purpose in order to generate qualified residence interest. Such loans can be used for any purpose desired by the taxpayer.

Example: Bubby purchased a home three years ago for $400,000. His acquisition indebtedness on the home was $350,000. This year the fair market value of the residence is $450,000. Bubby takes a home equity loan of $75,000 secured by the residence and uses the money to buy a racing car for his use as an amateur racer. The interest payments on both the original mortgage and the home equity loan are deductible because each of the loan principal amounts are less than the applicable dollar amount limitations, are secured by the residence, and when added together ($425,000) do not exceed the fair market value of the residence ($450,000) even though they do exceed its cost.

Qualified residence interest is deductible by individual taxpayers as an itemized deduction on Schedule A of Form 1040.

Prepaid Interest and Mortgage "Points"

Sometimes a debtor will prepay interest on a loan. Prepaid interest is generally an amount paid on a loan that represents a charge for the use of borrowed funds that is allocable to a future tax year or accounting period. For taxpayers on the cash basis method of tax accounting (including almost all individual taxpayers), the general rule for prepaid interest payments is that such payments are not deductible in the year paid but rather must be allocated to the tax year or years with respect to which the interest payments actually represent a payment or charge for the use of the borrowed funds. In other words, prepaid interest is generally not deductible in the year it is paid. However, there are special rules that apply to so-called mortgage "points" paid to a mortgage lender in the year when a loan secured by the taxpayer's principal residence is obtained.

"Points" can be described as a charge imposed by mortgage lenders at the inception of a loan. They are calculated as a percentage of the principal amount of the loan and are not fees for a mortgage application or other services provided by the lender. Points paid in connection with certain loans secured by a principal residence are deductible in the year paid rather than being subject to the general rule just described for prepaid interest.

In order for taxpayers to be assured that points paid upon the origination of a loan will be currently deductible, the following requirements must be met:

- The loan must be incurred in connection with the acquisition of the taxpayer's principal residence.
- The loan must be secured by the taxpayer's principal residence.
- The points must be calculated as a percentage of the principal amount of the loan.
- The points must be paid to the lender directly by the taxpayer rather than added to or derived from the principal amount of the loan.
- The lender's charging of the points must be consistent with an established business practice in the area in which the loan is made and must not exceed the amount generally charged for points in such area.
- The settlement statement describing the acquisition of the home must designate the payments as points by using a term such as "points," "discount points," "loan origination fees," or similar terminology.

The above "safe harbor" rules provided by the IRS for the deductibility of points do not include points paid for a loan used for the improvement, rather than acquisition, of a principal residence. However, the Code expressly provides that such points may also be deductible. If the loan is used to make improvements to the taxpayer's residence, and all the requirements other than the first and last requirements listed above are met, the points will in all probability be currently deductible. However, points paid in connection with a simple refinancing of the taxpayer's mortgage on a residence are generally nondeductible.

Personal Interest

Under current law no interest on loans borrowed for personal use is deductible unless the interest is either qualified residence interest or interest on "qualified education loans."

Deductible interest on qualified education loans, also referred to as the "student loan interest deduction," includes interest payments of up to $2,000 ($2,500 beginning in 2001) per year per taxpayer for certain loans borrowed for the funding of higher education. The deduction is available only during the first 60 months in which interest is charged under the loan. The deduction is phased out completely for married taxpayers filing jointly with adjusted gross income (subject to certain modifications) in excess of $75,000 and for other taxpayers with AGI in excess of $55,000. There are additional restrictions and limitations on the student loan interest deduction that are beyond the scope of this text. If available, the deduction is claimed not on Schedule A of Form 1040 but as an above-the-line deduction taken in determining the taxpayer's adjusted gross income.

Virtually all other interest on loans borrowed for personal use is nondeductible. Such interest would include interest on an individual's credit card purchases, car loans not secured by the taxpayer's home, and interest on most loans arranged between friends or family members.

Expenses and Interest Relating to Tax-Exempt Income

As a general rule of tax law, an otherwise allowable deduction for an interest payment or any other expense will be disallowed if the interest expense or other expense is incurred in the course of producing income that is exempt from income tax. The most common example of this general rule would probably be where a taxpayer borrows money to purchase tax-exempt bonds. Interest on such a loan would not be deductible, even though the interest would qualify as investment interest if the bonds generated taxable rather than excludible interest payments. If other expenses, such as fees for financial advice, were incurred in the course of purchasing tax-exempt bonds and directly connected to that purchase, then the fees would also be nondeductible.

Uncertainty may arise in interpreting this disallowance of deductions because there is not always conclusive proof of a connection between the interest or other expense and the production of tax-exempt income. For example, the proceeds of a loan do not necessarily have to be directly traceable to the purchase of a tax-exempt investment for the disallowance to apply to a given taxpayer. In this regard, the Internal Revenue Service has provided guidelines under which it will infer or conclude that a portion of a taxpayer's interest payments or other expenses should be allocated to those activities of the taxpayer that produce tax-exempt income.

The disallowance of deductions relating to tax-exempt income applies in addition to all other limits and restrictions on interest deductions imposed by the tax law.

CHARITABLE CONTRIBUTION DEDUCTIONS

Introduction

People make gifts to charity. Whether motivated by a combination of social, moral, or economic reasons, individuals have traditionally contributed large amounts to public charities. The vastness of both these sums and the possible tax savings to individuals make it imperative for the financial adviser to have a working knowledge of the charitable contribution deduction rules.

Charitable contributions have tax value. They result in current income tax savings, they may reduce federal estate taxes, and they can be made gift tax free. From the charity's point of view, charitable contributions are also tax favored. The charity itself pays no tax upon the receipt of either a lifetime gift or a bequest, and generally no income tax is paid by the qualified charity on income earned by donated property.

A charitable contribution deduction is allowed for contributions to certain charitable, religious, scientific, educational, and other specified organizations. Deductions may be taken by either individuals or corporations. The deduction by individual taxpayers is allowed only from adjusted gross income. Therefore it may be wise from a tax standpoint for individuals to make charitable contributions only in years in which they have itemized deductions in excess of the standard deduction amount.

Four Requirements for Deductibility

The first requirement for deductible charitable contributions is that they must be made to organizations that are *qualified*. Qualified organizations include nonprofit schools and hospitals, churches and synagogues, the United Fund, community chests, YMCA, YMHA, YWCA, YWHA, the American Red Cross, the Salvation Army, and police boys' clubs. The Boy Scouts, Campfire Girls, CARE, the Heart Association, and The American College are some of the other organizations that are considered qualified.[*]

A donee cannot be considered a qualified charity unless it meets three conditions. First, it must be an organization operated exclusively for religious, charitable, scientific, literary, or educational purposes, or for the prevention of cruelty to children or animals. Second, no part of the organization's earnings can benefit any private shareholder or similar individual. Third, no substantial part of such an organization's work can consist of propaganda or legislation-influencing activities.

Technically there are two types of qualified charities: (1) the public charity and (2) the private charity. Gifts to public charities are subject to higher deductible limits than gifts to private charities. Public charities (also called 50 percent charities because individuals can take a deduction of up to 50 percent of their contribution base for gifts to these charities) include most well-known charities such as the American Red Cross, the United Way, and The American College. All other qualified charities that are not public (50 percent) charities are considered private (20 or 30 percent) charities. (See the Charitable Contribution Deduction Limitations Chart later in this chapter.) Included under the category of private charities would be most private foundations or organizations. It is important to recognize that an organization is not automatically a qualified charity merely because it is tax exempt.

For example, civic associations, social clubs, chambers of commerce, and other business leagues are generally exempt from tax. However, they are not considered qualified organizations. Therefore gifts to these organizations are not deductible as charitable contributions, but they may be deductible as ordinary and necessary business expenses. Even direct contributions of cash or other

---

[*] A list of qualified organizations is contained in IRS publication no. 78 entitled, "Cumulative List, Organizations Described in Section 170(c) of the Internal Revenue Code of 1986," published by the Superintendent of Documents, U.S. Government Printing Office in Washington, D.C. A taxpayer is not entitled to rely on the statements of an organization as to whether contributions to it are tax deductible.

property to a needy family are generally nondeductible because of the rule that contributions must be made to a qualified charity to be deductible.

A second requirement necessary for a charitable contribution deduction is that *property* must be the subject of the gift. The value of a taxpayer's time or services, even if contributed to a qualified charity, is not deductible. For example, if Whipsaw, a carpenter, spent 10 hours building a podium for his church, he could not deduct his normal hourly wage as a charitable contribution. However, if he built the podium at home and gifted it to the church, he could deduct the cost of the materials used in producing the finished product (not including the value of his working time) as a charitable contribution.

If Marlon Brandi—the famous streetcar conductor turned actor—entertained at a charity ball, he could not deduct the value of his personal services, mainly because he has not been charged with income as the result of rendering such services. However, he could deduct any out-of-pocket expenses incurred in rendering such services. For example, if he had to fly into New York from Chicago solely to appear at the charitable event, his transportation expenses incurred in rendering services for the charity in question would be deductible. If a car is used to render charitable services, a deduction of 14 cents per mile is currently permitted.

A third requirement for a charitable contribution deduction is that there must in fact be a contribution to the charity in excess of the value received. In some cases, donors will receive a benefit in conjunction with their charitable gifts. Such contributions are deductible only to the extent that the value of the contributed property exceeds any consideration or benefit to the donor. For example, if Pam purchases bonds issued by a nonprofit hospital to finance a new building, the purchase price of the bond would not be deductible as a contribution. However, if Pam later donated the bonds to the hospital, she would then become entitled to a deduction. A similar question often arises in the case of dues, fees, or assessments paid to qualified organizations. These items are deductible as contributions only to the extent that they exceed the monetary value of benefits received by the *donor*. Charitable organizations are now required to inform donors of the extent to which the contribution exceeds the value of benefits received in return if the contribution is more than $75. Dues, fees, or assessments paid to country clubs, veterans and fraternal organizations, or lodges are specifically nondeductible as charitable contributions.

If the local church or synagogue was to sponsor a bingo night, amounts paid to play (or for raffle tickets or other games of chance) would not be considered contributions. They would be treated as wagering losses. Likewise, if a qualified charitable organization sponsors a picnic (or a night at the theater, a charity ball, a sporting event, or a show), only the difference between the fair market value of the picnic lunch purchased and the amount actually paid is considered a charitable contribution. The balance is treated as a nondeductible personal expenditure. For example, if you paid $20 for a box lunch at a church picnic and the lunch plus entertainment was worth $3, only the difference—$17—would be a charitable contribution assuming the entire net proceeds of the picnic went to the church. The $3 balance is considered a personal outlay that is specifically nondeductible.

It is often difficult to distinguish between a tax-deductible *contribution to charity* and a nondeductible personal expense. A commonly litigated example is the cost of tuition paid by taxpayers to a parochial school for their children. Even where the tuition payment was not legally required by the church (only *expected*), no deduction was allowed because the outlay was considered essentially an expense in payment of personal educational services received rather than a charitable contribution.

A fourth requirement that must be met for a deduction to be allowed is that the contribution must actually be paid in cash or other property before the close of the tax year in question. This rule applies regardless of the accounting method used by the taxpayer. In other words, even an accrual-basis taxpayer must actually pay cash or contribute other property before the close of the tax year. A contribution made by credit charge is equivalent to payment in cash when the charge is made. Taxpayers are entitled to charitable deductions in the year they charge the contributions to their bank credit cards and not in the year they actually make payment to the bank.

Often a donor will give a charitable organization a promissory note. The issuance and even the delivery of the note are not enough to meet the requirement that the contribution be paid within the tax year. However, the donor will be allowed a deduction when payments on the note are actually made.

Deductible contributions of $250 or more are now subject to substantiation requirements involving a written acknowledgment from the donee organization that must be either provided to the donor or reported in substance to the IRS.

Deductible Amounts

Taxpayers are entitled to a deduction for contributions to qualified charities; that is, governmental bodies, public or private corporations, trusts, and foundations organized as well as operated predominantly for charitable, religious, scientific, literary, or educational purposes. However, the taxpayer's deduction is limited.

The amount of a charitable contribution deduction depends on the following five factors, which will be discussed in detail:

1. *the type of property given away.* This chapter will consider the following items under the heading of *property:* (1) rent-free occupancy, (2) cash, (3) capital-gain property, (4) ordinary-income property, (5) tangible personal property where the use of that property by the donee is related to the exempt functions of the donee, (6) tangible personal property where the use of that property is unrelated to the exempt purposes of the donee, and (7) future interests in property.

2. *the identity of the donee.* Generally contributions to publicly supported domestic organizations—so-called "public charities"—are more favorably treated than contributions to foreign organizations or most

CHARITABLE CONTRIBUTION DEDUCTION LIMITATIONS CHART						
		Percentage Limitation		Excess Carryover*		
Type of Property (1)	Donee (2)	Individual (Adjusted Gross Income) (3)	Corporation (Taxable Income) (4)	Individual (5)	Corporation (6)	Amount Deductible (7)
(A) Rent-free occupancy	Public Private					No deduction No deduction
(B) Cash	Public Private	50% 30%	10% 10%	5 yrs. 5 yrs.	5 yrs. 5 yrs.	Full deduction Full deduction
(C) Capital-gain property (1) Real estate and intangible personal property	Public	30% or	10%	5 yrs.	5 yrs.	Full deduction for fair market value (FMV)
		50% on election (see column 7)	No corp. election	5 yrs.		FMV minus 100% of appreciation (donor's cost basis)[†]
	Private	20%	10%	5 yrs.	5 yrs.	Full deduction for FMV[‡]
(2) Tangible personal property						
Use related	Public	30% or	10%	5 yrs.	5 yrs.	Full deduction for FMV
		50% on election		5 yrs.		Donor's cost basis
	Private	20%	10%	5 yrs.	5 yrs.	Donor's cost basis
Use unrelated	Public	50%	10%	5 yrs.	5 yrs.	Donor's cost basis
	Private	20%	10%	5 yrs.	5 yrs.	Donor's cost basis
(D) Ordinary-income property	Public	50%	10%	5 yrs.	5 yrs.	Donor's cost basis
	Private	30%	10%	5 yrs.	5 yrs.	Donor's cost basis

* No carryback.

† Example: Basis is $3,000. FMV is $5,000; 100 percent of appreciation is $2,000. Therefore deduction is limited to $3,000 ($5,000 − $2,000).

‡ Applicable only to qualified appreciated stock that is limited to 10 percent of the outstanding stock of a corporation for which market quotations are available.

private foundations. The deduction for an individual's contributions to nonpublic (private) charities, regardless of the type of property given away, is limited to the lesser of (1) 20 or 30 percent (see the preceding chart) of the taxpayer's contribution base, which is basically AGI, or (2) 50 percent of the taxpayer's contribution base minus the amount of charitable contribution deductions allowed for contributions to the public-type charities. For example, if Richblood donates property worth 40 percent of his contribution base (AGI) to a public charity, such as the Boy Scouts, his additional contributions to 20 or 30 percent charities (private charities) are deductible only up to 10 percent of his contribution base. Donations to individuals are not deductible.

2. *the identity of the contributor.* Individuals are limited to specified percentages of adjusted gross income, while a corporation is limited to a deduction based on a percentage of its taxable income.

4. *the amount of property given away.* Generally there is a carryover of excess contributions—contributions above their deductible limit—for up to 5 years. (See the preceding chart.)

5. *the place where the charity is organized.* Gifts made to foreign charities are not deductible (except where allowed by treaty).

As mentioned above, the actual amount of charitable contribution deduction depends on a number of factors. The primary questions to ask in each case are the following: (1) What type of property was gifted? (2) Was the donee a private organization or publicly supported? (3) Was the donor an individual or a corporation? (4) How much property was given? In order to illustrate the effect of these factors on the amount of charitable contribution deduction that will be allowed in a given case, review the Charitable Contribution Deduction Limitations Chart as well as the accompanying text.

Deductible Contributions

Right to Use Property and Partial Interests

Contributions consisting of a mere right to use property (such as a rent-free lease to the Boy Scouts) are not deductible. To be deductible, contributions must be made in cash or other property. The mere right to use property is considered neither cash nor other property. The IRS considers a contribution of the right to use property as a contribution of less than the donor's entire interest in the property.

Generally a charitable contribution of less than a donor's entire interest in property is nondeductible. Gifts of a partial interest in property are deductible in the following three narrowly defined situations:

1. The first is a gift of an undivided portion of the donor's entire interest. For example, if Xavier gave his original Ramlo sculpture to the Philadelphia Museum of Art but agreed with the museum that he could

keep it as long as he or his wife lived, no current deduction would be allowed. However, if Xavier gave an undivided one-half interest in the sculpture (that is, if he gave the museum an immediate, absolute, and complete right of ownership for display purposes or otherwise) for one-half of each year, he would likely be successful in obtaining a current deduction.

2.   The second situation involves a gift of a remainder interest in a personal residence or farm. If Tammy gives a qualified organization her home or farm with the stipulation that she may live there for life, Tammy may take a current income tax deduction for the present value of the future gift. This assumes, of course, that the gift is irrevocable.

3.   Finally, a gift of a partial interest would be deductible if transferred in trust. This exception allows a charitable deduction for outright transfers of property, even if less than the taxpayer's entire interest is transferred. The deduction is allowed to the same extent that a deduction would be allowed had the same property been transferred in trust rather than directly to the charitable organization. Gifts in trust will be discussed in detail later in this chapter.

Cash

Depending on who is the donee, cash contributions are fully deductible subject to a maximum that is a percentage of adjusted gross income. If the donee is a publicly supported charity, the deduction ceiling is 50 percent of the individual taxpayer's adjusted gross income. The deduction ceiling for private charities is 30 percent of adjusted gross income. A corporation's deduction is limited to 10 percent of its taxable income (with certain adjustments). Regardless of the type of property gifted, a corporation can always take a current deduction of 10 percent of its taxable income (column 4 of the Charitable Contribution Deduction Limitations Chart). Likewise, regardless of the identity of the donee, a corporation may carry over excess contributions for up to 5 years (column 6 of the Charitable Contribution Deduction Limitations Chart).

Individuals who make contributions to public organizations in excess of the deductible limit for the taxable year may carry over their excess deductions (column 5 of the Charitable Contribution Deduction Limitations Chart) for a period of up to 5 years. In other words, excess contributions are not wasted and can be used as itemized deductions in future years. For example, if Goldberg contributed $20,000 in cash to a synagogue this year, but his adjusted gross income was only $36,000, he could currently deduct only 50 percent of his adjusted gross income, which is $18,000. However, he could carry over the $2,000 excess ($20,000 contribution − $18,000) to next year. Individuals who make excess cash contributions to private charities may deduct the excess contributions in subsequent years.

A full deduction, up to the percentage limitation of 50 percent of adjusted gross income for individuals (or 10 percent of taxable income for corporations), is allowed for gifts of cash to a public charity (column 7 of the Charitable Contribution Deduction Limitations Chart).

If a taxpayer makes a contribution to a college or university and receives the right to purchase tickets for an athletic event in one of the institution's athletic stadiums as a result of the contribution, only 80 percent of the amount contributed will be deductible by the taxpayer. This provision applies to contributions made, for example, by an alumnus of a university that requires the alumnus to make the contribution in order to be eligible to purchase season tickets for the university's basketball team.

Capital-Gain Property

Capital-gain property for purposes of the charitable contribution deduction is property that the taxpayer has held for more than 12 months as of the date the property is contributed. Capital-gain property can be divided into two types. The first type would consist of intangible personal property and all real property. A gift of publicly traded stock purchased 11 years ago at $100 a share, now worth $400 a share, would be considered intangible, personal, capital-gain property. Appreciated land that is held for the requisite holding period would be an example of real property properly classified as capital-gain property. The second type of capital-gain property is tangible personal property, such as a car, a painting, a sculpture, an antique, or jewelry. Tangible personal property will be discussed later in this chapter.

Where intangible personal property or real property is given to a public donee (column 2 of the Charitable Contribution Deduction Limitations Chart), an individual's deduction may not exceed 30 percent of adjusted gross income (column 3 of the Charitable Contribution Deduction Limitations Chart). If the gift exceeds this percentage limitation, the taxpayer may carry over the deduction for up to 5 future years (column 5 of the Charitable Contribution Deduction Limitations Chart). The full fair market value of the gift is deductible (column 7 of the Charitable Contribution Deduction Limitations Chart).

For example, suppose Phil Anthropist donates stock worth $25,000 to the Gotham Library. The stock cost Phil $13,000 when he purchased it 4 years ago. If Phil's adjusted gross income was $30,000, his maximum contribution deduction would be $9,000 (30 percent of $30,000). He would be able to carry over the $16,000 balance and apply that as a deduction against future years' income.

There is an election that taxpayers may want to make in situations similar to the example above. The 30 percent limit can be increased to 50 percent of adjusted gross income if donors are willing to reduce the value of their gifts by 100 percent of their potential gain. In other words, Phil, in the example above, could elect to exclude 100 percent of his potential gain, $12,000, thus decreasing the deductible value to $13,000 ($25,000 − $12,000). By doing so, he is currently able to deduct the entire $13,000. This is because the election allows him to currently deduct up to 50 percent of his adjusted gross income of $30,000.

The election can be important for a taxpayer whose income fluctuates widely from year to year. It is of particular value when the amount of appreciation is small. For example, capital-gain property with a basis of $980 and a fair market value of $1,000 would be reduced by only $20. In this way taxpayers could qualify for the higher 50 percent limitation at the expense of losing only a very small portion of their deductions. However, note that the amount representing 100 percent of the potential gain may not be carried over and deducted in a later year if the election is made. Note that by reducing the deductible amount by 100 percent of the potential gain, the deduction is, in effect, limited to the donor's basis in the property.

Ordinary-Income Property

Ordinary-income property is an asset that would have resulted in ordinary income (rather than capital gain) on the date of contribution had it been sold at its fair market value rather than contributed. Ordinary-income property includes (1) capital assets held 12 months or less at the time contributed, (2) works of art, books, letters, and musical compositions, but only if given by the person who created or prepared them or for whom they were prepared, and (3) a business person's stock in trade and inventory (which would result in ordinary income if sold).

Other than the special exception discussed in the following paragraph, taxpayers' deductions are limited to their basis (cost) for ordinary-income property (column 7 of the Charitable Contribution Deduction Limitations Chart). For example, if Papa Chezman, the famous painter, donated a genuine Chezman painting worth $25,000 to an art museum, his deduction would be limited to his cost for producing the painting. This means that only the cost for canvas, paint, and so forth, would be deductible. No deduction would be allowed for the value of his time. Here is a similar situation: Phil Anthropist owned his National Motors stock for 5 months. A sale would have resulted in short-term capital gain. He purchased the stock at a cost of $12,000 and gave it to the Boy Scouts of America when it was worth $25,000. Only his cost (basis) is deductible. Therefore, since the property is considered ordinary-income property, Phil will be limited to a charitable deduction of $12,000 even though the property had a fair market value of $25,000 at the time of the gift.

One exception increases the charitable deduction for contributions by corporations of new tangible inventory-type property that is used for scientific research. As an increased incentive to corporations to make charitable contributions of scientific equipment to colleges or universities, a deduction is allowed in an amount equal to the cost of the property plus one-half of the unrealized appreciation limited to a maximum deduction of twice the basis of the property. In other words, the charitable deduction in such cases cannot exceed twice the cost of the property regardless of the amount of the unrealized appreciation. The property that qualifies for this increased deduction must be either new inventory-type scientific equipment or an apparatus manufactured by the donor corporation. This rule applies only to contributions of scientific equipment to colleges, universities, and certain research organizations to be used for research purposes including research training. The property must be donated to a college or university no later than 2 years after it was fully constructed or purchased. This deduction is available to business corporations only. S corporations, personal holding companies, and certain service organizations are not eligible for the increased deduction.

Ordinary-income property gifted to a public charity is subject to the 50-percent-of-AGI limitation. Consequently, in the previous example, Phil Anthropist would need an AGI of at last $24,000 to deduct $12,000 for his gift to the Boy Scouts if the property given had been ordinary-income property (rather than long-term capital-gain property).

Gifts of ordinary-income property should be avoided where the estate will be subject to federal estate taxes. Ordinary-income property left by will to charity can be more beneficial, since a federal estate tax deduction for the full value of the property can be taken. However, where it appears that the estate will not be subject to federal estate tax, a lifetime gift of ordinary-income property will permit a current income tax deduction, although it will be somewhat limited as described previously.

Tangible Personal Property

Tangible personal property (which would have produced capital gain if sold) includes cars, jewelry, sculptures, artworks, books, and so forth, but only if created or produced by persons other than the donor. With respect to this type of property, a distinction must be made between (1) gifts that will be used by the donee-charity in such a manner that the use of the gift is related to the exempt purposes of the donee, and (2) gifts that will not be used by the charity in a manner related to the exempt purposes of the donee.

For example, a gift of a painting (not by the artist) would be *use related* if the painting was donated to a museum that planned to exhibit the painting in its public galleries. The same gift would be *use unrelated* if given to the Red Cross or to the Campfire Girls. It is unlikely that either of these organizations would use the painting as a painting. In all likelihood the art would be sold and the proceeds used for the Red Cross or the Campfire Girls. However, it is the gift itself, and not the cash or other property that can be obtained for the gift, that determines whether the gift is use related or use unrelated.

Another example might be the contribution of a stamp collection to an educational institution. If the stamp collection is placed in the donee-organization's library for display and study by students, the use of the donated property is related to the educational purposes constituting the basis of the charitable organization's tax exemption. But if the stamps are sold, the use of the property is an unrelated one, even if the proceeds are used by the organization for educational purposes.

This distinction is important because where appreciated tangible personal property is considered use related, the entire fair market value at the date of the gift is deductible. In other words, a use-related gift of tangible personal property held for the requisite period is treated exactly the same as any other long-term capital-gain property. Thus the donor is subject to the 30-percent-of-AGI limitation or may elect to reduce the value of the gift by 100 percent of the potential gain realized if the gift was sold rather than contributed. By doing this, the percentage limitation on the donor's adjusted gross income ceiling would be increased to 50 percent. In some cases this would result in a larger, immediate deduction.

For example, Denise Donor has an adjusted gross income of $10,000. She contributes a collection of whaling harpoons for display purposes to the Cape May County Historical Museum (a public charity). The collection cost Denise $6,000, but it was worth $10,000 on the date of contribution. The type of property contributed is tangible personal property. The donee is a public charity, and the gift is use related to the exempt purposes of the museum. Therefore Denise can deduct up to 30 percent of her contribution base (AGI), $10,000, or $3,000. She gets credit for the full $10,000 contribution, enabling her to carry over the excess contribution, $7,000, for up to 5 years (subject to the 30 percent rule each year). Alternatively, Denise may elect to reduce the value of her gift by 100 percent of the potential gain, or $4,000 ($10,000 − $6,000). Under the election Denise would have a current deduction of $5,000 (50 percent of adjusted gross income), and the remaining $1,000 ($6,000 − $5,000) could be deducted in a later year.

If the gift is use unrelated (that is, made to a donee whose direct use of the asset is unrelated to the charitable function of the donee), the fair market value of the gift *must* be reduced by 100 percent of the potential gain. For example, the gift by Denise Donor would be *worth* only $6,000. However, it would be deductible up to 50 percent of her contribution base.

Future Interests in Property

A *future interest* is any interest or right that will begin at some time in the future. The term *future interest* includes situations where donors purport to give tangible personal property to a charitable organization but have made a written or oral agreement with the organization reserving to themselves or members of their immediate families the right to use, possess, or enjoy the property. For example, suppose Fulton Flushbucks donates a genuine Meccariello photograph to an art museum but arranges with the museum to keep the photograph in his home for as long as he lives. The museum has only a future interest in the photograph.

Some of the basic rules governing charitable contribution deductions are that contributions must (1) actually be paid, (2) be paid in cash or other property, and (3) be paid before the close of the tax year. Furthermore, no deductions are allowed for a contribution of less than the donor's entire interest in property. (Three narrow exceptions are the following: (1) an undivided portion of the donor's entire interest, (2) remainder interest in personal residences or farms, or (3) partial interest that would be deductible if transferred in trust.) A charitable contribution (not made by a transfer in trust) of a partial interest in property may not be deducted.

Since the benefit to the museum—and consequently to the public—was deferred in the Flushbucks gift of the Meccariello photograph above, no current tax deduction would be allowed. The implication is that a deduction will not be allowed until the charity receives actual possession or enjoyment of the artwork. The gift of tangible personal property must be complete in the sense that all interests and rights to the possession and enjoyment of the property must vest in the charity. This means that a transfer of a future interest in property to a charity is not deductible until all intervening interests in and rights to possession held by the donor or certain related persons or organizations have expired (or unless the gift is in the form of a future interest in trust that meets the requirements discussed below).

Remainder interests are a form of future interest in which an income interest is given by the donor to someone other than the donor, and at the death of that income beneficiary, the principal goes to a designated charity. An example would be a gift to Sue for life and at the death of Sue (the income beneficiary) the remainder (the principal at Sue's death) goes to charity (the remainder beneficiary). A gift "to Sue for life, remainder to The American College" would be considered a gift of a future interest to The American College. The American College is called the remainderman because the gift *remains* away from the donor after the death of Sue, the income beneficiary, and The American College receives the principal remaining at Sue's death.

Gifts in Trust

Gifts of a remainder interest either in real property or in trust are deductible only if made in one of three ways: (1) a *fixed-annuity* trust, (2) a *unitrust,* or (3) a *pooled-income fund.* These three permissible trust forms are a result of congressional concern over potential abuses of gifts of a remainder interest in trust to charity. For example, suppose Mr. and Mrs. Weltodo were a financially secure but childless couple. Mr. Weltodo might leave his property to his wife in trust. Mrs. Weltodo, according to the terms of the trust, would receive the income for life if she survived her husband. At her death, the principal in the trust would pass to a designated charity. Mr. Weltodo would take a current charitable contribution deduction for the present value of the gift that the charity would receive at the death of the income beneficiary. In order to counteract inflation and provide for contingencies, a clause might be inserted in the trust agreement authorizing an invasion of principal for Mrs. Weltodo's benefit.

The potential for abuse was that the trust principal was often invested in securities that produced an extremely high income but at the cost of a correspondingly high risk. This situation naturally worked to the detriment of the charitable *remainderman.* In addition, the trustee's ability to make substantial invasions into the trust principal further increased the likelihood that little, if any, of the original contribution would be received by the charity. The result was a decrease in the value of the charity's remainder interest.

For these reasons, rules were designed to prevent a taxpayer from receiving a current charitable contribution deduction for a gift to charity of a remainder interest in trust that is substantially in excess of the amount the charity may ultimately receive. (This is so because the assumptions used in calculating the value of the remainder interest had little relation to the actual investment policies of the trust.)

Pursuant to these rules, deductions are basically limited to situations where the trust specifies (1) a fixed annual *amount* that is to be paid to the noncharitable income beneficiary (an annuity trust); or (2) the amount the income beneficiary will receive in terms of a *fixed percentage* of the value of the trust assets ascertained each year (a unitrust); or (3) that property contributed by a number of donors is commingled with property transferred by other donors, and each beneficiary of an income interest will receive income determined by the rate of return earned by the trust for such year (a pooled-income fund).

Annuity Trust

More specifically, a charitable remainder annuity trust is a trust designed to permit payment of a fixed amount annually to a noncharitable (income) beneficiary with the remainder going to charity. In order to qualify for income tax (and estate or gift tax) deductions, the trust must meet a number of tests. The primary requirements are as follows:

- A fixed amount or fixed percentage of the *initial value* of the trust must be payable to the noncharitable beneficiary.
- This annuity must not be less than an amount equal to 5 percent of the initial fair market value of all the property transferred in trust.
- The specified amount must be paid at least annually to the beneficiary out of income and/or principal.
- The trust must be irrevocable and not subject to a power by either the donor, the trustee, or the beneficiary to invade, alter, or amend the trust.
- The trust must be for the benefit of a named individual or individuals who must be living at the time the property is transferred to the trust. An amount can be paid to a person for life or for a term of years not greater than 20 years. The remainder must go to charity (charities) and cannot be split between charitable and noncharitable beneficiaries.

If all the necessary tests are met, the donor of a charitable remainder annuity trust will be entitled to an income tax deduction limited to the present value of the remainder interest.

Unitrust

A charitable remainder unitrust, like a charitable remainder annuity trust, is basically designed to permit payment of a periodic sum to a noncharitable beneficiary with a remainder to charity. The key distinction is in how the periodic sum is computed. In order to qualify for income, estate, and gift tax deductions, a charitable remainder unitrust must meet a number of tests, the most important of which are the following:

- A fixed percentage of the net fair market value of the principal, *as revalued annually,* must be payable to the noncharitable beneficiary. Therefore the amount payable to the income beneficiary may fluctuate from year to year.
- The percentage payable must not be less than 5 percent of the annual value.
- The unitrust may provide that the noncharitable beneficiary can receive the lesser of (1) the specified fixed percentage or (2) the trust income for the year, plus any excess trust income to the extent of any deficiency in the prior years by reason of the limitation to the amount of trust income in such years.
- The noncharitable income beneficiaries must be living at the time of transfer in trust, and their interests must be for a term not exceeding 20 years or for their respective lives.
- The entire remainder must go to charity (or charities).

The tax deductions allowed are the same as in the case of a charitable remainder annuity trust.

Pooled-Income Fund

A pooled-income fund is a trust created and maintained by a public charity rather than a private donor. The basic requirements are the following:

- The donor must contribute an irrevocable, vested remainder interest to the charitable organization that maintains it.
- The property transferred by each donor must be commingled with the property transferred by other donors.
- The fund cannot invest in tax-exempt securities.
- No donor or income beneficiary can be a trustee.
- The donor must retain a life income interest for himself or herself or one or more named income beneficiaries.
- Each income beneficiary must be entitled to and receive a pro rata share of the income (annually) based on the rate of return earned by the fund.

If these tests are met, the donor will be entitled to income and gift tax deductions. The economic advantage to the donor of making this transfer is that the donor is obtaining diversification for the income beneficiary without incurring the capital-gains tax that would ordinarily be imposed if the donor exchanged securities for other securities.

Advantages of Charitable Gifts of Life Insurance

Life insurance, like any other property, can be and often is the subject of a gift. In fact, life insurance is a favored means of making charitable contributions for a number of reasons.

First, the death benefit going to charity is guaranteed as long as premiums are paid. This means that the charity will receive an amount that is fixed in value and not subject to the potential downside risks of securities.

Second, life insurance provides an *amplified* gift that can be purchased on the installment plan. Through a relatively small annual cost (premium), a large benefit can be provided for the charity. A large gift can be made without impairing or diluting the control of a family business interest or other investments. Assets earmarked for the donor-insured's family can be kept intact.

Third, life insurance is a self-completing gift. If the donor lives, cash values (which can be currently used by the charity) grow constantly from year to year. If the donor becomes disabled, the policy will remain in full force through the waiver-of-premium feature, guaranteeing both the ultimate death benefit to the charity as well as the same cash values and dividend buildup that would have been earned had the insured not become disabled. Even if death occurs after only one deposit, the charity is assured of its full gift.

Fourth, the death proceeds can be received by the designated charity free of federal income and estate taxes, probate and administrative costs and delays, brokerage fees, or other transfer costs. Thus the charity in fact receives one-hundred-cent dollars. This prompt cash payment should be compared with the payment of a gift to the selected charity under the terms of an individual's will. In that case, probate delays of up to several years are not uncommon.

Fifth, because of the contractual nature of the life insurance contract, large gifts to charity are not subject to attack by disgruntled heirs. Life insurance proceeds also do not violate the so-called mortmain statutes that prohibit or limit gifts made within a short time of death.

Finally, a substantial gift may be made with no attending publicity. Since the life insurance proceeds paid to charity can be arranged so they will not be part of the decedent's probate estate, the proceeds can be paid confidentially. Of course, publicity may be given if desired.

Taxation of Charitable Gifts of Life Insurance

If a life insurance policy is sold at a gain, the gain is taxed as ordinary income. Therefore a gift of life insurance is a gift of ordinary-income property. Assuming the value of the policy (interpolated terminal reserve plus unearned premium on the date of the sale) exceeds the policyholder's net premium payments, the deduction for a gift of a policy is equal to the policyholder's basis (cost), that is, the net premium payments paid by the policyholder. For example, suppose Mary McClu assigns a policy on her life to The American College. Her charitable contribution deduction is limited to her basis, that is, her cost in the contract (or the value of the policy if lower). If Mary paid net premiums of $15,000, even if the policy had a value of $18,000, her charitable contribution deduction would be limited to $15,000. On the other hand, if the value of the policy in this case was $15,000 and the net premium payments were $18,000, the amount of the charitable deduction would still be $15,000. The income tax value of a paid-up policy depends on the replacement cost of the policy. The replacement cost of a single-premium or paid-up policy is the single premium the same insurer would charge for a policy of the same amount at the insured's attained age (increased by the value of any dividend credits and reduced by the amount of any loans outstanding). The insurance company in question will generally calculate the exact value on IRS Form 712 upon request. Remember that the charitable deduction is limited to the policyowner's basis if that is less than the policy's value.

The charitable deduction for a newly issued policy is the gross premium paid by the insured.

Premium Payments as Contributions

Premium payments are considered gifts of cash and therefore are fully and currently deductible as charitable contributions if the charity owns the policy outright.

Occasionally, a donor will attempt to *split dollar* the charitable gift; that is, name the donor's personal beneficiary as the recipient of the policy's pure death benefit (the amount at risk) but make the charity the owner of the cash value. The IRS has maintained that this is a gift of a "partial interest" in property and denies a deduction for the premium payment. The same principle applies where the donor retains an interest in the policy cash value but assigns an interest in the *amount-at-risk* portion to the charity. Therefore the donor should make an absolute assignment of the ownership of the policy to the charity in order to qualify for the desired tax benefits. If the charity initially applies for and owns a life insurance policy, and the insured pays the premiums, the charity must have an insurable interest in the insured under local law in order for the insured to obtain the desired tax benefits. In general, it may be preferable to transfer ownership of an existing policy.

The donor should send a check directly to the charity and have it pay the premium to the life insurance company in order to ensure the most favorable tax results. The canceled check will serve as proof (1) of the fact that a gift was made to the charity, (2) of the date the gift was made, and (3) of the amount of the gift. It will also ensure a full deduction of up to 50 percent of the donor's adjusted gross income.

There should be no adverse gift or estate tax implications. Gifts to charity are deductible in full for federal gift tax purposes. There is no percentage limitation on the amount of the gift tax deduction. Likewise, the death proceeds of a life insurance policy payable to a charity do not generate any federal estate tax.

OTHER ITEMIZED DEDUCTIONS

The remaining categories of an individual's itemized deductions include deductions for theft and casualty losses, and miscellaneous itemized deductions (whether or not subject to the 2 percent floor). Deductions for theft and casualty losses were discussed in chapter 8, and miscellaneous itemized deductions were discussed in chapter 7. Therefore those subjects are not discussed in this chapter.

Individual Income Tax Credits

James F. Ivers III

The Eiffel Tower is the Empire State Building after taxes.

Anonymous

Chapter Outline

INTRODUCTION

Tax credits are highly beneficial to taxpayers because they constitute dollar-for-dollar reductions of the actual tax owed to the government. A tax deduction, on the other hand, only reduces the amount of the taxpayer's income that is subject to taxation. It produces a net tax benefit equal to the taxpayer's marginal tax rate multiplied by each dollar deducted. For example, a taxpayer whose top marginal rate is 31 percent would receive a benefit equal to 31 cents for each deductible dollar. Although deductions are certainly beneficial, credits are more beneficial because they are applied directly to the tax liability.

In this chapter, four important tax credits that are available to individual taxpayers will be examined: the tax credit for children, the adoption credit, the dependent-care credit, and the credits for higher education expenses. The higher education credits are actually two different credits: the "Hope" scholarship credit and the "Lifetime" learning credit.

All these credits reflect the concern of Congress with providing tax incentives for socially beneficial or economically necessary activities of individual taxpayers. Each credit has its own set of rules for eligibility, availability based on the taxpayer's income level, and credit amounts. Knowledge of how these credits operate is essential to a fundamental understanding of the income tax law.

TAX CREDIT FOR CHILDREN

The tax law provides an annual tax credit that may be claimed against an individual's tax liability for each qualifying child of the taxpayer. The amount of the credit is currently $500 per child. However, the credit is "phased out" for upper-income taxpayers as explained below.

Qualifying Child

A "qualifying child" under the credit rules is one for whom the taxpayer is entitled to claim a dependency exemption under IRC Sec. 151. The child must be a son, daughter, stepson, stepdaughter, or eligible foster child of the taxpayer. In addition, the child must be under the age of 17 at the close of the tax year. Finally, the child must be a citizen, national, or resident of the United States.

The taxpayer must include the name and Social Security number of the child on the tax return in order to claim the credit. If the amount of the credit exceeds the tax liability shown on the return, all or a part of the excess may be refundable under a complex formula that involves the earned income credit computation, the taxpayer's Social Security taxes, and the number of children the taxpayer has.

Phaseout of Credit

The credit is phased out for upper-income taxpayers. The phaseout occurs based on the taxpayer's adjusted gross income (AGI) with certain minor modifications ("modified adjusted gross income"). The phaseout begins at the following levels of modified AGI:

Married filing joint return	$110,000
Married filing separately	$ 55,000
Unmarried taxpayers	$ 75,000

The otherwise allowable credit is phased out by $50 for each $1,000 (or fraction thereof) by which modified AGI exceeds the threshold amount. For example, a married couple filing jointly with one child would have no child credit if their modified AGI was more than $119,000. This is because their AGI exceeds $110,000 by $9,000 plus a fraction of $1,000. Therefore the credit is phased out by 10 x $50, or $500, the total amount of the credit.

Under the language of the statute, the credit is apparently phased out sequentially (rather than simultaneously) per child for taxpayers with more than one child. Therefore taxpayers with more than one child will have a larger "phaseout range" for the credits. This is different from the phaseout of dependency exemptions for upper-income taxpayers as discussed in chapter 4. Such exemptions phase out simultaneously regardless of the number of exemptions claimed.

Relationship to Dependency Exemption

Remember that the taxpayer who claims the dependency exemption for the child is the taxpayer who is entitled to the credit. This rule is important in cases involving divorced, separated, or unmarried parents.

TAX CREDIT FOR ADOPTION EXPENSES

There is currently a tax credit of up to $5,000 per eligible child available for qualified expenses paid in the course of adopting a child. If the adopted child is a special needs child, a credit of up to $6,000 is available. The limit on the credit is a cumulative limit per child. In other words, no more than the maximum amount may be claimed for any one child regardless of the number of years for which the credit is claimed for that child.

Phaseout of Credit

The maximum adoption credit is phased out for taxpayers whose adjusted gross income for the year exceeds $75,000. The credit is completely phased out when AGI reaches $115,000. Adjusted gross income for this purpose is determined with certain minor modifications similar to those used for the tax credit for children.

To calculate the amount phased out, divide the amount of the taxpayer's adjusted gross income in excess of $75,000 by $40,000. Then multiply the resulting fraction by the allowable amount of the credit ($5,000 or $6,000).

Example: Jim and Denise Oliver pay $12,000 in legal fees and other costs in the year 2001 to adopt Michael, a 2-year-old U.S. citizen who is not a special needs child. The adoption is completed in 2001. The Olivers' adjusted gross income for 2001 is $95,000. The maximum allowable credit for their expenses is $5,000. This $5,000 amount must be reduced by a fraction equal to $20,000 (the amount of AGI in excess of $75,000) divided by $40,000, or 1/2. Therefore the amount of the allowable credit that is "phased out" is $2,500 ($5,000 x 1/2). The allowable credit is $2,500 ($5,000 – $2,500). It may be claimed in the year 2001 since the adoption is completed in that year.

Qualified Adoption Expenses

It is important for clients considering adoption or in the process of adoption to understand what expenses qualify for the credit and how the income limitation is applied. *Qualified adoption expenses* include legal fees, court costs, and other related fees and costs that have the principal purpose of a taxpayer's legal adoption of an *eligible child* or a *child with special needs.*

Costs associated with the adoption of a child of the taxpayer's spouse or costs for surrogate parenting arrangements are not qualified expenses. In the case of foreign adoptions only, the adoption must actually be completed in order for the expenses to be qualified adoption expenses.

An *eligible child* is a person who is either under the age of 18 or is physically or mentally incapable of self-care. A *child with special needs* is defined as a citizen or resident of the United States who is determined by state authorities to be unable to be placed for adoption without adoption assistance. Requirements for such a determination by state authorities include findings that the child should not be returned to his or her biological parents, and that there is a specific factor or condition that makes the child unable to be placed without adoption assistance.

When Credit Is Claimed

For tax years in which an adoption becomes final, the taxpayer is allowed to claim the credit for expenses paid during that year. For years in which qualified expenses are paid but in which the adoption does not become final, the taxpayer must claim the credit for those expenses for the tax year following the year in which the expenses are paid. If expenses are paid in a year following the year the adoption becomes final, the expenses may be claimed for the year in which they are made. Expenses for a foreign adoption qualify for the credit only if the adoption becomes final and must be claimed only in that year even if paid in a prior year.

There is a 5-year carryover period available for taxpayers whose allowable adoption credit exceeds their tax liability for the year the credit is first allowable.

The credit for adopting an eligible child is currently scheduled to be available for expenses paid until December 31, 2001. After that date the adoption credit will be available only for expenses paid for the adoption of a child with special needs.

Related Income Tax Exclusion

In planning for the adoption credit, it is important to know that there is also an income tax *exclusion* available for amounts paid by a taxpayer's employer for qualified adoption expenses on behalf of the taxpayer/employee. Such amounts must be furnished under a nondiscriminatory adoption assistance program. The rules defining and limiting this exclusion for adoption assistance payments are similar to the rules just described for application of the adoption credit. For example, the dollar amounts of the available exclusion are the same as the dollar amounts of the credit. Any amounts excluded from gross income under such a program are not eligible to be treated as qualified expenses for purposes of the adoption credit.

Planning Considerations

The adoption credit is one of the largest of any allowable tax credit for an expense of a personal nature in the history of the income tax law. For that reason alone, it is significant. In addition, the credit reflects a congressional awareness of family values in a context that has not been so strongly recognized in the past. Since the first $5,000 spent to adopt a child can be free for the majority of families, many fortunate children and their adoptive parents benefit from the credit.

Planners should remember that the adoption credit is a per *child,* not a per *year,* credit. This means that the credit can be claimed up to the maximum amount of $5,000, or $6,000 for a special needs child, only *once* for *each* child. If expenses are paid in different years for the adoption of the same child, the maximum aggregate expenses that may be taken into account in computing the credit for that child cannot exceed either $5,000 or $6,000, respectively, for all taxable years. However, the maximum amount of expenses can be claimed *again* for the adoption of *another* child.

It is also crucial to remember that families have only until the end of the year 2001 to pay expenses eligible for the credit (except for adoptions of special needs children). Whether that "sunset" date will be extended is still uncertain.

THE DEPENDENT-CARE CREDIT

Introduction

There is a tax credit that applies to expenses paid by individual taxpayers for the care of their dependents if the expenses are necessary to allow the taxpayer to be gainfully employed. The amount of the credit ranges from 20 to 30 percent of qualifying expenses based on the taxpayer's income level. The qualifying expenses upon which the credit percentages are based are subject to dollar amount limitations as explained below. The credit was enacted generally for the purpose of providing a tax credit for working parents with children in day-care facilities.

Expenses Eligible for the Credit

As stated above, the expenses must be made in order to allow the taxpayer to be gainfully employed for the credit to be available. The expenses must be paid by a taxpayer who maintains a household that includes as a member one or more "qualifying individuals." Expenses must be paid either for household services or specifically for the care of a qualifying individual. A qualifying individual must fall within one of the following definitions:

- the taxpayer's child who is under the age of 13 and who is the taxpayer's dependent for purposes of claiming a dependency exemption for the year
- an individual who is physically or mentally incapable of caring for himself or herself and is also the taxpayer's dependent for tax purposes
- the taxpayer's spouse who is physically or mentally incapable of caring for himself or herself

Generally the expenses must be paid for services rendered inside the taxpayer's home, unless the services are for the care of either the taxpayer's dependent child who is under the age of 13 (that is, day-care services), or for the care of another qualifying individual who regularly spends at least 8 hours per day in the taxpayer's household. In no event, however, can expenses paid for an overnight camp be eligible expenses.

There is a rule that disallows expenses paid to certain individuals who are related to the taxpayer. Eligible expenses do not include payments for care provided by a child of the taxpayer who is under the age of 19 (such as a sister or brother of the qualifying individual). Also, eligible expenses do not include those paid for services rendered by any individual who is a dependent of the taxpayer for dependency exemption purposes. The purpose of this rule is to prevent child-care payments made to certain family members from generating a tax credit.

There is a limit on the amount of expenses that can be counted in calculating the allowable credit. For taxpayers caring for one qualifying individual, the maximum amount is $2,400 per year. If there are two or more qualifying individuals, the maximum amount is $4,800. Qualifying expenses may not exceed the amount of the taxpayer's earned income for the year.

Calculation of the Credit

The allowable amount of the credit ranges from 20 to 30 percent of the amount of eligible expenses The allowable percentage begins at 30 percent and is reduced by one percent for each $2,000 (or fraction thereof) of adjusted gross income in excess of $10,000. The credit is not reduced below 20 percent.

Therefore once the taxpayer's AGI (regardless of filing status) exceeds $28,000, the credit remains at 20 percent.

> *Example:* Sue Broadstring is a single taxpayer with two children aged 8 and 10. The children attend a day-care facility to allow Sue to be gainfully employed. Sue's adjusted gross income is $40,000 this year, and she pays $10,000 this year to the facility for her children's care. Sue has $4,800 in eligible expenses (the maximum amount) and is permitted to claim a 20 percent credit for those expenses since her income exceeds $28,000. Therefore Sue's allowable credit is $960 ($4,800 x .20).

Other Rules and Restrictions

Coordination with Dependent-Care Assistance Programs

The same eligible expenses cannot be used for both the dependent-care credit and the income tax exclusion for amounts received from an employer-provided dependent-care assistance program (described in chapter 6). In addition, if a taxpayer is a participant in such a program, the maximum amount of qualifying expenses for credit purposes is reduced by one dollar for each dollar paid from the employer program and excluded from the taxpayer's gross income. Therefore taxpayers are often forced to choose between the income tax exclusion for such plans and the dependent-care credit. Generally speaking, if the taxpayer is in a marginal tax bracket of 28 percent or higher, the exclusion provides a more efficient method of funding dependent-care expenses than does the 20 percent credit.

Additional Rules for Married Couples

Certain special rules apply to married couples claiming the dependent-care credit. These rules include the following:

- Married couples must generally file a joint return to be eligible for the credit. However, if the spouses live apart for the last 6 months of the taxable year, the credit may be available even if separate returns are filed.
- Eligible expenses are limited to the earned income of the spouse with the lesser earned income. Therefore, generally speaking, both spouses must be working to claim the credit, although there is no requirement of full-time employment.
- A significant exception to the rule just described involves spouses who are either full-time students for at least 5 calendar months during the year or who are incapable of self-care during the year. Such spouses are deemed to have a monthly earned income of $200 for each month during which they are students or incapable of self-care. If there are two or more qualifying individuals in the household, then such spouses are

deemed to have $400 per month of earned income. Note that this rule allows such married couples to qualify for the maximum amount of eligible expenses ($2,400 or $4,800 per year), if they qualify for this "deemed" earned income for all 12 months.

THE "HOPE" AND "LIFETIME" EDUCATION TAX CREDITS

Individual taxpayers are permitted to claim tax credits for certain expenses for higher education. There are two credits for higher education: the "Hope" scholarship credit and the "Lifetime" learning credit.

Relationship of One Credit to the Other

Before describing the specific rules for these credits, it is important to know how they interact. First, the credits cannot be claimed together with respect to the education expenses of the same student. The Hope scholarship credit applies on a per-student basis, while the Lifetime learning credit applies on a per-taxpayer basis. This means that the Hope scholarship credit applies separately with respect to each student for whom the taxpayer pays education expenses, while the Lifetime learning credit applies on an overall basis to all qualifying expenses (for one or more students for whom the Hope credit is not claimed) paid by a given taxpayer.

The taxpayer elects the credits with respect to qualifying expenses. The elections must be separate. For example, if a taxpayer elects the Hope scholarship credit for the college expenses of one child, he or she may still elect the Lifetime learning credit for the qualifying education expenses of another child or children. Alternatively, the Hope scholarship credit can be elected separately for each child in college. As previously stated, the Lifetime learning credit cannot be elected with respect to expenses that have been treated under the Hope scholarship credit.

Expenses Qualifying for the Credits

Both credits are available with respect to "qualified tuition and related expenses." Such expenses include those paid for the attendance by the taxpayer, the taxpayer's spouse, or the taxpayer's dependents at a postsecondary educational institution offering credit toward a degree or other recognized postsecondary educational credential. Qualified expenses do not include expenses for courses involving sports, games, or hobbies unless the course is part of the student's degree program. Room and board, transportation, and living expenses are also not qualified expenses for these credits.

Special Rules for Hope Credit Expenses

The Hope scholarship credit is allowed only for expenses for the first 2 years of the student's postsecondary education and can be elected for only 2 taxable years for any one student. The student must be at least a "half-time" student; that is, he or she must carry at least one-half the normal full-time workload for the course of study being pursued. The Hope scholarship credit will not be allowed if the student has been convicted of a felony drug offense during the year.

Lifetime Credit Expenses

Unlike the Hope scholarship credit, the Lifetime learning credit may be claimed for all postsecondary years of education expenses including graduate and professional school expenses. The Lifetime learning credit is also available with respect to expenses of a student who is taking courses to acquire or improve job skills, even if that student is not a half-time student as required under the Hope credit rules.

Interaction with Dependency Exemption

If the student is a dependent of another taxpayer, he or she may not claim the education credits on his or her own return. The taxpayer who claims the student as a dependent is the taxpayer who may claim the credits. Under Treasury regulations, it is permissible for the parent who is eligible to claim the student as a dependent to choose not to claim the dependency exemption to allow the student to claim an education credit on the student's own return. This may be advisable in cases where the student has tax liability that can be absorbed by the credit, and the parent is subject to phaseout of the credit because of the income limitations discussed below.

Rules for Calculating the Hope Credit

The Hope scholarship credit can be claimed in amounts up to $1,500 per student per year. It is calculated based on 100 percent of the first $1,000 of qualifying expenses and 50 percent of the next $1,000 of expenses. Therefore the maximum credit is $1,500 for the first $2,000 of expenses. The expense limits will be indexed for inflation beginning in 2002.

Phaseout of the Hope Credit

The allowable credit is phased out proportionately for taxpayers with modified adjusted gross income (AGI with certain minor modifications) in excess of certain levels. For married taxpayers filing jointly, the phaseout range is between $80,000 and $100,000 (a $20,000 phaseout range). For single taxpayers, the phaseout range is between $40,000 and $50,000 (a $10,000 phaseout range). Married taxpayers filing separately cannot claim the credit.

Example: Paul and Margie have a dependent son, John, who is attending his first year of college as a full-time student. The couple's adjusted gross income this year is $90,000. Their tuition payment eligible for the Hope credit this year is $7,000. Their maximum allowable Hope credit of $1,500 is reduced by the ratio of the amount of their modified AGI in excess of $80,000 to the $20,000 phaseout range. This ratio is $10,000/$20,000 or 1/2. Therefore $750 of their maximum $1,500 Hope credit is phased out ($1,500 x 1/2).

The ranges of income to which the phaseouts apply will be adjusted for inflation beginning in 2002.

Rules for Calculating the Lifetime Credit

The Lifetime learning credit is equal to 20 percent of the first $5,000 of qualifying expenses paid by the taxpayer during the tax year. For 2003 and thereafter, the $5,000 figure is increased to $10,000 (these amounts are not currently scheduled for inflation adjustments). Therefore the maximum annual Lifetime learning credit is $1,000 through 2002 and $2,000 thereafter.

Phaseout of the Lifetime Credit

The Lifetime learning credit is phased out proportionately in the same way and in the same range of income as the Hope scholarship credit, as previously discussed.

Coordination with Other Income Tax Provisions

These credits are not applicable with respect to student expenses that are paid from an education individual retirement account under IRC Sec. 530(d)(2)(c). Expenses covered by a scholarship that are excludible from gross income under IRC Sec. 117 also do not qualify for the credits. Expenses that are claimed for the credits will also reduce the amount of the exclusion available under IRC Sec. 135 for certain U.S. savings bond interest used to pay expenses for higher education. Finally, expenses excluded from gross income under an employer-provided educational assistance program (IRC Sec. 127) do not qualify for the credits.

The purpose of these coordinating provisions is to prevent taxpayers from receiving multiple tax benefits for the same expenses.

11

Cost Recovery Deductions

James F. Ivers III

I have something my tax doctor calls "narcotaxis." Within 20 seconds of hearing someone launch into an explanation of tax laws, my eyes become glassy, my body loses all feeling, and I go into a shallow coma.

Russell Baker

Chapter Outline

INTRODUCTION

This chapter will cover the basic income tax rules for capital cost recovery. The most common type of cost recovery deduction is referred to as "depreciation." Cost recovery is an important concept in the tax law because it reflects the intent of Congress to provide income tax benefits for capital investment.

The concept of cost recovery in the income tax law allows taxpayers who invest capital in business and income-producing property to recoup their investment through tax deductions for the cost of the capital investment. Generally, the taxpayer's cost is "recovered" for tax purposes over a specified number of years. This type of cost recovery generally takes the form of depreciation deductions. However, the cost of certain assets may be recovered immediately or "expensed" in the year the asset is placed in service by the taxpayer, up to a specific dollar limit per year.

Of course, allowing deductions for the cost of assets does not completely reimburse the taxpayer for a capital investment. It only makes that cost deductible for income tax purposes over a certain period of time. Still, cost recovery is a powerful concept for taxpayers, since the total cost being recovered may often be leveraged. In addition, deductions for depreciation—the most common type of cost recovery deduction—are most often claimed in tax years in which there is no actual cash expense corresponding to the deduction during the year the deduction is claimed. As a result, tax benefits generated by depreciation are sometimes referred to as "paper" deductions or losses.

A special type of cost recovery deduction called obsolescence is sometimes allowable with respect to an asset that has become useless due to economic, technological, or other changes or advances.

Certain intangible assets (such as goodwill of a business) are eligible for cost recovery through a deduction called amortization. Amortization is a concept that corresponds to depreciation except that it is applied to intangible assets.

The law also imposes special limitations on the cost recovery of certain assets such as automobiles and computers.

Recovery Methods and Recovery Periods

Depreciation and other cost recovery deductions are calculated under a number of different formulas. The amount of the deduction in a given year is basically a function of the following two elements:

- the rate at which the asset's cost is recovered (the "recovery method")
- the period of time over which the cost is recovered (the "recovery period")

The recovery method is typically a mathematical formula that determines how much of an asset's cost can be deducted in a given year. This amount does not represent a loss in the actual economic value of the asset. In fact, many assets eligible for cost recovery may actually be appreciating in economic value during the time their cost is being recovered for tax purposes.

The recovery period is generally a fixed number of years over which the cost is recovered. The recovery period may or may not be based on an estimate of the actual economic useful life of the asset. The only true economic assumption made in connection with cost recovery deductions is that during the time such deductions are being claimed, the asset is somehow being used in connection with the production, or the attempt to produce, income.

The tax law provides recovery periods and recovery methods for each kind of asset that is eligible for cost recovery. These periods and methods may vary for a particular type of asset depending on the year that the asset was placed in service.

The year that an asset eligible for cost recovery is originally placed in service by a particular taxpayer generally determines which cost recovery period and method will be applied to that asset in calculating depreciation or amortization. Depreciable property is categorized by "class" depending on the type of property and the date it is placed in service.

One set of rules now applies to assets placed in service before 1981. Those rules are the more traditional types of cost recovery calculations. A second set of rules generally applies to assets placed in service between 1981 and 1986. These rules are often referred to as the "accelerated cost recovery system" (ACRS). A third set of rules applies to assets placed in service after 1986. This cost recovery system is called the "modified accelerated cost recovery system" (MACRS). The basics of each of these will be examined. First, however, some fundamental requirements for the allowance of cost recovery deductions should be explained.

BASIC CONDITIONS FOR THE ALLOWANCE OF COST RECOVERY DEDUCTIONS

The most basic condition for the allowance of cost recovery deductions is that the asset must be either used in the taxpayer's business activity or held for the production of income. Because of this requirement, assets held for the taxpayer's personal use or enjoyment are not eligible. Such assets would include the taxpayer's personal residence, home furnishings, jewelry, automobiles, and so forth. However, if any personal assets are used for business or for an income-producing activity, all or a part of their cost may become eligible for recovery, based on the percentage of business or investment use for which the asset is placed in service. An example of such a conversion of use would be where a taxpayer owns a car that was previously used only for personal purposes, and places the car in service in her business as a sales representative. In such a case, if the car is used less than 100 percent for business, the cost that is depreciable is correspondingly reduced.

A second condition for the allowance of cost recovery deductions is that the taxpayer must have an ownership interest in the asset. For example, even though depreciable property may be subject to a mortgage, and the mortgagee (lender) has a secured interest in the property, the mortgagor (borrower) is considered to be the equitable owner of the property for the purposes of eligibility for cost recovery deductions. It is also generally true that lessees of property may not claim cost recovery deductions with respect to the property being leased. However, if the lessee makes an improvement to the property, cost recovery may be allowable as discussed later in this chapter.

A third condition for the allowance of cost recovery deductions is that the taxpayer must have a depreciable basis in the property. Without an income tax basis in the property, no cost recovery can be deducted. If a taxpayer buys the property in a taxable sale, the basis is generally equal to the taxpayer's cost, plus the cost of any capital improvements to the property, minus any losses that are properly chargeable to the capital account. As cost recovery deductions are claimed, the taxpayer's basis in the property is correspondingly reduced. Once the taxpayer's basis is reduced to zero, no further cost recovery may be claimed for tax purposes.

A fourth condition for the allowance of cost recovery deductions is that the asset must be considered to have a limited useful life. Buildings, machinery and equipment, vehicles, and intangible assets such as patents, copyrights, and even the goodwill of a business are considered to have a useful life that is limited. On the other hand, the cost of land may not be depreciated since land is not an asset that is considered to be used up or "worn out" over time. One very limited exception to this rule involves deductions for depletion available to industries that extract natural resources from the ground. Generally, however, the portion of the cost of real property rented or used for business purposes that is attributable to the cost of the land is not eligible for cost recovery deductions. This means that when real estate is depreciated, the basis of the property must be properly allocated between the land and building(s) to determine the portion of the basis eligible for cost recovery.

DEPRECIATION DEDUCTIONS FOR PROPERTY PLACED IN SERVICE BEFORE 1981

Sec. 167 of the Internal Revenue Code generally applies to determine the amount of depreciation deductions for tangible assets placed in service by the taxpayer before January 1, 1981. Although the majority of such assets are either no longer in service or have been sold and placed in service by a different taxpayer after 1980, many assets, particularly real estate used in a business or held for the production of income, are still being depreciated under rules in effect before the advent of the ACRS, which applies to assets placed in service in 1981 or later.

With respect to pre-ACRS assets, there are four methods used to compute depreciation. These four methods are

- the straight-line method
- the declining-balance method (which is applied using varying rates of recovery, as explained below)
- the "sum-of-the years-digits" method
- any other consistent method that during the first two-thirds of the depreciable asset's recovery period does not result in cost recovery greater than that obtainable under the declining-balance method. Such methods, including the unit of production method, were employed less frequently than the first three methods listed above.

With respect to certain assets placed in service before 1981, a "salvage value" was subtracted from the property's basis in determining annual depreciation. This was an amount that was presumed to be the asset's economic value at the end of the recovery period. The salvage value concept does not apply with respect to assets placed in service in 1981 or later.

Straight-Line Method

The first method, the straight-line method, is the simplest. It is still used for real estate currently placed in service and for certain other property. Under this method, the taxpayer simply divides the depreciable basis in the property by the number of years of the property's applicable recovery period to arrive at an annual deduction that remains the same over the course of the recovery period. The deduction may be somewhat different in the first and last year of the recovery period if the property is placed in service for depreciation purposes under a "convention" that allows only partial depreciation for the first and last years of the recovery period.

> *Example:* Dominic places property in service in January of this year under the straight-line method of depreciation with a 25-year recovery period. Assume there is no special convention for determining depreciation in the year the property is placed in service. The basis of the property is $100,000. Dominic can claim $4,000 per year ($100,000 ÷ 25) in depreciation deductions for the property.

Declining-Balance Method

The second method, the declining-balance method, uses a somewhat more complex calculation. This method is also used as a recovery method for ACRS and MACRS property placed in service after 1980. Under the declining-balance method, a fixed percentage of the taxpayer's original basis in the depreciable property is allowed in the first year. The following year the same percentage is applied to the basis of the property as adjusted to that point. Unlike the straight-line method that applies a fixed percentage to the initial basis of the property and then allows the same dollar amount of depreciation each year, the declining-balance method applies the same percentage to the property's current adjusted basis each year.

The declining-balance method is typically an accelerated method of depreciation because a percentage higher than that used under the straight-line method is allowable. That percentage cannot be more than twice the percentage used in applying the straight-line method to the original basis of property in the year it is placed in service. For example, assume that property having a cost recovery period of 10 years is depreciated under the straight-line method. Depreciation equal to 10 percent of the property's initial basis would be allowable each year. Under the declining-balance method, up to 20 percent of the property's basis would be allowable each year (this would be the maximum allowable under the declining-balance method or, in this case, the "double-declining-balance" method), but the 20 percent would be applied to the property's basis each year as adjusted for previous depreciation claimed.

"Sum-of-the-Years-Digits" Method

The "sum-of-the-years-digits" method is more esoteric since it is not a standard method used under ACRS or MACRS with respect to property currently being placed in service. Under this method, a changing percentage, not a fixed percentage, is applied to the basis of the property to calculate allowable depreciation. The fraction is determined as follows:

- The numerator of the fraction is the number of years remaining in the cost recovery period as of the year the depreciation is being claimed.
- The denominator of the fraction is the sequential sum of the numbers representing each year in the total recovery period of the property.

In each successive year of the recovery period, the numerator of the fraction will change but the denominator will not. For example, suppose the recovery period for the property being depreciated under the sum-of-the-years-digits method is 5 years. The denominator of the fraction will be equal to 1+2+3+4+5, or 15. In the first year, the numerator of the fraction will be five. Therefore for tax purposes in the first year the property will be depreciated by multiplying its basis by 5/15 or 1/3. In the second year the fraction will be 4/15. Note that the fraction is applied to the original basis of the property under this method (the basis on the date the property was placed in service) and not to the basis as already adjusted for depreciation, as under the declining-balance method.

Other Methods

Other methods that were allowable for pre-ACRS property included the so-called "unit of production" and "machine hours" method along with other unusual depreciation methods. Generally these methods could not be used if they resulted in a more accelerated depreciation schedule than that available under the double-declining-balance method.

The foregoing explanation of basic methods of depreciation is intended to make the basic theory of depreciation computation more understandable. For purposes of this text, specific cost recovery periods and methods used for various assets will be discussed below only in connection with property placed in service after December 31, 1980, under ACRS or MACRS.

The Concept of "Useful Life"

Under ACRS and MACRS, there are fixed recovery periods for each category of depreciable assets. These recovery periods cannot be changed except in certain situations where the taxpayer elects an alternative depreciation system. Under the law in effect before 1981, however, it was sometimes allowable to calculate an asset's recovery period by making an estimate of the actual economic useful life of the property. Depreciation deductions would then be allowed under the applicable depreciation method for the period estimated to be the asset's useful life. Under ACRS and MACRS, the fixed recovery periods may or may not correspond closely to the actual economic life of the asset, and they cannot be altered to more accurately reflect its actual "life span." Therefore the concept of useful life has for the most part been supplanted by the application of fixed recovery periods to specifically defined categories of assets. However, the overall concept of claiming deductions for depreciation is still generally based on the concept that taxpayers should be able to deduct, or "recover" for tax purposes, the amount of an investment in an income-producing asset over the period of time that the asset is useful for its intended purpose.

One rule that still exists in the tax law and is related to the useful life concept is the rule that the basis of depreciable property must be reduced by the amount of depreciation allowable for a given year, even if the depreciation was not actually deducted on the taxpayer's return. This means that if the taxpayer omits a depreciation deduction for a certain asset from a tax return in a given year, the basis of the asset will still be adjusted over the term of its recovery period in a systematic way that corresponds to a systematic use of the asset. If a taxpayer so fails to claim depreciation for a given year, that deduction cannot be "made up" on a later year's return.

On the other hand, the laws applicable to depreciation do not require that the asset actually be used to the same extent for each year of the recovery period. The asset must be placed in service initially for an income-producing purpose. However, even if the asset is used sparingly (or even not at all) in a given year for economic or business reasons, depreciation is still allowable so long as the asset is still available for the purpose for which it was placed in service.

DEDUCTIONS FOR OBSOLESCENCE

Obsolescence occurs when an asset becomes economically useless to the taxpayer who owns it. It may occur as a result of technological or scientific advances in a given business or industry, through changes in applicable laws that essentially prohibit the use of the asset, or simply because of changes in economic conditions that remove profitability from the use of the asset. Another form of obsolescence is where the asset's actual condition deteriorates much more rapidly than was expected so that the asset can no longer be used for the purpose for which it was placed in service. Clearly, obsolescence involves a loss of usefulness resulting from abnormal conditions rather than from reasonable and expected wear and tear on the property.

In such cases, a deduction is available for the undepreciated basis the taxpayer has left in the obsolete asset. The deduction becomes available at the point in time when the taxpayer can determine with reasonable certainty that the asset has or will become obsolete. At that time, the taxpayer's remaining basis in the asset may be deducted ratably between the time when obsolescence becomes reasonably certain and the time of actual obsolescence. These two situations may happen at the same time or at different times. Obsolescence is still available under ACRS and MACRS, as distinguished from the concept of salvage value, which does not apply under ACRS and MACRS.

ACRS AND MACRS

The advent of the accelerated cost recovery system (ACRS) in 1981 significantly modified the way in which the tax law allows the recovery of investment capital for income tax purposes. Since ACRS, the term "depreciation" has been somewhat supplanted in tax parlance by the term "cost recovery." Although the difference in terminology does not indicate a radical departure from traditional concepts of depreciation, there are significant theoretical differences between the older system of depreciation and ACRS (along with its later counterpart, the modified accelerated cost recovery system or MACRS). For example, fixed recovery periods are assigned to assets eligible for cost recovery, rather than allowing an evaluation and estimate of the asset's actual economic life to be made to determine the applicable period of cost recovery. These fixed periods are generally shorter than what taxpayers would typically estimate to be the asset's actual span of "useful life." Most assets (but not real property) are eligible for "accelerated" methods of cost recovery (that is, depreciation). The term "accelerated" in this context means any method of cost recovery that provides a higher deduction in the earlier years of the asset's recovery period than that which would be provided by a straight-line recovery method.

ACRS applies to depreciable assets placed in service between January 1, 1981, and December 31, 1986. MACRS generally applies to assets placed in service after December 31, 1986. Therefore the determination of the date that property is "placed in service" for an income-producing purpose that qualifies it for cost recovery will dictate which system applies to it and consequently what the asset's applicable recovery method and applicable recovery period will be. ACRS and its progeny MACRS are substantially different with respect to both the recovery periods and the recovery methods assigned to specific types of assets. Both systems generally classify assets in groups according to their applicable recovery periods; hence the terms "5-year property class," "15-year property class," and so on. ACRS and MACRS are described under Sec. 168 of the Internal Revenue Code.

First, the applicable property classes and recovery methods for property placed in service after December 31, 1986, under the MACRS system will be examined. The property classes and recovery methods of the original ACRS system applicable to assets placed in service between 1981 and 1986 will then be summarized.

THE MODIFIED ACCELERATED COST RECOVERY SYSTEM (MACRS)

MACRS currently applies to most depreciable property placed in service after 1986. Certain property is not depreciated under the MACRS system including most public utility property, motion pictures, sound recordings, intangible property, and property for which a depreciation method not determined by an annual recovery period (such as the unit of production method that is available for certain property) has been elected by the taxpayer. However, most depreciable property placed in service after 1986 is governed by MACRS.

MACRS Recovery Periods

The property "classes" or applicable recovery periods for MACRS are as follows. (The components of this list are not all-inclusive.)

- 3-year property. This property class includes most racehorses, tractors, breeding hogs, certain manufacturing tools, qualified rent-to-own property, and certain computer software that is readily available to the public.
- 5-year property. This class includes cars, most trucks, computers, copiers, typewriters, solar and wind energy equipment, breeding and dairy cattle, and semi-conductor manufacturing equipment.
- 7-year property. This class includes office furniture and fixtures, most machinery and industrial equipment, and railroad equipment.
- 10-year property. This class includes property used in petroleum refining, fruit-bearing trees and vines, and barges, tugboats, and other water transportation vessels.
- 15-year property. This class includes telephone distribution plants, service station buildings, pipelines, billboards, and land improvements such as roads, sidewalks, and bridges.
- 20-year class. This class includes certain farm buildings and municipal sewers.
- 27 1/2-year class. This important class of property includes residential real estate.

- 39-year class. This class includes nonresidential rental property such as office buildings, factories, and warehouses. If the property was placed in service before May 13, 1993, the recovery period is 31 1/2 years.

MACRS Recovery Methods

The cost recovery methods used for MACRS property are assigned by property class. Assets in the 3-, 5-, 7-, and 10-year classes are generally depreciated under the double- (or "200 percent") declining-balance method with a switch to the straight-line method at the point where the straight-line method produces a higher deduction. Property in the 15- and 20-year classes is depreciated under the 150 percent declining-balance method with a similar switch to the straight-line method. Property included under the 27 1/2-year, 31 1/2-year, or 39-year classes is depreciated under the straight-line method. This includes all real estate, both residential and nonresidential. Therefore, as it applies to real estate, the modified accelerated cost recovery system is really not "accelerated" at all.

The following tables illustrate MACRS depreciation schedules in the form of depreciation percentages over the property's useful life.

TABLE 11-1
MACRS Depreciation System—Personal Property
**Method: 200 percent or 150 percent declining-balance switching to
      straight-line**
Convention: Half-year

If the recovery year is	If the recovery period is					
	200 percent				150 percent	
	3 years	5 years	7 years	10 years	15 years	20 years
1	33.33	20.00	14.29	10.00	5.00	3.750
2	44.45	32.00	24.49	18.00	9.50	7.219
3	14.81	19.20	17.49	14.40	8.55	6.677
4	7.41	11.52	12.49	11.52	7.70	6.177
5		11.52	8.93	9.22	6.93	5.713
6		5.76	8.92	7.37	6.23	5.285
7			8.93	6.55	5.90	4.888
8			4.46	6.55	5.90	4.522
9				6.56	5.91	4.462
10				6.55	5.90	4.461
11				3.28	5.91	4.462
12					5.90	4.461
13					5.91	4.462
14					5.90	4.461
15					5.91	4.462
16					2.95	4.461
17						4.462
18						4.461
19						4.462
20						4.461
21						2.231

Example: Jimmy places office furniture costing $10,000 in service this year. The recovery period for the property is 7 years. Jimmy's first-year depreciation deduction (assuming he does not use the expensing election discussed later in this chapter) is $1,429 ($10,000 x .1429).

TABLE 11-2
MACRS Depreciation—Real Estate
Method: Straight-line
Convention: Mid-month
Recovery period: 27.5 years

Residential Rental Property					
The month in the first recovery year the property is placed in service:					
	1	2	3	4	5	6
---	---	---	---	---	---	---
First Year	3.485%	3.182%	2.879%	2.576%	2.273%	1.970%
Years 2–27	3.636%	3.636%	3.636%	3.636%	3.636%	3.636%

	7	8	9	10	11	12
First Year	1.667%	1.364%	1.061%	0.758%	0.455%	0.152%
Years 2–27	3.636%	3.636%	3.636%	3.636%	3.636%	3.636%

TABLE 11-3
MACRS Depreciation—Real Estate
Method: Straight-line
Convention: Mid-month
Recovery period: 31.5 years

Nonresidential Real Property (Placed in service prior to May 13, 1993)					
The month in the first recovery year the property is placed in service:					
	1	2	3	4	5	6
---	---	---	---	---	---	---
First Year	3.042%	2.778%	2.513%	2.249%	1.984%	1.720%
Years 2–31	3.175%	3.175%	3.175%	3.175%	3.175%	3.175%

	7	8	9	10	11	12
First Year	1.455%	1.190%	0.926%	0.661%	0.397%	0.132%
Years 2–31	3.175%	3.175%	3.175%	3.175%	3.175%	3.175%

TABLE 11-4 MACRS Depreciation—Real Estate Method: Straight-line Convention: Mid-month Recovery period: 39 years					
Nonresidential Real Property (Placed in service on or after May 13, 1993)					
The month in the first recovery year the property is placed in service:					
1	2	3	4	5	6
First Year 2.461%	2.247%	2.033%	1.819%	1.605%	1.391%
Years 2–39 2.564%	2.564%	2.564%	2.564%	2.564%	2.564%

	7	8	9	10	11	12
First Year	1.177%	0.963%	0.749%	0.535%	0.321%	0.107%
Years 2–39	2.564%	2.564%	2.564%	2.564%	2.564%	2.564%

Example: Caroline places nonresidential real property in service for cost recovery purposes in April of this year. The portion of her basis in the property allocable to the building on the property is $150,000. Her first-year deduction for cost recovery will be $2,728.50 ($150,000 x .01819).

Cost Recovery Conventions

Certain "conventions" are required to determine how much cost recovery will be allowed for the year the asset is placed in service and the year when it is disposed of or otherwise retired from cost recovery. Assets in property classes of 20 or fewer years are subject to a "half-year" convention for cost recovery. This means that the equivalent of 6 months of depreciation is allowed for the asset in the year it is placed in service. The same convention applies in the year the asset is disposed of or in the last year of its recovery period. Since there is a half-year's depreciation in the first year of the recovery period and a half-year's depreciation in the last year, assets are actually depreciated over a period of taxable years that is one year longer than the statutory recovery period.

A special convention applies if more than 40 percent of all property placed in service that year and otherwise subject to the half-year convention is placed in service during the last 3 months of the taxable year. In such cases, a "mid-quarter" convention will be applied to all property otherwise eligible for the half-year convention. The property will be depreciated for the first year as if it had been placed in service in the middle of the quarter in which it was actually placed in service. The purpose of this rule is to prevent the taxpayer from claiming 6 months of depreciation for assets placed in service toward the end of the year.

For real estate, a "mid-month" convention applies. Depreciable real estate placed in service (or disposed of) during any month of the taxable year is treated as being placed in service or disposed of in the middle of that month in calculating allowable depreciation.

Alternatives under MACRS

There are elective alternatives available with respect to MACRS property. First, taxpayers may elect the straight-line method of depreciation for classes of property that are eligible for the declining-balance method. The straight-line method is then used over the property's MACRS recovery period.

There is a second type of elective treatment under an alternative depreciation system (ADS). ADS allows taxpayers to elect the 150 percent declining-balance method for certain property otherwise eligible for the 200 percent declining-balance method, or to elect the straight-line method for property otherwise eligible for the 150 percent declining-balance method. Under this election, such property is generally depreciated over a recovery period longer than its MACRS recovery period.

However, the longer ADS recovery periods do not apply to most tangible personal property placed in service after December 31, 1998, if the taxpayer elects the 150 percent declining-balance method in lieu of the 200 percent declining-balance method. In such cases, the regular MACRS recovery period is used with the election of the 150 percent declining-balance method and not a longer recovery period. The same calculation is used for such property in computing depreciation for purposes of the alternative minimum tax (AMT). The purpose of this election is to provide equivalent treatment for such property for both AMT and regular tax purposes by making the 150 percent declining-balance method available under the regular tax calculation. In other words, by using the election to depreciate property under the 150 percent method rather than the 200 percent declining-balance method, the taxpayer can use the same depreciation method and recovery period for both regular tax and alternative minimum tax purposes. The AMT is discussed in more detail in chapter 15.

As previously mentioned, straight-line depreciation may be elected for MACRS property over either its regular recovery period or over ADS recovery periods that are generally longer than the regular MACRS period (except for certain assets such as automobiles and qualified technological equipment). For real estate, which in any circumstance is subject to straight-line depreciation under MACRS, the ADS election is available to depreciate the property over a 40-year period.

Alternative depreciation may be elected on a property-by-property basis for real estate. For other property, it is elected on a property class basis.

Improvements by Lessees

If a lessee makes an addition or improvement to real property subject to a lease, the lessee may deduct the cost of the addition or improvement under MACRS. The prescribed recovery period is used regardless of the term or remaining term of the lease. The property class of the improvement is determined by reference to the property to which the improvement is made. If the lessee does not retain the improvement at the end of the lease, the lessee may deduct the amount of the remaining basis in the improvement at the time the lease is terminated.

DEPRECIATION OF PROPERTY PLACED IN SERVICE BETWEEN 1981 AND 1986 (ACRS)

The original accelerated cost recovery system (ACRS) generally provided faster cost recovery than does the current MACRS system. At this time only certain real property originally placed in service under the original ACRS would still be in service for tax purposes. Some of the major differences between the original system and the current MACRS are as follows:

- Automobiles. Autos were depreciated over a 3-year period using a recovery rate similar to the 175 percent declining-balance method. Under MACRS, autos are in the 5-year class of property.
- Office furniture, fixtures, equipment, and heavy machinery. These assets were depreciated over a 5-year period using a 175 percent declining-balance method. Under MACRS, these assets are depreciated over 7 years, although the 200 percent declining-balance method applies.
- Real property. Under ACRS, depreciable real estate was recovered over a 15-, 18-, or 19-year recovery period depending on the date the property was placed in service. Real estate was also eligible for an accelerated method of depreciation corresponding to the 175 percent declining balance method. Under the current MACRS, real property is depreciated using the straight-line method over a recovery period of 27.5 years (residential) or 39 years (nonresidential). Clearly, MACRS cut back substantially on the cost recovery benefits associated with real estate investments.

There were also elective alternatives under the original ACRS. The alternative to the ACRS recovery methods and periods was the straight-line method of depreciation with recovery periods significantly longer than the regular prescribed ACRS periods. For real estate, alternative depreciation could be elected on a property-by-property basis. For other classes of property, the election was made by property class.

RECAPTURE OF DEPRECIATION DEDUCTIONS

When an asset that has been depreciated for tax purposes is later sold or exchanged in a taxable transaction, all or a portion of prior depreciation deductions claimed with respect to the asset may be "recaptured." The term "recapture" in this context means the taxation of certain gain from the sale of the asset as ordinary income rather than as capital gain.

Personal Property

With respect to depreciable tangible personal property (as distinguished from depreciable real property), all depreciation claimed is generally subject to recapture upon the sale of the property regardless of the depreciation method used. This means that gain from the sale of the property will be taxable as ordinary income to the extent of the cumulative depreciation deductions claimed for the property.

> *Example:* Sophie sells a piece of machinery that was used in her business as an architect. Her adjusted basis in the machine at the time of the sale is $3,600. The machine is sold for $6,800. Sophie has claimed a total of $3,000 of depreciation deductions for the machine. Her realized gain from the sale is $3,200 ($6,800 sale price – $3,600 adjusted basis). Of that $3,200 in gain, $3,000 is taxable as ordinary income because of depreciation recapture. The balance of Sophie's gain ($200) is taxable as capital gain.

Real Property

The recapture rules for depreciable real estate are different from those that apply to personal property. Whether there is recapture on real property depends on the method of depreciation used for the property and the date the property was placed in service.

Only real estate that has been depreciated under an accelerated method (that is, a more rapid recovery method than the straight-line method) will be subject to depreciation recapture. Therefore real property placed in service after 1986 under MACRS is not subject to recapture since it is depreciated under the straight-line method. Property placed in service between 1981 and 1986 under ACRS may be subject to recapture. The amount of depreciation recaptured depends on whether the property is residential or nonresidential real property. For residential property, only that amount of depreciation claimed that is in excess of the amount allowable under the straight-line method is recaptured. For nonresidential property, there is generally recapture of the full amount of depreciation unless the straight-line method is elected for the property.

For real property placed in service before 1981, somewhat different recapture rules apply that are beyond the scope of this text.

It is also important to know that a special long-term maximum capital-gains tax rate of 25 percent applies to the portion of capital gain that is attributable to depreciation upon the sale of real property by an individual taxpayer. This 25 percent rate is higher than the regular maximum capital-gains rate of 20 percent that applies to individual taxpayers. The rule imposing a 25 percent capital-gains rate is separate from the depreciation recapture rules and may be applied in addition to those rules. The recapture rules, as previously stated, may tax a portion of the capital gain as ordinary income. The capital-gain and loss rules are discussed in more detail in chapter 14.

ELECTION TO EXPENSE CERTAIN DEPRECIABLE BUSINESS ASSETS

Under IRC Sec. 179, taxpayers other than trusts, estates, or certain noncorporate lessors may elect to deduct or "expense" the full cost of certain depreciable property in the year such property is placed in service. This election applies only to depreciable tangible personal property that is acquired by purchase for active use in the taxpayer's trade or business; such property is referred to as "Sec. 179 property." Under this definition, real estate does not qualify for the "expensing election." Also other depreciable property that is held for the production of income but not used in a trade or business (that is, investment property) does not qualify.

There are dollar amount limitations on the amount of property that may be expensed under this rule. The limit is currently on an increasing schedule—by reference to the calendar year in which the taxpayer's taxable year begins—as follows:

2000	$20,000
2001, 2002	$24,000
2003 and thereafter	$25,000

There is an additional rule that may further limit the first year expensing election for Sec. 179 property. The applicable dollar amount limitation is reduced by one dollar for each dollar of the cost of qualifying property in excess of $200,000 that the taxpayer places in service during the taxable year.

Example: In the taxable year 2001, Bear Foot places $215,000 of Sec. 179 property in service. Mr. Foot must reduce his expensing allowance by $15,000 ($215,000 – $200,000). Therefore he may elect to expense an amount up to only $9,000 of the cost of the property ($24,000 – $15,000). To avoid the $200,000 threshold amount, Mr. Foot may have been better off taxwise if he had placed some of the property in service in the following taxable year.

The amount of the expensing allowance for any year is also limited by the taxpayer's taxable income derived from the business for the year (determined without regard to the expensing election). Any amount disallowed under this limitation may be carried forward to future tax years.

Any amount claimed under the expensing election reduces the tax basis of the asset. Therefore, the amount of depreciation deductions allowable for the expensed property will be reduced, perhaps to zero, by the election to expense the property's cost.

Also, to the extent that the cost of property is "expensed" in its first year, gain on the subsequent sale of the property will be taxable as ordinary income rather than as capital gain under the recapture rules.

The expensing election is a substantial incentive for capital investment by business taxpayers. For tax purposes it essentially treats property that would otherwise have to be depreciated over a cost recovery schedule as a current expense that is immediately deductible.

COST RECOVERY LIMITATIONS ON AUTOMOBILES AND OTHER "LISTED" PROPERTY

"Listed" Property

Certain depreciable assets are subject to special limitations on cost recovery deductions. These assets include passenger automobiles having unloaded gross vehicle weight of 6,000 pounds or less, computers and peripheral equipment, and any property of a type generally used for entertainment, recreation, or amusement.

If such property is not used more than 50 percent for business purposes, depreciation of the property must be computed under the MACRS alternative depreciation system (ADS). This means that straight-line depreciation must be used over the applicable ADS recovery period. For automobiles, the ADS recovery period is 5 years, the same as the regular MACRS period. For computers, the recovery period is also 5 years.

The amount eligible for cost recovery of any asset is limited to the percentage of the cost of the asset that corresponds to the percentage of its business use. If such business use is not more than 50 percent, expensing of such assets under IRC Sec. 179 is effectively prohibited because of the requirement that ADS depreciation be used.

If an employee uses personally owned listed property in the course of his or her employment, no depreciation is permitted unless the use of the listed property is for the employer's convenience and is required as a condition of employment.

With respect to computers, the term "listed property" does not include computers used exclusively at a regular business establishment that are owned or leased by the person operating that establishment. An office in a home is treated as a business establishment for this purpose only if it is a qualified home office under the home office deduction rules. For such computers, the percentage of business use does not have to be monitored in order to claim full cost recovery.

"Luxury" Automobiles

There are also annual dollar amount limitations on cost recovery for so-called "luxury automobiles." The limitations apply to both MACRS depreciation and the first-year expensing election. Therefore the first-year expensing election described previously in this chapter cannot be used to avoid the limitations. The dollar amount limits are indexed annually for inflation. For vehicles placed in service in 2000, the limitations are as follows:

Year of Recovery Period	Cost Recovery Limit
First	$3,060
Second	$4,900
Third	$2,950
Fourth and subsequent years	$1,775

Example: Susie purchased a car in 2000 that she uses 100 percent for business. The cost of the car was $40,000. Under the MACRS tables, Susie's depreciation deduction for 2000 would be $8,000 ($40,000 x .20). However, her deduction is limited to $3,060 in 2000 regardless of whether she depreciates the car or uses the first-year expensing election.

If the dollar limitations result in the taxpayer having unrecovered basis in the vehicles after the normal 5-year recovery period is over, the maximum amount for the fourth year can be claimed in succeeding taxable years until the vehicle is fully depreciated. Note that these amounts are maximum amounts. If the depreciation deduction under the normal MACRS calculation is less than the maximum dollar amount, then the MACRS calculation applies. If the vehicle is not used 100 percent for business, the dollar amount limitations are applied first. They are applied before the reduction in allowable depreciation that reflects the percentage of personal use is applied. This ensures that deductions allowable for vehicles used partially for personal purposes will not be eligible for 100 percent of the dollar amount limitations.

The limitations apply to passenger vehicles that are treated as "listed property." Not included in the definition of "listed property" are trucks or vans having gross vehicle weight of over 6,000 pounds, ambulances, hearses, and vehicles used directly in the business of transporting people or property for hire. Modified limitations apply to certain clean-fuel passenger automobiles.

DEDUCTIONS FOR AMORTIZATION OF INTANGIBLE ASSETS

Certain intangible assets may be "amortized" for income tax purposes as a means of allowing taxpayers to recover their cost. The concept of amortization is similar to that of depreciation, although from a conceptual standpoint it is unrelated to the idea of physical wear and tear over the period of an asset's "useful life." The cost of intangibles eligible for amortization is recovered ratably over a 180-month period under IRC Sec. 197. Since the recovery period is based on months rather than taxable years, no cost recovery timing "conventions" are applied to the asset when it is placed in service or when it is disposed of. The cost of the asset is recovered proportionately over the 180-month period. The amortization calculation is similar conceptually to the calculation under the straight-line method of depreciation.

Assets that are eligible for the 180-month amortization deduction include

- the goodwill of a business
- the "going concern" value of a business
- a company's "workforce in place" including its composition and terms and conditions of its employment
- business books and records, information bases, and operating systems (but not computer software available for public purchase and subject to a nonexclusive license)
- patents and copyrights acquired in a transaction involving an acquisition of an interest in a business
- formulas, processes, designs, know-how, and similar property
- licenses, permits, or other rights granted by a governmental unit
- franchises, trademarks, and trade names (but not including professional sports franchises)
- a covenant not to compete entered into in connection with an acquisition of an interest or a substantial portion of an interest in a trade or business

To qualify for amortization, the asset must be used in a trade or business or held for the production of income. If it is business property, it is also treated as being "depreciable" property specifically for purposes of special favorable tax treatment under IRC Sec. 1231 as discussed in chapter 14. However, the property eligible for amortization may not also be depreciated.

There are special limitations regarding the income tax recognition of losses realized upon the disposition of amortizable intangible assets. Basically, if a taxpayer acquires a group of such assets in the same transaction (or in a related transaction), no loss upon disposition can be recognized until the taxpayer disposes of all the intangibles so acquired.

These rules generally apply to intangible assets acquired after August 10, 1993.

12

Limitations on "Passive Activity" Losses and Credits

James F. Ivers III

[American tax laws] are constantly changing as our elected representatives seek new ways to ensure that whatever tax advice we receive is incorrect.

Dave Barry

Chapter Outline

INTRODUCTION

Sec. 469 of the Internal Revenue Code deals with the limitations on tax benefits associated with "passive activities." This section was enacted because Congress was concerned with the availability of substantial tax "losses" (deductions in excess of income) claimed by taxpayers with respect to business activities in which the taxpayer owns an interest but does not substantially participate in on a regular and continuous basis. The most common examples of such activities include rental activities (particularly rental real estate) and the ownership of limited partnership interests and similar types of business ownership. The rules were designed to reduce losses of tax revenues resulting from so-called "tax shelters."

LIMITS ON DEDUCTIBILITY OF LOSSES

Basically, the rules limit deductions for excess passive activity losses. Excess passive activity losses are the excess of otherwise allowable deductions from the taxpayer's passive activities over the amount of income from the taxpayer's passive activities. In other words, deductions for net losses from the taxpayer's passive activities are not allowed.

> *Example:* Sporty has $50,000 of income from passive activities and $65,000 of deductions from passive activities. The amount of Sporty's deductions in excess of his passive income ($15,000) may not be deducted on his current tax return.

In general, the taxpayer's passive losses and passive income are aggregated for purposes of the limitation, so that losses from one passive activity may offset income from another passive activity. There are restrictions on such aggregation of passive activities for purposes of the overall limitations that are beyond the scope of this text.

Excess passive activity losses are disallowed on the taxpayer's current tax return. However, for tax purposes such excess losses are not lost forever but are deferred. Excess passive activity losses are allowable in subsequent tax years in which the taxpayer has excess passive income. The losses carried over are then allowed to the extent of the taxpayer's excess passive income. Furthermore, any remaining excess passive activity losses are fully allowed in the year in which the taxpayer disposes of his or her entire interest in the passive activity.

PASSIVE ACTIVITY CREDITS

Similar limitations apply to excess passive activity credits. If the passive activity qualifies the taxpayer for tax credits that would otherwise create a net loss from the activity, thereby creating an offset for the passive activity credits against tax liability generated by the taxpayer's other (nonpassive) income, then such credits are disallowed in the current year to the extent they would offset tax liability not generated by the passive activity. Unused credits may be carried over to subsequent taxable years subject to the same limitation.

APPLICATION OF PASSIVE ACTIVITY LIMITATIONS

A "passive activity" may be generally defined as a trade or business in which the taxpayer does not "materially participate." (The term "material participation" will be defined below.) However, rental activities of the taxpayer are subject to the passive activity limitations, regardless of whether the taxpayer materially participates in the activity or not. There is also a special, and more favorable, rule that applies to extractive industries. Under this rule, any direct ownership of a working interest in a gas or oil venture is not treated as a passive activity, regardless of whether the taxpayer materially participates in the activity, so long as the taxpayer is not a limited partner in the activity. A limited partnership interest in a business activity is a prime example of the type of ownership that the passive activity limitations were designed to cover.

The passive activity limitations do not apply to all taxpayers. The limitations apply to individual taxpayers, estates, trusts, certain personal service corporations, and any "closely held" corporation. The limitations also effectively apply to partnerships and "S" corporations because they are "pass-through" entities in which the reporting of income and losses flows through to the individual owners. If the owners have an insufficient degree of participation in the business of the entity, then the passive loss limitations will be applied on their returns.

A corporation is a "closely held" corporation for purposes of the passive loss limitations if more than 50 percent of the value of its outstanding stock is owned by five or fewer individuals at any time during the last half of the corporation's taxable year. Although the passive loss limitations apply to such corporations, the rules are more lenient as explained below. The rules apply fully to personal service corporations, which for passive loss purposes are defined as corporations "the principal activity of which is the performance of personal services and such services are substantially performed by employee-owners." The passive loss limitations do not apply to C corporations that are not closely held corporations or personal service corporations.

DETERMINATION OF "PASSIVE" INCOME AND LOSSES

Categories of Income

The basic operation of the passive activity limitations is calculated by first dividing the income of the taxpayer into three general categories:

- portfolio income
- active income
- passive income

"Portfolio income" includes dividends, interest, royalties, income from annuities, and the gain or loss realized from the disposition of property that generates portfolio income for the taxpayer. It would also include gain or loss realized from the disposition of property held for investment, even if the property was not income producing. Portfolio income does not include any income generated in the conduct of a business.

After a taxpayer's portfolio income has been segregated, then the remaining income of the taxpayer is characterized as either active or passive income. This characterization essentially depends on whether the taxpayer has material participation in the activity generating the income. Wages and other compensation are treated as active income because they are generated by the efforts of the taxpayer. The characterization of income from a pass-through business entity such as a partnership or S corporation depends on whether the taxpayer materially participates in the activity of the entity.

After income has been characterized, the passive loss limitations are applied. If a taxpayer has a net loss from passive activities (that is, total expenses and other deductions from passive activities exceed the income from passive activities), the loss cannot be used to offset active income or portfolio income. In the case of a closely held corporation (but not a personal service corporation), excess passive losses can be used to offset active income but cannot be used to offset portfolio income.

Material Participation

A taxpayer will be treated as materially participating in an activity only if the taxpayer is involved in the operations of the activity on a regular, continuous, and substantial basis. Generally, no limited partner in a limited partnership is treated as materially participating in the partnership's activity. There are special rules for closely held corporations and professional service corporations regarding material participation. These rules involve the nature of the corporation's activity and the extent to which the owners materially participate in that activity.

Rental Activities

The general rule for rental activity is that such activity is treated as a passive one regardless of the taxpayer's participation. However, there is an exception for taxpayers who essentially work full-time in the real property business. If the taxpayer performs more than 750 hours of service during the taxable year in a real property business or businesses, and that participation represents more than one-half of the total hours of service provided by the taxpayer for active businesses during the year, then the rental activities for that taxpayer are not automatically treated as passive activities. Services performed as an employee do not count toward the 750-hour requirement. If the taxpayer qualifies for this exception to the rental activity rules, the taxpayer must still meet the requirements of material participation in the real estate activity to have income and deductions from the activity classified as active.

The "Active Participation" Exception

Even though rental activities are generally classified as passive, there is an important exception for rental real estate activities known as the "active participation" exception. This exception applies to individual taxpayers only. It provides a significant opportunity for individuals who own rental real estate to avoid the passive loss limitations. To qualify, the taxpayer must have "active participation" in the real estate activity. This definition is completely separate and different from the definition of "material participation" that generally applies to a taxpayer's activities to determine whether they are active or passive.

To meet the standard of active participation, a taxpayer must own at least a 10 percent interest in the rental real estate (determined by reference to the value of the property) and must also participate in the rental activity. However, the strict standard of material participation need not be met in order to qualify under the active participation standard.

Qualifying taxpayers may deduct up to $25,000 per year of net losses from the real estate activity from their active or portfolio income if the active participation standard is met. If the taxpayer's adjusted gross income (AGI) exceeds $100,000, the $25,000 allowance is reduced by 50 percent of the amount by which AGI exceeds $100,000. Any losses in excess of the active participation allowance may be carried forward to succeeding tax years, subject to the same limitations.

> *Example:* Buddy owns and manages a residential rental property. This year his net loss generated by the property for tax purposes is $21,000. Buddy's adjusted gross income this year is $120,000. Therefore his $25,000 allowance is reduced by $10,000 [($120,000 − $100,000) x .5]. His maximum allowance under the active participation exception is $15,000 ($25,000 − $10,000). As a result, only $15,000 of his $21,000 of losses can be deducted this year.

CONCLUSION

This chapter is merely a simplified summary of the passive activity limitations. Treasury regulations cover many complex issues regarding the definition of various activities, as well as the aggregation rules for multiple activities and many other related topics. Since many passive activities involve assets eligible for cost recovery deductions, those deductions as well as deductions for loan interest and other expenses may be restricted by the passive activity limitations where the total deductions attributable to a taxpayer's passive activity exceed the income generated by it.

13

Sales and Exchanges of Property

James F. Ivers III

Another difference between death and taxes is that death is frequently painless.

Anonymous

Death and taxes and childbirth. There's never any convenient time for any of them.

Margaret Mitchell

Chapter Outline

INTRODUCTION

The federal income tax law applies to the sale or exchange of property by generally requiring that the sale or exchange be treated as a taxable event. A taxable event can be roughly defined as a transaction that results in the recognition of income or loss for federal income tax purposes. There are many types of taxable events other than the sale or exchange of property (such as the receipt of wages or other compensation for services rendered, or the receipt of income from property held for investment). In any event, property sales are an important element in the collection of tax revenues, and these transactions involve some of their own basic principles of taxation.

REALIZATION AND RECOGNITION OF GAIN OR LOSS

In order to determine the taxable amount resulting from the sale of property, the amount of gain or loss realized from the sale must be ascertained. In order to calculate realized gain or loss, two elements of the transaction must be determined: the amount realized from the sale or exchange, and the taxpayer's basis in the asset transferred.

The "amount realized" is simply the value of all property received in exchange for the asset transferred. This would be the amount of any money received for the property, plus the fair market value of any other property received as consideration for the property transferred.

The taxpayer's "basis" in the property transferred (or "adjusted basis" as referred to in IRC Sec. 1001) is generally the taxpayer's cost for the property, subject to certain adjustments. These adjustments may include reductions in basis for previously claimed depreciation deductions, or increases in basis for additions or improvements that the taxpayer made to the property. The rules for basis adjustments will be discussed later in this chapter. If the taxpayer previously acquired the property in a taxable exchange, the cost for the property would be equal to the fair market value of the property given up at the time of that exchange. The cost basis rule generally applies to determine the taxpayer's initial basis in the property when it is acquired, unless the property is acquired in a nontaxable transaction, as explained below. The taxpayer's basis in an asset must be known to calculate the amount of realized gain or loss upon the sale of the asset, as well as the amount of any depreciation or other cost recovery deductions available with respect to that asset.

Once the amount realized and the taxpayer's adjusted basis in the property have been determined, realized gain or loss is calculated by subtracting the adjusted basis from the amount realized in the sale or exchange.

> *Example:* Alexandra pays $7,500 for a violin and later sells it for $10,000. There have been no adjustments to the violin's tax basis. Alexandra's realized gain from the sale is $2,500 ($10,000 − $7,500).

As so calculated, realized gain may be described as the economic gain that a taxpayer obtains from the sale or exchange of property. As a general rule, any gain *realized* on the sale or exchange of property must also be *recognized* for federal income tax purposes; that is, it must be included in the taxpayer's gross income for the year it is realized.

Any income a taxpayer realizes is includible in gross income unless some provision of the Internal Revenue Code specifically states otherwise. The Internal Revenue Code does contain several provisions that define sales or exchanges of property in which realized gain does not have to be recognized for tax purposes. These exchanges of property, such as like-kind exchanges or qualifying exchanges of insurance contracts (discussed later in this chapter), do not result in current recognition of gain. Still, in such transactions realized gain is not altogether eliminated but merely deferred to a later date when the taxpayer disposes of the property received in the tax-deferred exchange. This deferral (but not elimination) of realized gain is accomplished largely through the mechanism of a "substituted" or "carryover" basis, as explained below.

In a tax-deferred exchange, the taxpayer generally carries his or her basis in the old property for tax purposes over to the newly acquired property rather than obtaining cost or fair market value basis in the new property. In this way, any untaxed gain in the old property is carried over to the new property and preserved until the new property is sold in a taxable transaction.

In certain other situations, the Code provides that a sale of property will not be taxed at all. This is accomplished by providing that the gain realized from such a sale will be excludible from the selling taxpayer's gross income. In such transactions, no carryover of basis applies to any newly acquired property because the realized gain is not merely being deferred, it is being eliminated. This makes an exclusion a significantly more beneficial provision than one that merely defers tax on realized gain. The most common example of a sale of property that produces gain excludible from gross income is the sale of a taxpayer's principal residence. The rules for this exclusion will also be discussed later in this chapter.

If property is sold or exchanged at a loss (that is, the amount realized is less than the basis of the asset sold or exchanged), the loss is generally not deductible unless the transaction was in connection with a trade or business or an activity entered into for profit. The deductibility of losses is discussed in chapter 8, and the special rules for capital losses are discussed in chapter 14.

CONSIDERATIONS REGARDING A TAXPAYER'S BASIS IN PROPERTY

Nontaxable Exchanges

As previously stated, a taxpayer's basis in property is generally the cost of the property subject to certain adjustments. However, in a nontaxable exchange the basis of property acquired is determined by reference to the same taxpayer's basis in the property transferred or given up in the exchange. Such a basis is typically referred to as a substituted basis. This is different from the cost basis rule that applies to assets acquired in taxable transactions. A more detailed discussion of how basis is determined in a nontaxable exchange of property is presented later in this chapter.

Gifts

In the case of a gift, the taxpayer receiving the gift (the donee) generally has a basis equal to that of the same property in the hands of the taxpayer making the gift (the donor). This type of basis calculation is somewhat different from the calculation used in a nontaxable exchange. This is because the taxpayer's basis in the property is determined by reference to another taxpayer's basis in the same property rather than by reference to the same taxpayer's basis in a different property previously owned. This basis rule may be referred to as a carryover basis.

> *Example:* Conner receives stock in Specific Motors as a gift from his father. The father's basis in the stock is $5,000. Its fair market value is $20,000. Conner's basis in the stock will be $5,000, the same as his father's basis.

Variations in the Application of Cost Basis Rules

Regarding the general rule of cost basis, certain variations in how the rule is applied should be examined. The following circumstances illustrate how the cost basis rule is applied in certain specific types of situations:

- The taxpayer may have received the property as compensation for services rendered. In such a case, the taxpayer receiving the property will have a basis equal to the fair market value of the property at the time it was received. This amount would also generally be the amount of income that would be taxable as a result of the payment of compensation in the form of property.

- If the taxpayer purchases property and takes a mortgage (or assumes a mortgage) on the property to finance a purchase, the taxpayer's basis is equal to the entire cost of the property including the amount subject to the mortgage.

- Certain difficulties may arise in determining basis when a taxpayer wishes to sell publicly traded securities such as stocks or bonds. If the taxpayer has bought the same stocks or bonds at different times and has a different basis in the units or shares depending on when they were purchased, one of two rules will be used to determine cost basis. If the taxpayer can adequately identify the actual shares or units being sold, then the basis of those specific shares or units can be used as his or her basis in calculating realized gain or loss. If the taxpayer cannot specifically identify the shares sold, basis will be calculated using a "first-in, first-out" (FIFO) method of identification whereby the shares the taxpayer first purchased are deemed to be sold first. However, when a taxpayer sells or redeems shares in a mutual fund, the taxpayer is permitted to use the average cost of all the mutual fund shares he or she owns in determining the basis of the shares sold or redeemed. The average cost method may be used for mutual fund redemptions in place of either the FIFO method or the actual identification method.

PROPERTY ACQUIRED FROM A DECEDENT

"Step-Up" in Basis at Death

A special basis rule generally applies when the taxpayer acquires property through a decedent's estate. If the property is includible in the gross estate of the decedent for federal estate tax purposes, the taxpayer receiving the property takes a basis in the property equal to its fair market value as of the date of the decedent's death. If the fiduciary of the decedent's estate elects the so-called "alternate valuation date" (6 months from the date of death) for the valuation of property for federal estate tax purposes, then the taxpayer takes a basis equal to the fair market value of the property at that time. The basis adjustment at death is a significant tax advantage in cases where the property received from the estate has substantial untaxed appreciation. That appreciation will escape taxation because of the "step-up" in basis to the property's current fair market value resulting from its passing through the decedent's estate.

Example: Buck owns a personal residence with a basis of $75,000. Buck dies this year. His executor does not elect the alternate valuation date for estate tax purposes. The fair market value of Buck's residence is $300,000 on the date of his death. Therefore the income tax basis of the property in the hands of his estate (and of his heir) is $300,000.

The step-up in basis to its current market value applies to most property includible in the decedent's estate for federal estate tax purposes and not just to probate property passing under the terms of the decedent's will. Certain property does not qualify for this special basis rule.

The basis step-up does apply to property that was held jointly by the decedent with another individual or individuals. The portion of the jointly owned property that is includible in the decedent's gross estate will be eligible for a fair market value basis adjustment. In the case of property held jointly or by married couples in a tenancy by the entirety, federal estate tax law requires that one-half of the property's value be included in a decedent owner's estate. Therefore the surviving spouse in such cases receives a basis step-up (or step-down if the property has experienced a reduction in value) to fair market value with respect to one-half of the property. Different rules apply to property that is community property under applicable state law.

If the decedent acquired property in his or her estate as a gift within one year of death, and if the donor of the gift to the decedent is the same person (or that person's spouse) to whom the property passes from the decedent's estate, the basis step-up will not be available. This rule exists to prevent taxpayers from artificially acquiring a basis step-up in property by giving property to a donee in anticipation of the donee's death where the donee's will makes a bequest or devise of the property back to the donor. However, the disallowance of the basis step-up does not apply if the donee-decedent lives for more than one year after the date of the gift.

There are certain other transfers of property that do not qualify for a basis step-up. These include benefits that death beneficiaries receive under most nonqualified deferred annuity contracts. Also any money or other property that constitutes income in respect of a decedent ("IRD") under Sec. 691 of the Internal Revenue Code does not qualify for the special basis rule for property acquired from a decedent. A detailed discussion of the concept of IRD is beyond the scope of this text.

Comparison with Basis of Property Acquired by Gift

In contrast to the basis step-up rule, if a taxpayer receives property by means of a gift made during the donor's lifetime, a carryover basis rule applies. With respect to gifted property, the donee's basis is computed by reference to the property's adjusted basis in the hands of the donor. An additional basis rule applies to gifted property. If the donor paid gift taxes in connection with the donative transfer, an adjustment to the carryover basis is made as discussed below.

The basis rule for property acquired from a decedent's estate is much more beneficial to the taxpayer receiving the property than the basis rules that apply to a gift, unless the property's value has decreased significantly. This is particularly true with respect to depreciable property where the property's adjusted basis in the hands of the decedent was adjusted substantially downward to reflect depreciation deductions. Because of the basis step-up at death, the beneficiary of such property will never have to pay taxes on the gain that would have resulted from depreciation adjustments if the decedent had sold the property during his or her lifetime. This advantage will not be obtained by a donee if the property is given away before the donor's death.

SPECIAL BASIS RULES FOR GIFTED PROPERTY

Adjustment for Gift Taxes Paid

As previously mentioned, the basis of gifted property in the hands of the taxpayer who received the gift is the same as the property's basis in the hands of the taxpayer who made the gift. In other words, a carryover basis rule applies to gifted property. If the property had appreciated in value during the donor's ownership, and a gift tax was paid with respect to the gift of the property, a basis increase is allowable to the donee. That increase is equal to the percentage of the value of the gifted property that is attributable to the appreciation of the property in the donor's hands, multiplied by the amount of the gift tax paid with respect to the property.

Sales of Gifted Property

As a result of the carryover basis rule for gifted property, the gain realized upon a subsequent sale of the property by the donee will be equal to the amount realized on the sale minus the donee's carryover basis in the property (as adjusted for any gift tax attributable to appreciation at the time of the gift).

However, another special basis rule applies in order for a donee's sale of property received by gift to result in a realized loss for income tax purposes. In calculating a realized loss resulting from such a sale, the donee's basis will be the lower of the carryover basis received by the donee, as adjusted, or the property's fair market value at the time of the gift (not at the time of the sale). This rule discourages taxpayers from giving property that has experienced a significant reduction in value to other taxpayers who can use a realized loss from the sale of the property more efficiently for income tax purposes than the donor taxpayer can. If a donor makes a gift of such property that has depreciated in economic value, the loss of value during the donor's period of ownership will not produce a deductible loss for either the donor or the donee taxpayer.

> *Example:* John owns stock in the Siavash Corporation, a privately owned company. He gives his stock in Siavash to his friend, Oliver. John's basis in the stock at the time of the gift was $100,000, and the value of the stock was $10,000. Oliver sells the stock a year later for $8,000. Oliver's realized loss from the sale for tax purposes is $2,000 ($10,000 − $8,000), because the stock's value at the time of the gift ($10,000) was less than John's basis at that time ($100,000). Oliver cannot use John's basis of $100,000 to calculate a deductible loss on the sale of the property.

SIGNIFICANT CATEGORIES OF BASIS ADJUSTMENTS

There are certain items for which an adjustment must be made to the basis of a taxpayer's assets. These adjustments will generally occur regardless of whether the asset was acquired in a transaction that resulted in a carryover basis in the taxpayer's hands or in a transaction in which the cost basis rule was originally applied. Basis adjustments that may be required for various types of property include, but are not limited to, the following:

- Adjustments for cost recovery and related types of deductions claimed with respect to the property. These include adjustments for depreciation, first-year expensing for tangible personal property used in a trade or business, and deductions for amortization, obsolescence, and depletion.
- Adjustments for permanent improvements to property made after the taxpayer acquires the property. In this connection, any expenditures made for the property that are allocable to the property's capital account (as distinguished from items allocable to the income account) will generally result in a basis adjustment. Expenditures for normal maintenance or repairs to an asset that do not either increase the value of the asset or add to its useful life will generally not result in basis adjustments.
- Various adjustments that are made to the basis of a taxpayer's ownership interest in a business as a result of distributions, proportionate shares of the business entity's income or loss, and other items. These adjustments occur with respect to the ownership of a partnership interest, stock in an "S" corporation, and also stock in a "C" corporation. Each type of business entity is subject to its own rules for these adjustments, which will be discussed in later chapters of this text.

As stated above, one significant adjustment that a taxpayer makes to the initial cost basis in property is an adjustment to reflect deductions for depreciation or other cost recovery deductions. The amount of such deductions is subtracted from the taxpayer's cost basis in calculating the taxpayer's adjusted cost basis at the time of a property sale.

It is important to note that the paying down of a mortgage and the corresponding increase in the owner's equity in property does not result in any basis adjustment. Similarly, a refinancing of the property or the taking of an additional mortgage to increase the amount of debt on the property during the period of the taxpayer's ownership does not result in an adjustment to basis. However, if a property is sold subject to a mortgage and the buyer takes over the existing loan, any loan amount assumed is treated as part of the amount realized by the selling taxpayer on the sale, which may result in realized gain.

There are many other required adjustments to the basis of property listed under IRC Sec. 1016. The adjustments mentioned above represent the more common and more significant types of basis adjustments to property.

NONTAXABLE SALES AND EXCHANGES OF PROPERTY

Certain exchanges of property do not give rise to a taxable event for federal income tax purposes. This means that even though an economic gain or loss may be realized as a result of the exchange, that gain or loss is not recognized for income tax purposes. This concept of nonrecognition of realized gain takes one of two forms under the income tax law. It may be a "tax-deferred" event in which gain or loss is not completely eliminated but rather deferred through the application of a carryover basis rule for potential taxation at a later date. Alternatively, it may be truly a "tax-free" event in which the gain or loss is permanently eliminated from gross income without any basis rule or other provision that will expose the untaxed gain or loss to recognition at some future date. The latter type of tax rule is an exclusion from gross income, like those discussed in chapter 6.

Whether the transaction is treated as a tax-deferred exchange of property or a tax-free disposition of property, there must be a specific provision in the Internal Revenue Code authorizing such treatment. This is so because all items of economic income the taxpayer receives during the year are subject to income tax, unless the Code expressly provides otherwise.

Four general categories of nontaxable sales and exchanges will be discussed in this chapter. First, the rules for "like-kind" exchanges of property will be examined. Next, the rules for nontaxable exchanges of insurance contracts under Code Sec. 1035 will be explained. Third, the tax rules for the exclusion of gain upon the sale of a personal residence will be set forth. Finally, an overview of the "wash sale" rules will follow. The first two areas fall within the category of tax-deferred exchanges where untaxed gain is preserved for potential taxation at a future date. The third topic, the sale of a personal residence, is an exclusion from gross income specifying that the taxpayer's gain, subject to definitions and limitations, is "eliminated" and will never be taxed. The final topic, wash sales, is a provision that specifically disallows the recognition of tax losses resulting from certain sales of stock or other securities.

LIKE-KIND EXCHANGES OF INCOME-PRODUCING PROPERTY

Introduction

Under IRC Sec. 1031, no gain or loss will be recognized on the exchange of certain properties held either for an investment or for productive use in a trade or business. This provision allows tax-deferred exchanges of many types of business or investment property. These exchanges are referred to as "like-kind" exchanges. The general concept of the like-kind exchange rules is this: Where a taxpayer uses an exchange to continue an investment in a specific type of income-producing property but needs a different piece of such property from that which was needed before, the continuation of what is essentially the same investment in the same type of property should not give rise to a taxable event.

The like-kind exchange provisions have the effect of deferring, but not completely eliminating, unrecognized gain or loss because a substituted basis rule applies to the properties involved in the exchange, as explained below.

Qualifying Property

Property eligible for the like-kind exchange provisions includes domestic real estate, machinery, equipment, vehicles, office furniture, computers, and most other real and personal property that would typically be used for income-producing purposes. It must be understood that one type of qualifying property cannot be exchanged for another type of qualifying property under Sec. 1031. Rather, the qualifying properties must be of generally the same type; that is, they must be of "like-kind." For example, a vehicle used for business may be exchanged for another vehicle used for business without recognition of gain or loss. One piece of income-producing real estate may be exchanged for another. However, a computer could not be exchanged for a vehicle and receive tax-deferred treatment under Sec. 1031. Treasury regulations provide guidance as to which types of qualifying property are of like-kind and which are not. In most cases, common sense will guide taxpayers to the correct conclusion.

Qualification of property depends essentially on the nature of the property rather than the purpose for which the taxpayer uses it. For example, a residential apartment building could be exchanged for a commercial office building even though the properties being exchanged have not been used for the same purpose.

Nonqualifying Property

Certain types of property do not qualify under the like-kind exchange rules. Property that is specifically *ineligible* for like-kind exchanges includes

- inventory (or stock in trade) of a business taxpayer
- corporate securities (including stocks, bonds, or any debt or equity securities) or ownership of interests in an unincorporated business
- real and personal property held or used outside the United States that is exchanged for property held within the United States

Characterization of Property

In a manner similar to situations under the capital-gain rules and other provisions in the tax law, a factual issue may arise as to whether a certain property is inventory of the taxpayer (held for sale to customers) or whether the property is held for use in the taxpayer's business or other income-producing activity. The issue frequently arises in situations involving real estate. Is the taxpayer a dealer in real estate who holds the properties primarily for resale? Or is the taxpayer holding the properties for rental or other investment purposes, hoping for wealth accumulation through the properties' income stream or long-term appreciation? In the former case, an exchange of the property will not be treated as a like-kind exchange because inventory is not a property held for investment or for productive use in a business. In the latter case, however, the exchange will qualify.

Exchanges between Related Persons

A special limitation applies if an exchange that otherwise qualifies as a like-kind exchange is between taxpayers who are related persons. The definition of "related persons" for this purpose includes immediate family members, ancestors, descendants, and certain business entities that are owned or controlled by other business entities.

If the taxpayers taking part in an exchange are related persons, generally each taxpayer must keep the property for 2 years after the date of the exchange. If one of the parties to the exchange sells the property received in the exchange before the 2-year period is up, both the selling party and the other party to the exchange will have a taxable event. The party who received the property that is later sold will be taxed, and the party who transferred the property to the related person will also be taxed. The party who transferred the property sold by the transferee will be taxed as if the property was sold in a taxable transaction at the time it was exchanged, except that the recognition occurs at the time of the sale, not as of the date of the exchange. The party to the exchange who sells the property within 2 years of the exchange will also have a taxable event. The gain or loss recognized by the transferor (the party from whom the selling party received the property) is taken into account in determining the gain or loss to be recognized by the selling party.

> *Example:* Lem and Clem are brothers. One year ago Clem received a parcel of land from Lem in a like-kind exchange. Lem's basis in the land transferred to Clem was $50,000. The value of the land at the time of the exchange was $70,000. Clem now sells the land for $80,000. As a result of this sale, Lem will recognize $20,000 ($70,000 − $50,000), the amount of his gain that was deferred in the exchange. Clem will recognize $10,000 of gain ($80,000 − $70,000) when he sells the land. His gain is only $10,000 because the amount of gain recognized by Lem is "taken into account" (that is, added to Clem's basis) in calculating Clem's gain from the sale.

Like-Kind Exchanges Involving "Boot" Property

Partially Taxable Exchanges

In a like-kind exchange, often cash or other property will be involved in the exchange along with the like-kind property to make the total of the value of property surrendered in the exchange equivalent to the total of the value of property received. In such an exchange, the cash or other property that is not property of like-kind is referred to as "boot."

The inclusion of boot in a like-kind exchange does not disqualify the exchange from tax-deferred treatment. However, it does result in the exchange being treated as partially taxable. Note that the taxpayer who pays the boot property will not have to recognize gain or loss on an otherwise qualifying exchange. However, the taxpayer who receives the boot property must recognize any realized gain but only to the extent of the value of the boot received. For example, if a taxpayer exchanges a business computer plus $1,000 in cash for another business computer, that taxpayer does not recognize gain or loss on the exchange. However, the other taxpayer receiving the $1,000 pursuant to the exchange must recognize any realized gain up to the amount of the cash received. If the exchange resulted in $3,000 of realized gain to the taxpayer receiving the cash, that taxpayer would have to recognize $1,000 of the $3,000 of realized gain. Note, however, that no loss will be recognized by the taxpayer (only gain) as a result of the receipt of boot in a Sec. 1031 exchange.

Assumption of Liabilities

A common type of like-kind exchange is one involving real estate. There are certain cases where the properties being exchanged are subject to liabilities (that is, they are mortgaged), and the parties to the exchange take the properties subject to the liabilities by taking over the loans owed on the properties and relieving the other party from liability on the property being surrendered. In such cases the assumption of liability is treated as payment of boot. In other words, a party who has been relieved of a debt pursuant to an exchange is basically treated for tax purposes as having received an amount of money equal to the principal amount of the debt. However, if both properties in the exchange are subject to liabilities that are transferred, only the net amount of debt relief received by a taxpayer is treated as boot received.

> *Example:* Laura and Woody are exchanging rental apartment buildings. Laura's property is worth $1 million and is subject to a mortgage with a principal balance of $500,000. Woody's property is worth $900,000 and is subject to a mortgage with a principal balance of $400,000. In each property there is equity of $500,000, so the equities are balanced in the exchange. However, Laura will be treated as having received $100,000 of "boot" because the amount of the mortgage she is relieved of ($500,000) is $100,000 more than the amount of the mortgage she is assuming ($400,000). Laura's potential tax liability as a result of this relief from liability may be a factor in negotiating the terms of the exchange.

Determination of Basis in Like-Kind Exchanges

Basis of Property Received in an Exchange

A specific type of basis rule is applied in calculating the basis of a taxpayer's property received in a like-kind exchange. This rule may be referred to as a "substituted" basis. It provides that the basis of the property received in the exchange will be the same as the adjusted basis the taxpayer had in the property surrendered in the exchange. Note that the taxpayer's basis in the property received is not determined by reference to the other party's basis in the same property now owned by the taxpayer (as would be the case in a donative transaction). Rather, it is determined by the same taxpayer's basis in a different property: the property surrendered in the exchange.

> *Example:* Charlotte and Wilbur exchange farm properties in a transaction that qualifies as a like-kind exchange. Wilbur's basis in the property he transfers to Charlotte is $200,000, and its fair market value is $300,000. Charlotte's basis in the property she transfers to Wilbur is $250,000, and its fair market value is also $300,000. Wilbur's basis in the property he receives from Charlotte will be $200,000, the same as his basis in the property he transferred. Charlotte's basis in her new property will be $250,000.

Basis Rules for Exchanges Involving Boot Property

There are basis adjustments that must be made to the substituted basis of the taxpayer in cases where the exchange does not solely involve property of like-kind. The required basis adjustments fall within two general categories:

- The taxpayer's basis must be decreased by the amount of any money and/or the value of any other "boot" property received in the exchange.
- The taxpayer's basis must be increased by the amount of any gain that was recognized on the exchange or decreased by the amount of any loss recognized on the exchange. The Code provides for a basis decrease for any loss recognized on an exchange even though a realized loss is not permitted to be recognized as a result of the receipt of boot in a partially taxable exchange.

Remember that a transfer of a liability such as a mortgage that relieves the taxpayer from an obligation to pay a debt is treated as boot received in an exchange, and therefore triggers the requirement for a basis adjustment. Note also that if the realized gain in a partially taxable exchange is greater than the amount of cash or other boot received, then gain will be recognized to the full amount of the boot. In such cases, there will be a negative adjustment (or decrease in basis) for boot received followed by a positive adjustment (or increase in basis) of the same amount for recognized gain, resulting in a "wash" for purposes of the basis calculation.

Example: Assume the same facts as in the previous example except that the property transferred by Charlotte has a fair market value of $315,000 and is subject to a mortgage of $175,000, and the property transferred by Wilbur has a fair market value of $300,000 and is subject to a mortgage of $160,000. Each party to the exchange is to assume the mortgage on the transferred properties. Charlotte has a net "debt relief" of $15,000 ($175,000 − $160,000). Therefore Charlotte will recognize $15,000 of her realized gain. Her basis in the property received from Wilbur will remain at $250,000 after corresponding adjustments for boot received ($15,000) and gain recognized ($15,000). The adjustments are equivalent, thereby resulting in a "wash."

NONTAXABLE EXCHANGES OF INSURANCE CONTRACTS

Introduction

Sec. 1035 of the Internal Revenue Code provides that no gain or loss will be recognized for income tax purposes upon the exchange of one life insurance, endowment, or annuity contract for another life insurance, endowment, or annuity contract if certain requirements are met. This Code section, generally similar to the like-kind exchange provisions just discussed, allows non-recognition of gain with a corresponding basis rule to preserve untaxed gain in the new contract until a later taxable disposition or other transaction. It is—like IRC Sec. 1031, which describes like-kind exchanges—a provision for deferral of taxation rather than permanent exclusion of gain.

No loss will be recognized in a Sec. 1035 exchange. However, a loss is generally not allowable for the surrender of a life insurance policy anyway. The deductibility of a loss upon the surrender of an annuity contract is more of an open question that is beyond the scope of this text.

The purpose of Sec. 1035 is to allow taxpayers to continue what is essentially the same investment in an insurance or annuity contract by replacing a contract that no longer serves the taxpayer's best interests with a contract that is better suited to his or her needs. This may occur, for example, where the investment risk attributes of the old policy no longer suit the needs or preferences of the policyowner, or where a more modern and economically efficient policy has become available.

Rules for Qualifying Exchanges

A life insurance contract may be exchanged under Sec. 1035 for another life insurance contract, an endowment contract, or an annuity contract. An endowment contract may generally be exchanged for another endowment contract or for an annuity contract. An annuity contract may be exchanged without recognition of gain only for another annuity contract and not for a life insurance or endowment contract. For example, an exchange of a life insurance contract for an annuity would be a permissible exchange under Sec. 1035, while an exchange of an annuity contract for a life insurance contract would not be permissible.

In a somewhat surprising decision, the United States Tax Court has held that in an exchange involving annuities, it is not necessary to surrender the old annuity contract for a new contract to qualify under Sec. 1035.[1] The Court decided that a withdrawal of some of the funds from an existing annuity followed by a purchase of a new contract with those funds is sufficient to qualify as a tax-deferred exchange of annuity contracts. Currently, it is not known whether the IRS will continue to litigate this issue. Most commentators had previously thought that a complete surrender of the old contract was necessary to qualify under Sec. 1035.

There is a "same insured" requirement under Sec. 1035. Specifically, the insured under a life insurance contract must be the same person in both the old and the new contracts when a life insurance policy is exchanged for another life policy. Where an annuity contract is exchanged for another annuity, the same insured requirement is satisfied by having the primary annuitant under the new contract be the same person as under the old contract. Presumably, in a life policy to annuity exchange, the insured under the life insurance contract must be the same person as the primary annuitant under the annuity contract.

The IRS has taken the position that two life insurance contracts separately insuring the lives of a married couple cannot be exchanged for one joint life policy insuring both their lives.[2] Their rationale was *not* that two policies cannot be exchanged for one policy (this is generally permissible), but rather that all the contracts involved in the exchange did not cover the life or lives of the same insured. The logic involved in this position would appear to be somewhat specious.

Sec. 1035 does not apply to any exchange involving a foreign person, that is, a person other than a United States person.

It is clear that the policyowner may not receive cash from an old policy and then decide to invest it at a later time in a new policy and treat that series of transactions as a 1035 exchange. Rather, the surrender or use of funds from the old policy and the acquisition of a new one must be done as an integrated transaction in which the policyowner does not obtain unfettered control over cash.

Income Tax Mechanics of Sec. 1035 Exchanges

A substituted basis rule applies under Sec. 1035 in basically the same way as in a like-kind exchange under Sec. 1031, as previously explained. Essentially, the policyowner takes the same basis in the new contract as he or she had in the old contract. If the policyowner makes an additional premium payment for the new contract (which is permissible), the basis will then be increased. Note that if the policy being surrendered carries an economic loss (that is, the cash value is less than the basis in the policy), the substituted basis rule will actually result in a higher basis in the new policy than if the policyowner had surrendered the old contract and then purchased a new one in a separate transaction.

The like-kind exchange rules regarding "boot" also apply to an exchange of insurance contracts under Sec. 1035. If the policyowner receives cash or other property pursuant to an exchange that otherwise qualifies under Sec. 1035, the policyowner will have to recognize gain in the old policy to the extent of the "boot" received in the exchange. The payment of cash by a policyowner in an exchange does not constitute the receipt of boot.

> *Example:* Horace owns a life insurance policy covering his own life. He has paid a total of $100,000 for the policy, and the policy has paid dividends as a nontaxable return of capital to the extent of $15,000. Therefore the tax basis of the policy to Horace is currently $85,000 ($100,000 – $15,000). The current cash surrender value of the policy is $125,000. Horace exchanges the policy for a new policy issued by a different life insurance company. The cash value of the old policy is used to fund the purchase of the new policy. The exchange qualifies under Sec. 1035. Horace has $40,000 of realized gain on the exchange ($125,000 – $85,000), but the realized gain will not be recognized for income tax purposes. The basis in the new policy will be $85,000, the same as the basis in the old policy at the time of the exchange. If Horace makes additional premium payments into the new policy, his basis will then be increased.

Note that if the old policy had an outstanding policy loan against it, and the loan is simply extinguished pursuant to the exchange, the principal amount of the outstanding loan will be treated as boot. This corresponds to the rules governing like-kind exchanges.

EXCLUSION FOR GAIN REALIZED UPON THE SALE OF A PRINCIPAL RESIDENCE

Introduction

Under current law, there is a relief provision in the form of an exclusion from gross income for gain realized from the sale of a taxpayer's home. There has traditionally been tax relief available for the sale of a principal residence. Under prior law, however, there were two provisions:

- a rollover of gain provision that was similar to a tax-deferred exchange rule because it required the taxpayer to purchase another residence within 2 years
- a once-in-a-lifetime exclusion of gain provision that was available to taxpayers age 55 and over

Both of those provisions were repealed and replaced by the current law that grants an exclusion from gross income for the sale of a taxpayer's home, without any requirement for a replacement residence, any age requirement, or any fixed limit on the number of times the exclusion can be used in a taxpayer's lifetime.

Ownership and Use Requirements

To claim the exclusion, the taxpayer must have owned and used the home as a principal residence for an aggregate time period of 2 years out of the 5-year period immediately preceding the home's date of sale.

Taxpayers who are incapable of self-care and who reside in nursing homes or other similar facilities may treat such periods of residence as "use" of their principal residence for a total of up to one year of the 2-year use requirement for the exclusion. This wrinkle in the use requirement obviously helps such taxpayers qualify for the exclusion.

An unmarried taxpayer whose spouse has died before the date of the home sale can "tack on" any period of ownership and use by the deceased spouse prior to the taxpayer's ownership and use of the home.

If a taxpayer receives a home in a transfer incident to a divorce proceeding or settlement, the taxpayer may "tack on" the transferor's period of ownership under the ownership test. Similarly, if the taxpayer owns the property and his or her spouse or former spouse was granted use of the property under a divorce or separation agreement, the taxpayer can treat such occupancy as his or her use of the property for purposes of the use requirement for the exclusion.

Finally, if the taxpayer used the "rollover of gain" provision under prior law in the process of acquiring the home being sold (that is, the home was the replacement residence under that provision), the period of ownership and use of the taxpayer's prior residence sold pursuant to the rollover rules is counted as ownership and use of the residence currently being sold.

Amount of the Exclusion

For married taxpayers filing jointly, the maximum amount of realized gain that may be excluded from gross income is $500,000. The $500,000 limit applies if both spouses meet the ownership and use requirements, but also if only one spouse meets the ownership requirement as long as both spouses meet the use requirement. This law allows spouses to choose the ownership arrangement for a home without directly affecting the amount of the available exclusion. However, if only one spouse meets the use requirement, the maximum amount of the exclusion is $250,000. For other taxpayers, the maximum exclusion is $250,000. Taxpayers who have realized gain in excess of the applicable amount will have to pay tax on the amount of the excess as a capital gain.

> *Example:* Terry and Carol Outman sell their home this year for $950,000 (net of expenses of the sale). Their basis in the home is $400,000. Carol has owned the home for 20 years and the couple has

lived together in it for that time. The Outmans' realized gain is $550,000 ($950,000 − $400,000); the maximum exclusion is $500,000. Therefore the couple will have a recognized gain of $50,000 ($550,000 realized gain − $500,000 maximum exclusion).

Other Significant Rules

Generally, a taxpayer can claim the exclusion only once every 2 years. If a single taxpayer marries a person who has used the exclusion within the past 2 years, then the maximum exclusion available is $250,000 rather than $500,000 until such time as 2 years have passed since the exclusion was used by either spouse.

Under certain circumstances the maximum amount of the available exclusion is reduced. If the taxpayer fails to fully meet the ownership and use rules or the "once every 2 years" rule, and the sale of the home is due to a change of the taxpayer's place of employment, a change of health, or other "unforeseen" circumstances, the $250,000 or $500,000 maximum amount (whatever amount would otherwise be available if the taxpayer fully met the requirements) is reduced. The maximum exclusion is multiplied by the ratio of the amount of time that the taxpayer's qualifying period of ownership and use bears to 2 years. The resulting figure is the maximum amount of gain that the taxpayer is permitted to exclude from gross income.

Unlike the former "rollover of gain" provision, there is no requirement that the taxpayer purchase a replacement residence. Also the taxpayer does not have to make an election to have the exclusion apply. The exclusion will apply automatically unless the taxpayer elects out of it. There is no apparent reason for him or her to do so.

If the taxpayer has used a portion of the home for business or rental purposes and claimed depreciation deductions, the amount of depreciation the taxpayer claimed with respect to the home after May 6, 1997, will reduce the amount of his or her realized gain that is eligible for the exclusion. This means that the exclusion does not apply to gain that is realized as a direct result of basis adjustments for depreciation claimed on the residence.

WASH SALES

Taxpayers are not permitted to recognize a realized loss from the sale of corporate stock or other securities if the same stock or security is repurchased by the taxpayer within a 30-day period beginning before or ending after the sale in which the loss was realized. The purpose of this provision is to prevent a tax avoidance technique in which a taxpayer could (in the absence of the wash sale rule) sell stock, claim a tax loss from the sale, then quickly repurchase the same stock so that the taxpayer's economic position regarding the stock is essentially unchanged, but a tax savings is generated.

The 30-day period imposed under the wash sale rules for repurchase of the same stock or security helps to ensure that if the taxpayer does repurchase the stock sold at a loss and wishes to claim a tax loss for the sale, he or she will be subject to market fluctuations affecting the stock price during the 30-day period before or after the sale. Therefore the taxpayer cannot be assured the repurchase price will be substantially identical to the sale price.

For purposes of the wash sale rules, options to buy or sell a stock or security will generally be treated as a purchase or sale of the stock or security.

The wash sale rules do not apply to transactions made by the dealer in stock or securities in the ordinary course of the dealer's business.

Finally, note that the wash sale rules operate only to disallow the recognition of certain realized losses from the sale of securities. The rules do not apply to exclude or defer gain realized from a stock sale.

NOTES

1. *Conway v. Comm'r.,* TC No. 22257-96,111, T. C. No. 30, 12/30/98.
2. PLR 9542037.

14

The Taxation of Capital Gains and Losses

James F. Ivers III

Any reasonable system of taxation would be based on the slogan "Soak the Rich."

Heywood Broun

Don't soak the rich, soak the poor. There's more of them.

Eric Wright

Chapter Outline

INTRODUCTION

There are special, and generally more favorable, rules that apply to the taxation of capital gains and losses as distinguished from the taxation of ordinary income. The income tax rules for capital gains and losses apply to the proceeds realized upon the taxable sale or exchange of property that fits the Internal Revenue Code's definition of a capital asset.

The tax treatment of capital gains and losses has long been a social, political, and economic issue in the United States. Some observers believe that capital gains should not be taxed at all on the grounds that such gains are often attributable only to inflation, or on the grounds that appreciation of a capital asset held for investment is an accretion of wealth that should not be intruded on by the government. Other observers believe that capital gains and losses are merely one type of economic income, that there is nothing unique or special about such gains and losses, and that they should be taxed under the same rules as ordinary income such as wages and salaries. For the most part, however, Congress has taken a path somewhere in the middle ground of these two opposites poles, taxing capital gains but providing more lenient treatment for such gains than that which is applicable to ordinary income.

Under current law, there is generally a maximum tax rate of 20 percent applicable to most long-term capital gains of individual taxpayers. Under certain circumstances the maximum rate may be higher or lower depending on the type of asset involved and the income level of the taxpayer. Corporate taxpayers do not receive any special rate differential for capital gains as compared with other corporate income. There are special rules for the deductibility of capital losses, and these provisions also differ depending on whether the taxpayer is an individual or a corporation.

The specific rules for taxation of capital gains and losses will be discussed below. First, however, when considering the taxation of a specific transaction, the following questions should generally be asked:

- Is the asset giving rise to the gain or loss a capital asset under the Internal Revenue Code?
- Was there a taxable sale or exchange of the asset?
- In the case of an individual taxpayer, was the gain or loss long-term or short-term gain or loss?

In addition to the rules applicable to specific transactions, there are procedures for combining or "netting" all of a taxpayer's capital gains and losses for the year. There are also provisions defining and limiting under what circumstances capital losses can be deductible. Finally, there is a special category of assets called "Sec. 1231" assets that combine the tax features of capital assets with those that give rise to ordinary income or loss. Those assets will also be discussed.

THE DEFINITION OF A CAPITAL ASSET

Under Sec. 1221 of the Internal Revenue Code, a capital asset is defined as any property the taxpayer owns (whether or not connected with a business activity) except for the following types of property that are specifically excluded from the definition:

- "stock in trade" (that is, inventory) of the taxpayer or other property held by the taxpayer primarily for sale to customers in the ordinary course of the taxpayer's business
- depreciable or real property used in the taxpayer's trade or business
- a copyright, a literary, musical, or artistic composition, a letter or memorandum, or similar property held either by the creator of the property, or by a taxpayer whose basis in the property is determined in whole or in part by the creator of the property, or by (in the case of a letter or memorandum), the taxpayer for whom the property was prepared or produced
- accounts or notes receivable acquired in the ordinary course of business for services rendered or for the sale of inventory or inventory-type property
- publications of the United States government that are held by a taxpayer who did not purchase the publication or by a nonpurchasing transferee of such a taxpayer

The types of assets listed above are those that are *not* treated as capital assets. Any other property held by a taxpayer is defined as a capital asset for income tax purposes. Consequently, most assets owned by taxpayers are treated as capital assets.

THE REQUIREMENT OF A SALE OR EXCHANGE

Generally, there must be either a sale or an exchange of a capital asset in order for the capital gain and loss rules to apply. For example, the mere holding of investment property over a period of time does not give rise to capital gain or loss, even though the property may have substantially appreciated. As discussed in chapter 13, there must be a realization of gain or loss for a taxable event to occur. In the case of capital assets, realization of gain or loss generally occurs through a sale or a taxable exchange of the asset.

Example: Hannah owns stock in General Motors with a current value of $10,000. Her basis in the stock is $7,500. If Hannah sells the stock, she will realize a gain of $2,500, which is taxable. However, if she keeps the stock, no taxable event has occurred.

If some specific rule of the Internal Revenue Code provides that a particular asset can be sold without recognition of gain (such as the sale of a principal residence, subject to limitations), the sale of such an asset is not a taxable event. Also there are tax rules that limit the deductibility of various types of losses incurred by an individual taxpayer, as described in chapter 8. Basically, losses of individual taxpayers are deductible only if they are incurred in a business activity or in a transaction entered into for profit, or if they are casualty or theft losses. The sale or exchange of the asset must give rise to a taxable gain or deductible loss under other requirements of the Internal Revenue Code before the specific rules determining the treatment of capital gain and loss are applied.

LONG-TERM VERSUS SHORT-TERM GAINS AND LOSSES

With regard to individual taxpayers, different rules and tax rates apply depending on whether the capital gain or loss is long-term or short-term. This discussion will be restricted to the current rules applicable to sales of assets occurring after December 31, 1997. The rules in this area have frequently been changed.

Holding Periods

Whether a sale or exchange of an asset results in long-term or short-term gain or loss for tax purposes depends on the period of time the asset was held by the taxpayer (the "holding period"). Sales of capital assets held by the taxpayer for "more than" 12 months result in long-term gains and/or losses. Sales of capital assets held by the taxpayer for 12 months or less result in short-term gains and/or losses. Note that the long-term holding period is not exactly 12 months but "more than" 12 months. For example, publicly traded stock the taxpayer held as an investment would give rise to long-term gain or loss if sold one year and one day after it was purchased but not if it were sold exactly one year later.

Carryover of Holding Period

In certain situations, the holding period of one taxpayer who previously owned an asset carries over to the holding period of another taxpayer who currently owns it. This typically occurs in donative transactions where one person gives property to another. In such a case, the property's basis in the hands of the taxpayer who currently owns it is determined by reference to its basis in the hands of the previous owner, so the holding period will "carry over." Similarly, if property has a basis in the hands of the taxpayer that is determined by reference to other property previously held by the taxpayer, the holding period will also carry over from the ownership of the other asset. This typically occurs where a taxpayer surrenders one property in exchange for another in a transaction in which no gain is recognized under the Internal Revenue Code.

Example: Gail owns an antique ring that she gives to her daughter, Daria. Gail's cost for the ring was $1,000, and she had owned it for 5 years. Its value is now $2,000. Daria's basis in the ring for purposes of computing taxable gain is $1,000, and her holding period is 5 years.

Corporations

For corporations, there is no tax significance regarding the holding period of a capital asset. This is so because no special tax rates apply to corporate capital gains and losses; such gains and losses are simply netted against one another. If there is a net capital gain for the year, the corporation pays tax on the net gain. If there is a net loss, the corporation cannot deduct the net capital loss against its other income but can only carry it over to offset past or future capital gain. These corporate rules will be discussed again in chapter 18. For individual taxpayers, the rate system and the netting procedures applicable to capital gains and losses are more complicated.

TAX RATES APPLICABLE TO CAPITAL GAINS OF INDIVIDUALS

Sales of capital assets held by an individual for more than 12 months are generally eligible for the maximum rate of 20 percent on long-term capital gains. Sales of capital assets held for 12 months or less are treated as short-term capital gains and are subject to ordinary income tax rates, unless the short-term gains are offset by capital losses under the netting procedures discussed later in this chapter. Therefore there is a significant maximum rate differential between long-term and short-term capital gains. The maximum statutory tax rate on ordinary income under current law is 39.6 percent.

Not all long-term capital gains of individuals are eligible for the maximum rate of 20 percent. First, the portion of long-term gain from the sale of depreciable real property that is attributable to unrecaptured depreciation claimed on the property is taxed at a 25 percent maximum rate. Second, long-term gain from the sale of "collectible" capital assets is taxed at a maximum rate of 28 percent rather than 20 percent. "Collectible" assets include works of art, rugs, antiques, stamps or coins, precious stones and metals, and alcoholic beverages. Third, to the extent that the 15 percent marginal tax rate on ordinary income would otherwise apply to the capital gain, the maximum rate on long-term gain is reduced from 20 percent to 10 percent. This means that individuals in the 15 percent tax bracket will pay a 10 percent tax on their long-term capital gains up to the point where their total taxable income, including such gains, exceeds the maximum amount subject to the 15 percent bracket. Any additional gains will be subject to the 20 percent maximum rate.

There are special rules that apply to sales of capital assets by individuals taking place after December 31, 2000. These rules can be summarized as follows:

- The 10 percent rate, if applicable, is lowered to 8 percent for sales after December 31, 2000, but only if the taxpayer's holding period is more than 5 years regardless of the date the asset was acquired.
- The maximum rate of 20 percent is lowered to 18 percent if the taxpayer's holding period is more than 5 years and the asset was

acquired after December 31, 2000. An election can be made for certain publicly traded securities allowing taxpayers to treat such securities acquired before 2001 as acquired after December 31, 2000. This election is for the purpose of qualifying the taxpayer for the 18 percent rate. To make the election, the taxpayer recognizes for tax purposes any gain that exists in the asset at the time of the election. At that point, the required 5-year holding period for the 18 percent maximum rate will begin to be counted. Under this rule, the 18 percent rate will not actually be used until 2006 and thereafter, although the 8 percent rate described above can be used for qualifying sales beginning in 2001.

TAX TREATMENT OF CAPITAL LOSSES

For corporations, capital losses are deductible only against capital gains. If capital losses exceed capital gains for the year, the corporation will have a capital loss carryover as previously mentioned.

For individuals, there are more involved rules for the treatment of capital losses. First, capital losses are fully deductible against capital gains for the year. If a taxpayer has both short-term and long-term capital gains and/or losses, there are specific procedures for the "netting" of those gains and losses that will be discussed below. If the taxpayer has only capital losses and no capital gains, or if, under the netting procedures, the taxpayer's capital losses exceed capital gains for the year, the capital losses may be deducted from the taxpayer's ordinary income in an amount up to $3,000 per year. If such net capital losses exceed $3,000, the excess may be carried forward to future tax years by individual taxpayers until the excess losses are used up. For married taxpayers filing separately, the $3,000 capital loss limitation is reduced to $1,500.

HOW CAPITAL GAINS AND LOSSES ARE NETTED FOR INDIVIDUAL TAXPAYERS

Because there are different tax rates applicable to different categories of capital gains, and because capital gains and losses may be either long-term or short-term, the taxpayer needs to organize these gains and losses and take specific steps to determine whether he or she will have a net capital gain or loss and what type of net gain or loss it will be. To accomplish this result, gains and losses are first separated into various groups (commonly referred to as netting "baskets") and netted separately against each other. Next, the net gains and/or losses from the various groups or baskets are once again netted against each other to calculate the amount and the character of a net gain or loss. The steps in this netting process may be summarized in the following way:

- Any short-term capital gains and losses are netted together to determine the amount of the taxpayer's net short-term capital gain or loss.

- Any gains and losses from the sale of "collectibles" (the gain from which would be taxed at a maximum rate of 28 percent) are netted together to determine the taxpayer's net "collectibles" gain or loss.
- The portion of any gains from the sale of real estate attributable to unrecaptured depreciation (the gain from which would be taxed at a maximum rate of 25 percent) are added together to determine the taxpayer's total gain in this category.
- Long-term gains and losses from the sale of capital assets (the gain from which would be subject to the 20 percent maximum tax rate) are netted together to determine the taxpayer's net long-term capital gain or loss in this category.

   Example: Natalie has $10,000 in long-term gains from the sale of assets eligible for the 20 percent maximum capital-gains rate this year. She also has $4,000 of losses from sales of the same type of assets. Her net gain in the 20 percent rate basket is $6,000 ($10,000 – $4,000).

After the gains and losses have been separated into these various baskets and netted against each other, there are additional netting procedures if one or more of the baskets contains a net capital loss. However, if there are only capital gains in the separate baskets there is no additional netting, and each category of capital gains is taxed at its applicable rate. For example, net short-term gains would be taxed at the rates applicable to the taxpayer's ordinary income. Net "collectibles" gain would be taxed at a maximum rate of 28 percent. Net long-term gains eligible for the 20 percent maximum rate would be taxed at that rate (or a lower rate if the taxpayer's marginal rate of tax on ordinary income is 15 percent as previously discussed), and so on.

If the taxpayer has net capital loss in any of the original netting baskets, the following additional netting steps apply:

- Any net short-term capital loss is first netted against gains subject to the maximum rate of 28 percent ("collectibles" gain), then to gains subject to the maximum rate of 25 percent, then to gains subject to the maximum rate of 20 percent (or a lower rate, if applicable). In other words, net short-term capital losses are netted against the capital gains subject to the highest rates first.
- Any net long-term loss from collectibles is netted against any net 25 percent gain first, then against any net 20 percent gain. If the collectibles loss still has not been fully utilized, the balance may be netted against the taxpayer's net short-term capital gain for the year. Any remaining loss would be deductible against ordinary income subject to the $3,000 limitation.
- A net long-term capital loss from the sale of assets that would result in 20 percent gain if sold at a gain is handled in basically the same way: the excess loss is netted first against any net 28 percent gain, then

against any net 25 percent gain, then against any net short-term capital gain. Any remaining loss would be deductible against ordinary income subject to the $3,000 limitation.

> *Example:* Assume the same facts as in the previous example except that Natalie also has a net long-term loss from the sale of collectibles of $5,000 this year. Natalie may offset $5,000 of her $6,000 of net capital gain subject to the 20 percent maximum rate with the $5,000 of losses from her collectibles. She will then have $1,000 of long-term capital gain subject to the maximum rate of 20 percent.

Although this netting process seems quite complicated, it is actually rather logical and arises from a simple concept. The long-term loss netting "baskets" (those containing 28 percent, 25 percent, or 20 percent net losses) are first netted against the long-term gain baskets that have gain subject to the highest maximum rate first, then the next highest, and so forth. Net long-term losses are netted against net short-term capital gains only after all the long-term gain baskets have been "netted out." Similarly, net losses in the short-term baskets are netted against net gains in the long-term baskets subject to the highest maximum rates first. In this way, net long-term capital gains subject to higher rates are netted out before the baskets subject to the lower rates. This is a reasonably fair netting system for taxpayers, although the structure of the overall tax system for capital gains and losses still looks more complicated than it really should.

"SEC. 1231" GAINS AND LOSSES: THE "BEST OF BOTH WORLDS"

Introduction

In the foregoing discussion of the taxation of capital gains and losses, it was noted that the Internal Revenue Code defines a capital asset as property owned by the taxpayer except for certain specifically enumerated types of property that are excluded from the definition of a capital asset. One of the exceptions to the definition of a capital asset is "depreciable or real property used in the taxpayer's trade or business."

Generally, property that is excluded from the definition of a capital asset will produce ordinary income or loss if sold rather than capital gain or loss. However, depreciable or real property used in the taxpayer's trade or business is a special type of property for tax purposes that is treated under the rules of IRC Sec. 1231. That section requires that in order to receive the special tax treatment provided to Sec. 1231 assets, the property must have been held by the taxpayer for more than one year. In other words, depreciable and real property used in the taxpayer's trade or business will be treated as a Sec. 1231 asset if held by the taxpayer for more than one year. If such property is held for a year or less, it will be treated as ordinary income property in a manner similar to property that falls within any of the other exceptions to the definition of a capital asset (such as inventory or stock in trade).

The Taxation of Sec. 1231 Assets

Simply stated, upon the sale or taxable exchange of property that meets the definition of a Sec. 1231 asset, gain will be treated as long-term capital gain and loss will be treated as ordinary loss. This means that gain from the sale of such property will be eligible for the lower maximum tax rates on long-term capital gain, while loss from the sale of such property will be deductible from the taxpayer's ordinary income without regard to the capital loss limitations.

> *Example:* Michael owns a pickup truck that he uses exclusively in his business. His adjusted basis in the truck is $19,000. He sells the truck for $12,000 and does not acquire another vehicle at the time of the sale. His $7,000 loss on the sale of the truck is treated as an ordinary loss. If he had sold the truck for $25,000, his $6,000 of gain would be treated as capital gain (except for that portion of his gain subject to recapture of depreciation).

If a taxpayer has more than one sale or taxable exchange of Sec. 1231 assets during one year, all gains and losses from such sales are grouped or "netted" together to calculate the net gain or loss from the disposition of Sec. 1231 assets. If the result is a net gain, the gain is taxed as long-term capital gain. If the result is a net loss, the loss is treated as an ordinary loss deductible in full from the taxpayer's ordinary income. This is a unique type of treatment under the federal income tax law, and it really does give the taxpayer the "best of both worlds": long-term capital-gain treatment and ordinary loss treatment with respect to the same type of asset.

Note that if an asset is sold that is subject to depreciation recapture as discussed in chapter 11, capital-gain treatment under Sec. 1231 will apply only to that portion of the gain that is not subject to depreciation recapture.

Special "Recapture" of IRC Sec. 1231 Losses

There is a "catch" to this best of both worlds treatment. To the extent that a taxpayer in the prior 5 taxable years has deducted net Sec. 1231 losses from ordinary income, any net gains from Sec. 1231 property otherwise taxable as capital gain will be taxed as ordinary income. This rule in effect creates a 5-year window for looking back to previously deducted Sec. 1231 losses to determine whether Sec. 1231 net gains for the current year must be converted from long-term capital gains to ordinary income. If there have been net losses from Sec. 1231 assets during the previous 5 years, the best of both worlds treatment does not apply until an amount of net Sec. 1231 gains equal to the amount of such previously deducted losses has been reported by the taxpayer as ordinary income.

Example: Jake sells real property used in his business this year at a gain of $50,000. Two years ago, Jake sold other real property used in his business at a loss of $35,000 and deducted the loss as an ordinary loss. Therefore $35,000 of Jake's gain in the current year will be treated as ordinary income, and only $15,000 of the current gain will be eligible for capital-gains tax rates.

SUMMARY OF PROPERTY CLASSIFICATIONS

To determine the proper tax treatment for the sale or exchange of an asset as described in this chapter, the asset must be properly classified by the taxpayer. Generally assets can be thought of as falling into one of three categories:

- capital assets
- Sec. 1231 assets
- assets that are neither capital assets nor Sec. 1231 assets

Capital assets will be subject to the rules applicable to capital gains and losses. Sec. 1231 assets will receive long-term capital-gains treatment for net gains (subject to the recapture rule just discussed) and ordinary loss treatment for net losses. All other assets will result in ordinary income or ordinary loss if sold. Remember, however, that the tax law allows loss deductions to individual taxpayers only for sales of assets that are used in a business, or assets that are used in an activity engaged in for profit, or for casualty and theft losses. Specific rules for each of these types of losses limit and define how the losses can be deducted. Remember also that not all sales and exchanges that result in a realized gain will result in a taxable event. If the sale or exchange qualifies under a provision in the Code that provides nonrecognition of realized gain (such as a like-kind exchange as described in chapter 13), the gain from the sale of the asset may not be recognized for income tax purposes even though it is realized from an economic standpoint.

For business taxpayers, perhaps the most common type of ordinary income asset (one that is neither a capital asset nor a Sec. 1231 asset) is the taxpayer's inventory or property held primarily for sale to customers in the ordinary course of business. The sale of inventory will give rise to ordinary income or loss. For investors, a common type of property sold would be publicly traded stocks and bonds. Such property falls within the definition of a capital asset because it does not meet any of the exceptions to the definition (for example, it is not inventory and it is not depreciable property used in a business). The sale of such property will fall squarely into the tax rules for capital gains and losses. On the other hand, property eligible for depreciation deductions that is used in the taxpayer's business (such as machinery and equipment) is Sec. 1231 property that would receive the unique tax treatment available under that section. Before the tax consequences of a sale or exchange of property can be determined, the property must be correctly classified for income tax purposes.

Tax Uncertainty in Property Classifications

There may be uncertainty as to how a particular piece of property should be classified for income tax purposes. For example, some sales of real estate may raise the issue of whether the real estate was held as an investment or held for sale in the ordinary course of the taxpayer's business. If the former classification applies, gain will be taxed as capital gain. If the latter classification applies, the gain will be taxed as ordinary income. The answer to such a question may depend on whether the taxpayer was primarily engaged in renting properties as a profit-making activity (which would make the property a Sec. 1231 asset) or in buying properties for the purpose of reselling them (which would make the property the taxpayer's inventory).

These and other issues are factual questions that a court will examine if a dispute with the IRS results in litigation. Among the factors a court may consider are how often the taxpayer bought and sold properties, how long the taxpayer typically owned such properties, and the purposes the property served during the time it was held by the taxpayer. Similar questions may also arise with regard to sales of tangible and intangible personal property.

Rights to Receive Income

It should be noted that a right to receive income is generally not treated as "property" for purposes of the capital asset or Sec. 1231 definitions. Such a right is not even tested to determine what type of property it is under those definitions because, for tax purposes, it is not considered to be "property" at all. It is merely an anticipatory right to receive income. Therefore, if such a right is assigned for a price, the amount received for the right is treated as a receipt of the income generated by that right, and it is taxable as ordinary income. Examples of such rights to receive income include royalty and licensing rights, and income rights from extractive industries such as oil and gas drilling.

15

The Alternative Minimum Tax

James F. Ivers III

> The art of taxation consists in so plucking the goose as to obtain the largest possible amount of feathers with the least possible amount of hissing.
>
> Jean Baptiste Colbert
(attributed)

Chapter Outline

The alternative minimum tax, or AMT, is a separate method of calculating income tax liability. It is often referred to as a "parallel" system of income taxation. It applies in cases where the calculation of the AMT results in a higher tax liability than the calculation of the regular income tax. The purpose of the AMT is to prevent the taxpayer from reducing his or her tax liability below reasonable levels through the use of certain tax benefits targeted by the AMT rules. Therefore, in calculating the AMT, certain tax benefits available under the regular tax rules are limited or prohibited under the AMT calculation. Consequently when the AMT is calculated using different rules for these tax benefits, certain taxpayers will have a higher tax liability under the AMT calculation. Such tax benefits that are restricted under the AMT system may be loosely referred to as "tax preference" items.

The AMT is calculated by first determining the taxpayer's alternative minimum taxable income (AMTI). The calculation of AMTI uses the taxpayer's regular taxable income as a starting point, and then makes adjustments to reflect the impact of tax preference items including the elimination or reduction of certain deductions and/or credits and the addition of certain items of income that are excludible for regular tax purposes. These items will be summarized below.

ITEMS OF TAX PREFERENCE

Some of the more significant tax preference items that are handled differently in computing AMTI as compared with taxable income for regular tax purposes are as follows:

- Some itemized deductions allowable on Schedule A of Form 1040 for regular tax purposes cannot be claimed for AMT purposes; that is, they are tax preference items. However, certain itemized deductions of individuals *are* permitted to be claimed as deductions in calculating AMTI. These include
  - charitable contributions
  - casualty and theft losses
  - interest on indebtedness used to acquire or improve a qualified residence of the taxpayer
  - investment interest not in excess of qualified net investment income
  - the deduction for estate taxes attributable to income in respect of a decedent
  - medical expenses deductible for regular tax purposes. Note, however, that the deduction "floor" for medical expenses under the AMT rules is 10 percent as distinguished from the 7.5 percent floor that applies for regular tax purposes.

  The overall limitation on itemized deductions does not apply in calculating AMTI.
- The standard deduction is not allowable in computing AMTI. If an individual taxpayer uses the standard deduction for regular tax purposes, the amount of the standard deduction is added back to taxable income in calculating AMTI.
- Personal and dependency exemptions are not allowable in computing AMTI. Like the standard deduction, any exemption amounts claimed for regular tax purposes must be added to the taxpayer's regular taxable income in calculating AMTI.
- Certain research and experimental costs paid by individuals who own interests in a business in which they do not materially participate are not allowable in computing AMTI.
- Certain publishing circulation expenses that individuals incur are not allowable in computing AMTI.
- When the actual value of an incentive stock option at the time the option holder's rights become nonforfeitable exceeds the price paid for the option, the excess must be included in calculating AMTI.

- A portion of certain deductions for depreciation allowable for regular tax purposes is not allowable for AMT purposes. For example, in claiming deductions for depreciation on real property, only straight-line depreciation using a 40-year recovery period is allowable in calculating AMTI. Any excess of that amount claimed for regular tax purposes is disallowed. Also, with respect to depreciable personal property placed in service after 1998, the 150 percent declining-balance method must be substituted for property that qualifies for the 200 percent declining-balance method for regular tax purposes. Certain different adjustments must be made to depreciation deductions for personal property placed in service before 1999. These adjustments apply to both individuals and corporations.

- Interest on nongovernmental purpose bonds issued after August 7, 1986, that is excludible from gross income for regular tax purposes must be included in the calculation of AMTI by both individuals and corporations.

- Other deductions allowable for regular tax purposes are disallowed or otherwise partially restricted for AMT purposes for both individuals and corporations. These preference items include
  - amortization of pollution-control facilities
  - certain mining exploration costs
  - certain intangible drilling costs incurred by businesses engaged in the extractive industries

- Corporations are subject to an AMT adjustment for "adjusted current earnings." This preference will be discussed in more detail later in this chapter.

THE AMTI EXEMPTION

After AMTI is calculated, it may be reduced by an exemption amount. The applicable exemption amount is determined by the taxpayer's filing status and is phased out for upper income taxpayers. The phaseout of the AMTI exemption is determined by calculating the amount of the taxpayer's AMTI that is in excess of a specified threshold amount and then multiplying that excess by 25 percent. The resulting figure is the amount of the AMTI exemption that is disallowed. If the amount disallowed is more than the AMTI exemption, then the exemption is zero.

The exemption amounts and the threshold amounts for phasing out the exemption are shown in the following table:

Filing Status	Exemption Amount	Phaseout Threshold
Married filing jointly	$45,000	$150,000
Single and head of household	33,750	112,500
Married filing separately and estate or trust	22,500	75,000
Corporation	40,000	150,000

Example: Anthony, a single taxpayer, has $175,000 of AMTI for the current year. Anthony's AMTI exemption of $33,750 is phased out by 25 percent of the amount by which $175,000 exceeds $112,500. The amount phased out is $15,625 [($175,000 – $112,500) x .25]. Therefore his AMTI exemption will be $18,125 ($33,750 – $15,625). The amount of his AMTI subject to tax will be $156,875 ($175,000 – $18,125).

AMT TAX RATES

Once the taxpayer's AMTI has been reduced by the applicable exemption amount, the amount of the remaining AMTI is multiplied by the applicable alternative minimum tax rate. The applicable rates are shown in the following table:

Taxpayer	AMT Tax Rate
Individuals other than married filing separately	26 percent of the first $175,000 28 percent of the excess over $175,000
Married filing separately	26 percent of the first $87,500 28 percent of the excess over $87,500
Corporations	20 percent

Example: Mary, a single taxpayer, has AMTI of $230,000 this year after the application of her AMTI exemption. Her alternative minimum tax liability is the sum of $45,500 (.26 x $175,000) plus $15,400 [($230,000 – $175,000) x .28], or $60,900.

OTHER FACTORS IN THE CALCULATION OF THE AMT

Net Operating Loss

If a taxpayer has a net operating loss (NOL) from a business activity, the NOL may be used to eliminate up to 90 percent of the taxpayer's AMTI. The

NOL allowable for AMT purposes may be somewhat different from that calculated under the regular tax rules in that it is adjusted for any preference items that were used in determining the regular NOL.

Tax Credits

Generally, any foreign tax credit allowable in computing the regular tax may be used to eliminate up to 90 percent of AMT liability.

Other nonrefundable personal tax credits such as the child tax credit and education credits are also allowable to reduce AMT liability without the 90 percent limit applicable to the foreign tax credit. However, the allowance of these other credits against the AMT is currently scheduled to expire after 2001.

APPLICATION OF THE AMT TO CORPORATIONS

S Corporations

The AMT does not apply to S corporations because they are pass-through entities that are not subject to income tax at the entity level. However, shareholders in S corporations may be subject to the AMT on their individual returns.

C Corporations and the "Small Corporation" Exemption

C corporations are generally subject to the AMT. However, certain C corporations are exempt from the application of the AMT. This exemption applies to corporations that fit a specific definition of a "small corporation." To fit this definition, the corporation must meet an average annual gross receipts test. This test is applied as follows:

- For new corporations, average annual gross receipts must not exceed $5 million for the corporation's first 3 taxable years. The corporation's first year is counted under the 3-year test, but the corporation will not be subject to the AMT for its first year. After the initial test is passed, the corporation must not have 3-year average annual gross receipts in excess of $7.5 million or its exemption will be lost.
- For corporations in existence before 1997, a $5 million average annual gross receipts test is applied to the 3 taxable years beginning with the first taxable year ending after December 31, 1993. If the corporation was not in existence for 3 years when this test is applied, it is then applied on an average basis to the period of the corporation's existence. Note that all corporations in existence in 1997 must have passed the test for the 1997 tax year and qualified for the exemption or else the exemption was permanently lost. Once the gross receipts test is passed, the corporation must not have 3-year average annual gross receipts in excess of $7.5 million or the exemption will be lost.

The "ACE" Adjustment for Corporations

One tax preference item that applies only to corporations subject to the AMT and not to individual taxpayers is the "adjusted current earnings" or ACE adjustment. Essentially, this adjustment takes into account certain items that are not treated as taxable income for regular tax purposes but are treated as so-called "book" income for accounting purposes. "Book" income may be loosely defined as a calculation of income for accounting purposes that is computed somewhat differently than the calculation of income for tax purposes.

An important element included in the ACE adjustment is book income attributable to life insurance owned by a corporation. Such income for purposes of calculating adjusted current earnings includes both death benefits that are received tax free for regular tax purposes and increases in a life insurance policy's cash value that are not subject to the regular income tax. The ACE adjustment is calculated by adding to AMTI 75 percent of the amount by which the corporation's adjusted current earnings exceeds its AMTI. To avoid a circular calculation, the excess of adjusted current earnings over AMTI is computed using AMTI without regard to the adjustment. Seventy-five percent of the excess is then added to the corporation's AMTI base.

This adjustment can potentially result in up to 75 percent of a corporation's life insurance proceeds being subject to the AMT. Using a 20 percent AMT tax rate, an effective tax rate of up to 15 percent on life insurance proceeds could result (that is, the amount of proceeds x .75 x .20 tax rate).

Note that premiums paid on a life insurance contract reduce the ACE adjustment. Therefore premiums paid can reduce the amount of the corporation's income subject to the AMT. Correspondingly, increases in cash value of insurance contracts (as well as the receipt of death benefits) raise the adjustment.

It is also important to understand that the effective AMT rate of 15 percent on life insurance proceeds is the most severe tax result possible under the ACE adjustment. The actual result of the adjustment in many cases will be considerably less than the 15 percent effective rate. This is so because the AMT is only payable to the extent it exceeds the regular income tax. Corporations with few tax preference items other than the ACE adjustment may not have AMT liability substantially in excess of regular tax liability. Consider also that the highest corporate tax rates under the regular tax are much higher than the 20 percent AMT rate. Even though 75 percent of adjusted current earnings may be includible in AMTI, this does not necessarily mean that there will ultimately be a 15 percent additional tax on life insurance benefits and cash values because AMT liability may not be significantly higher (or higher at all) than regular tax liability. In cases where the corporation's regular tax exceeds its AMT, there will be no additional tax resulting from the ACE adjustment.

The term *adjusted current earnings* corresponds somewhat closely to the calculation of a corporation's earnings and profits. Earnings and profits, as discussed in chapter 19, is a calculation used as a measure to determine the taxability of distributions to corporate shareholders. It is related to, but not the same as, a corporation's taxable income. Similarly, the ACE adjustment includes items not included in the regular taxable income computation.

There are items other than life insurance values and benefits included in the ACE adjustment for AMT purposes. However, discussion of other specific items is beyond the scope of this text.

Income Taxation of Life Insurance

Fred J. Dopheide and James F. Ivers III[*]

I'm proud to be paying taxes in the United States. The only thing is—I could be just as proud for half the money.

Arthur Godfrey

Chapter Outline

Life insurance has received favorable tax treatment since 1916 when the federal income tax law first exempted life insurance death benefits from taxation. Although the laws concerning taxation of life insurance have changed since then, Congress has continued to recognize both the social value and utility of sheltering life insurance from the erosion of the federal income tax.

---

[*]Fred J. Dopheide, JD, CLU, is a retired vice president, Educational Resources, the American Society of CLU & ChFC (now known as the Society of Financial Service Professionals), Bryn Mawr, Pennsylvania.

It is the purpose of this chapter to present the general rules of income taxation of life and health insurance as well as to discuss the tax consequences of certain specific life insurance arrangements. In examining these arrangements, the following three interrelated questions are discussed:

1. When are proceeds received at death or as living benefits subject to income taxation?
2. When are premiums a deductible item for income tax purposes?
3. When are premiums paid by an individual or entity taxable to the party receiving the economic benefit from such payment?

GENERAL RULES

Life Insurance Death Benefits

Lump-Sum Payments

Generally, life insurance death benefits payable by reason of death of the insured are excluded from the gross income of the beneficiary,[1] regardless of whether the beneficiary is an individual or an entity. In addition to death benefits payable under individual life insurance policies, the term *death benefit payments,* for purposes of exclusion from income tax, includes death benefits payable under accident and health insurance contracts as well as workers' compensation insurance,[2] but does not include death benefits payable under an annuity contract.

Interest Option

When death proceeds are held by the insurer for future withdrawal or distribution and only interest on the proceeds is paid to the beneficiary, the full interest payment is taxable.[3]

Installment Options

For policies that matured by death before August 17, 1954, proceeds distributed under policy settlement options are fully tax free even though each payment contains an interest element. For policies maturing by death after August 16, 1954, that portion of each payment made under the fixed-period, fixed-amount, or life income installment options representing the principal of death proceeds is received tax free, but that portion representing interest is taxable. To calculate the taxable portion, the lump-sum death benefit that could have been received tax free is prorated over the payment period of the option, and the portion of each payment representing principal is tax free. The remainder representing interest is reportable as ordinary income.[4] In this calculation, the *payment period of the option* must be determined. Where the fixed-period option is in operation, the payment period is the number of guaranteed annual installments; where the fixed-amount option is in operation, it is the number of annual installments of a specified amount produced under the guaranteed interest rate in the policy; and, under the life income option, the payment period is the life expectancy of the beneficiary. (If the life income option has a refund or period-certain feature, the present value of such feature must be subtracted from the lump-sum death proceeds before proration.) Life expectancy and valuation of refund features are determined on the basis of mortality tables prescribed by the secretary of the Treasury in the regulations.[5]

Amounts paid as a survivor annuity on account of the death of a public safety officer killed in the line of duty are generally excludible from gross income and not subject to the rules just described.

Interest Exclusion

With respect to deaths of insureds occurring before October 23, 1986, a surviving spouse-beneficiary may still exclude from income up to $1,000 of interest payable under a settlement option, but only where the option is installment in nature; that is, if the payments are a true combination of both interest and principal. This special interest exclusion has been repealed for deaths occurring after October 22, 1986.[6]

Accelerated Death Benefits Paid to Terminally or Chronically Ill Insureds

Amounts received under a life insurance contract covering the life of an insured who is terminally or chronically ill are now excludible from gross income as amounts payable by reason of the death of the insured if certain requirements are met. The amounts received qualify for the exclusion if paid by the insurance company or by a licensed viatical settlement provider. The exclusion does not apply if the amounts are paid to a taxpayer other than the insured if the insured is a director, officer, or employee of the taxpayer or has a financial interest in a business conducted by the taxpayer.

A "terminally ill" insured is one who has been certified by a physician as having an illness or condition that can be expected to result in death within 24 months of the date the certification is given.

There are additional requirements for the exclusion to apply if the insured is "chronically ill" rather than "terminally ill." Basically, the exclusion for accelerated benefits paid to a chronically ill insured applies only if the benefit is paid under a rider or provision of the life insurance contract that is treated as a qualified long-term care insurance contract within the meaning of IRC. Sec. 7702B. Therefore, a life insurance contract without such a provision or rider can pay excludible accelerated benefits only to a terminally ill insured. A "chronically ill" insured has the same meaning as it has for purposes of the income tax rules applicable to long-term care insurance contracts. The tax rules applicable to benefits paid from such contracts also generally apply for purposes of the accelerated benefits exclusion.[7]

Life Insurance Living Benefits

Policy in Force

Prior to the Tax Reform Act of 1984, any increase in the cash value of a policy was not taxable, because a taxpayer's right to receive such income was subject to substantial limitations. A taxpayer did not have constructive receipt of increases, because to receive the gain he or she must have surrendered the policy and forfeited his or her rights.[8] Today, of course, many permanent life insurance policies permit withdrawals without policy termination. However, tax-deferred buildup of internal policy values is still allowed if the insurance policy meets certain actuarial tests. If these tests are not met, then the policy will be treated as a combination of term life insurance and a currently taxable fund.

Dividends are generally not taxable income but are viewed as a return of a portion of the premium, whether they are received in cash, used to either reduce or purchase additional coverage, or left with the company.[9] However, if aggregate dividends received or credited exceed the taxpayer's cost basis in the contract, such excess is taxable as ordinary income.[10] Interest earned on dividend accumulations is taxable in the year the taxpayer has the right to withdraw the interest. The taxpayer has constructive receipt of the interest income whether or not the income is withdrawn.

Withdrawals of cash value from a life policy are generally taxed on a first-in first-out (FIFO) basis; that is, withdrawals are treated as a nontaxable return of capital to the extent of premiums paid. Withdrawals in excess of premiums paid are taxable.

However, it is critically important to understand that withdrawals will be taxed as income first (a last-in first-out (LIFO) treatment) if the policy is classified as a modified endowment contract (MEC). The MEC rules are discussed in detail in the next chapter in this book.

In addition, withdrawals from a life insurance policy that are made during the first 15 policy years and are associated with a reduction in the policy's death benefit will also be subject to LIFO tax treatment, even if the policy is not a MEC.

Withdrawal features are typically associated with universal life policies. Taxable withdrawals during the first 5 policy years will have a higher taxable portion than withdrawals made during policy years 6 through 15. The maximum portion of any such withdrawal subject to income tax is that amount by which the policy cash value exceeds aggregate premiums paid on the policy.

There is a ceiling on the amount of taxable income associated with such withdrawals, however. The ceiling is based on the policy year during which the taxable withdrawal is made and the applicable test for life insurance used to satisfy the definition of life insurance after the withdrawal. The applicable test could be either the cash value accumulation test or the guideline premium test.

Lump-Sum Payments

Where the owner of a life insurance contract receives the lifetime maturity proceeds or cash surrender value of the policy in one lump-sum payment, the amount received in excess of the owner's cost basis is subject to ordinary income tax.[11] Cost basis is defined as the investment in the contract, which is the sum of premiums paid, less policy dividends actually received, less any policy loans,[12] less extra premiums paid for certain supplementary benefits, such as waiver of premium and accidental death protection.[13]

Gain realized upon surrender or maturity of United States Government Life Insurance (WW I) or National Service Life Insurance (WW II) is exempt from tax.[14]

No loss is recognized where, upon maturity or surrender, the amount received is less than the cost basis. The difference represents the cost of pure insurance protection—a nondeductible expense.

When the owner of a life insurance contract sells the policy to a third party, such a transaction is not considered a *sale or exchange* for income tax purposes. Thus the gain in such a transaction is taxed as ordinary income and not as capital gain.[15] Any gain is taxable as ordinary income and is determined in the same way as it would be upon surrender of the contract.

Interest Option

Where the policyowner leaves maturity or cash surrender values with the insurance company under the interest-only option, the interest earned will be taxable as ordinary income when received or credited to the payee.[16] In addition, at the time of maturity or surrender, if the values available to the policyowner exceed the cost basis, the gain will be taxed as ordinary income even though the lifetime proceeds are left with the insurance company, *provided* the policyowner also reserves the right to withdraw the proceeds at any time.[17] This right of withdrawal places the policyowner in constructive receipt of the gain. To avoid constructive receipt and thereby postpone the tax on any gain, the policyowner must elect the interest option *before* maturity or surrender and give up the right to withdraw the proceeds.[18] In such a case, the person who ultimately receives the proceeds will bear the tax liability for the gain.

Installment Options

When the policyowner places maturity or cash surrender values under any of the installment options, the annuity provisions of the Internal Revenue Code apply.[19] Part of each installment payment is considered a return of principal and is not subject to tax. The percentage of each installment received tax free is found by dividing the investment in the contract by the expected total return.[20] The Code provides a "60-day rule"[21] that affects the definition of "investment in the contract." The rule has significance when, at the time of maturity or surrender, the lifetime proceeds exceed the owner's cost basis. The rule enables the policyowner to avoid immediate tax on the gain, but as a result a larger percentage of the installment payments will be subject to tax. The rule works this way: If the policyowner elects the installment option no later than 60 days following the date of maturity or surrender of the policy, there will be no tax on the unrealized gain until installments begin, and *investment in the contract* will be the aggregate of premiums paid less dividends, loans, and premiums for certain supplementary benefits.[22] If, on the other hand, the owner delays electing the installment option until beyond the 60-day period, the owner will be taxed on the total unrealized gain as of the time of maturity or surrender, but the investment in the contract will be increased to the total maturity or surrender value, thus enlarging the tax-free portion of future installments. This will be accomplished, however, at the expense of exposing the total gain on the contract to taxation in one year.

Where the option selected is the life income option, the *investment in the contract* is reduced by the actuarial value of any refund or period-certain feature.[23]

The expected total return under the fixed-period option is determined by multiplying the fixed number of years or months by the amount of the guaranteed payment provided in the contract for such period.[24] Under the fixed-amount option, the expected total return is determined by multiplying the fixed-installment amount by the number of guaranteed installments.[25] Under the life income option, the expected return is determined by multiplying the periodic payment by the payee's life expectancy as determined by government tables.[26]

Contingent Beneficiaries

Where the primary payee dies before receiving all installments under the fixed-period or fixed-amount options, the contingent beneficiary will be taxed in the same manner as was the primary payee. That is, the contingent beneficiary will exclude the same portion of each installment from income and include the same portion of each installment in income.[27] However, where the primary payee is receiving a life income settlement and dies during a period of guaranteed payments, the contingent beneficiary will have no taxable income until the total amount received, when added to the amount that was received tax free by the primary payee, exceeds the investment in the contract.[28] Thereafter the full amount of each payment will be taxed as ordinary income.

Health Insurance Benefits

Disability Income Payments

Disability income insurance can be provided as a rider to a life insurance policy or through a separate contract. In either event, income payments on policies owned and paid for by the insured are received by the insured tax free.[29] When payments are made to a policyowner other than the insured—for example, to a corporation that has purchased the disability income insurance as key person insurance—the benefits paid by the insurance company continue to be tax free.[30]

A different situation arises, however, where disability income insurance is paid for by an employer to fund a wage continuation plan for employees, and the benefits are paid by the insurance company directly to the individual employees. Upon receipt of disability income from such a policy, an employee must include amounts received under the policy in income.

Medical Reimbursement

Benefits payable from hospital and surgical policies, major medical policies, and other insured medical expense coverages, whether from an individual or group policy, are exempt from income tax.[31] This rule also applies to qualified long-term care contracts, subject to certain limitations. However, any benefits received must be used to reduce the amount of related medical expenses otherwise deductible for the year. In addition, to the extent that reimbursement is received for medical expenses taken as a tax deduction in a prior year, it will be taxable in the current year.

Income Tax Treatment of Premiums

Personal Life Insurance

The general rule with respect to the income tax treatment of life insurance premiums is that they are a personal expense and as such are not deductible.[32] The rule applies whether the premium is paid by the insured, the beneficiary, or the policyowner. Exceptions to the general rule exist in certain situations based upon the use to which the life insurance is put. Examples include premiums paid for life insurance owned by a qualified charitable organization, premiums paid for life insurance by an ex-spouse as part of an alimony decree, and premiums paid by a business for life insurance used to fund certain employee compensation plans.

Business Life Insurance

Generally premiums paid on business life insurance are not deductible. The Internal Revenue Code is explicit: "No deduction shall be allowed for . . .

premiums on any life insurance policy, or endowment or annuity contract, if the taxpayer is directly or indirectly a beneficiary under the policy or contract."[33] Moreover, premiums on business life insurance have been characterized by the Internal Revenue Service as a capital investment and not a business expense, even though the policy is term insurance.[34] However, in certain situations where an employer is not a policy beneficiary, premiums paid on a policy covering the life of an employee may be deductible, as discussed later in this chapter.

Personal Health Insurance

The Internal Revenue Code provides that premiums paid for personal disability income insurance are not deductible.[35] Included in the definition of disability income insurance are policies that pay a weekly income payment to the insured while hospitalized.[36]

Premiums paid for medical reimbursement insurance are considered a medical care expense under the Code[37] and are deductible to the extent that they, along with other itemized medical expenses, exceed 7.5 percent of the taxpayer's adjusted gross income. Different rules apply to self-employed taxpayers as discussed in chapter 7.

Business Health Insurance

Where an employer pays premiums on a disability income policy on the life of an employee and benefits are payable to the employer, no premium deduction is allowable,[38] but benefits are received tax free. This tax treatment is similar to key person life insurance owned by a business on a key employee.

However, where the employer pays premiums on disability income insurance with benefits paid directly to the employees under a wage continuation plan, such premiums are deductible by the employer and are not taxable to the covered employee,[39] provided such premium payments, when added to all other compensation paid to the covered employees, do not exceed a reasonable allowance for personal services rendered.[40]

Premiums paid by an employer on a policy providing medical reimbursement to the employee are deductible to the employer and are not taxable to the employee,[41] if they meet the test of reasonableness and are part of an employee benefit plan.[42]

LIFE INSURANCE ARRANGEMENTS GIVING RISE TO TAX CONSEQUENCES

Transfer for Value

Perhaps the most prominent exception to the general rule that life insurance death proceeds are tax exempt is the transfer-for-value rule.[43] Where a policy transferred by assignment or otherwise for a valuable consideration matures by reason of death, the transferee will be liable for income tax on the amount of death proceeds in excess of the actual value of the consideration paid for the contract plus the total of net premiums and other amounts subsequently paid by the transferee.[44] This rule, which seems to be deeply grounded in public policy, is designed to prevent a tax-free windfall that might come about from speculation in life insurance policies. Life insurance enjoys an income-tax-favored position because of its unique economic function of protecting families and business interests that would profit more by the insured's continued life than by death. Therefore one who buys life insurance policies for speculation with the hope of realizing a substantial monetary profit on the death of the insured will not enjoy a tax exemption.

However, Congress did recognize that certain transfers of life insurance for consideration are not motivated by a desire for profit but for valid personal or business reasons. Therefore Congress included five exceptions in the Code to the transfer-for-value rule.[45] When any one of these exceptions applies, the full death proceeds will be income tax free in the hands of the beneficiary even though the policy was transferred for a valuable consideration.

The five specified exceptions are (1) transfers to the insured, (2) transfers to a partner of the insured, (3) transfers to a partnership in which the insured is a partner, (4) transfers to a corporation in which the insured is a shareholder or an officer, and (5) transfers in which the transferee's basis in the transferred policy is determined in whole or in part by reference to the transferor's basis. This latter exception (occasionally referred to as the *carryover-basis* exception) would apply in a tax-free exchange, where, for example, one corporation transfers a corporate-owned key person policy to another corporation in a tax-free reorganization. The carryover-basis exception may also apply where a policy is transferred in a part-sale/part-gift transaction.[46] In part-sale/part-gift transfers the basis of the property transferred in the hands of the transferee is determined by reference to the transferor's basis where the amount paid by the transferee for the property is less than the transferor's adjusted basis in the property.[47] This exception also applies to transfers of policies between spouses incident to a divorce, since such transfers are nontaxable.[48]

It is worthwhile to reflect on the conspicuous absence in the Code of other transfer situations that are not excepted and yet may be motivated by personal or business reasons that are equally as valid as those surrounding the exceptions enumerated in the Code. One can think of many family transfers that would not involve speculation but would be made for sound estate planning reasons. One glaring omission is the transfer of a policy from an insured who is a shareholder in a closely held corporation to a fellow shareholder. As in the transfer of a policy from a partner-insured to a fellow partner, there may be sound business reasons for such a transfer, yet the rule excepts the latter but not the former. Conscientious planners need to be especially mindful of these nonexceptions.

The tax results of a transfer-for-value problem can be onerous. Because of the aleatory nature of a life insurance contract, the amount exposed to ordinary income in one year can be substantial. Thus careful attention must be paid to every transfer of a life insurance policy in order to avoid the tax pitfall of the transfer-for-value rule. Examples of transfers that are not uncommon but that violate the rule include the following:

- A policyowner sells a policy on his or her life to a corporation in which he or she is an employee and/or member of the board of directors. (The insured must be a shareholder or officer.)
- Alice and Bruce own all the stock of a corporation and enter into a buy-sell agreement on a cross-purchase basis. Instead of buying new life insurance on each other's lives to fund the agreement, Alice and Bruce each transfer to the other an existing policy on their lives. (Coshareholders are not exempt transferees.)
- The Alice-Bruce Corporation has a stock redemption agreement with Alice and Bruce funded with corporate-owned insurance on Alice and Bruce. The parties wish to change the stock retirement arrangement to a cross-purchase plan. The corporation transfers Alice's policy to Bruce and Bruce's policy to Alice.

The above transactions are clearly transfers for value subject to tax at the death of the insured. Planning techniques may be available to achieve the desired results without falling into the transfer-for-value "trap." Other more subtle situations may bring the rule into play. In some instances the parties may be unaware that a transfer is being made or of the consideration involved.

For example, assume that corporate owners, Alice and Bruce, enter into a cross-purchase buy-sell arrangement and elect to fund it with group life insurance—a procedure not normally recommended. Alice, on her group certificate, names Bruce as beneficiary; and Bruce, on his certificate, names Alice as beneficiary. Alice and Bruce may not be consciously aware that they are transferring anything to each other, but the broad definition of "transfer for a valuable consideration" given in the regulations seems to suggest that Alice and Bruce are transferees for value:

> . . . a "transfer for a valuable consideration" is any absolute transfer for value of the right to receive all or a part of the proceeds of a life insurance policy. Thus the creation, for value, of an enforceable contractual right to receive all or a part of the proceeds of a policy may constitute a transfer for a valuable consideration of the policy or an interest therein.[49]

Thus it might be argued that Alice and Bruce have transferred for consideration an interest in their group life insurance to each other. The consideration seems to consist of reciprocal promises to fund their business agreement with cross-beneficiary designations.

A policy that has been transferred for value can be cleansed of the taint by a subsequent transfer of the policy, for value or otherwise, to an exempt transferee; for example, the insured.[50] However, the transfer-for-value taint is not removed by a subsequent gift of the policy to a nonexempt transferee. Thus where Robert, the insured, sells his $10,000 policy to Stanley, his son, for $3,000 and Stanley then gives the policy to his sister, Dawn, the policy is still subject to the transfer-for-value rule. At the insured's death, the proceeds in excess of $3,000, plus premiums paid subsequent to the transfer to Stanley, will be subject to ordinary income tax.[51]

Lack of Insurable Interest

The concept of insurable interest has had an influence on the taxation of life insurance proceeds. Lacking the requisite of insurable interest, life insurance has been viewed as a mere wagering contract entered into for profit. This was the view of the court in a case[52] where a corporation paid the premium on accidental death insurance on its truck drivers, with the corporation named as beneficiary of the death proceeds. When a driver was killed, the proceeds collected by the corporation were held to be profits subject to ordinary income tax. It was the view of the court that the truck driver was not a key person and that the corporation did not at any time have an insurable interest in the truck driver's life. The decision reminds us that the question of insurable interest in a business insurance situation is one that continues to merit careful attention.

In an earlier case[53] the Tax Court went so far as to tax the proceeds of a key person policy where an insurable interest existed at the inception of the contract but presumably not when the policy matured as a death claim. On appeal, however, the U.S. Court of Appeals for the Sixth Circuit reversed and held that the proceeds were not taxable for lack of an insurable interest. The court pointed out that local law required an insurable interest only at the time of inception of the contract. The requirement of insurable interest generally applies only at the time of policy inception.

It is possible for a business to have an insurable interest in a key person who is not an employee. In one Tax Court decision,[54] the IRS argued that key person life insurance proceeds received by a corporation on the life of an independent contractor were taxable as ordinary income. But the Tax Court disagreed, holding that the insured's services as a real estate developer were essential to the success of the corporation and that the corporation had a valid insurable interest in the real estate developer's life. As a result, the tax-free nature of the death proceeds was preserved. The question of insurable interest is important and should be considered at policy inception.

Proceeds as Corporate Distributions

If business life insurance is arranged so that proceeds of policies that are owned and paid for by a corporation are paid to beneficiaries other than the corporation, complex tax problems will arise. For example, when the beneficiaries are shareholders of the corporation they may think the proceeds paid directly to them by the life insurance company retain their tax-free character. The IRS has refused to accept this point of view, maintaining instead that such insurance proceeds are taxable as dividends because the result is the same as if the proceeds had been received tax free as life insurance proceeds by the corporation and then distributed to the shareholder as a dividend.[55] The IRS's position has the logical advantage, and this was acknowledged in at least one case.[56] Therefore in situations where a corporation owns and pays for life insurance to fund a buy-sell arrangement or to protect the corporation against the loss of a key employee, the corporation, and not the shareholders, should be the beneficiary.[57]

A collateral problem raised by unorthodox business insurance arrangements is taxability of the premiums. If a corporation pays premiums on business life insurance where shareholders are beneficiaries, or where shareholders are beneficiaries as well as owners of the life insurance, the premiums are taxable to the shareholders as dividends.[58]

An earlier assignment discussed the three types of losses that are deductible to an individual: (1) losses incurred in a trade or business, (2) losses incurred in a transaction entered into for profit, and (3) casualty losses. Section 165 of the Code generally allows deductions for such losses provided they are "not compensated by insurance or otherwise." The quoted language has been interpreted by the Tax Court in the *Johnson* case to include the death proceeds of life insurance. Therefore where a taxpayer purchased life insurance on the life of a partner to protect the investment in the partnership, and in fact such a loss was incurred on the partner's death, a loss deduction under Section 165 was disallowed because, according to the Tax Court, the life insurance proceeds compensated for the loss.[59]

The result in the *Johnson* case normally should not present a tax problem for businesses obtaining key person life insurance protection to provide funds to find a replacement or to fund a 303 stock redemption, a salary continuation arrangement, or a stock purchase or partnership purchase plan. The *Johnson* case will hopefully be applied as a precedent only in similar cases, namely, when the key person life insurance is specifically obtained to protect the surviving partner's investment in the partnership. There is a clear and direct link between an anticipated Section 165 loss and the acquisition of life insurance to compensate that loss—a link that is not normally associated with the acquisition of key person life insurance.

Charitable Contribution

Premiums paid on life insurance owned by a qualified charitable organization are deductible to the donor as a charitable contribution, subject to the charitable contributions limitations.[60] It is important that the charity be the owner of the policy and have the exclusive right to cash in the policy, borrow on it, or change the beneficiary.

One technique for achieving deductibility of life insurance premiums that is occasionally suggested is simply to name the charity as irrevocable beneficiary of the policy proceeds. This technique should be avoided because it is fraught with uncertainties. We know that the irrevocable beneficiary is given some ownership interest in the policy, but the exact nature is frequently clouded, especially in the area of charitable giving. Perhaps, more importantly, the Internal Revenue Code denies a charitable deduction for gifts to charities where less than the taxpayer's entire interest in the property is contributed.[61] The Code enumerates certain exceptions that do not seem to encompass partial gifts of life insurance.[62]

Separation and Divorce

Income tax consequences need to be considered carefully where life insurance is involved in separation agreements and divorce decrees.

Life Insurance in the Property Settlement

The transfer of property between husband and wife incident to a divorce is generally nontaxable. The spouse who receives the property has a carryover basis and pays income tax on appreciation if the property is sold. This means that there is no taxable event with respect to cash values when life insurance is transferred as a result of a divorce.

Premium Payments

Premium payments by one spouse or former spouse for life insurance owned by and benefiting the other spouse are deductible as alimony by the payer-spouse under Section 215 of the Code and taxable to the payee-spouse under Section 71 of the Code if the following occurs:

- Payments are made in cash and terminate at the death of the payee-spouse.
- Payments are made under a divorce decree or separation agreement.
- The parties are not members of the same household and do not file joint tax returns.
- Payments are not for child support.
- Payments must be made for at least 3 years unless either spouse dies or the payee-spouse remarries.

Death Proceeds

Life insurance proceeds on the life of one spouse payable to the other spouse to discharge legal obligations imposed by a divorce decree, separation agreement, or support decree are exempt from income tax.

Additional Compensation

Where the employee is the policyowner and the employer has no beneficial interest in the policy, premium payments by an employer on an individual policy insuring the life of an employee may be deductible by the employer.

Such an arrangement is often referred to as an "informal pension plan," whereby an employer selects certain favored employees for this nonqualified fringe benefit. The employee applies for the policy and possesses all incidents of ownership. The employee names his or her own personal beneficiary for the death benefit, and the employer pays the annual premium. Such payment, if considered reasonable additional compensation to the employee for services rendered, will be deductible under Section 162 of the Code as an ordinary and necessary business expense.[63] An important element in the success of this arrangement is that the payments must qualify as additional compensation and not as dividends should the employee also be a shareholder. It is also important that the total amount of compensation realized by the employee, including the premium payment, meet the test of reasonableness. Finally, the employer must not be a beneficiary of the policy, either directly or indirectly.[64]

Such premium payments by the employer are taxable to the employee when paid. The questions are often asked, Why arrange such a plan? Wouldn't it be equally effective if the employer simply increased the employee's salary by the amount of the premium and let the employee buy the life insurance with the increase in salary? It is true that the same tax result would follow, but whether the effect would be equal is the question to ponder. The employer has an opportunity to place himself or herself in a psychologically advantageous position by selecting one or more *key employees* for the benefit *plan*. The package of benefits embodied in a life insurance contract such as a substantial death benefit, disability features, and lifetime guaranteed retirement income may be more appreciated by an employee (and especially by the family) than a nominal salary increase to cover the premium payment.

Split-Dollar Life Insurance

A popular fringe benefit for selected employees is the split-dollar life insurance plan. Under a typical split-dollar arrangement, an employee and employer share or *split* the premium payments. Cash-value-type policies are universally used with the employer's share of the annual premium being measured by each year's increase in cash value. The employee's share of each premium payment is generally the difference between each year's cash value increase and the amount of net premium due. The employer is named beneficiary to the extent of the cash value, and the employee has the right to name his or her own beneficiary for the difference between the total death proceeds payable and the cash value.

Under such a plan an employee receives a substantial amount of life insurance at a relatively low cost. The employer pays the major share of each premium (at some point in the life of the policy, the employer may be paying *all* the premium) and thus bestows an economic benefit on the employee.[65] The employee thus must include in gross income each year the value of the economic benefit received, which is measured by the government's P.S. 58 rates.[66] The value of the employee's economic benefit each year is determined by multiplying the applicable P.S. 58 rate at the employee's age by the amount of net death protection provided that year. The employee's part of the premium paid for that year (if any) may be subtracted from the total value of the economic benefit taxable to the employee.

Note, however, that in the opinion of the IRS, if the split-dollar arrangement results in the cash value of the contract being greater than the amount that will ultimately be repaid to the employer, that excess is also taxable to the covered employee.[67]

No deduction is available to the employer for contributions to a split-dollar plan because the employer is also a beneficiary under such policy within the meaning of Section 264(a)(1) of the Code.

There are several different variations of split-dollar arrangements. Some are quite sophisticated. The individual circumstances of both the employer and employee must be considered in determining the features of a particular plan.

Income Tax Restrictions on Certain Amounts Paid in Connection with Insurance Contracts

IRC Sec. 264 imposes severe restrictions on the deductibility of two types of payments typically incurred in connection with insurance contracts: premium payments and interest payments on policy loans.

Nondeductibility of Premiums

As previously discussed in this chapter, premium payments on life insurance contracts are generally nondeductible, regardless of whether the policy is held as a personal asset or for business purposes. The only exceptions to this general rule arise when the taxpayer paying the premiums is not directly or indirectly a beneficiary under the policy, and the premiums qualify for a deduction under some specific rule of tax law. Such situations include certain premium payments deductible as charitable contributions, or as alimony payments, or as compensation paid to an employee. It must be emphasized that a deduction for premium payments may not be claimed in any case in which the taxpayer is a policy beneficiary.

This restriction applies to life insurance, endowment, and annuity contracts. The taxpayer need not be the named beneficiary of the policy for the disallowance of a premium deduction to apply. Basically any beneficial interest in the policy (such as the right to name or change the beneficiary) will prevent any deduction for premium payments.

Nondeductibility of Interest Payments

The current income tax law restrictions on the deductibility of interest paid or incurred in connection with insurance contracts are complex and severe. There are multiple layers of restrictions, one or more of which may apply depending on the context in which the policy is held, the policy's date of issue, and the specific nature of the circumstances surrounding the financial transaction involving the policy.

The general rule is that no interest deduction is allowable with respect to indebtedness incurred in connection with a life insurance, endowment, or annuity contract issued after June 8, 1997. Exceptions to this general rule provide for limited interest deductions for loans in connection with certain business-owned contracts, as discussed below. There are complex and overlapping sets of rules regarding interest deductions for policy loans with respect to policies issued on or before June 8, 1997. Those rules will be briefly discussed.

The "Key Person" Rule. This provision is the most significant exception to the general rule that interest deductions on policy loans are disallowed. The key person rule provides that interest on loan amounts not in excess of $50,000 per insured person is deductible if the insured or other covered person under the contract is a "key person." The definition of a key person is an officer or 20 percent owner of the taxpayer. Clearly, this definition restricts the application of the key person rules to contracts owned by business taxpayers. Such taxpayers include both incorporated and unincorporated business entities.

There are further restrictions on the definition of a key person. The total number of key persons per business taxpayer may not exceed the GREATER of:

- five individuals or
- the LESSER of
  - 5 percent of the total number of officers and employees of the business taxpayer, or
  - 20 individuals

This restriction means that in order for a business taxpayer to have more than five key persons for purposes of the tax rules for interest deductions on policy loans, the taxpayer has to have more than 100 employees. In addition, in order to have the maximum number of 20 key persons, the business taxpayer claiming the interest deductions would have to have at least 400 employees.

If the taxpayer is a corporation, the ownership rule of 20 percent is applied based on stock ownership. For unincorporated entities, the ownership test is based on ownership of a capital or profits interest in the business.

There are also limitations on the interest rate that may be used in calculating allowable interest deductions under the key person rule. The applicable interest rate for purposes of calculating deductions is the lesser of the interest rate specified in the contract or the rate of interest described as "Moody's Corporate Bond Yield Average—Monthly Average Corporates" as published by Moody's Investors Service, Inc., for the month in which the interest is paid or accrued.

The key person rules generally apply to policy loan interest paid or accrued after October 13, 1995. Different limitations applied to certain interest payments under so-called "transitional" rules pursuant to 1996 tax legislation. These transitional rules do not apply to any interest paid or accrued after 1998, so they will not be discussed here.

"Grandfather" Rule and Effective Dates. If an insurance contract was entered into before June 21, 1986, the key person rules and the $50,000 of indebtedness limitation do not apply. Interest on loans connected with such contracts may be deductible, subject to other layers of rules imposed by IRC Sec. 264. However, the monthly "Moody's" rate applies to current payments to limit the interest rate that may be used in calculating allowable deductions. Contracts entered into between June 21, 1986, and June 8, 1997, that are owned by business entities are generally subject to the key person rules and $50,000 of indebtedness limitations with respect to interest paid or accrued after October 13, 1995. Under certain circumstances loans from policies owned by taxpayers other than business entities may be deductible if the contract was entered into on or before June 8, 1997. Contracts issued after June 8, 1997, can be eligible for interest deductions for policy loans only under the key person rules (which require business ownership of the contract), subject to the $50,000 of indebtedness limitation and other restrictions discussed below.

Interest on Loans from Nonbusiness Policies. As already stated, contracts issued after June 8, 1997, can generate interest deductions on policy loans only under the key person rules. This means that no personally owned policy issued after that date can generate interest deductions. What about contracts issued on or before June 8, 1997? If all the other requirements of IRC Section 264 are met, interest on such personally owned policies may be deductible as investment interest (as discussed in chapter 9) if the taxpayer can demonstrate that the loan was used for investment purposes according to the loan "tracing" rules pursuant to IRC Sec. 163. This is probably the only avenue for individual taxpayers to claim interest deductions with respect to loans from personally owned policies.

Additional Restrictions on Interest Deductions for Policy Loans. If the indebtedness is incurred or continued to purchase or carry a single premium life insurance contract, no interest deduction for policy loans is allowable even if the interest qualifies under any of the other rules just described. For this purpose, a "single premium contract" is one in which substantially all the premiums are paid within a 4-year period from the date of purchase, or a contract for which an amount is deposited with the insurer for payment of a substantial number of future premiums on the contract.

Also no interest deduction will be allowed if the interest is paid pursuant to a plan of purchase that contemplates the systematic borrowing of part or all of the increases in cash value of the contract. This rule applies to contracts purchased after August 6, 1963. However, there are four exceptions to the disallowance rule for contracts involving a "systematic borrowing" plan:

- *The 7-year or "four-out-of-seven" exception.* The systematic borrowing rule will not apply if at least four of the first seven annual premiums under the contract are paid without using borrowed funds.
- *The $100-a-year exception.* The systematic borrowing rule will not apply if the taxpayer's total interest paid for the year that would be subject to the rule does not exceed $100.
- *The unforeseen event exception.* If the indebtedness was incurred because of an unforeseen substantial loss of income or unforeseen substantial increase in the taxpayer's financial obligations, the systematic borrowing rule will not apply.
- *The trade or business exception.* The systematic borrowing rule will not apply if the indebtedness was incurred in connection with the taxpayer's trade or business. Note that borrowing to finance split-dollar or key person life insurance plans is not treated as indebtedness incurred in connection with a business. There must be a business purpose apart from the insurance coverage itself.

Note that the exceptions to the systematic borrowing rule do not apply to single premium contracts. The single premium contract rule is separate from the systematic borrowing rule.

Coordination of Rules Limiting Interest Deductions on Policy Loans. The restrictions under IRC Sec. 264 generally apply separately and cumulatively. This means, for example, that interest payments qualifying under the key person rules must also satisfy the rules for single premium contracts and systematic borrowing plans. In addition, the limitations of Sec. 264 apply after all other tax rules that limit or prohibit interest deductions have been applied. This means that the general rules regarding interest deductions must first be applied to policy loan interest before the additional rules under Sec. 264 are considered. Those general rules are discussed in chapter 9.

Allocation of Interest Expenses to Policy Cash Values

This rule is a different type of restriction that also applies to life insurance, annuity, and endowment contracts issued after June 8, 1997. Under an allocation formula that takes into account both a taxpayer's policy cash values and the tax basis of any other assets owned by the taxpayer, deductions for interest on *any* loan payable by the taxpayer may be disallowed to the extent that the allocation formula determines that the interest payment is "allocable" to the taxpayer's unborrowed policy cash values. The taxpayer's entire asset portfolio is counted in determining what portion of an interest payment is "allocable" to the taxpayer's unborrowed policy values, and therefore is treated as nondeductible interest.

The rule has two important exceptions that limit its applicability to certain types of taxpayers. First, it does not apply to contracts owned by natural persons (human beings). Second, it does not apply to contracts insuring or covering 20 percent owners, officers, directors, or employees of a business taxpayer. The second exception means that interest qualifying under the key person rules described above will not be disallowed by this allocation rule. The original legislative intent of the allocation rule was to limit interest deductions of financial institutions that own life insurance contracts on the lives of their debtors and that borrow money from sources other than insurance contracts.

SUMMARY

Although death proceeds of life insurance enjoy shelter from the impact of federal income tax in the vast majority of instances, the very nature of life insurance as valuable property as well as its flexibility in solving human problems has led to its imaginative use in business and personal situations where careful planning is required to avoid income tax pitfalls. Thus all proposed transfers of life insurance should be closely examined to avoid transfer-for-value problems; the requirement of insurable interest should be taken into account as a tax-oriented dimension of concern; the proper arrangement of policy ownership and beneficiary designation should be given thorough consideration where premiums are paid with corporate dollars; and the disposition or use of life insurance in separation and divorce cases should be accomplished with specialized guidance to avoid unfavorable tax results. It should also be understood that there are now strict limitations on deductibility of policy loan interest.

The questions of life insurance premium deductibility and taxation are of special concern in charitable giving and in planning life insurance fringe benefits for selected employees. Again, in these complicated yet common transactions, the desired tax results can best be accomplished through an awareness of the tax principles involved.

NOTES

1. IRC Sec. 101(a)(1).
2. Treas. Reg. Sec. 1.101-1.
3. IRC Sec. 101(c).
4. IRC Sec. 101(d)(1).
5. P.L. 99-514, Tax Reform Act of 1986, Sec. 1001(b).
6. P.L. 99-514, Tax Reform Act of 1986, Sec. 1001(a).
7. IRC Sec. 101(g).
8. *Griffith v. United States,* 360 F.2d 210 (CA 3, 1966), affirming 245 F. Supp. 678 (1965).
9. IRC Sec. 72(e)(1)(B); Treas. Reg. Sec. 1.72-11(b)(1).
10. Ibid.
11. IRC Sec. 72(e).
12. Treas. Reg. Sec. 1.72-6(a)(1).
13. Rev. Rul. 55-349, 1955-1 C.B. 232.
14. 38 USC Sec. 3101(a).
15. *Commissioner v. Phillips,* 275 F.2d 33 (CA 4, 1960).
16. IRC Sec. 72(j).
17. Treas. Reg. Sec. 1.451-2; *Blum v. Higgins,* 150 F.2d 471 (CA 6, 1945).
18. *Constance C. Frackelton,* 46 B.T.A. 883, acq. C.B. 1944, p. 10.
19. IRC Sec. 72(a).
20. IRC Sec. 72(b).
21. IRC Sec. 72(h)(2).
22. Treas. Reg. Sec. 1.72-12.
23. IRC Sec. 72(c).
24. Treas. Reg. Sec. 1.72-5(c).
25. Treas. Reg. Sec. 1.72-5(d).
26. Treas. Reg. Sec. 1.72-5(a).
27. Treas. Reg. Sec. 1.72-11(c)(1)(2), Example 4.
28. Treas. Reg. Sec. 1.72-11(c)(1)(2), Example 1.
29. IRC Sec. 104(a)(3).
30. *Castner Garage, Ltd.,* 43 B.T.A. 1, acq. (1935).
31. IRC Sec. 105(b).
32. Treas. Reg. Sec. 1.262-1(b)(1); IRC Sec. 264(a)(1).
33. IRC Sec. 264(a)(1).
34. OD 699 C.B. 3, 1261.
35. IRC Sec. 213(d)(1).
36. Rev. Rul. 68-451, 1968-2, C.B. 111.
37. IRC Sec. 213(d)(1)(C).
38. Rev. Rul. 66-262, 1966-2 C.B. 105.
39. IRC Sec. 106.
40. IRC Sec. 162(a)(1).
41. IRC Sec. 106.
42. Treas. Reg. Sec. 1.162-10(a).
43. IRC Sec. 101(a)(2).
44. Treas. Reg. Sec. 1.101-1(b).
45. IRC Sec. 101(a)(2)(A)(B).
46. Rev. Rul. 69-187, 1969-16 I.R.B. 8.
47. "Where a transfer of property is in part a sale and in part a gift, the unadjusted basis of the property in the hands of the transferee is the sum of—(1) Whichever of the following is the greater: (i) the amount paid by the transferee for the property, or (ii) the transferor's adjusted basis for the property at the time of the transfer . . . ." Treas. Reg. Sec. 1.1015-4(a).
48. IRC Sec. 1041.
49. Treas. Reg. Sec. 1.101-1(b)(4).
50. Treas. Reg. Sec. 1.101-1(b)(3).
51. See citation in footnote 49, *supra.*

52.   *Atlantic Oil v. Patterson,* 331 F.2d 516 (CA 5, 1964).

53.   *Francis H. W. Ducros,* 272 F.2d 49 (CA 6, 1959).

54.   *M. Lucille Harrison,* 59 T.C. No. 57 (1973).

55.   Rev. Rul. 61-134, I.R.B. 1961-2.

56.   Golden v. Commissioner, 113 F.2d 590 (CA 3, 1940); Rev. Rul. 71-79, I.R.B. 1971-7, 17. But see Estate of J. E. Horne, 63 T.C. No. 98 (1975), acq. in result, 1980-1 C.B. 1, where proceeds payable to a shareholder on a corporate-owned policy were held not to be dividends where the proceeds could also be included in the gross estate of the deceased for federal estate tax purposes by Treas. Reg. Sec. 20.2042-1(c)(6). The Horne case is perhaps an aberration. Its result was a unique attempt by the court to achieve a degree of equity between conflicting ownership concepts. Although in fact the corporation owned the life insurance policy, the Treasury's own estate tax regulations attributed ownership to the insured. In a 1981 Technical Advice Memorandum (LTR 8144001), the IRS took the position that when the death proceeds of a corporate-owned life insurance policy on a majority shareholder were paid to the deceased shareholder's spouse, the proceeds were excludible under IRC Sec. 101(a) because the beneficiary spouse was not a shareholder.

57.   Where the insured is a controlling shareholder of a corporation, life insurance on the insured's life owned by the corporation but payable other than for the benefit of the corporation will be includible in its entirety in the insured's estate for federal estate tax purposes. Treas. Reg. Sec. 20.2042-1(c)(6).

58.   Rev. Rul. 59-184, 1959-1 C.B. 65.

59.   *A. N. Johnson,* 66 T.C. 897, (1976), aff'd. 78-1 USTC (CA-4, 1978). When the insured partner died, the surviving partner claimed a capital loss on liquidation of the partnership. It was this loss that the court held as compensated for by life insurance. The surviving partner argued unsuccessfully that (1) the life insurance compensated him for the loss of his partner's life, not for the loss of his investment in the partnership; (2) IRC Sec. 165 does not apply to life insurance; (3) unlike casualty insurance, the payment of life insurance death proceeds is not dependent on an investment loss; and (4) the disallowance of his loss deduction had the effect of taxing the life insurance death proceeds in contravention of IRC Sec. 101(a).

60.   IRC Sec. 170; *Eppa Hunton IV,* 1 T.C. 821.

61.   IRC Sec. 170(f)(3).

62.   The IRS, in two Revenue Rulings, reinforced this view. Rev. Rul. 76-1, I.R.B. 1976-1, 8 denied a charitable deduction for premiums paid on "split-life" insurance and in Rev. Rul. 76-143, I.R.B. 1976-16, 9 deductibility was denied for split-dollar plan premiums. In each instance the charity had a partial ownership interest in the plan.

63.   *Twin City Tile and Marble Co.,* 32 F.2d 229 (CA 8, 1929); *Hubert Transfer and Storage,* 7 T.C.M. 171; Treas. Reg. Sec. 1.61-2(d)(2)(ii)(a).

64.   IRC Sec. 264(a); Rev. Rul. 70-148, I.R.B. 1970-14, 9; 1970-1 C.B. 60.

65.   Rev. Rul. 64-328, 1964-2 C.B. 11.

66.   The insurance company's one-year term rates may be used to measure the economic benefits, if lower than the P.S. 58 rates. Rev. Rul. 66-110, 1966-1 C.B. 12.

67.   TAM 9604001.

Tax Treatment of Modified Endowment Contracts[*]

Edward E. Graves and James F. Ivers III[†]

Internal Revenue Service: The world's most successful mail order business.

Bob Goddard

Chapter Outline

---

[*] This chapter is an updated revision of an excerpt from *The Financial Services Professional's Guide to the State of the Art: 1989,* Stephan R. Leimberg et al. (Bryn Mawr, Pa.: The American College, 1989).

[†] Edward E. Graves, CLU, ChFC, is associate professor of insurance and Charles J. Zimmerman Chair in Life Insurance Education at The American College.

HISTORICAL PERSPECTIVE ON SINGLE-PREMIUM POLICIES

Single-premium life insurance policies experienced an 800 percent increase in sales volume between 1984 and 1988. This was mainly due to the Tax Reform Act of 1986, which eliminated many of the tax advantages of what had been popular tax-sheltered investments. After that legislation was enacted, many investors purchased single-premium life insurance policies. In many cases the income tax deferral was the primary motivation for the purchase. Some stock brokerages were promoting and selling single-premium life insurance policies as tax shelters. These policies were often described as the last remaining tax shelter under our tax law.

Single-premium life insurance policies and other limited pay policies enjoyed the same tax treatment as other life insurance policies (that is, cash value buildup is generally income tax free until the policy is terminated). The policyowner was able to borrow against the policy in the form of policy loans and gain possession and management of the purchase price of the policy without being taxed.

CONGRESSIONAL ACTION

Members of Congress were disturbed by the marketing of single-premium life insurance. The Technical and Miscellaneous Revenue Act of 1988 (TAMRA '88) changed the income taxation of any policy entered into on or after June 21, 1988, that fails a test titled the *7-pay test* and consequently is classified a modified endowment contract (MEC).

Policies entered into *before* June 21, 1988, have been grandfathered and are not affected by this law unless they undergo a "material change." The material changes that can jeopardize the grandfather protection will be explained below.

The objective of the changes in tax treatment for insurance policies classified as modified endowment contracts is to discourage the use of high-premium life insurance policies as short-term investments. This treatment makes the use of high-premium life insurance policies as short-term investments more costly and thereby decreases the return to the policyowner who takes possession of the cash value through loans, withdrawals, or terminations. However, the rules in no way decrease the return to policyowners who leave the funds with the insurer and look to the death benefit as the primary benefit of the contract.

The 7-Pay Test

The modified endowment contract rules affect the tax treatment of any policy entered into on or after June 21, 1988, in which the aggregate premiums paid at any time during the first 7 years of the contract exceed the sum of the "net level premiums" that would have been paid by that time if the contract provided for paid-up benefits after the payment of seven level annual premiums. This is called the *7-pay test.*

Policies that fail the 7-pay test because too much has been paid within the first 7 years are considered *modified endowment contracts* (MECs). For example, if the annual net level premium for a $100,000 7-pay policy is $4,500, then any $100,000 policy for the same insured will be considered a modified endowment contract if the aggregate premiums *exceed* the following:

- $4,500 during the first policy year
- $9,000 during the first 2 policy years
- $13,500 during the first 3 policy years
- $18,000 during the first 4 policy years
- $22,500 during the first 5 policy years
- $27,000 during the first 6 policy years
- $31,500 during the first 7 policy years

If the aggregate premiums paid during the first 7 years are *equal to or less than* the aggregate premiums that would have been paid on a level-annual-premium basis using the net level premium amount ($4,500 a year in this example) for a 7-pay policy (for the same insured), the policy will *not* be a modified endowment contract and will receive the same tax treatment previously applicable to all policies.

The definition of a net level premium under these rules is based on the net single-premium concept under IRC Sec. 7702, which provides the definition of a life insurance contract. The net level premium is *not* the same as the actual premium payable under the contract. It is also not the same as what many life insurance professionals refer to as a net premium. *Net level premium* is a technical term of art created and defined by the tax law. Stated simply, however, net level premium is an artificially constructed amount based on reasonable mortality charges, an assumed interest rate, and (in some cases) reasonable insurance company expense charges. Therefore it is possible that even policies that require 7 level annual premiums in some cases will not pass the 7-pay test because the net level premium will be less than the actual premium. In other words, if the net level premium is less that the actual premium payable, the payment of the actual premium due will cause the policy to fail the 7-pay test.

Those policies entered into on or after June 21, 1988, that are classified as modified endowment contracts may be subject to income taxes and penalty taxes not applicable to other life insurance policies. Policy loans and partial withdrawals of funds from such modified endowment contracts are subject to last-in first-out (LIFO) treatment to determine the applicable taxes. This means that any income earned on the contract fund is taxed as if it was withdrawn *before* the policyowner's cost basis in the contract. In addition to the regular income tax, a 10 percent penalty tax is generally applicable to taxable gains withdrawn from a modified endowment contract before the policyowner reaches age 59½. However, the 10 percent penalty does not apply to payments attributable to disability or to annuitized payments.

Example: Penelope purchased a life insurance contract 5 years ago. Her basis in the policy is $100,000, and the contract has a cash value of $140,000. The policy is a MEC. She borrows $50,000 from the policy's cash value on her 50th birthday. Penelope's taxable gain from the loan is $40,000 ($140,000 cash value – $100,000 basis in the policy). If Penelope is in the 36 percent tax bracket, she must pay an income tax of $14,400 ($40,000 x .36). She must also pay a 10 percent penalty on the taxable amount. The penalty will be $4,000 ($40,000 x .10). Therefore Penelope's total tax bill on the loan from the policy is $18,400 ($14,400 + $4,000).

Note that all amounts included in Penelope's gross income as a result of taking a loan from the policy are added to her basis in the policy for purposes of determining future taxable amounts. Therefore Penelope's basis in the policy after taking the loan will be $140,000 ($100,000 original basis + $40,000 taxable portion of loan). The $10,000 nontaxable portion does not affect Penelope's basis in the contract because the transaction is a loan and not a withdrawal.

These rules are similar to those applicable to deferred-annuity contracts issued after August 13, 1982. Income earned within such contracts is deemed to be withdrawn (and therefore taxable) before the cost basis of the contract is recovered when withdrawals are made before the annuity's starting date. However, life insurance policies that are not classified as modified endowment contracts, as well as so-called "pre-TEFRA" annuity contracts (those funded before August 14, 1982), are subject to a more favorable first-in first-out (FIFO) tax treatment on withdrawals.

Contracts with Death Benefits of $10,000 or Less

There is a variation on the application of the net level premium amount in the 7-pay test that applies to policies of $10,000 or less in face amount. The law provides an annual allowance of $75 to be added to the 7-pay test premium. The $75 additional allowance permits some small 7-pay policies to pass the 7-pay test when they otherwise might not. The smaller the policy is, the more likely it is that the actual premium will be less than the net level premium plus $75. The full $75 can be used for any amount of coverage between $1,000 and $10,000, resulting in a maximum allowable additional expense loading of $7.50 per $1,000 of coverage.

Congress anticipated the added attractiveness of this small policy expense allowance and its potential abuses. Therefore the statute requires that all policies issued by the same insurer to the same policyowner be treated as one policy for purposes of determining that the face amount does not exceed $10,000. This prevents policyowners from purchasing a large number of small policies to take advantage of the allowable expense loading. Note that the statute does not require that policies from *different* insurers be aggregated for this purpose. This may present a planning opportunity for taxpayers purchasing several small policies from different insurance companies.

Grandfathered Policies

Policies entered into prior to June 21, 1988, (as well as policies entered into on or after that date that pass the 7-pay test) will generally be treated the same as they have been in the past. There is no income tax applicable to withdrawals until after the cost basis has been recovered tax free. This is the first-in first-out (FIFO) treatment long associated with life insurance policy taxation. Generally no penalty tax is applicable to taxable gains from life insurance policies unless the policy is reclassified as a MEC.

It is important to remember that under the Tax Reform Act of 1986 withdrawals from policies that are associated with a reduction in policy benefits during the first 15 policy years are subject to a limited LIFO-type federal income taxation. The MEC rules were imposed *in addition to* these rules. However, the 1986 rules do not apply to policy loans. The MEC rules do apply to loans as well as to withdrawals.

Subsequent Exchanges of a MEC

Once a policy is classified as a MEC, it will automatically make any policy subsequently received in exchange for it also a MEC. Even if the new policy received in the exchange passes the 7-pay test, it will be classified as a MEC.

> *Example:* Merlin purchased a single-premium policy 3 years ago. The policy failed the 7-pay test and is treated as a MEC. This year, Merlin exchanges his single-premium policy for a level premium whole life policy that clearly passes the 7-pay test. However, the new policy will be treated as a MEC because it was received in exchange for a MEC.

At first glance this appears to be a harsh result. However, Congress was apparently concerned about the potential for using untaxed internal policy gains to purchase additional life insurance coverage. In the absence of this provision a tax benefit similar to a deduction for premium payments would have existed.

MATERIAL CHANGE RULES

A policy that at first passes the 7-pay test when it is issued can later become a MEC if there is a "material change" in the policy. In addition, a single-premium policy entered into before June 21, 1988, is not a MEC but could become one if the policy is materially changed anytime after June 20, 1988, and fails the 7-pay test after the change.

What constitutes a material change under the MEC rules? An increase in future benefits under the contract will generally be considered a material change. However, the following will *not* be treated as material changes:

- cost-of-living increases in death benefits that are based on a broad-based index (such as the consumer price index)
- death-benefit increases inherent in the policy design because of the crediting of interest or other earnings. (This appears to exempt the increasing death benefits of a type II universal life policy from classification as a material change.)
- increases in death benefits because of the premiums paid for the policy to support the level of benefits for the first 7 contract years. (This appears to exempt from material change classification any increase in death benefits necessary to keep the required relationship between the death benefit and the policy guideline cash value or guideline premiums as specified in Sec. 7702.)

A policy that was previously not classified as a MEC will be subject to the 7-pay test after a material change. If the policy then fails the test, it will be a MEC and therefore subject to LIFO taxation of policy loans, withdrawals, and terminations. The change in taxation will be applicable only for the year of the material change and subsequent years. There will not be retroactive taxation of loans or distributions in years prior to the application of the 7-pay test unless the distributions were made in anticipation of the failure or made within 2 years before such failure. In such cases the distribution will be taxed in the year it was made.

Special Rule for Death Benefit Increases over $150,000

A policy entered into prior to June 21, 1988, that experiences an increase of death benefits in excess of $150,000 on or after October 20, 1988, will be subject to the material change provisions. This means that such a policy could lose its grandfathered status if it does not pass the 7-pay test. The policy will be subject to the 7-pay test at each increase unless the death benefit increases were due to cost-of-living adjustments, to interest or earnings increases, or attributable to premiums needed to fund the lowest level of benefits during the first 7 policy years.

What increase in death benefits would be attributable to premiums needed to fund the lowest level of benefits during the first 7 policy years? If the increase in the cash value of the contract forces an increase in the death benefit in order to satisfy the definition of a life insurance contract under IRC Sec. 7702, such an increase in the death benefit is attributable to those premiums. Therefore such an increase will not cause the policy to be reclassified as a MEC.

However, the loss of grandfather status applies only to policies that require fewer than seven level annual premiums. If a policy required at least seven level annual premiums as of June 21, 1988, and the policyowner actually makes seven level annual premium payments, the $150,000 death benefit increase provision will not apply, and the policy will retain its grandfathered status.

Conversion Rights

Term insurance policies entered into before June 21, 1988, that are converted to cash value policies after June 20, 1988, will be treated as if originally entered into on the date of conversion. This means that they will have to satisfy the 7-pay test at the time of conversion.

> *Example:* Angelica purchased a term life insurance policy in 1987. On January 1, 2001, she converts her term policy to a whole life policy. Angelica's new policy is subject to the 7-pay test.

Reduction in Benefits

If there is a reduction of policy death benefits during the first 7 policy years, the 7-pay test will be applicable to the policy after the reduction. The test will be applied as if the contract had originally been issued at the reduced benefit level.

The law does allow a 90-day grace period for policy reinstatement that will prevent the conversion of the policy to MEC status if there is a reduction of benefits during the first 7 policy years because of nonpayment of premiums. In other words, a policy that lapses during the first 7 years but is reinstated within 90 days will not be reclassified as a MEC because of the temporary reduction of benefits prior to the reinstatement.

> *Example:* Bret purchased a $100,000 universal life policy in January 1997. In the fifth policy year, on January 31, 2001, he negotiates a reduction in the death benefit to $70,000. Bret must now pass the 7-pay test for a $70,000 policy entered into in January 1997. If the policy does not pass the test, the policy will be treated as a MEC beginning on the date the benefits were reduced, January 31, 2001.

With respect to policies entered into or materially changed on or after September 14, 1989, that insure more than one life (so-called survivorship policies), a reduction in death benefits *after* the first 7 contract years will also cause the policy to be subject to the 7-pay test as if the policy had originally been issued at the reduced benefit level. This provision was designed to plug a technical loophole in the MEC statute, which seemed to permit survivorship policies with fewer than seven annual premiums to pass the 7-pay test by taking advantage of benefit reductions after 7 years and the low probability of the death of both insureds during the first 7 policy years.

Benefit Increases without Additional Evidence of Insurability

As previously explained, if the death benefit of a grandfathered policy increases by more than $150,000, the policy may be subjected to the material change rules and be reclassified as a MEC if it fails the 7-pay test. In addition, Congress anticipated other potential abuses with respect to grandfathered policies.

One potential abuse would be the granting of benefit increases on policies that originally did not contractually provide for such increases without additional evidence of insurability. If the insurance company provides a benefit increase on a policy after June 20, 1988, that would have required additional evidence of insurability for such an increase before June 21, 1988, the policy will be treated as if it were entered into on or after June 21, 1988. This means that the policy will be subject to the 7-pay test based on the benefit increases, regardless of whether the benefit has increased by more than $150,000. However, if the policy originally provided for benefit increases for events such as birth or marriage without additional evidence of insurability, the policy will retain its grandfathered status until the aggregate of all such benefit increases exceeds $150,000, as previously discussed.

Treatment of Premiums Returned

There is a 60-day grace period for returned premiums to keep the premiums paid under the 7-pay net level premium amount. The insurer can return excess premiums within 60 days after the end of the contract year. The returned amount will reduce the sum of premiums paid under the contract during such contract year. If any part of such payment from the insurance company is interest, it will be includible in the gross income of the recipient.

Aggregation Rules

Congress foresaw potential abuses in withdrawing funds from MECs by splitting up funds between many policies and withdrawing funds from one policy. In that manner the gain on that one policy could be withdrawn and the remainder of the withdrawals would be a nontaxable return of the policyowner's basis in the contract. To prevent this the law requires that all MECs issued by the same insurer to a policyowner during any calendar year be treated as one MEC. This forces recognition of all gain from all such policies before the policyowner is able to withdraw the investment in the contract.

Example: Four years ago Arnie purchased 10 single-premium life insurance policies. He paid $100,000 for each one. This year, the policies have a cash value of $117,000 each.

Arnie is now 57 years old. He withdraws $50,000 of cash value from one of his policies. The aggregate untaxed gain on all of Arnie's policies is $170,000 ($17,000 x 10). Therefore the entire $50,000 withdrawal is subject to both federal income tax and the 10 percent penalty, even though the gain in the policy from which the funds were withdrawn is only $17,000.

Burial Contracts

Another provision in the law exempts assignments or pledges of MECs with face amounts of less than $25,000 from current taxation if the assignment or pledge is for funeral services or prearranged funerals. It is important to remember that all other pledges or assignments of MECs are treated as loans from the policy. Therefore the pledge or assignment will result in both the federal income tax and the 10 percent penalty.

MEC Checklist

The following are checklists for policies that originally were not classified as MECs. They involve changes that could affect the application of a new 7-pay test.

Can a *grandfathered* life insurance policy become a MEC if	Yes	No
it remains in force with no policy changes		X
it has a death-benefit increase of more than $150,000 after October 20, 1988	X	
its death benefit increases due to a premium "dump" on or after June 21, 1988	X	
it is terminated		X
it is a single life policy and is kept in force, but the death benefit is reduced after the 7th policy year		X
it is a survivorship policy and is kept in force, but the death benefit is reduced after the 7th policy year	X	
it experiences death-benefit increases due to interest or earnings internal to the policy		X
it has death-benefit increases in order to satisfy the definition of life insurance, and the premium has not increased above the level during the first 7 policy years		X

Can a *grandfathered* life insurance policy become a MEC if	Yes	No
it has death-benefit increases due to a cost-of-living provision linked to the consumer price index (CPI)		X
it experiences death-benefit increases from exercising the guaranteed purchase provisions in the policy		X
it experiences death-benefit increases as a result of purchase options exercised when the insured has a newborn		X
it has an increase in benefits for which there is no policy guarantee or provision waiving evidence of insurability requirements, and such increase would normally require additional evidence of insurability	X	

Can a policy entered into after June 20, 1988, that initially passes the 7-pay test be subjected to the test again if	Yes	No
the death benefit is decreased during the first 7 policy years (or thereafter in the case of a survivorship policy)	X	
the death benefit increases due to premium increases after the first 7 policy years	X	
the death benefit increases due to paid-up additions from premium amounts greater than required to fund the benefit levels provided during the first 7 policy years	X	
the death benefit increases due to cost-of-living adjustments tied to the CPI or some other widely accepted index		X
the death benefit must be increased to satisfy the definition of life insurance, but the premiums paid are not in excess of those required to fund the level of benefits maintained in the first 7 policy years		X
the death benefit must be increased to satisfy the definition of life insurance because of excess interest or earnings credited inside the policy, but premiums are not in excess of those required to fund the level of benefits maintained in the first 7 policy years		X

EFFECTIVE DATE

The law does not apply to policies that were entered into prior to June 21, 1988, unless a material change occurs as previously described. Those owning policies entered into on or after June 21, 1988, are subject to the MEC rules.

PLANNING CONSIDERATIONS

Individuals who own purchased policies that are classified as MECs should not be hasty to terminate them (especially those still subject to policy surrender charges in addition to the regular income tax and 10 percent penalty tax). In summary, funds received under the policy (including policy loans or other loans secured by the modified endowment contract and dividends paid out by the policy) will be considered taxable income first. Amounts in excess of the gain in the policy will be considered tax-free recovery of cost basis. This is similar to the treatment of withdrawals of funds during the accumulation phase under a deferred annuity.

Those individuals owning single-premium or limited pay policies that were entered into before June 21, 1988, should be aware of the grandfathering they enjoy and that their policy loans will not be subject to LIFO-based income taxes. However, owners must be cautioned that their grandfathered status can be lost if the policy is exchanged for a new policy that requires additional premiums or if the death benefit on the existing policy is increased in such a way that it is treated as a material change.

Owners of non-MEC contracts should be reminded that the law still imposes LIFO taxation on non-MEC policies that have funds withdrawn during the first 15 policy years, in association with a reduction of benefits. This is most likely to occur under certain universal life policies and grandfathered single-premium policies.

Those policyowners who purchase policies that fail the 7-pay test should be aware that they are subject to the MEC rules. They should carefully consider the cost of terminating such policies before deciding what to do. At first these policies probably have relatively small gains subject to taxation and penalty, but they may face significant surrender charges. The surrender charges will decrease with policy duration, but the taxable gains will increase with duration. Each individual policy has its own pattern and trade-offs. Individual evaluations are required to determine the optimal treatment of these policies. In some cases the policyowner may be justified in terminating early and limiting taxation even though it means paying surrender charges. Some may choose to keep the policy in force but not take possession of policy cash values. All policyowners should be able to find less costly sources of funds than policy loans from a MEC.

By congressional design, single-premium policies are no longer useful as a strictly investment-oriented tax-deferral vehicle. However, it is important to realize and emphasize that single-premium policies can still be viable and desirable. They provide a way to pass assets to others without subjecting them to the costs, delays, and uncertainties of probate; attacks on or elections against the insured's will; or the claims of creditors. These policies also provide a way to fully prefund future debts or pledges with discounted tax-advantaged dollars. At death they are still income tax free and can be arranged to be both estate and inheritance tax free.

18

Taxation of Corporations and Shareholders

James F. Ivers III and Stephan R. Leimberg

If Patrick Henry thought that taxation without representation was bad, he should see how bad it is with representation.

The Old Farmer's Almanac

There can be no taxation without misrepresentation.

J.B. Handelsman

Chapter Outline

Cheesman, Reebel, and Baily are engineers. They have developed a relatively inexpensive process for manufacturing an aircraft safety component that is in great demand for new jet airliners.

Cheesman is a sole proprietor currently engaged in producing aircraft parts. Reebel, a young man who has a postgraduate degree in business administration and an undergraduate degree in engineering, has worked for Cheesman for a number of years. He first started as an engineer and almost by accident moved into the firm's sales division. Reebel's sales efforts have been so successful that Cheesman would like to offer him an interest in a new business venture. Baily is slightly older than Cheesman and Reebel. He is a well-known and highly respected authority in the area of aircraft safety parts. He does quite a bit of consulting work for both government and private enterprise. He met Cheesman and Reebel on such a consulting project, and the three men have become good friends. Baily is quite wealthy, and he is interested in keeping both his money and his mind at work.

The three engineers have decided to form a business and have invited Bob Kress, a CPA attorney who is an expert in tax planning, to help them decide on a course of action. Kress has suggested that the best vehicle for their new business venture might be a corporation. They have asked Kress to discuss the taxation of a corporation on a detailed basis so that they could get an idea of what advantages and disadvantages corporate status entails, as well as some of the tax implications of doing business in corporate form.

LEGAL ASPECTS OF A CORPORATION

Kress: A corporation is essentially a legal entity created under state law for the purpose of conducting a business or philanthropic activity. Under traditional principles of state corporation law, there are four legal characteristics that distinguish a corporation from other forms of business operation. These four corporate characteristics are:

- limited liability
- transferability of interest
- centralized management
- continuity of life

Cheesman: Bob, would you go into more detail on exactly what you mean by those phrases?

Kress: Yes. An organization possesses *limited liability* if the organization's creditors cannot proceed against its individual owners personally in satisfaction of a corporate debt. This is one of the best-known reasons for choosing the corporate form.

If the formalities of corporate procedure are followed, then the corporation is really operating as a business and financial unit entirely separate from its shareholders for legal purposes. Shareholders will not be personally liable for the corporation's debts or other liabilities. As a practical matter, principal shareholders of small corporations will often be required to cosign a note or give a personal guarantee for the corporation and therefore become personally liable for loans to the corporation from banks or other lending institutions. Generally, however, the most a shareholder can lose is his or her investment in the business.

Transferability of interest generally means that a shareholder of a corporation can transfer interest in the profits, assets, and control of the business freely and without restraint. If each shareholder, without the consent of the other shareholders of the organization, can transfer interest to a person who is not a shareholder, there is *free transferability of interest*. It is permissible, however, to impose reasonable restrictions on shareholders to preserve the nature of close corporate membership. These restrictions are often contained in *buy-sell* agreements and facilitate family estate planning with respect to a business interest.

Centralized management exists if the operating authority is concentrated in one person or a relatively small class within the group as opposed to the sharing of management decisions commonly found in partnerships. If any person or group of persons (which does not include all of the members) has continuing, exclusive authority to make the decisions necessary to the management and daily operation of the business, there will be centralized management.

The group in which that authority is legally vested is called the board of directors. The board of directors uses its best judgment and independent discretion to determine and execute corporate policies. Although these individuals are in fact elected by the shareholders and are removable by them for cause (and possibly without cause), the directors are not agents of the shareholders. They are fiduciaries whose duties primarily run to the corporation itself.

It is the board of directors, not the shareholders, who make policy decisions with respect to the products, services, prices, and wages of the company. Likewise, even in the smallest corporation, legally speaking it is the board of directors that has the right to select, supervise, and remove officers and other personnel. For example, the board of directors, and not the shareholders, fixes compensation and decides on the installation and benefit levels of pension and profit-sharing plans, as well as other employee benefits. In short, the supervision and vigilance for the welfare of the entire corporate enterprise is vested in the hands of a very select group.

Continuity of life means that death, disability, incapacity, addition of a new shareholder, or withdrawal of an old shareholder will not cause legal dissolution of the business. If the effect of the death of a shareholder is the automatic death of the business, a vital element of corporate status would be lacking. A corporation is the only form of business enterprise that—theoretically at least—has the advantage of perpetual existence. For example, even the death of a 100 percent shareholder would not automatically cause the legal termination of the business. Practically speaking, however, without successor management, such a corporation will *die* as quickly as a sole proprietorship.

Under modern business law, business entities other than corporations, such as limited partnerships and limited liability companies, may also exhibit one or more corporate characteristics.

CLASSIFICATION UNDER FEDERAL INCOME TAX LAW

If an organization is classified as a corporation for federal tax purposes, it will be treated as a separate taxable entity, distinct and apart from the owners of its stock. A corporation therefore has a tax existence separate from its shareholders. The result is that a corporation must compute its own income and deductions, file its own return, and pay its own tax at the applicable corporate rates.[1]

In the past, the courts and the Internal Revenue Service applied the traditional concepts of corporate law to determine whether a business organization should be taxed as a corporation or as a partnership. If an organization was found to possess three out of those four characteristics, it would be taxable as a corporation under federal law, regardless of how it was formed under applicable state law.

The IRS has recently revised and simplified its approach in determining the federal tax classification of business organizations. Generally, an organization that is incorporated under state law will be taxed as a corporation under federal law.[2] Organizations that are unincorporated under state law (such as partnerships and limited liability companies) can generally elect whether to be treated as partnerships or corporations for federal tax purposes.

TYPES OF CORPORATIONS

There are many different types of corporations. For example, there is the ecclesiastical corporation that is organized to hold property in connection with the advancement of a particular religious faith. An eleemosynary corporation is created to hold property for the benefit of a charity or benevolent society. The type of corporation you gentlemen are contemplating is a subsection of a third general type, the civil corporation. The civil corporation encompasses all corporations other than ecclesiastical or eleemosynary. The civil corporation can be political, quasi-public, or private.

Reebel: Would we be considered private?

Kress: Yes, political corporations are created by governments to manage public affairs. The Post Office Corporation is a good illustration. Sometimes companies are privately owned but exist to serve the public. Where the state maintains close control and supervision over the conduct of a corporation's business, it is considered quasi-public. An example would be a gas or electric company.

The organization you are considering would be organized for the benefit of its members, the three of you. Such a private corporation, operated for a profit, is called a "stock" company. This means that the capital of the business is divided into transferable portions known as shares that are evidenced by stock certificates. These certificates will entitle holders to participate in a distribution of profits. As you know, a certificate represents a stockholder's proportionate interest in the profits, the net assets, and the control of the corporation.

Initially your organization will probably be a private stock corporation classified as a "close" rather than a publicly traded corporation. Commonly a close corporation is one that has no shares of its stock available for purchase by or in the hands of the general public.

Someday you may want to expand the business and finance the growth with money from outside investors. In a sense, you would be *opening* the close corporation by offering to issue shares of stock through a listing of the stock on a stock exchange or on the *over-the-counter market.*

As long as a corporation remains *close,* however, there will likely be only a few shareholders. These same people will probably also serve as directors and working officers. Therefore ownership, management, and key employees in your organization will be identical in fact—although separate for legal and tax purposes.

DISADVANTAGES OF CORPORATE STATUS

Baily: Are there reasons why we wouldn't want to operate as a corporation?

Kress: There are several disadvantages to the corporate form. Let's look at the non-tax-oriented disadvantages first. The corporate form lends itself to control of the minority by the majority. In the absence of appropriate control devices, the holder of a minority interest cannot readily cause the venture to be dissolved or force payment of dividends. For example, in the event of a shareholder's death—absent agreement on the subject—there is no easy way for the decedent's family to force a distribution of its share of corporate profits.

Another non-tax disadvantage is that a corporation has to strictly observe corporate form. This entails charter documents, bylaws, and board of directors' as well as shareholders' meetings—all a bit complicated in comparison with a sole proprietorship or partnership. Incorporating may also entail legal and accounting costs, as well as state filing fees and franchise taxes over and above those of a partnership.

Now let's consider the tax disadvantages. The basic tax disadvantage is the potential of double taxation of earnings. Since the corporation is a separate tax entity, earnings will be taxed to the corporation as earned, and then again to the shareholders if a corporate distribution to them is classified as a dividend.

ADVANTAGES OF CORPORATE STATUS

However, once corporate status is attained, you'll obtain a number of benefits that may substantially outweigh the costs.

I'll discuss the non-tax advantages first. Primary among non-tax-oriented advantages is the ability to freely transfer ownership. It is relatively easy when using the corporate form to provide for a new owner's entrance and an old owner's exit. Second, the corporate form affords a limited liability to its shareholders. The corporation, and not its shareholders, is responsible for corporate obligations.

Now let's examine some of the tax-oriented advantages of corporate status. Since the three of you would be *employees* of the corporation, you would become entitled to a number of benefits that would be tax free to you and tax deductible by the corporation. For example, as an employee you would be permitted to borrow from the corporation's pension or profit-sharing plan. The corporation—as your employer—could establish a sizable group life and health insurance plan to cover you and your family, again at little or no tax cost to you. Since this would be considered an "ordinary and necessary" business expense, premium payments could be deducted by the corporation. A third benefit is that premiums on the disability income policies you each personally own and pay for with after-tax dollars could be taken over by your company, again tax free to you and tax deductible to the business.[3]

Reebel: I understand that by incorporating we would be eligible for loans from qualified deferred-compensation plans and certain other tax-favored fringe benefit arrangements.

Kress: That is correct. The Code permits the corporation to offer you—as an employee—a number of fringe benefits. Keep in mind that these benefits must be reasonable in amount and in return for services you have rendered.[4]

There are other tax-oriented factors you may find advantageous. For instance, assuming your corporation does not have to pay out substantial dividends, the overall tax result may be lower federal income taxes. It might be easiest to illustrate this point by comparing partnership with corporate tax treatment. If you formed a partnership, the three of you would be taxed on all the income you earned as partners—even if you didn't actually withdraw all your partnership earnings from the firm. However, as stockholder-employees, you would be taxed only on your salaries (assuming no dividend had to be paid). Lower total federal income tax under the corporate form may result because a new taxpaying entity, the corporation, has been created. The total tax payable depends upon how much taxable income is left inside the corporation. Let's look at the current tax rate structure for corporations.[5]

Certain corporations engaged in the business of rendering personal services are taxed at a flat rate of 35 percent. We'll discuss this further when we talk about the taxation of a corporation as a separate entity.

A corporation can generally declare and pay dividends—as well as salaries—so as to avoid *bunching* income in those years when your personal income is highest. On the other hand, if you established your business in the partnership form, you'd have little control over the receipt and taxation of income. This ability to *time* income is important, since you may be able to reduce your ultimate tax liability by allowing some income to remain in the corporation and be taxed at a 15 or 25 percent rate.

Corporate Tax Rates	
Taxable Income	**Tax Rate**
$0–$50,000	15%
$50,001–$75,000	25
$75,001–$100,000	34
$100,001–$335,000	39
$335,001–$10,000,000	34
$10,000,001–$15,000,000	35
$15,000,001–$18,333,333	38
Over $18,333,333	35

Cheesman: Is there a way to have our cake and eat it too? That is, can we get the loss flow-through so that we can deduct any corporate losses against our personal income but still get many of the benefits you just mentioned?

S CORPORATIONS

Kress: What you are referring to sounds like an *S corporation.* The Internal Revenue Code allows a closely held corporation to elect not to be taxed as a regular corporation if it meets certain requirements. Basically the result is that the corporation is not taxed as a separate entity.[6]

In other words, the corporation itself does not (with certain exceptions) pay tax.[7] Instead, corporate net income is taxed directly to its shareholders. This enables shareholders of a small, closely held corporation to obtain the tax and non-tax advantages of corporate form without its disadvantages. The S corporation election avoids *double taxation* of a corporate income upon the payment of dividends. It also avoids the problems of a penalty on accumulated earnings as well as the personal holding company tax. Depreciation as well as corporate income and losses will be immediately passed through to the shareholders. However, some of the tax-advantaged fringe benefits that are available to employees of a regular corporation cannot be taken advantage of by shareholders of an S corporation.

All these characteristics are consistent with the underlying purpose of an S corporation, which is to promote tax neutrality when choosing the form in which to do business (for example, a sole proprietorship, partnership, or corporation). Congress felt that, to the extent tax treatment influenced the choice of business form, the result was a potential distortion of normal business practices. Therefore provisions were made in the Code to allow for S corporation treatment.

To qualify for S corporation status, the following requirements must be met:

- An S corporation can have only one class of stock.
- An S corporation must have no more than 75 shareholders. A husband and wife are treated as one shareholder.
- An S corporation can have no shareholder other than an individual, an estate, or certain types of trusts (except for qualified Subchapter S subsidiary corporations).
- An S corporation must be a domestic corporation—that is, incorporated in the United States.
- An S corporation may not have nonresident alien shareholders.

Types of trusts that are permitted to be S corporation shareholders include the following:[8]

- voting trusts
- grantor trusts
- trusts treated as owned by an individual other than the grantor under IRC Sec. 678
- qualified subchapter S trusts (QSSTs)
- electing small business trusts

Any such trust that owns S corporation stock or trusts that receive the stock under the terms of a will may hold the stock for a 2-year period after the death of the grantor of the trust or previous owner of the stock. A "QSST" is a trust that, among other requirements, must distribute all of its income currently to one individual. In general, an "electing small business trust" is a trust whose beneficiaries are all individuals or estates. Charitable organizations may, however, hold a contingent remainder interest in an electing small business trust. No interest in an electing small business trust may be acquired by purchase.

An S corporation does not pay corporate tax on its income. The result is that the shareholders are taxed on the taxable income of the corporation in proportion to their shareholdings. If the corporation has a loss, it can be deducted directly by the shareholders. As I have already noted, using this type of election, the corporation and its shareholders are taxed in most (but not all) respects in a manner similar to the way they would be taxed if they were operating as a partnership.

The S corporation election is used in a number of situations. For example, if you expected high initial losses in your first year or two of business operations, you would want to *pass through* the corporation's losses since you are all in high individual income tax brackets, so that you could use them against your own income tax liability.[9]

An S corporation election might also be indicated where business owners want to take advantage of limited liability but do not want to incur a double taxation when income earned and taxed by the corporation is later distributed to its shareholders.

An S corporation election may also be indicated when shareholders intend to withdraw substantially all corporate earnings and (1) not all stockholders are employees who could justify their shares as salary payments, (2) the amount of earnings is so great that any attempt to pay them out as salaries would result in unreasonably high salaries, or (3) the corporation has taxable income that would be taxed at a corporate rate higher than the shareholders' individual marginal rates without an S election. The S corporation election avoids the double tax that occurs to both a corporation and its shareholders when an actual or constructive dividend is paid out of earnings. Note, however, that the current top individual rate of 39.6 percent slightly exceeds the current top corporate rate of 39 percent.

By an irrevocable and unqualified gift of shares of stock, a taxpayer can arrange to *split income* with another family member. Thus it is possible to transfer income to lower-bracket donees. By getting stock into the hands of various family members, it is possible to shift income to other taxpayers despite the fact that the income may be used to satisfy support or other family obligations that the donor would otherwise have to pay with after-tax dollars.

In fact, you could even use the S corporation election to allow the corporation to continue income payments to you at retirement (or to your widow should you predecease her) without double tax consequences. You know that the IRS questions high salaries to older stockholder-employees, often claiming that part of the pay is really a nondeductible, fully taxable dividend in disguise. The election generally avoids this question since payments to shareholders are not taxed as dividends. Thus where a shareholder is inactive, less able to contribute time or services, or where he or she needs income upon retirement but does not want to create a double tax, the S corporation election may be the answer.

Baily: How long is the S corporation election effective?

Kress: Once made, an S election is effective indefinitely. However, the election can be terminated in any of the following ways:

First, the corporation can elect to revoke the election with the consent of the shareholders who own more than 50 percent of the stock.

Second, the election terminates if the corporation no longer qualifies as a "small business corporation"—that is, if it has more than 75 shareholders, or a nonresident alien acquires stock, or if an entity other than permitted shareholders acquires stock. Also the issuance of a second class of stock would terminate the election.

Third, if more than 25 percent of the S corporation's gross receipts for 3 successive tax years is from certain types of passive income and the corporation has accumulated earnings and profits from its days prior to the S election, the election will be terminated.[10]

The revocation can be elected on or before the 15th day of the third month of the present taxable year and will be effective for that entire taxable year, unless the revocation specifically requests a revocation date in the future. If so, the revocation will be effective on the date selected. If no future date of revocation is specified but the revocation election is filed after the permissible period, the revocation is effective at the beginning of the following taxable year. Voluntary revocations generally result in an inability to reelect the S status for 5 years without obtaining IRS consent to the reelection. The IRS can, in appropriate circumstances, waive the 5-year waiting period and permit the corporation to make a new election effective for the following taxable year. Also, if an S corporation election is invalid or late, the IRS may grant relief if the proper remedial action is taken by the corporation.

Let's get back to our discussion of regular corporations. Technically, there are no clearly discernible stages of a corporation's life. However, for illustrative purposes, let's think of the tax life of your proposed corporation in terms of the following four stages: (1) birth, (2) adolescence, (3) maturity, and (4) death.

FORMATION OF A CORPORATION

Kress: All three of you have something to contribute to the corporation. In return you will want to participate in the control and profits of the business while it is running or in a distribution of the assets of your business if the corporation's life ends. In other words, you will expect *shares* of the corporation. For discussion purposes, let's assume Cheesman will contribute his business (his sole proprietorship). Baily will contribute cash or securities. Reebel wants to contribute his services and a small amount of cash in return for his stock.

Assuming this is the case, here is what might happen: if Baily decides that his contribution to the capital of the corporation will be cash, the stock he receives will normally have a value at the time of the exchange equal to the cash. For example, if he transfers $10,000 of cash to the corporation, he will ordinarily receive back stock with a fair market value of $10,000. Since the value of the stock he receives is no more or less than the value of the cash he transfers to the corporation, he realizes neither a gain nor a loss. If he later sells his stock, the cash he paid will determine the basis of his stock. If he realizes $21,000 on the sale of the stock, his gain would be $11,000, the difference between his basis for the stock ($10,000) and the amount he realizes on the sale ($21,000).[11]

Reebel: Is it correct to assume that, as long as the value of the cash and/or property we transfer to the corporation is equal to the value of the stock we get, we will have neither gain nor loss?

Kress: Not exactly. The general rule is that when property is exchanged for stock in a corporation, there is a *sale or exchange.* In the absence of any other provisions in the Code, you would have a recognized gain or loss. The amount of gain or loss would be measured by the difference between the amount you realize in the transaction (the value of stock you get) and the adjusted basis (the cost) of the property transferred to the corporation. Therefore, if you transferred mutual funds that had a present fair market value of $100,000 in exchange for $100,000 of the newly formed corporation's stock, you might still have a taxable gain. For example, if you had paid only $10,000 for the mutual funds (now worth $100,000) and you exchanged the mutual funds for stock, there would be a taxable gain of $90,000. This same general principle applies if Cheesman was to exchange his appreciated business for cash—he would have a gain. The same result could occur when you transferred appreciated property to the corporation in exchange for its stock.[12]

Reebel: I guess that rules out Cheesman putting in his sole proprietorship and also Baily transferring his appreciated securities into a new corporation.

Kress: Not really—what we have just discussed is the general rule. But, like most provisions of the Code, there is an exception to the general rule. The exception was designed to encourage the formation of new corporations. It enables a taxpayer to transfer appreciated property or even a going business into a new corporation without the transferor recognizing income on the appreciation at the very time when his or her other expenses—the expenses involved in the organization and operation of the corporation—are the highest. The exception provides that even if the transferor *realizes* a gain when appreciated property is transferred to his or her new corporation, gain does not have to be *recognized* for tax purposes.[13]

NONRECOGNITION PROVISION FOR TRANSFER TO A CORPORATION CONTROLLED BY TRANSFEROR(S)

This nonrecognition provision must meet two basic requirements. Where a person or persons transfer property to a corporation (1) solely in exchange for the corporation's own stock (other than certain "nonqualified" preferred stock), and (2) the transferor(s) control the corporation immediately after the transfer, no gain will be recognized on the appreciated property or securities contributed to the new corporation.

The philosophy here is similar to that of a tax-free like-kind exchange. The transferor who receives stock in exchange for property has really maintained interest in the original property. It has merely changed form. The new form continues his or her interest in the original property, though it now has the physical identity of *stock.* This *continuity-of-interest* concept is the key to nonrecognition of the gain on the appreciated property transferred.

For example, suppose Cheesman, who is now operating as a sole proprietor, decides to transfer his going business to the new corporation. If his basis for the sole proprietorship is $10,000 and the fair market value of his business is $50,000 at the time he transfers it to the new corporation, he would probably receive $50,000 worth of stock. Under the general rule for taxing sales and exchanges, he would recognize a $40,000 gain. However, the nonrecognition provision provides that since he got back only stock and through that stock controlled the corporation (just as he previously controlled his sole proprietorship), what has happened is really only the substitution of stock certificates for his former physical possession of the property. In other words, he now owns stock that is evidence of ownership in the same property owned before. His interest has changed merely in form, not in substance.

This rule is logical since to recognize gain there must be a taxable event that usually occurs in the form of a sale, or exchange, or other disposition of property. Although technically there may be a sale (a transfer of property in return for money or a promise to pay money) or exchange (a transfer of property in return for other property or services), there has been no exchange in substance. Cheesman, in our example, hasn't disposed of his property. He has merely received certificates that evidence that he changed the form (and not substance) of his ownership in the original property. This would apply no matter how many people transfer property to the corporation. As long as it was done collectively, if the taxpayers transferring property to the corporation still have both (1) control and (2) interest in the property they originally owned, they would not have to recognize any gain on receipt of the new corporation's stock. Thus Cheesman would not have to recognize the $40,000 gain until and unless he later sells his stock.

REQUIREMENTS FOR NONRECOGNITION

There are three formal requirements that must be satisfied to obtain an exception to the general rule so that there will be no recognition of a gain. Perhaps this chart will help.

Nonrecognition Provision		

If the transfer of property is
    a. solely in exchange for the corporation's own stock and
    b. transferor(s) control the corporation immediately after the
        transfer, then no gain (or loss) is recognized.		

Money or Other Property Received to Boot		

Receives
    Stock
    Cash
	$30,000
	$20,000
		$50,000

Transfers
    Property (Basis)
    Gain
    Reportable*
		$10,000
		$40,000
		$20,000

*Gain ($40,000) is recognized to extent of *boot* ($20,000).		

First, there must be one or more persons transferring property (which may include cash) to the newly formed corporation. The example we have just discussed meets the *transfer-of-property* requirement, since we assumed Cheesman transferred his business to the corporation.

Second, the transfer must be *solely in exchange* for stock in such a corporation. Since all Cheesman received from the corporation was the stock of the new corporation, the example above meets this requirement. If, however, Cheesman had received stock plus *other property* (such as cash or corporate notes) his transfer would not have met this requirement. If he had received stock (which does qualify) plus that other property *to boot* (other property or cash which does not qualify), he would have had to recognize part of his gain. Generally to the extent of this *boot* received, or to the extent of the gain on his transaction (whichever is less), the transferor of appreciated property will have to recognize income. For example, in the situation above, if Cheesman had received $30,000 worth of stock plus $20,000 of cash, he would have received $20,000 worth of boot. He would have to recognize income to the extent of the cash he received ($20,000), since the figure is the lower of (a) $20,000 boot or (b) the $40,000 gain realized ($50,000 amount realized minus $10,000 basis for the sole proprietorship transferred).[14]

The third requirement for nonrecognition is that the transferors (the person or persons transferring cash and/or property to the corporation in return for stock of the corporation) must be *in control immediately after* the exchange. This requirement also makes sense. For nonrecognition to follow, the incorporation must be merely a change in the physical form of ownership—that is, an exchange of cash and/or property in return for stock.

If the original transferors no longer own their original property (where there has been a drastic shift in the proportion of ownership interest and control), the transaction takes on the effect of a sale or exchange and, as such, will be taxable. Control is defined as ownership of stock possessing at least 80 percent of the combined voting power, plus at least 80 percent of the total number of shares of the new corporation. This 80 percent test of control must be met for tax purposes even though, from a legal standpoint, a shareholder could actually control a corporation with as little as a 51 percent interest.

If the three tests are met (that is, if any one of you or even all three of you transfer property to a corporation, if the transfer is solely in exchange for the stock of the new corporation, and if you as transferors are in control immediately after the exchange), the following will result.

First, no gain will have to be recognized on the exchange either by the transferor(s) or by the corporation. Second, the corporation takes the transferor's basis for the property contributed. If Cheesman's basis for the property he transfers to the corporation was $10,000 and the corporation later sells that same property, its basis for tax purposes would be $10,000. Thus if it sold the property for $30,000, its gain would be the difference, or $20,000. Third, the stockholder who receives stock from the corporation takes a substituted basis—that is, for tax purposes his or her basis for the stock acquired from the corporation is typically the same as the stockholder's basis for the property he or she transferred.

If a stockholder receives boot, he or she must (1) decrease the stock's basis to the extent of the fair market value of any boot property as well as any cash received, but (2) his or her basis can be increased by the amount of any gain that must be recognized. If Cheesman, for example, received $40,000 worth of stock plus $20,000 in cash boot, he would report the $20,000 of cash as income. Therefore Cheesman must (1) decrease the basis of his stock by $20,000 since this is the amount of the boot he received; then (2) he may increase his basis by the amount of any gain that he must recognize. Since he recognizes $20,000 of income in this particular situation, the net result of the boot transaction is a $10,000 basis. Basis is first decreased by the amount of boot received but then increased by the amount of boot that was taxable. In this case it resulted in a *washout* so that Cheesman's basis remains at $10,000.

The basis to the corporation of the property received would be the transferor's basis ($10,000), plus the amount of gain the transferor had to recognize because of the boot he or she received ($20,000). Suppose the corporation later sold the property it received. If the amount the corporation realized on the sale of the property was $40,000, its gain would be only $10,000 ($40,000 amount realized less $30,000 adjusted basis [$10,000 original basis, plus $20,000 increase in basis because of the recognition of income by the transferor]). No gain or loss is recognized by a corporation for the receipt of cash or property in exchange for stock of the corporation.

ORGANIZATIONAL EXPENDITURES

Baily: Are the expenses of forming a corporation currently deductible in determining corporate taxable income?

Kress: The costs of creating a corporation ordinarily constitute capital expenditures. This means that those costs may be amortized (that is, taken as equal annual deductions against income of the corporation), since in a sense they create an *asset* that will be exhausted over the lifetime of the corporation.

There are a number of such expenses created in the organization of the corporation. For example, there are state filing fees and legal expenses in obtaining the charter, costs for accounting services incident to the organization, and fees paid for drafting the corporation charter and bylaws as well as for the terms of the original stock certificates. A corporation can elect to recover the cost of these organizational expenditures through amortization deductions. In other words, the corporation can elect to deduct these costs in even amounts over a period of 5 years or longer beginning with the month in which the corporation begins business. In most cases this would be after the charter is issued.[15]

OTHER METHODS OF FINANCING

One of the key advantages of business in the corporate form is that many different types of ownership interests in corporations can be created. We have just discussed the general definition of stock. This includes common stock, preferred stock, convertible securities, warrants, and options. The interests of any particular investor can be met by creating a security that fits his or her special needs and desires. This factor facilitates the acquisition of capital. Suppose the corporation issued bonds to acquire working capital as well as capital for long-term planning. As you know, a bond is a written obligation to repay a definite sum of money on a definite date, usually at least 10 and more often 20 or more years, from the date the bond was issued.

Bonds are a favored means of raising corporate capital. One reason for this is that a corporation will obtain a deduction for the interest paid on the indebtedness. By contrast, no deduction is allowed for dividends paid on either preferred or common stock. As long as a corporation can earn money at a higher rate (with the cash raised by issuing the bond) than it costs the corporation (in interest necessary to *service the debt),* it usually makes sense for the corporation to borrow money. This is known as "leverage."

Of course, issuance of the bonds themselves would create no tax liability to either the corporation or the bondholder. This is because the corporation has merely borrowed money and agreed to return it. Conversely, the bondholders have merely loaned money. When the bond *matures,* the principal becomes payable and the bondholders are entitled to a tax-free return of their capital investment. In contrast, when a corporation makes payments to its shareholders with respect to their stock, the general rule is that the payment will be taxed as a dividend.

Any money bondholders receive in the form of interest will be taxable as ordinary income, while any money they receive at the maturity of their bonds in excess of their capital investment may be taxed as capital gain. This occurs when bonds are purchased at a discount but are paid off at face value. (When bonds are issued at a discount by the issuing corporation, a bondholder generally must include a ratable portion of the discount in income each year as the bond matures. For example, if a bond with a par value of $1,000 was issued for $800 and is payable in 10 years, the $200 discount would be included in the taxpayer's income at the rate of $20 a year.)

Another reason bonds are favored over stock is that the accumulation of earnings and profits within the corporation to pay debt obligations can be justified more readily than accumulating earnings to redeem stock. This helps avoid an additional tax on an unreasonable accumulation of earnings.

Reebel: Is there any reason stockholders couldn't lend money to the corporation in return for bonds?

Kress: No, it is quite common for a shareholder to forgo an equity (stock) interest with regard to some of his or her contribution in return for the greater security of a loan. As you know, the bond promises to pay a specified sum of money by a specified date. This date is usually at least 10 years from the date of issue. Of course, bonds generally pay a fixed rate of interest each year until that specified date. Typically, in the event the corporation fails financially, bondholders have preferred rights to corporate assets. Since the interest paid on corporate indebtedness is deductible, the after-tax cost of raising capital through long-term corporate debt is substantially reduced.

However, some shareholders attempt to overdo it—they contribute almost no equity investment and characterize the major portion of their contribution as debt owed to them by the corporation. This is known as "thin capitalization," since the equity investment is *thin* in relation to the debt, but the *debt* is really disguised stock.

Reebel: What is the effect of thin capitalization?

Kress: Once the form of the debt is disregarded by the IRS and the substance is treated appropriately, corporate deductions for *interest* payments to shareholders are disallowed. Second, receipt of interest payments by shareholder-creditors are reclassified and treated as dividends. Third, when the corporation pays off its debt to the shareholders, that payment is taxed as a dividend. This means that instead of treating the amount received as a tax-free repayment of a debt, the shareholder-creditor must report the entire distribution as ordinary income. Finally, money that the corporation purportedly was accumulating to pay off the debt is now subject to the accumulated-earnings tax, which we'll discuss in a few moments. Also a debt that is reclassified as stock could cause a termination of an S election since an S corporation is allowed to have only one class of stock.

Baily: How do the courts distinguish between debt and equity?

Kress: The courts usually examine a number of factors such as, Was there an intention by shareholders to enforce payment of the debt? Was there collateral for the debt? Was there a debt instrument (note), and did it give the shareholders management or voting rights (like stock)? What was the ratio of debt to equity? A rule of thumb is that if the amount of debt exceeds shareholders' equity by more than four to one, the corporation is thinly capitalized. Basically the court would examine all the factors relevant to determine if a "loan" by shareholders was in reality more like an ownership interest (stock) than a debtor-creditor relationship.[16]

Keep in mind that while bonds are a tax-favored means of obtaining corporate funds, frequently a corporation does not want to become obligated to make fixed payments for interest and debt amortization. To avoid a cash-flow problem, therefore, corporations often finance long-term operations or investments with common stock, which entails no obligation to pay dividends, or preferred stock, on which dividend payments can frequently be avoided. Furthermore, stocks are used in preference to bonds because, unlike bonds, stocks never *mature*—there is no requirement that a corporation pay off either preferred or common stock.

Cheesman: Assuming we've properly capitalized the corporation, how is its income actually taxed?

TAXATION AS A SEPARATE ENTITY

Kress: A corporation is taxed as an entity separate from its shareholders. The rates are 15 percent of the first $50,000 of taxable income, 25 percent of the next $25,000, 34 percent on amounts of taxable income between $75,001 and $100,000, 39 percent on amounts between $100,001 and $335,000, 34 percent on amounts between $335,001 and $10 million, 35 percent on amounts from $10 million to $15 million, 38 percent on amounts from $15 million to $18,333,333, and 35 percent on amounts over $18,333,333. Thus if your corporation (let's call it the Bradwell Corporation) has $60,000 of taxable income, its tax will be $10,000 (15 percent of $50,000, plus 25 percent of the $10,000 excess above $50,000).[17]

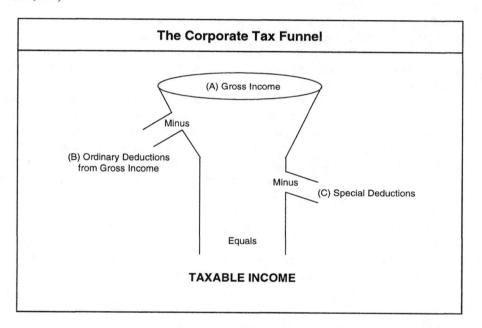

The Corporate Tax Funnel

(A) Gross Income

Minus

(B) Ordinary Deductions from Gross Income

Minus

(C) Special Deductions

Equals

TAXABLE INCOME

However, under current law the taxable income of a "qualified personal service corporation" is taxed at a flat rate of 35 percent. A qualified personal service corporation for this purpose is one in which (1) substantially all the activities involve the performance of services in the fields of health, law, engineering, architecture, accounting, actuarial science, performing arts, or consulting, and (2) substantially all the stock (95 percent or more) is held by employees or retired employees or by their estates.

Since the Bradwell Corporation will be engaged in a manufacturing business, the flat rate of 35 percent will not apply. However, should the Bradwell Corporation become a consulting business in the future, the flat tax rate would apply since all three shareholders will be working for the business. This, of course, is only the federal income tax. Corporations, like individuals, are liable for a number of other state and local taxes as well. Bradwell Corporation would report its federal income tax on IRS Form 1120.

Graphically, Bradwell Corporation's return might look like the illustration above.

COMPUTATION OF TAXABLE INCOME

Gross income would include such items as profit from sales and receipts from services. It would also include gains on sales or exchanges, income from rent, royalties, interest, and dividends.

A corporation is entitled to two types of deductions—ordinary deductions and special deductions. Ordinary deductions would include compensation of officers and salaries, bonuses, rent payments, charitable contributions, repair expenses, interest paid on indebtedness, casualty losses, deductions for depreciation and amortization of research and experimental costs, advertising, and corporate contributions to pension and profit-sharing plans. A corporation would also receive a carryover deduction for a net operating loss.

Several deductions are classified as "special." One of these items is known as a "dividends-received" deduction. This deduction reduces gross income by 70 percent of dividends received from certain other corporations. In other words, a corporation will pay tax on only 30 percent of the amount of such dividends. The deduction may be either 80 percent or 100 percent of dividends received, rather than 70 percent, if the receiving corporation owns specified percentages of the stock of the paying corporation.[18]

Taxable income is what is left after taking ordinary and special deductions. It is the amount to which the corporate income tax rates are applied. Certain credits are then directly applied against this tax, such as corporate overpayments of tax in previous years, payments for estimated taxes (paid on a quarterly basis), credit on certain foreign taxes paid, and investment credit.

Kress: Let me go into more detail on some of those items.

DEDUCTIONS FOR SALARIES

The first item we discussed under the category of "ordinary deductions" was salaries. Bradwell Corporation would be entitled to a deduction for salaries or any other compensation for personal services, but only if the services were actually rendered and the amount paid as compensation for those services was considered *reasonable*. Reasonable means only the amount that would ordinarily be paid for similar services by corporations like Bradwell under similar circumstances.

This reasonableness test is imposed most frequently on closely held corporations because of the large degree of coincidence of executive and shareholder interest. It is designed to prevent the shareholders of Bradwell from draining out corporate profits in the disguise of tax-deductible salaries.

Corporate profits are usually paid out in the form of dividends that are taxable to the shareholders but are nondeductible by the corporation. The portion of the salary considered unreasonable is usually classified as a disguised dividend, and to that extent the corporation's deduction is disallowed. However, even though that amount may not be deducted by the corporation, it is still taxable as ordinary income to the shareholder-recipient.[19]

Reasonableness is a question of determining the amount that would ordinarily be paid for like services by like enterprises under like circumstances. Generally, where an executive employee does not own or have options to purchase stock, arm's-length bargaining as to the amount of salary is assumed. One element that could be considered in determining reasonableness is the fact that a given individual was not adequately compensated in prior years. Thus if high compensation in the current year can be attributed to services rendered in prior years, the total current salary might be considered reasonable.

However, the amount of cash compensation is not the only relevant factor. Corporate contributions to pension and profit-sharing plans are considered business expenses and are allowed as deductions as long as the total amount of all forms of compensation paid on behalf of an individual does not exceed a reasonable total. Some of the other indirect forms of compensation may be premiums for life insurance, hospitalization, medical care, and salary continuation plans.

Costs of these plans, although deductible by the corporation, often do not result in taxable income to the individual. Since the corporation is a separate and distinct tax entity, and since the three of you would be considered salaried employees, you would be eligible for these forms of indirect compensation. This is true even though you would be not only employees, but also officers, directors, and shareholders of the corporation.

With respect to reasonable payments to executives or key employees, you should be aware of a concept called *excess golden parachute payments.* These are payments to executives or key employees (1) that are contingent upon a change or threatened change of ownership or control of a corporation, and (2) that have a present value equal to or in excess of three times the individual's average annual compensation for the 5 preceding years. These payments are not deductible by the corporation, and they subject the individual to an excise tax of 20 percent of the excess payment in addition to the regular income tax.

In addition, if compensation paid to an executive fits the definition of "excessive employee remuneration," the compensation will not be deductible by the employer.

Cheesman: What is "excessive employee remuneration"?

Kress: First, the compensation must be paid by a publicly held corporation to fall within the rule. Second, the definition applies generally to compensation of over $1 million per year paid to one employee.

Compensation for purposes of this definition does *not* include commissions, contributions to qualified plans, and tax-free fringe benefits. It also does not include any compensation that is "performance based." In order to be treated as performance based, the compensation must be payable solely on account of the attainment of one or more performance goals determined by a compensation committee of the corporation's board of directors. Such a committee must be comprised solely of two or more outside directors. Also, in order to be treated as performance based, the compensation must be both disclosed to the corporation's shareholders and approved by a shareholder vote.

The $1 million limitation applies only to the chief executive officer of the company and its four most highly compensated officers for the taxable year. Therefore it will apply only to a maximum of five employees in any given corporation. If the corporation has made so-called excess golden parachute payments that are nondeductible under IRC Sec. 280(G), such payments will reduce the $1 million annual cap.

CHARITABLE DEDUCTION

It is generally felt that corporations owe some type of obligation to the communities in which they exist. Consequently the corporate statutes of most states permit corporations to make charitable contributions. The Internal Revenue Code permits a charitable deduction for contributions by a corporation. However, the deduction is limited to a maximum of 10 percent of the corporation's taxable income. (Certain adjustments are made to taxable income before the 10 percent maximum deduction is computed. For example, taxable income for this purpose is computed without regard to the deduction for charitable contributions in order to avoid a circular calculation.)   If the corporation should make a contribution in excess of 10 percent of its adjusted taxable income, it can carry the deduction forward for up to 5 years and use that carryforward to reduce its future taxable income. For example, if taxable income was $100,000, and the corporation made a charitable deduction of $100,000, it would get a $10,000 ordinary deduction it could use in the current year. The balance could be carried over and applied against future years' income.[20]

NET OPERATING LOSS

Suppose Bradwell Corporation didn't do as well as originally planned. In fact, suppose the expenses of operating the business exceeded the corporation's income. Because a corporation is treated as a separate tax entity, losses will not be allowed to pass through to Bradwell's shareholders. Unlike the case in a partnership or S corporation, a normal corporation's shareholders will not be able to use a loss to offset personal income. The loss may only be used by the corporation itself. Bradwell could use this net operating loss to reduce income in certain other tax years. In other words, if the corporation has more operating expenses than it has income, it could carry the loss as a deduction to certain other tax years. The loss would then reduce tax liability for the year to which it is carried. Unlike charitable deductions where the corporation is only allowed to carry a deduction forward, in the case of a net operating loss, the corporation can *carry back* the loss and then also carry it forward.

The corporation can generally carry the loss back 2 years and carry it forward 20 years. The effect of this provision is to enable a corporation to average operating gain or loss over a continuous 23-year period. The process works like this: First, the corporation carries back its loss just as if that loss had been incurred 2 years before the year in which the loss was actually sustained. Appropriate adjustments are made on that year's tax return. Then any unused loss is carried back to the first year preceding the actual year when the loss is sustained. If there is any excess loss not applied to the previous 2 years, the remaining net operating loss is carried forward over the next 20 years.

A corporation may elect not to utilize the carryback period, even though this does not extend the carryforward period. A corporate taxpayer may waive the carryback period when it was in an unusually low bracket or when it was already shielded by tax credits that could not be carried to later years.

The purpose of the carryback or carryforward of operating losses is to enable the corporate taxpayer to stabilize business income. If there were no provisions for carrying operating losses backward or forward, the entire gain from successful years would be taxed, but in loss years only a portion of the loss could be utilized. A loss in a given year that exceeded earnings for that year would be useless.

CAPITAL GAINS AND LOSSES

Often a corporation will sell or exchange capital assets. If Bradwell sells a capital asset at a loss, then, unlike an individual, it may not apply any portion of that loss against ordinary income. A corporation can use capital losses only as an offset against capital gains. Corporations are permitted to carry an unused net capital loss back 3 years and then, if further loss still remains, carry the excess over to the 5 succeeding years. Note that the loss still cannot be used to reduce ordinary income. Corporate capital losses must be utilized only to offset capital gains. Such losses must first be applied to the earliest of the years involved (3 back—5 forward), then to the next year, and so on until the losses are exhausted.[21]

Cheesman: What if the sale resulted in a gain?

Kress: A corporation must include its full capital gain in income. However, there is an alternative method of taxation that may apply to a corporation's capital gains in some cases. The alternative method provides for a flat rate of 35 percent instead of the regular corporate tax rates. The alternative tax applies only if the applicable regular tax rate is higher than 35 percent (compared without regard to the 38 percent bracket). If the corporation's taxable income (including the capital gain) does not exceed $100,000, the regular rates must be used for capital gains. For corporations with taxable income in excess of $100,000, the determination is more complex. The following chart is a comparison assuming that the corporation has $75,000 of taxable income this year, which includes $5,000 of net long-term capital gain.

Corporation Has $75,000 of Taxable Income			
Regular Tax Computation		Alternative Tax Computation	
(1) 15% of $50,000 of taxable income	$7,500	(1) Taxable income (2) Less—$5,000 net long-term capital gain	$75,000 $ 5,000 $70,000
(2) 25% of taxable income between $50,001 and $75,000	$6,250	(3) Tax on $70,000 at regular rates (4) 35% of $5,000 capital gain	$12,500 $ 1,750
Regular tax	$13,750	Alternative tax	$14,250

Note: The alternative method of taxation would not be used in this example because it is more than the regular tax.

DEDUCTION FOR DIVIDENDS RECEIVED FROM CERTAIN CORPORATIONS

I mentioned before that a corporation may be entitled to certain *special* deductions. The most common of the special deductions is the deduction for dividends received from certain corporations. For example, Bradwell Corporation might purchase stock in other corporations, such as AT&T or General Motors, as an investment. Perhaps Baily will transfer stock of other corporations to Bradwell Corporation as part of his original contribution of capital in return for Bradwell's stock. Bradwell would be allowed a special deduction for a percentage of dividends received during its tax year from stock it holds in certain other corporations. Specifically, it may deduct (subject to certain limitations) 70 percent of the dividends it receives.

These dividends must be distributions from the earnings and profits of taxable domestic corporations. Since dividends on deposit or withdrawal accounts in domestic building and loan associations or mutual savings banks are not really dividends at all, they are treated as interest and do not qualify for this deduction.

Likewise, Bradwell cannot deduct 70 percent of the dividends received from many tax-exempt corporations, because the deduction for dividends received is intended to prevent triple taxation of corporate income. Since tax-exempt corporations and many foreign corporations are either not taxed at all or not taxed at full corporate rates, to allow a *dividends-received* deduction for dividends received from these corporations would be to favor them rather than to treat them equitably.[22]

The amount of the dividends-received deduction can vary depending on how much stock in the paying corporation is owned by the receiving corporation. The dividends-received deduction is 70 percent if the receiving corporation owns less than 20 percent of the paying corporation. If the receiving corporation owns 20 percent or more but less than 80 percent of the paying corporation, the dividends-received deduction is 80 percent. Different rules apply if the corporation receiving the dividends owns 80 percent or more of the corporation paying the dividends. If certain conditions are met, the dividends-received deduction is 100 percent.

There is a reduction in the dividends-received deduction when the corporation owns a portfolio of stock acquired by incurring debt. The theory is that the benefit of the dividends-received deduction should be neutralized, since the corporation obtained the added benefit of a deduction for interest on the debt incurred to purchase stock.

The dividends-received deduction is not available to S corporations.

THE ACCUMULATED-EARNINGS TAX

Assuming that Bradwell Corporation is as successful as the three of you have been individually, in a few years the corporation will reach its maturity stage. As the corporation begins to be profitable, it will need money to grow and expand, just as it needed capital at its formation. One of the easiest ways of financing growth is by accumulating earnings and plowing them back into the corporation to purchase new machinery, buildings, and other necessary capital assets. These *plow-back* earnings and profits begin to add up very quickly. You may want to use your business as a vehicle for accumulating money. You can do that merely by having the corporation retain earnings rather than make distributions to shareholders in the form of nondeductible dividends. If Bradwell Corporation allows earnings to accumulate in order to fund current or anticipated needs or projects that the corporation has planned, there is no problem. However, once earnings are allowed to accumulate beyond the reasonable needs of the business, those earnings may be subject to an additional tax.[23]

The accumulated-earnings tax is a tax imposed on every corporation that is formed or used for the purpose of avoiding personal income tax with respect to its shareholders by permitting earnings and profits to accumulate instead of being distributed. The purpose of the tax is to discourage the use of a corporation as an accumulation vehicle to shelter its individual stockholders from taxation resulting from dividend distributions. Without such a tax on improper accumulations, stockholders could arrange to have dividends paid in years when their incomes were low, or they could indefinitely accumulate earnings and profits inside the corporation until the corporation was liquidated. Accumulations of $250,000 or less will automatically be considered to be for the reasonable needs of the business. Accumulations of $150,000 or less will be considered to be for the reasonable needs of the business in the case of professional service corporations.[24] However, if Bradwell is profitable and begins to accumulate amounts in excess of $250,000, it should be prepared to show a bona fide business reason for not distributing these earnings in the form of dividends.

As I mentioned, the purpose of this tax is to discourage the corporation from retaining profits in the absence of legitimate business motives. If earnings could remain in the corporation indefinitely, then its stockholders might never have to pay personal income tax on corporate earnings and profits. As a regulatory device, the accumulated-earnings tax was designed to force the distribution of retained earnings at the point where they no longer serve a legitimate business purpose.

The accumulated-earnings tax is designed to tax only earnings retained beyond the reasonable needs of the business. The question then becomes, What reasonable needs would Bradwell Corporation have for accumulating profits? The regulation states that working capital needs and capital for building expansion or for the replacement of plant or equipment are among the needs that would allow Bradwell to properly accumulate earnings. In addition to these needs, a sinking fund to retire corporate bonds at maturity has often been found to be a reasonable need to accumulate cash. In other cases, funds set aside to acquire minority interests or quarreling stockholders' interests were also deemed to be retained for reasonable business needs.[25]

Baily: Our CLU suggested we purchase cash value key person insurance. Would accumulated earnings in the form of cash values be a reasonable business need?

Kress: That depends on whether or not the insurance answers a valid corporate business need. There must also be a close correlation between the type of policy and amount of death benefit and the alleged corporate need. Generally, hedging against the loss of a key employee's service because of unexpected death is considered to be a reasonable business need.

Key person life insurance is insurance owned by the corporation insuring the life of a key employee. The purpose of such a policy is to provide a fund at the employee's death that will compensate the corporation for the financial loss resulting from the unavailability of the employee to render services to the corporation. Often key person insurance death proceeds are also used to help in finding and compensating a suitable replacement. Therefore the purchase of life insurance as well as the earnings used to pay policy premiums should not be, per se, subject to the penalty tax.[26]

In one case enough insurance to generate $1.5 million worth of life insurance proceeds was considered reasonable. The point is that it is not the amount but the purpose of the accumulation that is important.

The same question often arises as to the effect of a split-dollar plan. If a corporation attempts to prevent taxation of income to shareholders by accumulating its earnings rather than distributing them, the existence or nonexistence of a split-dollar policy will not, by itself, deter the imposition of the tax penalty provided by the law. Conversely, the existence of a split-dollar policy will not, per se, incur the accumulations tax penalty if the corporation is not, in fact, accumulating earnings beyond the reasonable needs of the business. It is important to remember that this section of the Code exists to deter tax evasion and not to prevent a business from operating in a normal businesslike manner. The same principle applies in cases where the corporation has obligated itself to make preretirement death benefits to a key executive under a deferred-compensation agreement. An accumulation of corporate earnings to meet obligations under such an agreement is generally considered a reasonable business need (just as the funds accumulated to retire an outstanding corporate bond would be considered reasonable).[27]

This question also often arises when accumulated earnings are used to provide surplus cash for the redemption of stock. In this case, if the redemption is to be utilized to shift partial or complete control to the remaining shareholders without depleting their personal funds (for example, if by shareholder agreement the corporation will retire shares on the death of a shareholder), it is doubtful that accumulations to reach this result would be found to be a reasonable need. However, if a business purpose can be found, such as an accumulation to purchase the shares of the dissenting minority, then the accumulation will be found to be reasonable. The primary purpose must be a corporate, rather than an individual, benefit from the stock redemption.[28]

Reebel: What is the maximum we could reasonably accumulate?

Kress: The critical factor is not the size of the accumulated earnings and profits but rather the reasonableness and nature of that surplus. For this reason, part of the surplus may be justifiably earmarked in the form of reserves for specific business needs.

Keep in mind that for the tax to be imposed it is not necessary that tax avoidance be the primary reason for the accumulation. As long as it is even one of the purposes for retention of earnings, the tax could be levied.

Most corporations will have little trouble in proving a reasonable business need for most of the earnings they retain. However, a corporation must be prepared to create and preserve adequate records to show that it had a specific plan to use the assets accumulated.

Among the evidence that could be used to support the corporation's case might be the fact that the business in question needs large amounts of cash for operating purposes at certain times during the year because of the nature of the business. It might show the actual use of the profits of past years as well as documented plans for future use of accumulated dollars. Corporations that rarely pay dividends are generally suspect, but if the corporation has a strong history of paying dividends, this would be another evidential factor that the current accumulation was not for the prohibited purpose of avoiding personal income tax.

The Internal Revenue Service will give weight to a pattern of expenditures or loans to or on behalf of shareholders to show that the corporation had the financial capacity to distribute retained earnings as dividends but has chosen instead to avoid payment of such funds as dividends in order to prevent personal income taxes at the shareholder level. For the same reason, the Service might question the purpose of corporate funds placed in passive investments, such as the stock of unrelated corporations.

Cheesman: What is the penalty for retaining earnings that are not for the business's needs?

Kress: The penalty for accumulating earnings "beyond the reasonable needs of the business" is as follows: Improper accumulations are taxed at a flat rate of 39.6 percent on all "accumulated taxable income."[29]

It is important to note that the tax, if applicable, is imposed only on *accumulated taxable income,* an amount derived from the taxable income of the corporation for the particular year in question. Thus the tax does not apply to all the accumulated earnings and profits of the corporation but only to the accumulated taxable income of the year or years in which the tax is asserted.

This tax on a corporation's accumulated taxable income is payable in addition to the regular tax payable by the firm. "Accumulated taxable income" basically means the corporation's taxable income for the year in question with certain adjustments (such as a reduction for federal income taxes paid) minus the sum of

- distributions from current earnings and profits that the shareholders have reported as ordinary income (dividends paid), plus
- amounts from earnings and profits that the shareholders have reported as dividends even though no actual distribution was made (disguised dividends), plus
- the accumulated-earnings credit[30]

Keep in mind that in determining whether or not this year's accumulated taxable income has been retained for the reasonable needs of the business, you must also consider the availability of prior years' accumulated earnings. If past years' accumulations are sufficient to meet current needs (that is, this year's business needs) you would have no justification for accumulating this year's earnings.

I just mentioned an accumulated-earnings credit. In Bradwell's case, this is a $250,000 minimum credit, but it is important to note that it includes earnings from prior years. For example, if prior years' accumulated earnings were in excess of $250,000, there would be no credit. Every dollar of this year's accumulated taxable income would be subject to tax, unless it could be proven that the income was reasonable. Let me go into more detail about this credit.

The minimum credit "shall in no case be less than the amount by which $250,000 exceeds the accumulated earnings and profits of the corporation at the close of the preceding taxable year."[31] Thus if the accumulated earnings and profits on December 31 of last year were $20,000, the minimum credit for this year would be $230,000. If no earnings or profits were accumulated in the past, a surplus of at least $250,000 can be accumulated this year without incurring an accumulated-earnings tax. This means that corporations can accumulate up to $250,000 of their earnings and profits without any possibility of being subject to the tax, even though they have no reason for the retention of those earnings. However, that is merely the minimum credit. The maximum credit equals the greater of (1) the minimum credit or (2) the earnings and profits retained for the reasonable needs of the business.

PERSONAL HOLDING COMPANY TAX

Reebel: Is a personal holding company a tax-avoidance device similar to the unreasonable accumulation of corporate earnings?

Kress: Yes. A personal holding company is a device stockholders have used to place income with a corporation to prevent themselves from being taxed on a personal level. The formulation of a personal holding company generally has taken two forms—the "incorporated-talent" form and the "incorporated-wallet" form. The incorporated-talent or personal-service form of a personal holding company is set up as a result of this type of situation. A highly compensated individual, such as a movie star or athlete, normally receives a very high fee in return for services. This earned income is subject to tax rates of up to 39.6 percent under current law.

Under the incorporated-talents scheme, the financial superstar chose not to receive his or her fee directly, and so formed a corporation and contracted to work for it at a modest, fixed salary. The corporation then contracted the superstar's talents out at the *going rate,* and it received the normally high fee his or her unusual talent brought. Because of the separate entity concept, income attributable to the superstar's services was taxed, not to the individual, but to the corporation at corporate tax rates which were lower than individual rates under prior law. For example, a baseball player would form a corporation and contract to render services to it for, perhaps, $50,000 a year. The corporation would then contract out the player's services for a great deal more, say $120,000 a year. The $70,000 balance would be held and accumulated by the corporation, subject to the lower corporate tax. The corporation could later be liquidated and the individual would pay only a relatively low capital-gain tax on the liquidation.

A second scheme was known as the incorporated-wallet personal holding company. Its purpose was to form a corporation to hold passive investments. Property would be transferred to such a personal holding company so that dividends and interest earned by that property would be taxed at corporate rather than individual rates. The *corporate wallet* would merely hold the assets; collect the dividends, interest, or rental income; and pay tax at relatively lower corporate rates, under prior tax law.

Congress enacted a penalty tax on the undistributed income on corporations that operate as incorporated-talent or incorporated-wallet corporations. In the event that certain mechanical standards of receipt of passive income, personal-service income, and stock ownership found in the Internal Revenue Code are met, such corporations known as personal holding companies will be subject to taxation in addition to the regular corporate taxes.[32] The additional tax imposed is now 39.6 percent of "undistributed personal holding company income," as this is basically taxable income minus taxes paid and dividends distributed.[33]

Baily: When will a corporation be considered a personal holding company?

Kress: To be classified as a personal holding company, two conditions must be present: first, most of the corporation's income (at least 60 percent of *adjusted ordinary gross income)* must come from personal-holding-company passive investment income. Second, more than 50 percent of the value of the stock must be held by five or fewer individuals (this test is broad because ownership attribution rules apply).

Assume Harry Hughes, a billionaire, forms and is the sole shareholder of the Harry Corporation, which holds his large corporate bond portfolio. It will be the policy of the corporation never to distribute dividends. When the Harry Corporation receives the interest, it is taxed at a 39.6 percent rate. However, such a corporation would be found to be a personal holding company under the passive income and stock ownership standards, and Harry Corporation would incur, in addition to the corporate tax, a personal-holding-company penalty tax.

Cheesman: Can the personal-holding-company tax be avoided?

Kress: Yes. The principal way to avoid such a penalty tax is to cause the corporation to distribute dividends. If liability for personal-holding-company tax is found, the Code allows a corporation to mitigate this tax liability by paying a retroactive deficiency dividend.[34] However, liabilities for interest and penalties will not be eliminated. Of course, the distribution of dividends defeats the attempt by taxpayers to have income taxed at lower corporate rates.

Several types of corporations are specifically exempted from the personal-holding-company tax. Among these are life insurance companies, banks, and other financial institutions that are required by law to maintain certain asset reserves.[35]

Reebel: What happens when distributions to shareholders are finally made?

Kress: The taxation of shareholders in this case is the same as under any corporate distribution to shareholders.

DIVIDEND DISTRIBUTIONS BY THE CORPORATION

Although close corporations are not usually inclined to distribute dividends, a corporation that is already paying the highest reasonable salaries possible must distribute some or all of its profits in the form of dividends. The general rule is that any distribution made by a corporation to its shareholders will be considered a dividend for federal income tax purposes and will be taxed as ordinary income.[36]

There is a limitation on this general rule as well as three basic exceptions. The limitation to the general rule is that a distribution is a taxable dividend only to the extent that it is paid out of either accumulated earnings and profits or current earnings and profits. The three basic exceptions to the general rule are that (1) certain stock dividends are tax free, (2) certain redemptions of stock qualify for capital-gains treatment, and (3) the proceeds of certain liquidations qualify for capital-gains treatment.

Cheesman: I'd like to know more about how we can avoid dividend treatment. Would you discuss these principles in detail?

Kress: Certainly.

First, it might be helpful to discuss exactly how the Code and regulations define the term *dividends.* As I have already mentioned, we start with the general rule that all distributions are dividends. However, there is an *earnings and profits test.* This test provides the tax limit—it tells us how much of any given distribution will be taxable as a dividend and also what portion of that distribution will be considered a tax-free return of capital.[37]

You might think of a corporation as if it were a money machine. We put money into the machine hoping to get a lot more out. Part of the money coming out could be considered earnings and profits, while the balance could be considered part or all that was originally put in. If we think of a corporation this way, then some method has to be devised to determine what portion of a given corporate distribution is taxable at ordinary rates as profit and what portion of each distribution is nontaxable as a return of capital. This is exactly what the tax law gives us—an arbitrary method for distinguishing between (1) what we put in (capital) and (2) what we get out (capital and/or ordinary income and/or capital gains). Therefore some distributions are considered dividends in part, return of capital in part, or even a capital gain in part. Perhaps an example would be helpful.

If current and accumulated earnings and profits are $20,000, and the stockholder's basis for his or her stock is $10,000, a $50,000 distribution would have the following effect:

- To the extent of earnings and profits ($20,000), the distribution is considered a dividend and must be included in the shareholder's gross income.

- Any remaining portion of the distribution has the effect of returning the shareholder's cost. In this case $10,000 of the distribution would be applied against and reduce the shareholder's basis and would therefore be recovered tax free.

- If any portion of the distribution remains, the balance is considered to be a gain from the sale or exchange of property. If the stock was a capital asset in the shareholder's hands and was held for the requisite holding period, long-term capital gain will result. In this example there would be a capital gain of $20,000. (From the $50,000 distribution, $20,000 was applied against earnings and profits and is therefore ordinary income; the next $10,000 was considered a recovery of cost and is therefore tax free; and the remainder, $20,000, is considered gain and will be taxed as a capital gain.)

Baily: What is the effect if the shareholder in this example sells his or her stock after the distribution?

Kress: If the stock is subsequently sold, the stockholder's basis for determining gain or loss on the sale will be zero. Let me point out an important thought on the subject of dividend distributions. When a distribution is made to all shareholders in proportion to the number of shares owned by each shareholder, the distribution will be typically considered a dividend. I want to emphasize that a dividend can be found even in the absence of a formal pro rata distribution. Without any other explanation, the word *dividend* implies any corporate distribution in any form to shareholders from the surplus of the corporation. Therefore ordinary dividends can be paid as cash, notes, or stock of other corporations, or even disguised in various forms.

When a distribution constitutes a dividend, it is taxable as ordinary income to the recipient-shareholder. Note that even though dividends are taxable to the recipient-shareholder, the distributing corporation receives no deduction for the distribution.

When the distribution consists of cash, the amount of cash determines how much taxable income must be reported by the shareholder-recipient. If the dividend is in the form of property, the fair market value of the property determines what is reportable. If the property distributed by the corporation is subject to a liability, the taxable amount is reduced by the amount of liability assumed by the shareholder.

Baily: Will the corporation itself have a gain if it uses appreciated property for corporate distributions?

Kress: The rule is that when appreciated property is distributed in any type of distribution, gain (but not loss) is recognized. This rule is applicable to distributions of dividends and in redemption of stock. The amount realized would be equal to the gain that would have been realized if the property had been sold at the time of the distribution.

Reebel: What effect does a dividend distribution have on the accumulated earnings and profits?

Kress: The accumulated earnings and profits of the corporation will be reduced by the amount of the dividend. When cash is distributed, corporate earnings and profits will be reduced by the amount of that cash. When property other than cash is distributed, the reduction in earnings and profits is measured by the basis of that property to the corporation.

NOTES

1. IRC Secs. 11 and 6012.
2. Prop. Reg. Sec. 301-7701-1, 2.
3. IRC Secs. 402, 403, 79, 105, and 106.
4. IRC Sec. 162(a).
5. The effect of state corporate taxes should not be overlooked.
6. IRC Secs. 1361-1363: IRC Secs. 1366-1368.

7. IRC Sec. 1374 (tax imposed on certain built-in gains).
8. IRC Sec. 1361(b), (c), and (d).
9. IRC Sec. 1366(a) and (d).
10. IRC Sec. 1362(d).
11. Reebel, who is transferring cash in exchange for stock, will also receive stock in exchange for services he is to render to the corporation. The stock he receives will be counted in determining whether the transferors of *property* have control of the corporation. However, the fair market value of the stock he receives for the future performance of services will be currently taxable to him as compensation.
12. IRC Secs. 1001.
13. IRC Sec. 351.
14. IRC Sec. 351(b).
15. IRC Sec. 248. (For purposes of determining the *earnings and profits* of a corporation for dividend payments, organizational expenses are to be capitalized and written off as part of the basis of the corporate asset[s] to which the expenditure applies.)
16. IRC Sec. 385; see also *Kraft Foods Co. v. Comm'r*, 232 F.2d 118 (Ratio of Debt to Equity); *J. S. Biritz Construction Company v. Comm'r*, 387 F.2d 454 (Initial Working Capital Requirements); *McSorley's Inc. v. U.S.*, 323 F.2d 900 (Loans Proportionate or Disproportionate to Shareholdings); *Nassau Lens Co. v. Comm'r*, 308 F.2d 39 (Terms of Loan).
17. IRC Sec. 11.
18. IRC Sec. 243.
19. IRC Sec. 162; see also *Chesapeake Mfg. Co., Inc.*, T.C. Memo 1964-214, aff'd. 347 F.2d 507; *R. J. Reynolds Tobacco Co.*, 260 F.2d 9, aff'g. T.C. Memo 1956-161; Treas. Reg. Sec. 1.162-7(b).
20. IRC. Secs. 170 and 162(b).
21. IRC Sec. 1211(a), 1212.
22. IRC Sec. 246.
23. IRC Secs. 531 and 532.
24. IRC Sec. 535(c)(2).
25. IRC Sec. 537; Treas. Reg. Sec. 1.537-1(b)(1) and (2); Treas. Reg. Sec. 1.537-1(a); *Hardin's Bakeries, Inc. v. Martin, Jr.*, D. C. Miss., 1/10/67; Rev. Rul. 67-64, 1967-1 C.B. 150.
26. *General Smelting Co.*, 4 T.C. 313; *Reynard Corp.*, B.T.A. 552; *Harry A. Koch Co. v. Vinal* (Dist. Ct., Neb.) 228 F. Supp. 782; *Vuono-Lione, Inc.*, T.C. Memo 1965-96; *Emeloid Co. v. Comm'r*, 189 F.2d 230; *Bradford-Robinson Printing Co.* (Dist. Ct., Colo., 1958) 1 AFTR 2d 1278.
27. *John P. Scripps Newspapers*, 44 T.C. 453; *Okla. Press Pub. Co. v. U.S.*, 437 F.2d 275; Treas. Reg. Sec. 1.537-2(b)(3).
28. *Mountain State Steel Foundries, Inc. v. Comm'r*, 284 F.2d 737; *Oman Construction Co.*, T.C. Memo 1965-325; *Dill Mfg. Co.*, 39 B.T.A. 1032; *Gazette Publishing Co. v. Self*, 103 F. Supp. 779. See also *Prunier v. Comm'r*, 248 F.2d 818; *Sanders v. Fox*, 253 F.2d 855; *Hedberg-Freidheim Contracting Co.*, T.C. Memo 1956-275, aff'd 25 F.2d 839.
29. IRC Sec. 531.
30. IRC Sec. 535.
31. IRC Sec. 535(c).
32. To be considered personal-service (incorporated-talents) income, the following two tests must be met: (1) the person with whom the corporation has contracted for the services of its "star" has the right to designate that the "star" is the one who must perform the services contracted for, and (2) the individual who must or did perform the services owns 25 percent or more of the stock in the corporation.

    In Rev. Rul. 75-67, 1975-9, I.R.B.-7, a doctor, a specialist, incorporated his practice. The Internal Revenue Service ruled that this one-man corporation would not be considered a personal holding company as long as the doctor was not designated orally or in writing to personally perform services, and the services would not be so unique as to preclude substitution.

33. IRC Sec. 541.
34. IRC Sec. 547.
35. IRC Sec. 542(c) and (d).
36. IRC Secs. 301 and 316.
37. IRC Secs. 301 and 316(a); Treas. Reg. Sec. 1.316-1(a) and (c).

19

Taxation of Distributions to a Corporation's Shareholders

James F. Ivers III and Ted Kurlowicz[*]

> In my own case the words of such an act as the Income Tax, for example, merely dance before my eyes in a meaningless procession; cross-reference to cross-reference, exception upon exception—couched in abstract terms that offer no handle to seize hold of—leave in my mind only a confused sense of some vitally important, but successfully concealed, purport, which it is my duty to extract, but which is within my power, if at all, only after the most inordinate expenditure of time.
>
> Learned Hand

Chapter Outline

---

[*] Ted Kurlowicz, JD, LLM, CLU, ChFC, AEP, is professor of taxation and is the Charles A. Drimal Professor of Estate Planning at The American College.

Many problems in financial and estate planning for shareholders in closely held corporations can be solved through redemptions of some or all of their stock. The Internal Revenue Code defines a redemption of stock as an acquisition by a corporation of its own stock from a shareholder "in exchange for property, whether or not stock so acquired is canceled, retired, or held as Treasury stock."

In many states local law provides that a corporation cannot purchase its own stock without adequate surplus funds. For this reason the planner should be aware of local corporation law, including how it determines the amount of a corporation's surplus, whenever a redemption of stock is considered.

For tax planning purposes the primary objective in arranging a stock redemption is to achieve capital-gain treatment as opposed to dividend treatment on the exchange of stock for money or other property. If the transaction is treated as a dividend distribution rather than as a capital transaction, the redemption proceeds will be taxable as ordinary income.

Capital transactions are subject to tax treatment that is more favorable than the treatment that applies to dividends. First, an individual's capital losses are deductible in full against capital gains for any given year. On the other hand, net capital losses are deductible against ordinary income only to the extent of $3,000 per year. Capital losses, therefore, can "shelter" capital gains fully. Second, in a capital transaction a taxpayer receives back his or her basis as a tax-free return of capital when property is sold. This can be very important, for example, if a shareholder's basis in redeemed stock is high. Of course, return of basis is much less significant if the redeemed shareholder's basis in the shares is very low. Third, long-term capital gains are now subject to maximum statutory marginal rates that are considerably lower than the maximum statutory marginal rates applicable to ordinary income.

It is important to note in this context that an estate receives a stepped-up basis in a decedent's stock that is generally equal to the value of the stock at the date of the decedent's death. Therefore the qualification of a redemption from an estate as a capital transaction is very important. Stock redemptions from estates that qualify as capital transactions will usually provide little or no income tax liability because the redemption price will be approximately equal to the estate's basis in the decedent's stock.

On the other hand, if a stock redemption from a decedent's estate is treated as a dividend, the estate's stepped-up basis in the stock is ignored, and the full amount of the redemption proceeds will be taxed as a dividend to the extent of the corporation's earnings and profits.

This chapter will first examine the technical requirements for qualifying a redemption as a capital transaction. Then planning opportunities that the tax law presents in this area will be explored.

GENERAL RULES FOR TAXATION OF CORPORATE DISTRIBUTIONS

Unless the Internal Revenue Code provides otherwise, a distribution of property from a corporation to a shareholder is taxed as a dividend to the extent of the corporation's current and accumulated earnings and profits. "Earnings and profits" are computed according to tax accounting principles. It may be said that the earnings and profits of a corporation for a given taxable year are determined by reference to the corporation's taxable income. Taxable income is the starting point in calculating earnings and profits. However, several significant positive and negative adjustments to taxable income are made to determine the amount of earnings and profits for tax purposes. The specific adjustments are beyond the scope of this chapter.

If a distribution that would otherwise be taxable as a dividend is in excess of the corporation's earnings and profits, the amount distributed by the corporation in excess of its earnings and profits is treated as a capital transaction. That is, the amount in excess is treated as a return of capital to the extent of the shareholder's basis in the stock. The balance, if any, will be treated as capital gain.

Stated another way, a three-part tax treatment generally applies to a corporate distribution to a shareholder:

- The portion of the distribution not in excess of the corporation's current and accumulated earnings and profits is treated as a dividend and taxed as ordinary income.
- The portion of the distribution in excess of the corporation's current and accumulated earnings and profits is then treated as a nontaxable return of capital to the extent of the shareholder's basis in his or her stock.
- The portion of the distribution not treated as a dividend that exceeds the shareholder's basis in his or her stock is taxed as a capital gain.

Example: Linda is the sole shareholder in the Allston Corporation, which has $40,000 in current and accumulated earnings and profits. Linda's basis in her Allston stock is $6,000. The corporation distributes to Linda $50,000, which is not compensation for her services. Of this amount Linda must treat $40,000 as a dividend, taxable as ordinary income. The next $6,000 of the distribution is treated as a return of Linda's capital investment in the Allston stock. Her basis in the stock is thereby reduced to zero. The remaining $4,000 of the distribution will be treated as capital gain.

These rules apply in basically the same way regardless of whether the distribution to the shareholder is made pursuant to a redemption of stock or simply paid with respect to the shareholder's ownership of stock, as in the above example.

THE PROBLEM OF CONSTRUCTIVE DIVIDENDS

Certain transactions may be taxed to shareholders of a corporation as dividends even though they are not cast in the structure of a dividend by formal resolution of the corporation's Board of Directors. Such transactions are not intended by the corporation to be treated as dividends for tax purposes or any other purpose. However, if the economic effect of such a transaction is the same as a dividend distribution, the IRS may recharacterize the transaction for income tax purposes as a taxable dividend. In general, and particularly in this context, it should be understood that dividends to shareholders do not necessarily have to be paid in the form of cash. Dividends can be paid in the form of property other than money. Such property might be real estate or personal property such as vehicles or equipment. The taxation of such dividends is generally measured by the fair market value of the property distributed. Transactions that could be treated as so-called "constructive dividends" include the following:

- where a debtor of the corporation makes payments directly to the corporation's shareholders rather than to the corporation itself
- where a corporation relieves a shareholder of liability for a debt the shareholder owes the corporation
- where a corporation receives life insurance proceeds and then later pays the amount of the proceeds to its shareholders on a pro rata basis
- where a corporation pays premiums on a life insurance policy that is owned by and insures its principal shareholder, and the corporation is not the beneficiary of the policy
- where a corporation sells property to its shareholders for less than the property's fair market value (a "bargain sale")
- where a shareholder-employee of a corporation is paid a salary that is more than the value of the services furnished to the corporation
- where a shareholder enjoys personal use of property owned by the corporation, such as a residence or a vehicle

The IRS will examine the actual economic effect of such transactions in determining whether dividend tax treatment should be applied. In many of these transactions, there may be a question as to whether the economic benefit was incurred in exchange for services rendered to the corporation, or simply as a constructive dividend payment. The above list is not all inclusive; there are many other transactions that may have the economic effect of a dividend distribution to a corporation's shareholders. A "substance over form" analysis would generally be applied by the IRS to such a situation in determining whether dividend treatment should be imposed.

There may be a valuation issue in such situations. For example, in the case of a bargain sale, the amount taxable as a dividend would be the fair market value of the property sold to the shareholders minus the amount of consideration paid by the shareholders for the property. In a case involving unreasonable compensation, the dividend amount would be the amount of compensation paid minus the value of the services provided to the corporation by the shareholder-employee. A transaction may be characterized as a dividend for tax purposes even if the dividend is not provided pro rata to all the shareholders of the same class. Under state corporate law, dividends are required to be paid pro rata with respect to shares of stock of the same class.

These are some of the basic tax principles that apply to corporate distributions to shareholders. The remainder of this chapter will focus on the specific rules applicable to stock redemptions. Redemptions generally involve distributions to shareholders, which may or may not be taxable as dividends.

REDEMPTIONS THAT ARE TAXED AS CAPITAL TRANSACTIONS

As already stated, the general rule provides that dividend treatment is applied to distributions to shareholders, including the proceeds of a redemption, to the extent of the corporation's current and accumulated earnings and profits. However, the tax law provides exceptions to the general rule. These exceptions apply to certain types of redemptions in which the redeemed shareholder's percentage of ownership of the corporation is materially affected by the redemption. These types of redemptions are treated as capital transactions rather than as dividend distributions.

One type of redemption treated under the general rule is a pro rata redemption. A redemption that is pro rata among shareholders does not change the percentages of ownership, so the redeemed shareholder's percentage of ownership is not affected.

Example: Two shareholders each own a 50 percent interest in a corporation, and the corporation redeems half of each shareholder's stock. After the redemption both shareholders still have the same proportionate interest in the corporation that they had before the redemption. The ownership of the corporation has not been materially affected by the transaction. Therefore the proceeds will be treated as a dividend distribution to the extent of current and accumulated earnings and profits.

The Internal Revenue Code contains specific provisions describing certain types of redemptions that materially affect a shareholder's percentage of ownership. If a given redemption qualifies under one of these provisions, the transaction will be treated as a capital transaction for tax purposes. Sec. 302 allows such treatment for the following four types of redemptions:

- a redemption that is "not essentially equivalent to a dividend"
- a "substantially disproportionate" redemption
- a "complete" redemption
- a distribution to a noncorporate shareholder in "partial liquidation" of the distributing corporation

Redemptions Not Essentially Equivalent to a Dividend

This first category involves questions of fact. Each redemption for which a taxpayer seeks treatment under this provision must be evaluated according to its particular facts if the IRS challenges capital-gain treatment claimed by the redeemed shareholder. There are several revenue rulings in which the IRS has conceded that certain redemptions resulted in a "meaningful reduction" in a shareholder's interest in a corporation. A meaningful reduction is required for a redemption to be considered not essentially equivalent to a dividend. This is not a mathematical test, but a subjective one.

Substantially Disproportionate Redemptions

The second category under Sec. 302 is that of a substantially disproportionate redemption. Sec. 302 provides for automatic qualification of a substantially disproportionate redemption as a capital transaction if a mathematical safe-harbor test is met. The test defines a substantially disproportionate redemption as follows:

- After the redemption the shareholder must own less than 50 percent of the total voting power of the corporation.
- The shareholder's percentage ownership of *voting* stock of the corporation after the redemption must be less than 80 percent of his or her percentage ownership of voting stock before the redemption.
- The shareholder's percentage ownership of *common* stock of the corporation after the redemption must also be less than 80 percent of his or her percentage ownership of common stock before the redemption.

Example: Sobel and Sherman (unrelated individuals) each own 400 of the 800 outstanding voting common shares of Thor Industries, Inc. Thor has no other classes of stock outstanding. A proposal is made to redeem 300 of Sobel's shares. Under the test for substantially disproportionate redemptions the following results occur:

- After the redemption Sobel will own 100 of the 500 outstanding Thor shares. This is less than 50 percent, so the first test is met.
- Before the redemption Sobel's interest was 50 percent of Thor. Eighty percent of 50 percent is 40 percent. After the redemption Sobel's interest will be 20 percent of Thor (100 of the 500 outstanding voting common shares). Since this is less than 40 percent, the 80 percent test is met for both voting and common stock, since only one class of stock is outstanding.

The redemption will qualify as substantially disproportionate.

It is important to note that for purposes of the 80 percent test, the shareholder's proportionate percentage of ownership is the ratio of his or her shares owned to the total shares outstanding. Therefore both parts of the ratio will change after the redemption. The postredemption ratio must reflect the reduction in the total number of shares outstanding. The planner should multiply the preredemption ratio of ownership by 80 percent. Any postredemption ratio that is less than 80 percent of the preredemption ratio is an acceptable reduction of percentage ownership under the 80 percent test.

Complete Redemptions

A complete termination of the shareholder's interest in the redeeming corporation is the third category under Sec. 302. To qualify for capital treatment under this category, the corporation must redeem all the stock the shareholder owns. If the redemption is a complete redemption, it will be treated in its entirety as a capital transaction.

Partial Liquidations

The fourth category under Sec. 302 is that of a distribution in which there is partial liquidation of the distributing corporation. In determining whether a redemption qualifies under this category, the nature of the distribution must be examined at the corporate level, rather than from the point of view of the shareholder receiving proceeds. Distributions in partial liquidation are beyond the scope of this chapter.

ATTRIBUTION OF STOCK OWNERSHIP

Attribution of ownership means that stock owned by one individual or entity is considered to be owned by another individual or entity for the purpose of determining how a particular transaction is taxed.

In evaluating a redemption under each of the first three categories described above, the rules for attribution of stock ownership must be considered.

Attribution may adversely affect the tax treatment of a redemption. Also referred to as constructive ownership, attribution can cause a redemption that would otherwise be taxable as a capital transaction to be treated as a dividend distribution to the extent of the corporation's current and accumulated earnings and profits, since attribution changes a shareholder's percentage of ownership for purposes of determining the tax effects of a redemption.

The rationale for attribution of ownership is that a shareholder may effectively control the operation of a corporation through shares owned by related individuals and entities as well as through shares he or she actually owns. Although this may not in fact be true in many instances, redemptions should always be structured to comply with the attribution rules when these rules are applicable.

Any redemption involving stock of a corporation owned by related parties should be evaluated with these rules in mind.

Family Attribution

Stock owned by an individual shareholder's parents, spouse, children, and grandchildren will be attributed to the shareholder for purposes of determining the tax treatment of a redemption. Stock owned by the shareholder's grandparents or siblings will not be attributed. There is a rationale for these distinctions. In most instances dealings between siblings are more likely to be at arm's length than are dealings between parent and child or between spouses. In addition, it is a more natural situation for stock of a grandparent to pass to a grandchild and remain effectively controlled by the grandparent than for a grandchild to attempt to effectively exercise rights of ownership in stock owned by a grandparent.

Attribution from an Entity

In general, ownership of stock is attributed to a shareholder from an entity in proportion to the shareholder's interest in the entity. However, partnerships, estates, trusts, and corporations are all treated somewhat differently in the application of this general rule.

Attribution from Partnerships

If a partnership owns stock in a corporation, a partner is deemed to own that amount of stock owned by the partnership that is in proportion to the partner's interest in the partnership.

> *Example:* The Hamilton partnership owns 100 shares in Commonwealth Realty Corporation. Harold is a 50 percent partner in Hamilton and owns 100 shares in Commonwealth Realty, which redeems 25 of Harold's shares. For purposes of determining the tax treatment of

Harold's redemption, he is also deemed to own 50 of the 100 shares in Commonwealth Realty owned by the Hamilton partnership.

Attribution from Estates

The general rule that ownership of stock is attributed to a shareholder from an entity in proportion to the shareholder's interest in the entity applies to attribution from an estate to a beneficiary of the estate. However, the beneficiary must have a direct present interest in the estate for attribution to occur. An individual holding a remainder interest in an estate would not have ownership of stock attributed from the estate. Also after an estate has completed its distribution of property to a beneficiary, any stock still owned by the estate will generally no longer be attributed to the beneficiary.

Attribution from Trusts

To determine whether stock owned by a trust is attributable to a trust beneficiary, another variation of the general rule is applied. An actuarial computation of a beneficiary's interest in a trust is made to determine the percentage of stock owned by the trust that will be attributed to the beneficiary. Therefore a beneficiary having only a remainder interest in a trust is subject to attribution of ownership from the trust, even though a remainder interest in an estate would not result in attribution to the beneficiary from the estate.

Attribution from Corporations

The general rule also applies in attributing ownership of stock from a corporation to a shareholder of the corporation, with one important modification. Stock ownership will be attributed from a corporation to a shareholder only if the shareholder is a 50-percent-or-greater owner of the value of all the outstanding stock of the corporation that owns the stock to be attributed.

> *Example:* Suppose Kevin is a 60 percent owner of the Building Corporation and also owns stock in the Hammer and Nail Corporation. The Building Corporation is also a shareholder in the Hammer and Nail Corporation. When the Hammer and Nail Corporation redeems a portion of Kevin's shares, 60 percent of the stock in Hammer and Nail owned by the Building Corporation will be attributed to Kevin for purposes of determining the tax treatment of Kevin's redemption. However, if Kevin were only a 49 percent owner of the Building Corporation, the stock in Hammer and Nail owned by Building would not be attributed to Kevin when Hammer and Nail redeems a portion of Kevin's shares.

Special Rule for S Corporations

It is important to note that the stock attribution rules treat an S corporation as if it were a partnership. Therefore to determine the attribution of stock ownership both to an S corporation and from an S corporation, the rules that apply to partnerships must be used.

Attribution to an Entity

When a corporation redeems shares owned by a partnership, estate, trust, or another corporation, the attribution rules must be examined to determine the tax treatment of the entity receiving proceeds of the redemption.

In general, all the stock owned by a partner, a beneficiary of an estate or trust, or a controlling shareholder in a corporation will be attributed to the partnership, estate, trust, or corporation.

> *Example:* The Horseshoe Corporation redeems stock owned by the Trail partnership. Louis, a partner in Trail, also owns stock in the Horseshoe Corporation. For purposes of determining the tax treatment of the redemption of Trail's stock in Horseshoe, Trail is deemed to own the stock in Horseshoe owned by Louis.

There are modifications to this general rule that apply to trusts and to corporations.

Stock owned by a contingent beneficiary of a trust will not be attributed to a trust if, considering the trustee's discretionary powers under the trust instrument, the beneficiary's largest potential interest in the value of the trust property, determined actuarially, is 5 percent or less of the value of the trust property.

Stock in one corporation owned by a shareholder who also owns stock in a second corporation will not be attributed to the second corporation unless the shareholder owns 50 percent or more of the value of the second corporation that is receiving proceeds of a redemption by the first corporation.

> *Example:* Paul is a 40 percent owner of Landscape Corporation. Both Paul and Landscape Corporation own stock in the Tractor Corporation. Tractor redeems the Tractor stock owned by Landscape. To determine the tax treatment to Landscape in this transaction, stock in Tractor owned by Paul is not considered to be owned by Landscape since Paul owns less than 50 percent of Landscape.

Note how attribution *to* a corporation is different from attribution *from* a corporation. A corporation is deemed to own *all* the stock in another corporation owned by one of its shareholders if attribution applies. However, attribution of stock from a corporation to a shareholder receiving proceeds of a redemption by another corporation applies only to the extent of the shareholder's percentage interest in the corporation from which ownership is attributed.

> *Example:* Suppose Paul in the above example is a 50 percent owner of Landscape Corporation. Paul and Landscape each own 100 shares of the Tractor Corporation. If Tractor redeems Landscape's stock in Tractor, Landscape will be considered to own all 100 shares in Tractor owned by Paul. However, if Tractor redeems Paul's stock in Tractor, Paul will be considered to own only 50 of the shares in Tractor owned by Landscape.

Reattribution

The term *reattribution* refers to situations in which constructive ownership rules are combined to attribute ownership from one shareholder to another shareholder not directly related under the rules.

> *Example:* A father will be considered to own the stock owned by a trust of which his son is the sole beneficiary.

> *Example:* A corporation will be considered to own 50 percent of the stock owned by a partnership in which the corporation's sole shareholder is a 50 percent partner.

There are certain situations in which the Internal Revenue Code prohibits reattribution. For instance, family ownership rules cannot be applied two times in succession.

> *Example:* A father will be considered to own stock owned by his son. Likewise, a daughter will be considered to own stock owned by her father. However, family attribution rules cannot be applied twice in succession to attribute ownership of the son's stock to the daughter. If this type of constructive ownership applied, it would result in sibling attribution.

Waiver of Family Attribution in Complete Redemptions

If a corporation redeems all the stock a shareholder owns, it is possible for the shareholder to avoid the application of the family attribution rules. In order to qualify for a waiver of family attribution in a complete redemption, a shareholder must comply with a number of requirements imposed by the Internal Revenue Code. These include the following:

- The redeemed shareholder may retain no interest in the corporation after the redemption. For these purposes "interest" includes the status of officer, director, or employee of the corporation. It is permissible for the redeemed shareholder to remain a creditor of the corporation.
- The redeemed shareholder must not acquire any prohibited interest in the corporation for a period of 10 years beginning on the date of the distribution of the redemption proceeds. However, if the redeemed shareholder receives stock in the corporation by bequest or inheritance, this provision is not violated.
- The redeemed shareholder must file an agreement with the IRS to notify it if any acquisition of a prohibited interest takes place within the 10-year period. The redeemed shareholder must retain the necessary records to comply with this requirement.
- The redeemed shareholder must not have acquired any portion of the stock redeemed during a 10-year period prior to the date of the redemption from a person whose stock would be attributable to the redeemed shareholder.
- The redeemed shareholder must not have transferred any stock in the redeeming corporation to any person whose stock would be attributed to the redeemed shareholder within a 10-year period before the date of distribution of the redemption proceeds. This requirement will not apply if the corporation also redeems such stock of the person to whom it was transferred by the redeemed shareholder.

The last two requirements may not apply if the redeemed shareholder can show that the transfer or acquisition in question did not have the avoidance of federal income tax as one of its principal purposes. The waiver of attribution is available only in the case of a complete redemption and generally only for the family attribution rules (not entity attribution).

However, an entity (estate, partnership, trust, or corporation) can also make use of the waiver of family attribution provisions, as long as all individuals whose stock would be attributable to the entity comply with the conditions for waiver of family attribution. Note, however, that waiver by an estate has limited application because in most cases stock in a family corporation will be owned by family members or left to family members under the decedent's will, so that beneficiaries of the estate will also be stockholders. Still, in certain situations an estate may be able to effectively claim the waiver.

Example: The Connecticut Corporation plans to redeem its stock owned by Biff's estate. Biff's estate is a 50 percent shareholder in Connecticut. The other 50 percent of Connecticut is owned by Bunny, Bill's wife. Biff and Bunny's son and daughter, Rollo and Muffy, are the sole beneficiaries of Biff's estate. Biff's estate can achieve capital-gain treatment on the redemption of Connecticut stock through the waiver of family attribution rules as long as Rollo and Muffy agree not to acquire any interest in the corporation that is prohibited by those rules during the time period prescribed by the rules. In effect, the waiver of family attribution rules in this situation operate as if the beneficiaries of the estate were the parties whose stock was redeemed.

SEC. 303 REDEMPTIONS

The Internal Revenue Code contains a relief provision that applies to estates in which stock of a closely held corporation constitutes a substantial portion of total estate assets. The purpose of this section is to provide liquidity for such estates in order to avoid forced sales of the closely held stock to meet tax obligations and administration expenses.

This relief provision, Sec. 303 of the Code, allows distributions in redemption of such stock to be treated as made in exchange for a capital asset and therefore eligible for capital-gains treatment, subject to certain requirements and limitations. Sec. 303 is totally independent of the other Code provisions describing the tax treatment of redemptions of stock. Therefore neither the rules under Sec. 302 nor the constructive ownership rules need to be considered in determining whether favorable tax treatment is available under Sec. 303. Sec. 303 operates independently, and as long as its own requirements are met, favorable tax treatment can be achieved.

What Estates May Qualify under Sec. 303?

In order for an estate to be eligible for a Sec. 303 redemption, the value of corporate stock includible in the gross estate for federal estate tax purposes must be more than 35 percent of the value of the adjusted gross estate. The adjusted gross estate is defined for this purpose as the gross estate less deductions for funeral and administration expenses, debts, and deductible losses of the estate. To determine whether the corporate stock meets the percentage test, all classes of stock in the corporation owned by the estate are counted; that is, preferred is counted as well as common.

For estates that own stock in two or more corporations there is a variation of the 35 percent test. If the stock in the two or more corporations owned by the estate represents 20 percent or more of the outstanding value of all the stock in each corporation, the stock in the two or more corporations may be combined and treated as stock in one corporation for purposes of the 35 percent test. If the test is met by combining stock in two or more corporations, a Sec. 303 redemption may be made with shares of any of the two or more corporations.

Example: Spike's estate needs liquidity to meet its tax obligations and administration expenses. The estate owns 100 shares in the Jersey Video Corporation. These shares represent 25 percent of the value of

Spike's adjusted gross estate and 33 percent of the value of Jersey Video, Inc. The estate also owns 100 shares in Philly Stereo, Inc. These shares represent 15 percent of the value of Spike's adjusted gross estate and 25 percent of the value of Philly Stereo, Inc. Because the stock in each corporation owned by the estate represents 20 percent or more of the value of the stock in each corporation, and because the stock in the two corporations has a total value in excess of 35 percent of Spike's adjusted gross estate, the estate will qualify for a Sec. 303 redemption.

There is one more wrinkle that applies *only* to the special rule for stock in two or more corporations. For purposes of the 20 percent requirement, 100 percent of the value of stock the decedent held with his or her surviving spouse as community property or in joint tenancy, tenancy by the entirety, or tenancy in common is treated as having been included in the decedent's gross estate. This wrinkle applies *only* when the rule for stock in two or more corporations is applied and not to the 35 percent test in general.

How Much Stock May Be Redeemed under Sec. 303?

There is a limitation on the dollar amount of proceeds received for redeemed stock that will qualify for favorable treatment under Sec. 303. Redemption proceeds eligible for favorable tax treatment may not exceed the sum of the estate, inheritance, legacy, and succession taxes for which the estate is liable (including interest, if any) and the amount of funeral and administration expenses allowable as deductions to the estate under the Internal Revenue Code.

The amount of proceeds qualifying for treatment under Sec. 303 will be further limited if the redeemed shareholder (usually the estate) is not legally liable for the full amount of the taxes and expenses. Only that portion of the taxes and expenses that the redeemed shareholder is legally obligated to pay is considered in determining the maximum amount of proceeds allowable under Sec. 303.

> *Example:* A trust owns stock in the Texas Corporation that is included in Alvin's gross estate. The trust instrument does not require the trust to pay a portion of the taxes or administration expenses of Alvin's estate. However, Fergus, the trustee, uses proceeds of a redemption of the trust's stock in Texas to pay a portion of Alvin's estate taxes. In this situation the trust may not treat the redemption under Sec. 303.

Who May Receive Favorable Tax Treatment under Sec. 303?

If the requirements of Sec. 303 are met, any shareholder owning stock included in determining a decedent's gross estate is eligible for a Sec. 303 redemption. Generally the eligible shareholder will be either the decedent's estate itself or a beneficiary of the estate. However, in this context it is important to remember that unless a beneficiary of the estate has an obligation to pay death taxes or administration expenses, the beneficiary will not be eligible for Sec. 303 treatment.

When Must a Sec. 303 Redemption Be Made?

Sec. 303 treatment is available for distributions in redemption of stock made after the decedent's death and within 3 years and 90 days after the filing of the estate's federal estate tax return. If the estate has filed a petition in the Tax Court concerning an estate tax dispute, the time limitation is extended until 60 days after the decision of the Tax Court becomes final. Furthermore, if the estate has elected to pay its estate tax in installments under Sec. 6166 of the Internal Revenue Code, redemption distributions may receive the benefit of Sec. 303 if they are made within the time period of the installment payments.

Under any of these rules if redemption proceeds are paid more than 4 years after the decedent's death, the amount of distributions eligible to be treated under Sec. 303 cannot exceed the lesser of the amount of taxes and administration expenses remaining unpaid or the amount of such expenses that are paid within one year after the redemption.

Planning Considerations under Sec. 303

Minimal Taxable Gain

Because of its fiduciary duties to its other shareholders, a corporation will generally redeem the stock of a decedent shareholder at a price equal to the stock's current fair market value. For income tax purposes an estate or its beneficiary receives a "stepped-up" basis in a decedent's assets that is generally equal to the value of the assets as of the date of the decedent's death. Therefore if a redemption is made under Sec. 303 within a short time after the decedent's death, the redemption price should be equal to or very close to the basis in the stock held by the estate or the beneficiary. Since proceeds in a Sec. 303 redemption are treated as received in the sale or exchange of a capital asset, and not as a dividend, the redeemed shareholder will generally realize little or no taxable gain. If the stock has increased in value between the time of the decedent's death and the time of the redemption, any amount in excess of the estate's or beneficiary's basis in the stock will be taxed as long-term capital gain. Therefore unless there has been a significant change in the corporation's fortunes during that time, the amount of taxable gain will probably not be significant.

Accumulated-Earnings Tax

One problem that may arise in planning for the corporation to fund a Sec. 303 redemption is the accumulated-earnings tax. The Internal Revenue Code states specifically that corporate accumulations may be made to fund a Sec. 303 redemption without being subject to the accumulated-earnings tax. However, such accumulations are specifically exempt only when made in the corporation's taxable year in which the decedent died or any taxable year thereafter. Therefore accumulations prior to the year of the decedent's death to meet an anticipated funding need for a redemption may present the corporation with an accumulated-earnings tax problem. This problem is amplified by the requirement mentioned earlier that in some states a redemption may be effected only if the corporation has adequate surplus to fund the redemption.

If the IRS can show that the funding objective was not for a corporate purpose, but only for the benefit of the shareholder or the shareholder's estate, the accumulated-earnings tax may become a problem. It may be difficult to convince the IRS that a Sec. 303 redemption serves a business purpose of the corporation. Therefore as a practical matter the use of life insurance owned by the corporation may be the most appropriate method of funding a Sec. 303 redemption. Even though the accumulation of earnings to meet premium obligations for such insurance may be subject to the accumulated-earnings tax, the dollar amount needed for premiums will be substantially less than the dollar amount needed for cash funding. As a result, any possible exposure to the accumulated-earnings tax is minimized. The proper life insurance funding will also provide any surplus required to effect the redemption.

Taxation of Partners and Partnerships

Michael R. Harris, James F. Ivers III, and Stephan R. Leimberg[*]

Two years ago it was impossible to get through on the phone to the IRS. Now it's just hard to get through. That's progress.

Charles O. Rossotti

Chapter Outline

In order to highlight some of the more essential areas of partnership taxation, the following reading is written as a narrative between a CLU (Steve), an attorney (Mike), and a CPA (Jim). Because of the complexity of partnership taxation, the following subject matter covered should be considered merely an introductory overview to this topic.

TAX LAW CLASSIFICATION OF UNINCORPORATED BUSINESS ENTITIES

Steve: Mike, how do we know whether a business organization will be treated as a partnership or a corporation under federal tax law?

---

[*] Michael R. Harris is in the private practice of law and is a member of the Montgomery County Bar Association in Pennsylvania.

Mike: In the past, the tax classification of any business organization having more than one owner depended upon the presence or absence of a certain number of traditional legal corporate characteristics in the structure of the particular organization. If an organization exhibited a preponderance of corporate characteristics, it would be taxed as a corporation. If not, it would be taxed as a partnership.

However, the process of classifying a business organization for tax purposes has recently been greatly simplified. In general, an organization formed as a corporation under state law will be taxed as a corporation under federal law. Organizations that are not incorporated under state law, including partnerships and limited liability companies, will generally be permitted to choose whether to be taxed as corporations or partnerships.[1] In most cases, they will choose to be taxed as partnerships.

Steve: I'm a little confused by this. You're saying that most business organizations (other than sole proprietorships) will be taxed as either corporations or partnerships. Yet there are other types of business entities under state law, such as limited liability companies.

Mike: That's true. Under state law, business organizations may be formed as corporations, general partnerships, limited partnerships, limited liability partnerships, limited liability companies, or as variations of these business forms. However, all of these various types of entities are classified as either partnerships or corporations for federal tax purposes. Limited partnerships, for example, will generally be treated as partnerships for tax purposes. Although some special tax rules apply to limited partnerships, they are still taxed in generally the same manner as other partnerships. A limited liability company that elects to be taxed as a partnership is also taxed in generally the same manner as a state law partnership. Although there are many varieties of business entities under state law, federal tax law has just two general categories under which business organizations are classified. Note, however, that there are some variations within those two categories. For example, a corporation might elect to be treated as an "S" corporation under federal tax law. This would make the corporation taxable in a manner similar to a partnership, even though the entity is still basically a corporation under both state law and federal tax law.

Steve: You mentioned that unincorporated business entities are now permitted to choose whether to be treated as partnerships or corporations for federal tax purposes. How did this come about?

Mike: State business law has developed to the point where there are popular business entities, such as limited liability companies, that may exhibit some characteristics of a partnership and some of a corporation. From a legal standpoint, a limited liability company in its most basic form is really a partnership with the corporate characteristic of limited liability. Other unincorporated entities, such as limited partnerships and limited liability partnerships, may also exhibit certain corporate characteristics. With the development of these "hybrid" business entities, it became administratively difficult for the IRS to classify them for tax purposes based upon the presence or absence of a preponderance of corporate characteristics. As a result, a more flexible system of classification (often referred to as "check the box") was developed. This is the means by which these entities select their federal income tax status.

IMPORTANCE OF CLASSIFICATION AS A PARTNERSHIP

Steve: Why is it important that we know how a given organization will be classified?

Jim: It is important to everyone concerned that a particular organization be taxed as the parties involved intended. There are important distinctions between a corporation and a partnership.

When the organization is taxed as a corporation, the organization and its members are treated as two separate and distinct taxable entities.[2] When profits are earned by a corporation, they are taxed once to the business and then taxed again to the shareholders if they are paid out in the form of dividends. This potential double taxation is avoided in a partnership. If the organization is treated as a partnership, these same profits earned by the same recipients will be taxed only once—on the recipients' individual returns. Also, if a business is classified as a corporation, losses may be claimed only by the corporation and are not available to offset the shareholder's other income. However, in the event that the partnership has a net loss, the partners may deduct their share of the loss on their individual returns.

THE AGGREGATE AND ENTITY THEORIES

Steve: Am I correct in thinking that there is no difference between partners and their partnership—so that for tax purposes a partnership is equivalent to the sum of its individual members?

Mike: This statement is only partially correct. Woven into the relevant sections of the Internal Revenue Code are two general theories used in developing the tax law relating to partnerships and their partners. These are called the *aggregate theory* and the *entity theory*.

According to the aggregate theory, a partnership is considered as an aggregate of individual co-owners who have bound themselves together with the intention of sharing gains and losses. The key point here is that under the aggregate theory, the partnership itself has no existence separate and apart from its members. As the word *aggregate* implies, to the extent this theory influences tax law, a partnership is nothing more than the sum of its individual members.

The Code recognizes this theory by requiring that each partner include on his or her personal income tax return his or her share of certain partnership gains, losses, deductions, and credits. This means that it is not the partnership that is taxable. Rather, it is the partners who are subject to the income tax as an aggregate of individuals. In other words, the individual partners are the taxpayers, not the partnership.

At the same time, however, the Code provides that for certain other purposes, the partnership is a separate entity that is distinct from its members. Accordingly, the partnership must file an income tax return for information purposes only—Form 1065—and show gross income, business deductions, and taxable income.

Three other indicia of the entity theory are that a partnership has a taxable year, its own accounting method, and the right to exercise various income tax elections.

Steve: Would you explain the aggregate and entity theories in more detail?

Mike: Let me start with the aggregate theory. According to the aggregate theory, since a partnership is not a separate entity, no tax is imposed on the partnership itself. The liability is instead passed through directly to each partner who pays tax on his or her share of the profits just as though he or she realized the share of income as an individual. Capital gains, Section 1231 gains, dividends, and other taxable items are also passed directly through to the partners, who add them to like items on their 1040s.

In keeping with this *conduit* concept, these items retain their character. For example, as capital gains flow through the partnership conduit to the taxpaying partners, the aggregate theory keeps the nature of the gain the same—capital gain.

However, even while the aggregate theory makes the partnership a conduit for some purposes, the entity theory treats the partnership as separate from its individual partners. The entity theory requires the partnership itself to file a return. The return provides a way to inform both the IRS and the individual partners how the profits and losses are allocated.

For example, the partnership return breaks down the partnership's ordinary taxable income or loss, its net capital gain or loss, its Section 1231 gains or losses, its charitable contributions, and its receipt of dividends. Then each partner can readily see from his or her separate Schedule K-1 on Form 1065 his or her share of the partnership's income, credits, deductions, and so forth.

Another good example of the entity theory is the way partners who deal with their own partnership are treated. Generally a partner who engages in a transaction with his or her partnership is treated taxwise like a stranger. This rule does not apply to certain sales or exchanges of property between partners and partnerships. This means that when a partner is not acting in his or her capacity as a partner, a transaction between that partner and the partnership is treated as if it was conducted between the partnership and an unrelated third person.

For example, Debra and Lillian form a partnership with equal capital and income interests. The partnership agrees to pay Debra, the working member, $10,000 a year as salary. If the income (after deductions for expenses other than salaries) of the partnership is $10,000 and that entire amount is paid to Debra, she has taxable income of $10,000. The partnership itself has no taxable income. But if that same partnership had income after deductions (other than the salary deduction) of $25,000, Debra would be taxable on $17,500. That $17,500 would be composed of $10,000 of salary and Debra's distributive share of the partnership's taxable income. Her distributive share is one-half of $15,000, that is, one-half of the $25,000 of partnership income (after deductions other than salary), less the business expense deduction of $10,000 for the salary paid to Debra.

Other instances occur where a partner dealing with the partnership is treated as if he or she was not a partner when the partner lends money or property to the partnership or purchases property from the partnership.[3]

TAX RAMIFICATIONS IN THE FORMATION OF A PARTNERSHIP

Steve: I know that it is possible to form a corporation without incurring a tax even if the members contribute appreciated property. Can you explain the tax ramifications of forming a partnership?

Jim: Say you and I are both engaged in the same type of work. We agree it would be mutually beneficial to pool our talents, money, and other property. We might just shake hands or we might draw up a formal agreement that allocates partnership income, deductions, gain, loss, and credits. Any fees paid in connection with the organization, such as legal fees, are considered capital expenditures that may be amortized and deducted over a 5-year period.

We agree to form an equal partnership. You contribute $24,000 in cash—I'll contribute a building with a fair market value of $24,000. Generally speaking, no gain or loss is recognized on the exchange of property or money for an interest in a partnership.[4]

Assume my building, valued at $24,000, has a basis depreciated to $10,000. I've realized a $14,000 gain on the trade of my title to the building for a partnership interest. But I don't have to recognize that gain for tax purposes.

Instead, the basis for my partnership interest remains the same as the basis I had in the property I contributed, or $10,000.[5] If I should immediately sell my partnership interest for $18,000, I'd have an $8,000 gain. So the general rule is this: The basis a contributing partner had for property he or she contributes to the partnership becomes his or her initial basis for his or her partnership interest. Stated more precisely, the amount of cash contributed plus the adjusted basis an individual had in the contributed property becomes the original basis for his or her new partnership interest.

When contributed property is subject to indebtedness, the original basis of the contributor's partnership interest must be lowered by the portion of the indebtedness taken over by the other partners.[6] So if the $10,000 property I contribute is subject to a $6,000 lien, and the partnership assumes this liability, the basis for my partnership interest will be reduced to the extent that you assume part of this $6,000 liability. In this example, being an equal partner, you'd assume half of the liability, so my basis would drop from $10,000 to

$7,000. If you contributed $7,000 in cash, your basis would be the $7,000 you contributed plus the $3,000 share of the liability you assumed, for a total basis of $10,000. Note that if the property contributed to the partnership is subject to a liability in excess of its basis in the hands of the contributing partner, more complex tax problems arise and the contributing partner may realize taxable gain.

The partnership's basis in contributed property is the same as the contributing partner's basis in the asset. Therefore in the previous example, the partnership would have a $10,000 basis in the property I contributed. If the partnership later sells the property for $20,000, the partnership has a taxable gain of $10,000. Note that there is a distinction between a partner's basis in his or her partnership interest and the partnership's basis in assets contributed by its partners.

Now I might not have cash to contribute—but I do have unique talents I can bring into the business. If I contributed property in return for my partnership interest, I would not have to recognize either gain or loss. But if I contribute either past services or the promise of future services, this general rule doesn't apply.

The receipt of an interest in partnership capital in return for services is regarded by the tax law as compensation for services rendered (or to be rendered).[7] So I may have to pay a current tax on the fair market value of the interest in partnership capital I receive in return for my services.

Sometimes an interest in partnership capital will be transferred to an individual subject to the condition that he or she must complete specified services at a future date. For example, you and I could form a partnership. You provide cash and I provide talent. You transfer an interest in the partnership capital to me conditioned on my completion of 5 years of service. I will realize income as soon as there are no longer any substantial restrictions or conditions on my right to receive my interest in the partnership capital.

THE PARTNERSHIP IN OPERATION

Steve: OK. Suppose we get a partnership in operation. Since the partners will pay the income tax on partnership income, is the partnership required to file a federal return?

Mike: Yes, the partnership must file a return—IRS Form 1065—but it is for informational purposes only. A civil penalty is now imposed on any partnership that fails to file a complete partnership information return, unless reasonable cause is shown. The penalty consists of $50 times the number of partners for each month that the failure continues, up to 5 months. This penalty is in addition to criminal penalties for willful failure to file a return, supply information, or pay tax.[8] The form is due 3 1/2 months after the partnership fiscal year ends. Under Code provisions the partnership tax year must be the same as the principal partners' (partners owning 5 percent of more of capital or profit interests), unless a business purpose for a different tax year can be established. Since most individuals are calendar-year taxpayers, most partnerships also will have a calendar-year reporting period and file their informational return on April 15 each year.

Steve: Let's discuss how the partner is taxed.

Jim: Each partner must include in his or her return for each taxable year his or her distributive share of the partnership income or loss items. Each partner's share of partnership income and loss is computed with regard to what was realized in the taxable year of the partnership.

Steve: Could you be more specific as to which items would be includible as distributive shares?

Jim: The partners must include in their individual tax returns their shares of the partnership income or loss. They must also take into account (and report on their 1040s) a number of separate partnership items,[9] including

- capital gains and losses
- Sec. 1231 gains and losses
- charitable contributions
- dividends received by the partnership from stockholdings

The partners would then add their share of each of the above items to their individual income and deductions. For example, one partner's share of partnership capital gains and losses would be added to his or her personal capital gains and losses. In the same way, a partner's distributive share of the firm's charitable contributions is added to his or her individual contributions, and the charitable contribution deduction limitations are applied to the total.

Steve: How do the partners determine who gets what, that is, how are the distributive shares of each item determined?

Mike: Generally speaking, the distributive shares of each item are to be determined in accordance with the partnership agreement. If the partnership doesn't cover a particular item, the partner's distributive share of that item is the same percentage as his or her percentage share of partnership income or loss.[10] If the partner would normally receive one-third of all profits and losses, he or she would receive one-third of all capital gains.

Sometimes partners, through the partnership agreement, attempt to shift an item to the taxpayer in whose hands the item will be most beneficial. This allocation of one type of item to the partner who can obtain the greatest tax benefit (such as an allocation of all depreciation deductions to the highest tax bracket partner) may be ignored by the IRS. If such a provision does not have "substantial economic effect,"[11] the partners' shares of that item will be readjusted by the IRS just as if the partnership agreement contained no provision as to the item; that is, each partner's distributive share of that item is determined in accordance with his or her share of partnership income or loss.

It's difficult to determine the distinction between an acceptable and unacceptable allocation. Generally the dollar amounts of income received by the partners must be substantially affected by any special allocations independent of tax consequences.

If the economic after-tax consequences to one partner are enhanced by an allocation, the economic after-tax consequences to some other partner or partners should be diminished if the allocation is to be treated as having substantial economic effect. Using present-value concepts, this principle is applied for calculating economic consequences over the course of a number of years. Treasury regulations state the application of these principles in detail. Those regulations need to be studied in detail to determine the effects of any special allocations that the partnership may be considering.

If special allocations do not satisfy the requirement of substantial economic effect, they will usually be allocated in accordance with the general provisions in the partnership agreement for sharing income and loss.[12]

With respect to contributed property by the partner to the partnership, the partnership will generally be required, rather than permitted, to allocate *built-in* gain or loss on contributed property to the contributing partner, and not in accordance with each partner's interest in the property.

Steve: Suppose that one partner feels his or her distributive share of partnership income is too little compensation for the efforts provided. Can that partner obtain some type of salary from the partnership?

Jim: Yes, a partner can obtain a salary or, as it is sometimes called, guaranteed payment. A guaranteed payment is a sum paid to a partner, regardless of whether the partnership has income. This payment is deductible by the partnership.

Guaranteed payments are ordinary income to the recipient partner. Perhaps an illustration of the treatment of guaranteed payments would be helpful. Ethan, a partner in the Ethan Ward partnership, is to receive a payment of $10,000 for services, plus 40 percent of the taxable income or loss of the partnership. Assume that after deducting payment of the $10,000 salary to Ethan, the partnership has a loss of $8,000. Of this amount, $3,200 (40 percent of the loss) would be Ethan's distributive share of partnership loss. In addition, Ethan must report as ordinary income the guaranteed payment of $10,000 made to him by the partnership. This guaranteed payment would be reportable by Ethan in the taxable year of the partnership in which it deducted the payment and that ended with or within Ethan's own taxable year.

Steve: Suppose a partner wants to sell his or her partnership interest 2 or 3 years after the partnership is in operation. The amount received on the sale minus his or her basis in the partnership will be taxed. Is that partner's basis in the partnership interest the same as his or her original basis?

Jim: No, the partner's basis will not be the same.

A partner's basis is increased by the following three factors:

1. his or her capital contributions
2. his or her distributive share of partnership income
3. his or her share of liabilities *assumed*

A partner's basis is also reduced by the following three factors:

1. his or her share of losses
2. his or her distributions or draws
3. his or her share of liabilities *relieved*

Steve: Let's see if I understand. When a partnership is formed, the basis of a contributing partner's partnership interest is (1) the amount of money plus (2) the adjusted basis of the property he or she contributes to the partnership.

This same rule applies to a new partner who contributes money or property. The initial basis of a partner who receives an interest as an inheritance is basically determined by valuing the interest at the date of the decedent's death. If an individual acquires a partnership interest by gift, the new partner's basis would be the same as the old donor-partner's basis plus any gift tax paid on the transfer.

If a partner loans money to the partnership, that partner's basis is increased by his or her share of the partnership's liability to him or her as an outsider.

If only services are contributed, and the contributing partner receives an interest in partnership capital (that is, an interest in the property contributed by his or her copartners), then the contributing partner realizes current ordinary income as long as there are no substantial restrictions on that partner's right to withdraw or dispose of his or her interest in partnership capital. When such income is realized, that income will be added to the partner's basis.

Abe and Benny open a delicatessen. Abe owned luncheonette equipment with an adjusted basis of $4,000 and a fair market value of $5,000. He entered into an agreement with Benny in which Abe would contribute his equipment to the partnership and Benny would contribute $5,000 in cash. By mutual agreement, each man will own a 50 percent interest.

Since the adjusted basis of Abe's property was $4,000, the basis for Abe's 50 percent interest is $4,000. On the other hand, Benny's basis is equal to the cash he contributed, which is $5,000.

Of course, the original basis is only a starting point. If we had to determine the basis of a partner's partnership interest one year after the formation of a partnership, we would have to adjust the original basis to reflect changes that have occurred.

We'd start with the original basis—increase that figure by any subsequent capital contributions, and also increase basis by the sum of the partner's share of the partnership's taxable income as well as its tax-exempt receipts. So, for example, if the partnership received life insurance death proceeds, this cash would serve to increase each partner's basis.

Since an increase in a partner's share of liabilities is treated as if cash had been contributed, a partner's basis increases to the extent of his or her share of increased partnership obligations, such as accounts or notes payable and mortgages assumed.

Next, we'd reduce basis (but not below zero) by the amount of a partner's share of partnership losses, distributions by the partnership to the partner, and by the amount that the partner's share of liabilities was decreased.

Suppose the two of you formed a partnership. This year the firm lost $10,000. Jim's distributive share of the loss was $5,000. If the adjusted basis of his partnership interest, before considering his share of the partnership loss, was $2,000, he could claim only $2,000 of the loss this year. The adjusted basis of his interest would be reduced to zero. An individual partner's loss deduction cannot exceed his basis for his partnership interest at the end of the year for which the loss occurred. However, the partner is entitled to an unlimited carryover of nondeductible partnership losses.

If your partnership realized an $8,000 profit next year, Jim's $4,000 share of that profit would increase the adjusted basis of his interest to $4,000 (if we don't take into account the $3,000 excess loss he could not deduct last year). Next year's return should show his distributive share of partnership income to be $1,000 ($4,000 distributive share less the $3,000 loss he was not allowed to take this year). The adjusted basis of his partnership interest at the end of next year would be $1,000.[13]

What's the purpose for those increases and reductions in basis?

Mike: When we increase a partner's basis, what we're doing in effect is shielding those amounts from a subsequent tax. For example, when you sell your partnership interest, you should not have to pay tax on income you've already paid tax on. By the same token, your share of the tax-exempt income (such as life insurance proceeds) received by the partnership should be considered an additional capital investment by you—so if you sell your partnership interest, you should not be taxed on that item, either. Likewise, if you assume a portion of the partnership's liabilities, it's the same as if you contributed a like amount of cash. You should be able to recover that amount of cash tax free.

Reductions in basis serve just the opposite purpose. By reducing basis, you account for recoveries of basis on capital invested in the partnership resulting from losses deducted against other income, distributions of property or money from the partnership to you, and decreases in your share of partnership liabilities.

Partnership basis is important in determining the amount of loss that can be recognized. It also affects taxation upon the disposition of a partnership interest on a partner's retirement or death.

TAX EFFECTS UPON RETIREMENT OR DEATH OF A PARTNER

Steve: Let's examine the tax effects when a partner retires or dies.

Mike: I think it's best to do this in two stages. Let's first talk about a sale by the retiring or deceased partner to his or her former partners or to an outsider. Later, we will discuss payments from the partnership itself to the retiring or deceased partner's estate or other successor in interest.

When a partner's interest in a partnership is sold, his or her gain (that is, the amount received minus that partner's basis in the partnership interest) is taxed. Such gain will be treated as all capital gain, unless a partnership has inventory items or unrealized receivables.

Unrealized receivables are essentially uncollected fees and other rights to income. The term includes the right to payment for (1) goods delivered (that were not capital assets or would not be treated as capital assets on a sale), or (2) services, to the extent that these rights are not currently includible in income under the partnership's method of accounting.[14]

In the event that a partnership has inventory or unrealized receivables, the selling partner must fragment his or her gain into both a capital-gain portion and an ordinary-income portion. The selling partner's share of the potential gain on inventory, if sold, plus the partner's share of unrealized receivables, is taxed as ordinary income.[15] As previously mentioned, the balance is capital gain, including payments for goodwill. The remaining partners have the option to increase the basis of partnership assets in proportion to the gain recognized to the retiring partner.

Upon the sale of a deceased partner's partnership interest, the basis to his or her estate or successor in interest will be the value of the partnership interest (other than the value of unrealized receivables) on the date of that partner's death.[16] Any unrealized receivables will be taxed as income in respect of a decedent.[17] The partnership can make a special election under another section of the Code that allows adjustments to the bases of certain items held by the partnership.[18]

Frequently partners will enter into a buy-sell agreement stating that on the death of a partner, the surviving partner or partners will purchase the deceased partner's interest. To fund this cross-purchase-type agreement, often each partner acquires, pays for, and is the beneficiary of a policy on each other partner's life. The premiums each partner pays are not deductible. The insurance proceeds, however, will be income tax exempt.

Steve: Is there some way that the partnership can buy a partnership interest? I'm thinking of something similar to a stock redemption in the corporate area.

Mike: Yes, the partners may agree that the partnership will buy, or as it is sometimes termed, "liquidate," a partner's interest. Generally the partners enter into a buy-sell agreement, which states that upon the death or retirement of a partner, the partnership will purchase the former partner's interest. To fund this type of agreement, partnerships purchase life insurance on the lives of their individual partners. Premiums paid by the partnership are not tax deductible, and the insurance proceeds, when received, will be income tax free.

Steve: How is the retiring or deceased partner taxed when payment is received from the partnership for his or her interest?

Mike: If the partnership purchases a retiring partner's interest, the purchase price and the partner's share of the partnership basis in assets must be broken down into several parts. The purchase price and basis of the partnership in its assets must be segregated into amounts attributable to

- partnership property
- inventory
- unrealized receivables
- goodwill

There are now two different ways in which the payments are taxed. In a partnership in which capital is not a material income-producing factor (a service partnership), the liquidation of a general partner's interest is taxed in four layers.

First, that portion of the purchase price attributable to partnership property, exclusive of inventory, unrealized receivables, and goodwill, must be determined. If the retiring partner receives an amount for his or her interest in partnership property that exceeds that partner's share of the partnership basis in such assets, he or she will have a capital gain. The remaining partners have the option of increasing the basis of partnership assets in proportion to the gain recognized to the retiring partner.

Second, the retiring partner's share of the potential gain on inventory will be treated as ordinary income to the recipient. The partnership increases its basis for these inventory items in the amount that ordinary income is recognized.

Third, the portion of the purchase price attributable to unrealized receivables of the partnership, such as accounts receivable that were not previously taxed as partnership income, is taxed as ordinary income to the recipient but is deductible by the partnership.

Fourth, the portion attributable to goodwill can be treated in one of two ways: If the partnership agreement states that payment will be made for goodwill, the recipients will report any gain as capital gain, but the payment is not deductible by the partnership. Of course, the amount paid for goodwill must be reasonable. If the agreement is silent as to goodwill, the payment is taxable to the recipient as ordinary income and is deductible by the partnership. In the case of such agreements, the Code treats any other amounts paid as "additional payments."[19] Additional payments are treated as ordinary income to the retiring partner. They are characterized as part of the retiring partner's distributive share or as a guaranteed payment to the retiring partner. Of course, amounts that are treated as part of the retiring partner's distributive share or as a guaranteed payment are not taxed to the remaining partners. Another way to look at this is that the partnership obtains a deduction for the amounts paid to the retiring partner. In this type of situation, the retiring partner prefers the partnership agreement to state that payment will be made for goodwill to ensure that capital-gains treatment will be obtained. The remaining partners prefer the partnership agreement to be silent as to goodwill, so the partners can obtain a deduction for the payment of additional payments. This issue must be negotiated by the partners. Often the retiring partner is willing to receive ordinary income rather than capital gain and allow the other partners a deduction, if a greater amount is received for his or her interest. Note that, in general, a partnership has no basis in its goodwill for tax purposes unless it purchased the goodwill in a taxable acquisition. In such cases, the partnership can amortize its cost for the goodwill over a 15-year period, thereby reducing its basis in the goodwill.

In the event of a liquidation of a deceased partner's interest, the partner's basis in his or her partnership interest will be increased to its date-of-death value under the rules for inherited property as discussed previously.

In the case of a liquidation of a partnership interest other than that of a general partner in a service partnership, both unrealized receivables and goodwill are automatically treated as partnership property. As a result, the partnership in such cases receives no deduction for payments for such property. This is a different rule than that which applies to a service partnership. There is also no deduction to the partnership with respect to payments for inventory, although a basis adjustment is made corresponding to such payments as in the case of a service partnership.

To the extent the partner receives more for his or her interest in the partnership's cash and other property than the partner's share of basis in those assets, he or she will have a capital gain. The remaining partners have the option of increasing the basis in partnership assets for the gain so recognized by the partner. However, any portion of the payments received for unrealized receivables and inventory that exceeds the partner's share of partnership basis in such assets is treated as ordinary income. The retiring partner must segregate the cash and other property from the inventory and unrealized receivables.

TABLE 20-1		
	Adjusted Basis	Fair Market Value
Cash	$ 9,000	$ 9,000
Real estate	30,000	36,000
Accounts receivable	0	30,000
Goodwill	0	45,000
Total	$39,000	$120,000
Liabilities	0	0
Capital accounts		
A = $ 40,000		
B = 40,000		
C = 40,000		
Total $120,000		

Steve: Could you give me an example of how these rules operate?

Jim: Assume that Catherine wishes to retire from the Cartland partnership, a service partnership that utilizes the cash-basis method. Assume that Catherine's basis in her partnership interest is $13,000. Assume that the balance sheet of that firm on the date of retirement may be stated as in table 20-1.

Assume that Catherine is willing to sell her interest for $40,000 cash. If her other partners purchase her interest, her taxable gain is $27,000. Catherine's gain is treated as a capital gain except for amounts attributable to her share of unrealized receivables and inventory.

Assume that this firm has no inventory items, and that its only unrealized receivables are its accounts receivable. Catherine's share of the unrealized receivables is $10,000 (1/3 x $30,000), and since the partnership basis in the unrealized receivables is zero, $10,000 of her $27,000 gain must be treated as ordinary income. The balance is capital gain. The remaining partners have the option to increase the basis of partnership assets in proportion to the gain recognized to the retiring partner.

Mike: If the partnership decides to liquidate Catherine's interest for $40,000, Catherine still has a $27,000 gain. However, her amount received must be fragmented into $15,000 for partnership property [1/3 x ($9,000 cash + $36,000 real estate)]; $10,000 for unrealized receivables (1/3 x $30,000 of accounts receivable); and $15,000 for goodwill (1/3 x $45,000).

There is no inventory. The payments for (1) partnership property, (2) unrealized receivables, and (3) goodwill are taxed as follows:

- *Partnership Property:* Catherine receives $15,000 for her share. Her basis in her partnership interest that is allocable to those assets is $13,000. She has a $2,000 capital gain. The remaining partners have the option to increase the basis of partnership assets in proportion to the gain recognized to the retiring partner.
- *Unrealized Receivables:* Catherine receives $10,000 for her share. Since the partnership has no basis in this asset (cash-basis taxpayers have a zero basis in accounts receivable), neither does Catherine. The $10,000 would be ordinary income to Catherine and the partnership would have a $10,000 deduction.
- *Goodwill:* She receives $15,000 for her share. Since the partnership has no basis in this asset, neither does Catherine. If the partnership agreement states that payment shall be made for goodwill, then Catherine may treat the $15,000 as capital gain. If the partnership is silent as to goodwill, Catherine will treat the $15,000 as ordinary income. If Catherine does have ordinary income, then the partnership may treat the $15,000 as part of Catherine's distributive share or a guaranteed payment to her.

If instead Cartland is not a service partnership, the cash and other property consists of one-third of $9,000 cash, $36,000 real estate, and $45,000 goodwill, or $30,000. Catherine has one-third of $30,000 unrealized receivables, or $10,000. As she has no basis in the unrealized receivables, she recognizes $10,000 ordinary income. The partnership has no deduction. Catherine recognizes a $17,000 capital gain on the excess of the $30,000 attributable to cash or other property over her $13,000 basis.

A summary of the foregoing is shown in table 20-2.

TABLE 20-2
Taxation of Payments to a Retiring Partner
or Deceased Partner's Estate

Nature of Partnership Asset	Type of Buy-Sell Agreement	Estate of Deceased or Withdrawing Partner	Partnership, Remaining, or Surviving Partner
Capital assets (cash, building, equipment, furniture, etc.)	Entity and cross purchase	Capital gain/loss	No deduction
Unrealized Receivables (service partnership)	Entity and cross purchase	Ordinary income	Deduction
Unrealized receivables (nonservice partnership)	Entity and cross purchase	Ordinary income	No deduction
Inventory	Entity and cross purchase	Ordinary income	No deduction
Goodwill	Cross purchase	Capital gain/loss	No deduction
Specified goodwill (service partnership)	Entity	Capital gain/loss	No deduction
Unspecified goodwill (service partnership)	Entity	Ordinary income	Deduction
Goodwill (nonservice partnership)	Entity	Capital gain/loss	No deduction

TAXATION OF LIMITED PARTNERSHIPS AND THEIR PARTNERS

Steve: Can we discuss the taxation of a limited partnership?

Jim: Basically limited partnerships and their partners are taxed the same as general partnerships and their partners. As you know, a *limited partnership* is an arrangement in which the liability of some of the partners is limited to what they have contributed to the partnership. This is a useful device when a number of individuals are investing in an enterprise, but only one or a few individuals will be the managing and active members. Generally the limited partners are limited in authority as well as liability. The taxation of a limited partnership follows the same general rules we have already discussed.

TAXATION OF FAMILY PARTNERSHIPS AND THEIR PARTNERS

Steve: Can you explain how the taxation of *family partnerships* differs from the taxation of other types of partnership?

Jim: A family partnership is one whose members are closely related through blood or marriage. The family, for this purpose, includes only husband or wife, ancestors, and lineal descendants, and any trusts for the primary benefit of such persons. Brothers and sisters are not included.

Family partnerships are not essentially different from other partnerships. However, because family partnerships are sometimes formed solely to shift income within a family unit in order to minimize taxes, such partnerships receive special scrutiny both as to initial formation and actual operation.[20]

If there is economic (non-tax-motivated) reality to the arrangement, the partnership allocations of income will be accepted for income tax purposes. If the arrangement lacks economic reality, the Internal Revenue Service may ignore the entire partnership arrangement and reallocate income to properly reflect the interests of the partners.

There are certain guidelines designed to test the reality of the partnership arrangement. For example, in the determination of whether income can be shifted from the original sole proprietor to a new partner, a family member will be recognized as a partner only if his or her capital interest was acquired in a bona fide transaction (even if by gift or purchase from another family member), where capital is a material income-producing factor. To be treated as a partner for tax purposes, the family member must actually own the partnership interest and be vested with dominion and control over it.

Capital is considered a material income-producing factor if a substantial portion of the gross income of the business results from the use of capital (as when substantial inventories or investments in plant, machinery, or equipment are required).

If a family member acquires a capital interest in a family partnership by gift in which capital is a material income-producing factor, there are limitations on the amount that may be allocated as his or her distributive share of partnership income.

First, the donor of the interest must be allowed an amount that represents reasonable compensation for services rendered to the partnership. The remaining income generally may be divided among the partners according to their agreement for sharing partnership profits and losses. However, that portion of the remaining income allocated to the donee may not be proportionately greater than that allocated to the donor on the basis of their respective capital interests.

An interest purchased by one member of the family from another member of the family is considered to be created by gift for this purpose. Let me give you an example. A partnership in which the father sold (considered a gift) a 50 percent interest to his son had a profit of $60,000 for the year. Capital was a material income-producing factor. The father performed services worth $24,000 as reasonable compensation, and the son performed no services. The $24,000 must be allocated to the father as compensation. With respect to the $36,000 of income attributable to capital, at least 50 percent, or $18,000, must be allocated to the father since he owns a 50 percent capital interest. The son's share of partnership income cannot exceed $18,000.

Steve: What happens when capital is not a material income-producing factor?

Mike: An individual can still be treated as a partner for tax purposes even if capital is not a material income-producing factor. However, in such cases the individual must contribute substantial or vital services.

Capital is not a material income-producing factor if the income of the business consists principally of fees, commissions, or other compensation for personal services performed by members or employees of the partnership. A law or accounting practice would be a good illustration. For a son to be recognized as a partner in his father's accounting firm for tax purposes, he'd have to contribute substantial services to the business. Otherwise, his share of partnership income would be reallocated by the IRS to the other partners.

Steve: In this brief review of the income tax treatment of partnerships, it's apparent to me that the area is quite complex, and that each situation merits thorough as well as thoughtful consideration and planning.

Mike: That's correct, but with proper structuring, the partnership is often the best means of conducting a profit-motivated undertaking when more than one individual has an interest. The benefits, however, may not be available if the partnership exists merely on a handshake, with no analysis, planning, or formalization of the understanding of the parties. For income tax purposes, a partnership may exist in such a situation, but it is likely that problems will arise in the future, without carefully thought-out and formalized arrangements.

NOTES

1. Prop. Reg. Sec. 301.7701-1, 2, 3.
2. S corporations are an exception to this rule.
3. An attempt to prevent a "disguised sale" by the partner to the partnership was the objective of the amendment of IRC Sec. 707(a) by the Tax Reform Act of 1984. If a transaction is characterized as a sale, then the partner would be acting as a nonpartner for this one transaction and, of course, would be required to recognize a gain or loss on the transaction.
4. IRC Sec. 721.
5. IRC Sec. 722.
6. IRC Sec. 752(b).
7. Treas. Reg. Sec. 1.721-1(b)(1). (A capital interest in a partnership means an interest in its assets that is distributable to the owner of the capital interest upon the owner's withdrawal from or the liquidation of the partnership. The mere right to share in the earnings and profits is not a capital interest in the partnership.)
8. IRC Sec. 6698(a) and (b).
9. IRC Sec. 702(a).
10. IRC Sec. 704(b).
11. IRC Sec. 704(b)(2).
12. Treas. Reg. 1.704-1(b).
13. Where a partner cannot practicably determine the adjusted basis in the partnership interest, the adjusted basis of his or her interest may be determined by reference to the partner's proportionate share of the adjusted basis of partnership property, as long as it is reasonable that the result produced will not vary substantially from the above basis rules. IRC Sec. 705(b); Treas. Reg. Sec. 1.705-1(b).
14. IRC Sec. 751(c).
15. IRC Sec. 736.
16. IRC Sec. 1014.
17. IRC Sec. 691.
18. IRC Sec. 754.
19. IRC Sec. 736(b)(2).
20. IRC Sec. 704(e).

Index

Editor's note: A lowercase *f.* following a page number refers the reader to a figure on said page; a lowercase *n.* indicates a note; a lowercase *t.* indicates a table. Thus 305 *f.* refers to the figure on page 305; 354 *n.* 13 refers to note 13 on page 354; and 310 *t.* refers to the table on page 310.